Long out of print, this new edition memoir by an intelligent and articulate "other rank", provides fascinating insights into the Great War infantryman's experience.

In autumn 1915, twenty-year-old Gerald Dennis enlisted in Kitchener's Army. Posted to the 21st (Service) Battalion of the King s Royal Rifle Corps, affectionately known as the "Yeoman Rifles", he experienced fierce fighting on the Somme 1916, during Messines Ridge and Third Ypres in 1917 prior to deployment to Italy in the immediate aftermath of the Caporetto disaster. Re-assigned to a battalion of the Cameron Highlanders in summer 1918, Dennis took part in the advance to victory before demobilisation in 1919.

A vivid and engaging record of wartime service and comradeship, his recollections are not those of the archetype disenchanted ex-soldier: "Whatever impressions the readers of this book draw, I would like to emphasise that I bear no resentment or bitterness. As far as I could, I have drawn a true and honest picture of my army life ... I realise that I did only the merest little bit for my King and Country, not that we gave either special thought. We had volunteered for them."

A KITCHENER MAN'S BIT

AN ACCOUNT OF THE GREAT WAR 1914-18

Rifleman Gerald Dennis (C/12747)
**21st Service Battalion, The King's Royal Rifle Corps
(The Yeoman Rifles)**

Helion & Company

Helion & Company Limited
26 Willow Road
Solihull
West Midlands
B91 1UE
England
Tel. 0121 705 3393
Fax 0121 711 4075
Email: info@helion.co.uk
Website: www.helion.co.uk
Twitter: @helionbooks
Visit our blog http://blog.helion.co.uk/

Published by Helion & Company 2016
Designed and typeset by Farr out Publications, Wokingham, Berkshire
Cover designed by Paul Hewitt, Battlefield Design (www.battlefield-design.co.uk)
Printed by Lightning Source Ltd, Milton Keynes, Buckinghamshire

Text © Gerald V. Dennis Estate
Images © as individually credited
Maps drawn by George Anderson © Helion & Company

ISBN 978-1-911096-20-7

British Library Cataloguing-in-Publication Data.
A catalogue record for this book is available from the British Library.

For details of other military history titles published by Helion & Company Limited contact the above address, or visit our website: http://www.helion.co.uk.

We always welcome receiving book proposals from prospective authors.

Contents

List of Photographs   vi
List of Maps   vii
Foreword   viii
Preface   ix
Introduction   xii

1   Helmsley – Featherbed Soldiers   13
2   Aldershot – A Dog's Life   23
3   Outtersteene and Plugstreet – Preparation and Initiation   36
4   Plugstreet Wood – the thin edge of the wedge   47
5   The Somme/Flers – Blood, Mud, Heroes and All   67
6   The Somme – A Sacrifice Attack?   86
7   Trench Warfare – The Brasserie Sector (The Salient – Ypres)   100
8   Messines Ridge – Preparation for, and attack   139
9   Messines Ridge – Ours now – Consolidation   153
10   The Third Battle of Ypres – Gas, rain and mud   161
11   Boeschepe – The Signalling Course   173
12   Blighty and Leave   177
13   Italy – Cushy   185
14   In Dock (Hospital Blues) – Genoa and Marseilles   200
15   Étaples – Base, Bombs and my new Battalion   213
16   School again – Meteren – Jerry in Retreat   219
17   Lannoy – Waiting for my ticket – Demobbed   225
18   And now – Aprés la Guerre   233

Appendices
I   "Thank You" printed by Second Army, presented to all ranks leaving the Army   239
II   People mentioned in the text   240

List of Photographs

Corporal Gerald V. Dennis (C/12747), autumn 1917. (Source: Richard Frost)   128

Rifleman Gerald Dennis, Aldershot December 1915. (Source: Richard Frost)   128

Duncombe Park (Source: Richard Frost)   129

Helmsley, North Yorkshire (Source: Richard Frost)   129

Sergeants' Mess, Aldershot 1916, Lieutenant-Colonel The Earl of Feversham left centre. (Source: KRRC Association)   130

Second Lieutenant Anthony Eden 1916. (Source: KRRC Association)   130

'A' Company 21st K.R.R.C., Aldershot 1916. (Source: KRRC Association)   131

Riflemen Herbert 'Bert' Rowsby and Herbert 'Tom' Hore 1917. (Source: Richard Frost)   132

Rifleman Norman Carmichael. (Source: Richard Frost)   132

Private Gerald V. Dennis (No. 50517) in his Cameron Highlanders uniform 1918. (Source: Richard Frost)   133

Anthony Eden during the unveiling of the Yeoman Rifle memorial plaque at Helmsley Visitor Centre 1935. (Source: Helmsley Visitor Centre)   133

Yeoman Rifles' Association Reunion, York 7 May 1949: Programme cartoons and caricatures. (Source: KRRC Association)   134

The Riley High School under twelve-and-a-half 'A' football team 1953–54. Gerald Dennis is seated at the far right. (Source: Richard Frost)   135

Riley High School teaching staff c. 1960. Gerald Dennis is standing in the back row, sixth from left. (Source: Richard Frost)   135

Helmsley 1991. L to R: Gerald Dennis, Lieutenant General Sir David House, Colonel Christopher Consett and Captain Sandy Fletcher. (Source: Richard Frost)   136

Gerald Dennis memorial programme 1994. (Source: Richard Frost)   137

A moving Last Post tribute to the late Gerald Dennis at Hull's Northern Cemetery. (Source: Richard Frost)   138

As per his wishes, Gerald's ashes are deposited at Duncombe Park. (Source: Richard Frost)   138

List of Maps

Map 1. Ypres, Armentières and vicinty   35

Map 2. Ploegsteert Wood   45

Map 3. Somme 1916   65

Map 4. Brasserie Sector 1916–17   114

Map 5. Messines 1917   151

Map 6. Italy 1917-18   183

Foreword

I am pleased and honoured to have been asked to write a foreword to Gerald Dennis's account of his service during the Great War. My distant relative and namesake gave his life in the cause, and for this he has been remembered with affection by the surviving Yeomen Riflemen; my 'bit', as Gerald would say, has been to offer hospitality to the survivors, their families and friends when they have come to Helmsley for their annual reunions, September by September – and this has been a pleasure to me if only a small recompense to them when compared to the sacrifice of so many of the 21st Battalion between 1915 and 1918.

Now that numbers of surviving Riflemen have dwindled almost to extinction, it has, sadly, been decided that the reunions shall cease; however, just as Yeomen Riflemen of the 21st Battalion were always welcome here, so their families and friends will be at Helmsley.

Thank you, Gerald, for the privilege of allowing us to share your reminiscences, and thank you, to all connected in any way, for allowing me to put my name to this introductory note.

The Lord Feversham
Duncombe Park, Helmsley
November 1993

Preface

Originally the account of my reminiscences of Army days during the Great War was written at the request of Captain P. Brooksbank of Healaugh Hall, near Tadcaster for a few pages to add to his large collection of living, true and human stories as told by men of the Yeoman Rifles. He was particularly keen on compiling such a collection because the official account of the 21st K.R.R.C. was uninteresting and lacking in life. However, instead of writing some thrilling story, I spent my spare time in the evenings of the winter of 1928-29 in trying to recall all my Army life; my left foot gave me much trouble and I had to rest a lot. To my surprise I filled a ledger of about one hundred and fifty pages and covered only my time in the old battalion. Old chums like Mac (Arthur McGahey), Pip (Percy Porter) and Ted Coulson, to whom I owe many thanks, helped me to fill in the gaps when I was on leave, and when I was lucky enough to miss certain days when the boys went over the top. Otherwise, this account is entirely from memory, except where post cards and letters sent home supplied some dates and, of course, from the diaries I kept. Whilst I was enjoying recalling my past, Remarque's "All Quiet on the Western Front" appeared in English, but I did not make any attempt to read it until my own work was completed. Up to the time of writing my book, I had not read any other books about the Great War.

I then put the work on one side and in 1930 I lost the one parent who had made so many sacrifices for my up-bringing. Later that year I let Mac read my rough effort, and again shelved it. However, another Old Boulevardian, Val Walpole, author of "Men in the Line", heard about my reminiscences and asked what they were like. After a little hesitation I let him read them on condition that he told me exactly what he thought about them. He thought that I ought to go further with them, and so keen was he that I bought a second hand typewriter and typed them out. But for Val I should not have gone so far with them. (Val had been gassed at Vimy, so very badly that he had had a lung taken away and, on the advice of the surgeons, had gone to live in South Africa, taking up work as a professor of English at Stellenbosche University. I met him whilst he was on leave).

As I wrote there came into my mind that well-known text. "Lest we Forget", and I kept asking myself. "Lest who forget?" Certainly not the Tommies who were out there; they remember as well as, if not any better, than I. Not the loved ones who worried at home, for they suffered heavily in a different way; they too will never forget. Those who came back from war's hell cannot forget, and in many instances do not want to forget because they made the acquaintance of men, met true friendship, saw the very best in men, and realised that other men were just as good, if not better, than themselves. Then who? Those who suffered no loss? Those who never experienced a raid from the sky? Those who never tasted the horrors of war? Those who made money because of it? The new generation, which cannot understand what their fathers went through? Yes, some of these, if not all.

To all the Tommies of the front line, they who lived just close enough to the barbed wire of No Man's Land, those who were lousy and lived in mud, that at undistinguished crowd and the men of the ordinary battalions that received very little mention – to them, and to those left behind out there, and to those of them who returned, I dedicate this book.

Gerald V. Dennis, October, 1928

Whatever impressions the readers of this book draw, I would like to emphasise that I bear no resentment or bitterness. As far as I could, I have drawn a true and honest picture of my Army life. I listened to rumours, grumbles, grousing and complaints, and there were hundreds of them – "Satan gives the idle mind much to do", and we had such a lot of spare time to oblige him. Much of it was not meant, it was just a case of getting things off one's chest. Why shouldn't we grouse or grumble? We were volunteers.

I realise that I did only the merest little bit for my King and Country, not that we gave either a special thought. We had not volunteered for them. I don't suppose many of us could give the real reason we had joined up. "We're here because we're here because ... " summed it up. I now know how very fortunate I was and what a lot of the worst I missed, but I am very proud that I did even a little "bit". I could have been marked "unfit", I could have "gone sick" and been discharged, but I preferred to stick to the finest men and boys I have ever known. I am proud that I lived with them in dugouts just below the barbed wire of No Man's Land and shared their danger.

I shall never forget the bravery of the unselfish battalion runners, the battalion stretcher-bearers, the very young Second Lieutenants and the gunners of the eighteen pounders. To me they were the heroes and deserved, richly, any medals which were awarded to them. Far more received medals "with the rations" and they should have been "putty medals".

I think that so little of the horrors and conditions of the Great War were known in the twenties because Tommies of the Front Line came home on leave and said nothing because they did not want to alarm their relatives; whereas the soldiers of the back areas, and those officers responsible for sending such a lot of men to their deaths, came on leave many times and said a lot, some probably boasting of what they thought it was like down the Line.

G.V.D.

A Word of Explanation Some explanation is needed, I feel, of my involvement with this book by Gerald Dennis, and to give this I must go back a long time – to December 1915, when the first raw recruits for the Yeoman Rifles gathered at Duncombe Park. Amongst them, along with Gerald Dennis, were my father, Frank Reed Hickes, and his brother, Victor Gordon Hickes.

To move on to 1949, when my personal connexion with the Y.R.A. began: my father having died nearly three years earlier, my mother was invited by Captain Eddie Worsley to attend the annual reunion of 'A' Company at the Crown Hotel at Helmsley, and I went too, as I did for the next three or four years, until I left school.

Some years later, about 1980, my interest in family history led me to contact Gerald, having read in the local paper about the ever-flourishing reunions, despite the dwindling number of World War I survivors still able to attend. It was not until about two years ago, however, that I chanced to learn that Gerald had kept a diary throughout his Army days, and that ten years after the Armistice, while convalescing after an operation on his war-wounded left foot, he had used this diary as the basis for *A Kitchener Man's Bit*. This he had attempted to have printed and published, but was told it was not likely to be of interest because (a) it was too long and detailed, (b) it needed indexing, and (c) – and this in 1929! – there was not enough sex in it!

Having been a teacher of English for over thirty years and with early retirement a strong possibility, and having recognized that *A Kitchener Man's Bit* was very competently and convincingly written, I took the plunge and volunteered to do what I could to get it into print; the rest as they say, is history. Many hours have been devoted to preparing the text, but every minute has been both enjoyable and rewarding; I feel it is a privilege to have been able to help Gerald to make his experiences, which he writes about so calmly and sensibly, available to a much wider circle than the few who hitherto know of the memoirs.

Gerald is now 98 and is somewhat frail, but he comes of a long-lived family – his great-grandmother, he tells me, died aged 108 in 1914, having been born the year after Nelson's victory at Trafalgar! From listening to Gerald's comment about his comrades-in-arms, I realized there was much that had not been included in his Bit; consequently, some of his recollections of these people (which he gives with a promptness that suggest it might have been only yesterday that they were together "over there") are given in the Appendix – family and local historians alike will, I feel, be pleased to have such original detail, and of so many men and places, particularly where Hull is concerned.

This book is very substantially Gerald's own work and words; only in the Appendix, in this explanatory foreword, and in a few very brief instances (where there was ambiguity, for example) are the words mine.

Every reader will, I hope, feel as gratified by *A Kitchener Mans Bit* as I do; would that everyone professing an interest in putting the world to rights could have the opportunity to discover, and absorb, Gerald's philosophy for him or herself.

Michael E. Hickes
September 1993

Introduction

The King's Royal Rifle Corps Association

52/56 Davies Street, London W1K 5HR

As Honorary Secretary of the King's Royal Rifle Corps Association for the past 36 years I have had the privilege of meeting many remarkable old soldiers, most whom have since passed on. I would like to pay particular tribute to Gerald Dennis, an unassuming man who had that remarkable skill of making everyone who met him feel instantly at ease.

My first contact with him was when I became the Hon Sec of my Association; Gerald regularly sent the Yeoman Rifles report for inclusion in the Annual KRRC Journal. In the 1978 Journal he reported that six members of the Yeoman Rifles had been invited to Westminster Abbey for the Memorial Service of Lord Avon. They were wonderfully placed in the Abbey and warmly welcomed by the Green Jackets outside. Affectionately known as the "Boy", 2nd Lt R A Eden was at first posted to "C" Company and later became Adjutant. The six who attended were Bert Whittaker, Norman Carmichael, MM, Ernest Nicholson, MC, William Poucher, George Welford and Rowland Otley. Gerald was unable to travel due to ill health.

I regularly made the long trip from Kent to Helmsley for the Annual Reunion Lunch in September at the Feathers Hotel that was organised by Gerald and well remember him saying in his after lunch speech 1989 that there were only four surviving members of the Yeoman Rifles. This book is testament to Gerald and all those who made the supreme sacrifice. I fear we shall never see their like again.

Richard Frost MBE
Hon Sec
The King's Royal Rifle Corps Association
September 2016

1

Helmsley – Featherbed Soldiers

When the Great War was still being carried on after fifteen months and the much-heard remarks, "Oh, it will soon be over," or "It'll be over by Christmas," were proving untrue, and were yet believed to a certain degree, I, like many another youth, began to think of that war. The British communiques never gave much news – not enough at least to make English people be war-minded at first. However, after the first year of war, we began to wake up. Many men, youths and even boys began to join up.

In October 1915, Arthur McGahey (hereinafter known as Mac) and I regularly turned over in our minds the matter of joining up and felt sure of one thing, that when we did join up, we should be able to pick our unit. Some old school friends had joined, in a body, the Royal Garrison Artillery in order to be stationed near home. Men were encouraged to join local units and many Pals' Battalions were formed. No one was turned away from the unit he wished to join. Compulsory enlistment was hinted at but, at that time, men followed their choice. Mac was eager to join the local Cyclist Battalion because he was a keen rider and well built for hard riding. I was not so muscular and lacked his stamina, but would have gone with him for we were staunch friends and wanted to be together. Actually I thought of the R.E.s (Royal Engineers), not because of the danger of the infantry man for that was not painted as it ought to have been, but because in such a unit there would be more scope for the exercise of one's intelligence.

November found a very restless air throughout the Men's Hostel of a certain East Riding (of Yorkshire) College for the Training of Teachers. Lectures were listened to during the day, but no one worked in the evenings. Private study and prep were out of the question. The nightly topic was the war. The Principal was as variable as the wind. His advice was never the same two mornings in succession. One morning he thought that the Seniors ought to enlist if they wished to and the Juniors should hang on. The very next morning he advised the Juniors to enlist if they wished to, and the Seniors to wait. He meant well. He was trying to think what the Board of Education's attitude would be. What allowances concerning length of training would it make according to the year, first or second at the Training College? No wonder we were in doubt. So Mac and I, being Juniors, let youth and its attendant thoughtlessness settle the question. One Saturday, two juniors, MacWilliam and Jimmy Hannah, announced at supper time that they had enlisted in a certain battalion, the 21st King's Royal Rifles – the Yeoman Rifles. Perhaps they gave the impression that they had joined a mounted regiment. This, the idea of cavalry, appealed to George Bramley and myself; I had always liked horses, my father's family being farmers. On Monday, 22nd November, we wandered to the City Square and saw the K.R.R. Recruiting Sergeant on the steps of the City Hall. Didn't he look smart in his uniform, somewhat different from the usual khaki! He wore a green and black rig-out which we thought was army dress. It was the peace time uniform and not the active service one. We went up to him and said that we wished to join his regiment and were taken indoors and directed to a Tommy at a table on which were many forms, pens and ink. Again we stated what we required or desired, but we were told that we would not be accepted for anything but the infantry as men for the line were most wanted. Our names were taken, we answered many questions, gave quite a lot of what seemed to be unnecessary information and particulars and were passed further along. We now stripped and were medically examined. Bram got through easily enough but the M.O. gave me a very doubtful look just after his first test with the stethoscope. "What? You are wasting my time. You know what's wrong with you, don't you?" he barked out. I showed that I did, I knew of my heart weakness and the fact that I had a medical certificate for games, drills and the like, but I murmured that many of my pals were joining up and that I wanted to be with them. "It will kill you!" he said, and as an afterthought he added, "or cure you!" He put me through and I was in. After I had dressed myself I stood again before a Tommy at a table. He wanted more particulars. He asked me if I wished to make an allotment to my mother and I told him that I did, in fact I do not suppose that I would have enlisted if such a thing could not be done. He assured me that the Army would add so much according to what I agreed to allocate to her. Being an only son and mother a widow I felt very satisfied at being able to help her a little, the one parent I would be leaving behind. Finally each of us received a slip of paper, a Certificate of Enlistment showing the date, 22nd November 1915; the name of the unit, the 21st King's Royal Rifle Corps; and rubber stamped with the name of the recruiting officer of the district (..?..Boyd). At the same time we were told to report there at the City Hall at nine o'clock on the 6th December, a Monday. By that date it was expected that more men would join our unit and we would all travel together. In the meantime we were thus allowed a fortnight in which to settle our affairs, finish with our studies, or rather talks, pack up our books and other belongings and return to our homes. Just to think of it, a soldier, a soldier for the duration. I did not then feel any different, though that slip of paper, which I did not use at all, meant a change in my life.

Bram and I returned to the College and said nothing to anyone for some time. We entered the Common Room, which was almost deserted as it was a free afternoon. A few students sat round a fire evidently trying to think of something ordinary to say. Invariably they were unsuccessful. Now that the situation affected their position as students and there was a chance of their training being interrupted, their thoughts always turned to the subject of the war. What ought they to do? What a serious problem now faced them. Now and again a few words were spoken, thus disturbing the quietness of a somewhat gloomy room, which was usually very noisy. All seemed very relieved when the bell for tea sounded and we hastily made our way to the dining hall. After tea amid such an atmosphere, Bram and I wondered if we had done the right thing. Anyhow we should have to report our enlistment to the "Prinnie" and then let the hostel matron, who saw to the catering, know that we would not be requiring meals at the College much longer. We decided to break the news to the matron first because she could not criticise what we had done. I was just telling her the news when a fellow Junior entered and heard me. "What? They've taken you?" he asked in utter amazement. "Yes," replied the matron, "they seem to take anyone nowadays." Perhaps she was right, though her reply to him was not meant to be personal. She, of course, knew my medical record. That evening we four who had joined the same unit met in my study bedroom and discussed the step we had taken. There it did not seem to be serious. The "thin red line" (which had become the "thin khaki line") out in France could manage without us – wasn't the war going to be over by Christmas? We might be sent on coast defence for a short time and then return to our studies again. The next morning Bram and I went to the "Prinnie" in his study.

"We enlisted yesterday afternoon, sir." A pause as he looked out of the window, as if looking for that mysterious fourth dimension. "Juniors? I think that you have done the wrong thing. You should have waited till the end of term and then weighed up the position." We were not discouraged. We could not turn back and we did not want to. We were satisfied with what we had done.

Immediately after that short interview, I slipped home. As I dropped off a tram car I saw my mother who, of course, was very surprised to see me. I told her that I had enlisted. We went straight home. I had acted very selfishly; certainly I had never given a thought to my only parent. I had acted quite independently and thoughtlessly. Just as if it did not matter I had bluntly told the one person who had striven to put me where I had reached. In a second it seemed I had undone many years of sacrifice and love. What she thought then and felt inwardly I did not know but now can imagine. Not a word of reproach, not a look of doubt, not a sign of fear, not a question as to whether it was the right thing but just: "When do you go?"

The fortnight's respite took the edge off the blow, temporarily holding off the parting so we did not look at it and carried on as if nothing had happened.

Why, I asked myself, why was England's youth acting so recklessly, throwing up or interrupting careers and positions and crushing hopes all in a few minutes? Were the recruiting posters responsible? Were some of them haunted and driven to enlisting by Kitchener's poster: YOU, with the pointing finger and appealing eyes which seemed to follow the looker as he moved by. Did the words of the well-known song stir some internal chord of feelings: *Your KING and COUNTRY need YOU We think you ought to go?* Did the talk of "conscription next year" spur them on? No, none of these could claim youth's action. Youth just went, often heartlessly and thoughtlessly, never worrying or looking ahead. Those at home were left to worry. (Later I guessed that the words to the popular song out there summed it up: *We're here because we're here, because we're here*).

I went back to the College and stayed on for a few days doing very little work, taking things easy and not liking to sever so abruptly the new friendships I had formed. Occasionally I slipped home taking a few of my things gradually. More time was spent merely on talking about the war. A few more of the Juniors had joined the same battalion and one Senior too, but I did not know this at the time. Mac (Arthur) had joined on the Tuesday and Frank Markham later in the week. Don Wardell and Ted Nixon, two friends of long standing had been granted leave of absence to go to London to see about joining an Officers' Training Corps. They were unlucky, all cadet training camps were full to overflowing such was the rush of young men to become subalterns. They were asked where they had come from and were recommended to return north and join a certain new unit at Helmsley, arriving there before we did. So did Johnny Watson, the Senior.

The imminent departure of quite a lot of the men students caused the women students to organise a farewell dance on the Saturday evening. The very name of it robbed it of some happiness and light-heartedness usually found at a dance. The air seemed heavy with thoughts of the partings, though we had known one another only six weeks. Dozens of goodbyes were spoken; *Auld Lang Syne* was sung rather sadly, the College war cry with gusto, and the *National Anthem* with sincerity. Then with lagging footsteps we dispersed. How different were the women students at the same training college when some of us returned to it four years later; we were not wanted and it was shown only too well.

I spent the next week at home and then it began to dawn on me that I was in for my first separation from home. I had not even enlisted in a local battalion and so weekend leaves would be out of the question. I should be leaving my home town. It was to be a real goodbye. Both mother and I appeared not to see it thus, and we tried to hide what we felt. Mother succeeded very well, certainly in front of me. Openly she was pleased and proud, but alone what did she think?

On Monday, 6th December, a few minutes before nine o'clock about sixty-three men and boys reported at the City Hall. Each looked at all the others, wondering if he knew any of them. I knew only the men from the College and so Jimmy Hannah, Mac Williams, Frank Markham, McGahey, George Bramley and myself stuck together. The same Recruiting Sergeant came up and ordered us to fall in. He was rather gentle with us, shepherding us into two lines and then putting us into fours. He assumed that we knew nothing at all about drill. "Right turn, quick march," he continued, almost in a whisper. He led the way down Waterworks Street and Paragon Street straight for the railway station. We tried to appear orderly and did not draw too much attention to ourselves. A few people, and only a few, turned to look at us and they and we were not at all concerned. They had seen far more recruits heading for the station earlier in the year and had shown greater interest in the local or pals' battalion like the East Yorks. They probably knew someone on those occasions.

At the Paragon Railway Station the sergeant left us whilst he verified the train on which he had to put us. He returned and picked someone to be in charge and told him the times of the trains, for we had to change en route. We were put on the Hull – York train and we six managed to get into the same compartment; there was no turning back now. We detrained at York and the man put in charge went to find out the time of our departure from York to Helmsley. He returned and told us that there was a long wait, three hours, and he left us to our own devices. We strolled about the platforms, sat down, visited the cafe and had a bite to eat before going back to the spot where we had left the one in charge.

When we reached Helmsley it was dark. One of our battalion, still in civvies, awaited us. After leaving the small station we passed along a short street, then took a road going uphill through a natural park. This first climb did not seem too hard. From the entrance gates to a large residence on the left was less than a mile. We were led into a large marquee. It was the Mess. Meals were served to all the newcomers here and we were given our tea. The long tables, boards on trestles, had just been washed down and were still very wet, sodden and greasy. We sat on the forms and the orderlies placed the supplies at one end of the tables and in a very light-hearted manner yelled out, "Coming down! Pass along, please." What a strange way of going on, and what a change! From the white tablecloths, cups and saucers and more or less dainty slices of bread to one and a half inch thick slices of bread and "Pheasant" margarine, both slid along the wet tables and becoming wet in the process. Basins were flung along in a similar manner and then the orderlies came round and filled them with tea. The latter was thick and strong and tasted like poison. No turning up our noses at this fare and we showed the beginnings of good soldiers-to-be in being able to adapt ourselves straight away to changed conditions.

Having finished the meal we went out into the darkness and stood about wondering what was going to happen next. In the distance across the park we could see very faintly some huts with strange tops. We were not taken in that direction but across a road towards the large house, our first billet in the Army. The buildings were in the shape of an arc and we were taken into one of the wings, a stable. What a night's rest! By no stretch of the imagination could it be called rest or sleep. The first in went upstairs into the loft, and I was one of them fortunately, for it had a wooden floor, but those downstairs had to get down on a stone floor. Crowded together, we did not notice the cold so much as we lay on the boards in our civilian clothes with our topcoats as blankets. I lost count of the number of times I turned over, off my right side and on to my back then on to my left side, then starting the rounds all over again. My hip bones ached and felt very sore and as the night wore on they felt as big as footballs. Eventually sleep came to me, when I had worn down those bones, as it were. That very first night in the Army proved a blessing in disguise for, after that experience, I could sleep anywhere or anyhow under far worse conditions. How poor the kip was; we needed no calling in the morning and were thankful that that kind of trial was to prove so short. We were given a breakfast of bread, margarine and jam with a basin of tea on dry tables, in the same marquee. Outside was a huge expanse of grass and clearly in the distance we could now see the huts; they were made of straw.

On making some enquiries, I learned that Johnnie Watson, Ted Nixon and Don Wardell from the College had arrived in Helmsley a few days before we did and had been put into 'A' Company and were already down in the village in a billet that caused us to smile, the Workhouse.

From earlier recruits we learned a little more about the battalion and its formation. Pals and Commercials Battalions had been formed in the cities and it was thought that men of the country and of the yeoman type could be encouraged to join a similar sort of battalion. A most suitable commanding officer seemed to be the Earl of Feversham who, in April 1915, had been with the Yorkshire Hussars in France. Upon his unit being broken up into Divisional Cavalry, the Earl was surplus to needs and, when offered the command of a new unit of the King's Royal Rifle Corps to be raised in the Northern Command, he gladly accepted. The recruits from the North and East Ridings were put into 'A' Coy.; those from the West Riding into 'B' Coy.; those from Northumberland and Durham into 'C' Coy.; and those from Lincolnshire, Leicestershire and Nottinghamshire into 'D' Coy. These recruits, boys for the most part were of a very high standard physically, educationally and socially and hundreds of them at first were personally interviewed by the Earl and either accepted or not.

The Earl had had built around the edges of the park some straw huts, like African kraals, for the first recruits, chiefly of 'A' Coy. A surprise fall of snow in October made them unsuitable for billets and they were condemned as unfit for use. The men were brought down to the town Workhouse, whose inmates were transferred to Kirkbymoorside. As more recruits arrived, 'A' Coy. men were removed to billets at Beadlam and Nawton, two charming villages a few miles from Helmsley. All further recruits were put into billets in the town – 'B' and 'D' Coys. in the Workhouse, in High Street, Castlegate and Station Road. Of the nine of us from the College, three were put into 'A' Coy and six into 'C'.

Almost all the junior officers who joined us at Helmsley were from the northern counties: P. Lloyd-Graeme of Sewerby near Bridlington, R.P. Graham, A. Howard of Sheffield and E. Worsley of Hovingham were in 'A' Coy; P. Brooksbank of Tadcaster had come from Canada where he had served in the Mounties, and A.T. Watson of Bishopthorpe to 'B' Coy; O. Coates, A. Eden of S. Durham, C. Thorpe of Alnwick and J. Waldy of Morpeth (Thropton) to 'C' Coy; G. Burton and G. Sheardown of Beverley to 'D' Coy.

R.A. Eden, ex Eton O.T.C., the youngest officer, arrived on the same day as the next youngest officer, R.P. Graham. They were greeted by the C.O., given a meal and a temporary billet. Later the C.O. and the Adjutant went to see if they were settled in and found them asleep. The Colonel looked at the former and said, "Why, he is quite a boy." The Adjutant, pointing to the other young officer said, because of his fresh colouring "He is like a pansy." The pet names stuck; they were terms of respect and affection.

We were all soon brought down into the town and found billets. Helmsley was a small market town amid beautiful surroundings and the six of us were put into 'C' Company. Our numbers were gradually increasing – farmers, farmers' sons, clerks, accountants, lawyers, teachers, students and businessmen all having been accepted for this particular battalion by its Colonel, the Earl of Feversham, whose residence was Duncombe Park here in Helmsley. He had been out in France with a cavalry regiment or squadron, the Hussars, and had been asked to raise an infantry battalion in the north. He gave it the name "Yeoman Rifles"; whether this was because of the number of men who enlisted in it who came from the land, I do not know. All I know is that the name made such a lot of us think that we had joined a mounted battalion.

My first billet was a few yards down Bond Gate on the right hand side as I left the Square. Six of us were put into a very small bedroom like a box room, empty save for the mattresses on which we slept, we being George Bramley, his newly made friend Jack Thompson, Jimmy Hannah, Mac, (McGahey), Frank Markham and myself. We all had to be inside before the bedding could be put down for the night and then it was almost impossible to open the door more than a few inches. It did not take long for Mac and I to realise that the best position was near the small window at that side of the room furthest from the door. Still more did we know it when one of our party, after a merry evening was taken short in the middle of the night. Anyone else needing to go out did not trouble for he in time solved his own problem.

This state of affairs did not last long. At the end of the first week like this the Adjutant came round to see how we fared in the billets. He saw that we were very cramped, that the bedroom became very stuffy during the night and considered it rather unhealthy. So we were paraded and he picked out McGahey and myself to be moved across the road to a much larger house in which there were two or three large beds, real beds. Our hosts were Mr. and Mrs. Arthur Ward of number 25. There were so many Wards in the town that we had to refer to these kind people by their Christian names. Already in this billet were two senior N.C.O.s, Jack Wade and Walter Woollons of Hull, in another room. Mrs. Arthur Ward was a typical country woman in that she made us very welcome and became a mother to us all, although she had a baby in arms. So well treated were all of us and so comfortable that a well-known English paper dubbed us "Featherbed Soldiers". Yet, despite the little things Mrs. Arthur Ward did for us, and she certainly attended to many of our wants, I hardly recollect her appearance and do not remember her family, due to my youthfulness and shyness.

All of us billeted in Bond Gate belonged to 'C' Company, like each of the other Companies having our own part of the town. We received our Army numbers, I was no Rifleman G.V. Dennis, C/12747 – men of Light Infantry regiments being known as Riflemen and not Privates. To all intents and purposes, I was now only a number.

In the meantime, the khaki-green uniforms had arrived and we paraded before the Quarter-Master Sergeant of the Company, Q.M.S. Woodward, an Edinburgh Scot, to receive them. Off went our tailor-mades and on went our ready-mades, which fitted us only where they touched. The tunics were very slack and were particularly ill-fitting at the neck. What a job it was putting on the puttees and trying to get them to look smart. Nobody neglected to let the trousers overlap the puttee tops the regulation two inches. The boots were somewhat heavier than our light discarded ones. The hats, which we later often referred to as cheese-cutters, did not seem to suit us. We must have looked strange. Surely only our mothers could have recognised us on our first appearance in uniform. I looked like an awkward, long-legged country lad. As soon as the change had been made, we gathered up our civvies. Our overcoats were stretched out on the floor and on them our other clothes were placed in as neat a pile as possible. Then the corners of the coats were drawn up around them and the whole lot tied with string. A few of us managed to acquire some brown paper. Labels or pieces of cardboard cut out to represent labels were addressed and were fixed to rather badly made bundles which were handed in to the Quarter-Master Sergeant's office. He sent them off and, to the surprise of many of us, arrived safely at their destinations. Our first chore was with our bright buttons and keeping them clean with the help of the button stick and a tin of "soldier's friend". Why that name I do not know! The words used during cleaning time were hardly friendly ones so that, when we learned that K.R.R.C. battalions wore black buttons, we very quickly bought a set without waiting for the issues, which might, or might not, arrive. They were quite different from the bright ones, having only a bugle on them. Yet some of us were so keen to be smart that we cleaned and polished them with "Cherry Blossom" boot polish. Our cap badges, very similar in appearance and shape to German Iron Crosses, especially appealed to us and showed up remarkably well with the issued red piece of cloth which was put behind them. The badge motto *CELER ET AUDAX* was impressed upon us by our Company Sergeant-Major, C.S.M. Kent. We had to be SWIFT and BOLD and live up to the reputation of the K.R.R.C., the old 60th Foot, the regiment with the most honours in the British Army. We were given to understand that this was true up to August, 1914.

C.S.M. Kent, a regular soldier, had the full history of the Regiment at his fingertips. When we got to know him we all said, "Good old Kent," and nobody said anything bad. We liked our 'C' Company Sergeant-Major only too well. Soon we had all the necessary parts of our equipment, and parades proper commenced. Old Territorials and Volunteers were asked for and made Lance-Corporals, Corporals and even Sergeants. So we of No.12 platoon met Wade, Woollons, Newmarsh and Green, our newly made N.C.O.s. Physical jerks in the Park seemed to be great fun, mostly to the regular drill instructors from Aldershot or Winchester who delighted in putting us through it. Squad drill straightened us up a bit and the slow ones clicked the "awkward squad", but most of us tried to do well so as to miss it.

On two occasions our help was wanted in order to corner the Earl's deer. We deployed and advanced in a long line beyond the Earl's residence on the far side of the Park and tried to drive those animals to a special corner, but we failed. After quite a long spell during which we thought that we were doing nicely, the deer dashed back past us and we did not stand the slightest chance of stopping them as, in their stampede, they even jumped over us.

During the training in the Park we often saw the Earl's young son in a red jacket, riding a pony. I wonder what he thought of our presence there, considering that he was about the toy soldier age.

On our little route marches we soon did justice to, "By the left, quick march!" We were fit, we had open air and plenty of it; exercise not too strenuous to affect us was good for growing lads. The food was sufficient and good. In fact I do not remember any complaints at meal times, even after the meals. We were always ready to tackle whatever the cooks had prepared for us, and the cooks did not have diplomas – they were picked at random, or volunteered. We put our best into our parades which finished daily at about four o'clock for it got too dark to carry on after that hour. There were no worries, so we laughed and grew fat (?). Khaki-green made friendships. Whereas we may have been reserved as civilians, now we made friends with anyone in uniform.

In No.12 platoon there were three of the surname of Dennis, but not one of us was related to the other two. This fact did not cause any trouble for the N.C.O.s for men were so friendly even on parade that our Christian names were used as being more suitable under the circumstances. Percy, Charlie and Gerald were used on parade as one might have thought. The other two by the name of Dennis were both from South Cave. The fact that I had a double by the name of Charlie Bulmer did puzzle the Sergeant-Major on several occasions. We were both fair-haired and blue-eyed and both of us wore rimless glasses that just clipped onto the nose. Fortunately, neither of us got into any trouble and neither did the three named Dennis, so that no very awkward situations arose. C.S.M. Kent, being the sport he was, laughed every time he was put right as to my identity. He lived up to that very well-known statement, "On parade – on parade; and off parade – off parade". He expected the best from us all on parade and got it. Off parade he was very much like one of us, always friendly and ready to give a cheerful smile.

The officers began to make more appearances and, of course, we quickly got to know their names and fads, if they had any. Captain Pitt was our C.O.; 2nd Lt. Eden was No. 9 Platoon Officer; young Yeaman was with No.10; Waldy with No.11 and Thorpe with No.12. Waldy, short and stolid had evidently come from farming; Thorpe was typical Northumberland in dialect, quite a burr. Some of his words amused us at first because he could not sound the letter "r" which appeared to sound like a "w". Captain Honey was Second in Command of the Company and the Adjutant. He specialised in teaching us to salute. He saw that we gave an extra special salute when we went up to the table on pay days and received our pittance, and then another good salute when we had got it and were leaving the table. We dare not do otherwise than bring the right hand up to the cap with a semi-circular sweep, pause, and cut it smartly down. Still, as some of us said, it was worth the special effort to draw the money, even if it were not so much. The amount depended on whether an allotment was made or not and, of course, on the size of that allotment. I did not draw on average five shillings a week, about three shillings and sixpence! It was not much, yet it was sufficient for my needs. I was a non-smoker and non-drinker. Roughly speaking my only out of the ordinary needs were writing paper, a few picture postcards and postage stamps.

On the way up from the Park entrance gates to the Earl's residence, on either side of the roadway were some very fine tall trees. The trees represented officers and here we learned some of our saluting. We were taught to raise our right hand up to the cap three paces from the tree, carry the salute as we marched past it and then lower the hand smartly after we had marched past the tree another three paces.

Nights set in very early and there was nothing much to do after tea at five o'clock Some of us spent the evenings in our billets, teetotal like I was. Other met at the "Crown" or the "Black Swan" (known as the "Mucky Duck") and whiled their time away there. Others made friends in the town and even in the neighbouring villages and spent their leisure hours very pleasantly. A publican in a nearby village with an eye to business, yet sympathising with the boys who did not wish to drink beers etc., opened up a private room for them where they could buy lemonade etc. Many of the youngsters flocked there and spent many an enjoyable evening there. It was too far away for me, so I stayed in my billet and read a lot, played cards or wrote many letters. I sometimes retired to bed very early because I was often very tired. Saturday and Sunday afternoons were free and Mac and I would explore the neighbourhood, which was very beautiful, and we found many charming villages and enchanting paths. The quiet path to Rievaulx Abbey was very attractive. From the Abbey another path wound steeply through the woods and brought us up to a crescent-shaped terrace nearly half a mile in length. An interesting temple stood at each end and the views from here were very beautiful.

Helmsley too had its attractive points – the market square with a cross, a Court House and interesting old houses.

Christmas was drawing near and the earliest recruits were sweating on leave, weren't we all, hopefully? I do not remember if lots were drawn to see who the lucky ones were to be, or if the companies were to go alphabetically. I do recall that 'C' Company's men were to stay at Helmsley for Christmas, so it was decided to make as good a show of enjoying ourselves as possible and that a grand spread was to be the most important part of Christmas Day.

'C' Company hired the large room upstairs at the Court House. As we dined excellently on the day, the Colonel looked in and wished us all the very best of wishes. C.S.M. Kent was acting "off parade" and was in great form. One of the Companies had its spread in the workhouse and may, or may not, have inspired the well-known ditty, "It was Christmas Day in the Workhouse".

My turn for leave came in the New Year of 1916, as did that of all 'C' Company men, and we spent the days from January 10th to 15th at our homes. The leave, being an ordinary one from Helmsley to which we had to return, could be enjoyed to the full and was not marred by thoughts of going "out there". I visited all my friends, old and new – the new ones being those at the College who had not enlisted. One of my early calls was to the old Secondary School, the Boulevard, where I talked with the masters and with some of the scholars who knew me when I was a Prefect at the Lower End. I learned that some of the O.B.s had been killed in action. The scholars were particularly interested in my cap badge and the black buttons. At the College some of the men asked what the Army life was like. "Fine, especially for those who like an easy time," I said, half in fun. To those who asked, "When are you going out to France?" I replied: "It does not look as if we shall go out at all."

We were all optimistic at that time, we did not look ahead even though Christmas had not brought the expected peace. My old school pal, John Bell, who was a draughtsman at a local shipbuilding works doing Government work on submarines, passed our house going for his dinner. I set him back afterwards, just as in peacetime we had taken evening walks together. We were idealists and talked much of conditions but I kept off talking about Army life.

I spent the rest of my time with my mother. She was anxious to know if I would be going "out", and fortunately I could not say that we were. She persuaded me to have my photo taken, although I did not want to. We were taken together and also had a separate one of me on my own. The photographers were doing a roaring trade – it's an ill wind that blows nobody good. My boyish face seemed to be out of place under a soldier's cap. I laughed at the figure I cut, but Mother looked at it from a different angle altogether. I guess that she was proud of me and her voice showed it when she introduced me to her friends. Everybody was very friendly and the short leave seemed to pass very quickly. When the end came the goodbyes were not all sad for there was no need to worry. Wasn't I returning to Helmsley to continue my Army life as a "Featherbed Soldier"?

We got back from leave and found a change in one direction. All the numerous instructors from Winchester had returned to their base depot as it was now believed that our own N.C.O.s could do all the necessary instructing. The former had, when taking us, often shocked us with certain words they used. We weren't familiar with some words that started with "b", at least not in every sentence; and a much shorter word that really shook us. Their frequent jibes in the early days amused us and they soon realised that they could ease off, especially the jibe about our upbringing. Up to this time I was just a rifleman and had no idea whatever when the specialist formations were made. We knew that our youngest officer, Eden, had gone on a bombing course and that some recruits were keen on the machine gun. We noticed an N.C.O. of another section somewhat strangely dressed for a Tommy. He wore breeches and puttees put on from knee down to ankle; he wore a collar and tie and an officer's cap at a jaunty angle. He carried a light cane and kid gloves. He was a specialist N.C.O. having been on a tour weeks' course before I had arrived at Helmsley. I was to learn who he was some weeks later.

The battalion being now at full strength, we had an inspection by the G.O.C. Northern Command. We were drawn up in columns of platoons for the occasion and on reaching No.12 platoon he spoke to a young boy quite close to me and asked him a question. Lance Wakefield replied by telling him that he had been put into 'C' Company whilst all his friends had been placed in 'D' Company. I think that the G.O.C. had asked him if he was happy or satisfied and, on hearing what Lance had replied, he said, "Would you like to join them?" Of course, Lance did, and a short time later he was transferred to the Company that he wanted. He became a runner, a specialist job and a very hard and dangerous one out at the front.

The workhouse was the billet for some of the cooks, George for 'B' Company, Brickie for 'C' Company, Sergeant Kilham for the H.Q. (yes, that was his true name, not his objective!). Despite the large number of deer on the estate, we never had venison, though in season it was sold in the market place at four pence a pound.

2

Aldershot – A Dog's Life

Shortly after my return to Helmsley from leave, things began to get busy. Parades were more frequent and we seemed to be racing against time in order to learn, if not practise, all drills and duties. Up to that time we had never heard any rumours, but suddenly it was whispered that we were shortly to move and then all knew that we were about to go south, to Aldershot – the training base of the Southern Command. I wrote home and warned my mother that if she did not hear from me for a few days it would be because the battalion was about to move. I would give her my new address when the move had taken place. One Sunday morning January 22nd, 1916, we paraded in full pack, marched to Helmsley railway station and entrained. What a crush! Ten men with full kit to one compartment. We did not grumble as we stacked our equipment on to the luggage racks. Five of us had to try and sit down whilst the other five struggled to put their kits up and then we were able to dispose of ours. There had been a struggle to get near the windows to wave goodbye to many of the Helmsley people who had come to see us go. We were all very happy and carefree and we all wanted to see the countryside, and especially to wave to anyone on any small country railway station. A very pretty girl on Raskelf station drew everybody's attention and she waved to all of us, right along the train. Then we settled down and sat still as we realised that our train was missing all the large stations and making its way non-stop.

We had a rough idea of what towns we would be passing en route, but as the day wore on we saw no people anywhere. Dusk came and we might have been near London, but we did not know. Most probably our train side-tracked it. Darkness came and eventually we reached our destination where we detrained. We lined up and marched off led by a band that played our Regimental March, a very quick and lively tune suitable for a light infantry battalion, and we stepped out very briskly to it. We entered the North Camp, marched to the Stanhope Lines and halted at the Barossa Barracks, which were to be our new quarters. Barracks? On our first view of them that very first night there, in darkness, they looked like a prison, not billets. We were ordered to take off our packs, put them down and sit on them if we wished to do so whilst our N.C.O.s went off for instructions. They found out all right and told us where each platoon had to go, but then came a most startling order. "Barrack rooms to be scrubbed out before you settle down. Hot water, buckets and soap can be drawn from the cookhouse, over there. JUMP TO IT!"

Cheerfully, well quite cheerfully, we dashed to thec ookhouse where the staff had plenty of buckets etc waiting for us and most kindly and with much good humour, handed them out. We hurried to the rooms allocated to us and got busy. Many willing hands made light of the work, each of us getting down on our knees and cleaning the floor as quickly as we could. We arranged the little bedsteads around the walls and the N.C.O.s gave us our positions. Then we had to draw blankets and a "donkey's breakfast" as a mattress, and finally make up our own beds. We were very tired and wasted no time in getting down to it. What a change! Those beds were nothing like the featherbeds that we had left behind in Helmsley, but we soon fell asleep. A short sleep it was too, for at half past six a bugle sounded Reveille and we realised that Aldershot already looked like soldiering proper. There was no turning over for a few extra minutes' nap because what seemed to be very thunderous voices yelled out, "Jump to it! Show a leg!" and the N.C.O.s, our own, were the owners of those rousing words, and gave us no chance of hesitating. No loitering though the morning was cold. "Give me the man who can sing in the morning," called out one of the boys. In reply, another one yelled, "Give me the man who can sing at night," that is after a day's training! Quickly we half dressed, found out where the wash house was, a more thorough wash than usual because of the dirty work we had had to do the evening before, returned to our room and completed our dressing. We ran down to the mess room and obtained some bread, a bit of bacon and a drink of tea – our breakfast. Having done full justice to that first meal, for we were very hungry, we cleaned the lid of the dixie because we had drawn our bacon in it; after rinsing under a tap we dried the other part of the dixie in which we had drawn our tea.

We returned to our barrack room in order to smarten ourselves up for the first parade at nine o'clock. Those men who had not shaved before breakfast now did so, but I did not have to. I had never had to use a razor, perhaps there was just a little show of down on my face but it could not be seen very well because of my fair complexion. I was fortunate and even lucky, as I realised many months later. "Double up there on parade!" shouted the Sergeants. "At the double!" From the barracks to the square had to be done at the double. No-one had to be seen walking or even stepping smartly to the parade ground, where we did squad drill and company drill in the Light Infantry extra

quickstep. "Pick 'em up, pick 'em up!" Though we had perhaps broken our mothers' hearts, the instructors soon forgot that well-known jibe, "If you broke your mother's heart, you won't break mine. Pick 'em up, pick 'em up! Left, right, left, right, left, right, left!" It was soon noticed that no Drill Sergeant varied the number of "lefts" and "rights". Always a group of three "left, rights" and an extra "left". I often wondered what would happen if he accidentally cut out one "left, right" or even added another "left, right". Would it upset the whole rhythm of his commands?

The little bit of training at Helmsley was nothing to this real soldiering. My, didn't we improve – in leaps and bounds. We were all keen, not only to be able to do the drills, but also to know all about them. So we went to Gale and Polden's in Aldershot and bought them out of many of their military publications, such as *Infantry Training, Company Drill, Squad, Section, Platoon and Company Drill* and *Rifle Exercises Made Easy*. With their help we knew as much as the officers and the N.C.O.s, if not more. We could tell when any one gave the wrong order and yet do the right thing.

Aids to Scouting by Baden-Powell was another of my purchases in the book line. It was a mine of information about a different kind or warfare and I realised after I had read it that it could not be of much use for trench warfare. We had to make sure that the books we bought were suitable for light infantry training for some of the orders were quite different from those used by ordinary line regiments. We did not always receive an order: "Attention!", but came to that position from "Stand at ease!" position when another order like. "Move to the left in fours" was given. We carried our rifles at the trail and not at the slope, so we would receive the order "Trail arms" or do it without an order when moving off, it being understood that we trailed them. When lining up we of 'C' Company would be instructed to "Leave plenty of woom in your wanks for your wifles", as our Northumbrian officer put it.

Bayonet drill "On guard". Thrusting, parrying etc and then practice in trench taking driving home the bayonet into the sacks that represented the enemy; pretending to let off the cartridge in the spout if the bayonet seemed to stick; trench digging; in fact everything from route marching to night operations. We took in everything, in practice. To test our fitness we had long route marches in full pack. Perhaps lucky was the man who was able to substitute an oblong box instead of his greatcoat. His valise certainly looked much more tidy than the one in which a folded up greatcoat was fixed in with difficulty. Many were the sore feet and many were the blistered feet. The treatment for blisters was to thread a large needle with grey wool and pass it through the blister, thus drawing out the liquid inside it. Just as we thought that we were making great strides to becoming real soldiers, one certain day showed us how weak some of us were. It was on the day of inoculation. 'C' Company had to parade for that ordeal at two p.m. Some two hundred of us formed a single line stretching from the medical room to the barrack room. Tunics were taken off and the left shirt sleeves rolled up. I, being in No.12 platoon, was in the last quarter and could watch all those in front of me get nearer to the M.O. who stood on the steps just outside the medical room. His orderly dabbed something on cotton wool on the upper part of each man's left arm, then the M.O. did a slashing movement with the needle as it making the kind of diagram used in playing noughts and crosses (two horizontal slashes, crossed by two vertical slashes). The sight of this operation unnerved a few before they reached the M.O. for their turn and they just fell down in a faint. And what seemed odd was the fact that the men who fainted were the tallest men in the Company. It was not till 5.30 p.m. that I received my needle thrust. Inoculation earned each man twenty-four hours off duty, although it had no ill effects on anyone.

When the time for vaccination came, the same procedure was followed. Eric washed the spot with a vaccine on the left arm; the M.O. scratched that place in the same manner. A few unlucky men developed badly swollen arms, whilst most of us merely felt a little stiff and sore. What appeared very strange was the fact that there was no off duty allowed after vaccination which affected us more than the inoculation.

We had to learn the bugle calls and we soon became familiar with "Cookhouse", "Reveille", "Letters", "Fall in all the Company" and even "Defaulters". The battalion soon had its own buglers, including Musson from Co. Durham and Jimmy Hannah of 'C' Company, the latter being one of the six Juniors who often practised in the barrack room much to the annoyance of some men. His efforts amused us at first, even the excitement when he went on and on practising the Regimental March, but he really had the last laugh for he had a very easy time of it. Even when on duty he just stood by ready to do his blowing but we were in kip when he sounded "Lights out" and he was up before us to blow "Reveille".

The "Cookhouse" usually caused a wild dash to see who could be first in the queue at the mess room.

Breakfasts were good on the whole; teas varied, but once a week on Sundays there was always "high tea" reminding me of my young days at home – an extra course of a piece of fruit cake, or tinned fruit, or tinned fish. Anyhow there was nothing to grumble about when we compared tea with dinner. The latter invariably went down badly if it went down at all. Some of the dinners were hardly fit to eat. Many a time dozens of us threw our curried stew into the waste food bins and wished that we had not soiled our dixies by drawing it. Curried stew was served from a large copper or boiler, similar to the old washboiler at home, and the top of it was covered with a green slimy skin which probably scared us off liking it. Anyhow, the pigs belonging to the waste food collector would enjoy it. Always after a meal of this kind there was a mad dash to the canteen where a long queue would wait for tea and cake or sausage and mash. By the time all were served it was almost time for the afternoon parade.

We paid rather dearly for our purchases at the canteen – those who could afford to go there – one shilling for a thin slice of currant loaf was rather exorbitant. We lined well the pockets of the profiteers. We were growing lads and had very healthy appetites and, as the Army did not provide supper, another visit was made to the canteen by the better off. Yes, of course, the Orderly Officer for the day came round at dinner times, sometimes just as the meal was being dished out or more often when the meal was nearly finished. "Orderly Officer!" bawled out the N.C.O. accompanying the officer and banging his stick on a table so that we all heard him. "Any complaints?" True to the British way of putting up with almost anything after a little grousing, there were no complaints. The Orderly Officer passed on and whether he saw the wasted food or not, or saw the queues at the canteen on his way, when late, I do not know. He was probably glad that there were no complaints.

Considering that we were "in the Army now", a rather humorous incident happened to me in the later Aldershot days. At tea in the mess room one Sunday, a bread crust struck me on the head. I looked around but could not then detect who had thrown it. Again, a second piece of bread struck me, and I turned round very quickly just in time to notice that Mac Williams was the culprit. So the next time I was hit I retaliated and let him have it back. Just my bad luck! At that moment the Lance Corporal on duty entered the room. Immediately he came up to me and said, "You'll be for Company Office in the morning! Crime, ungentlemanly behaviour." Nine o'clock the next morning, "C/12747 Rifleman Dennis -shun! Hat off, quick march! Halt!" I was before the O/C of the Company in the Orderly Room. When the crime had been read out to him, Captain Pitt gave me a severe dressing down for such disgusting behaviour. "The Army tries to make a gentleman of you, and here you are ... .. at tea."

I could not help thinking how funny his words were. He was a Londoner and I would have like to have told him where most of his Company came from and the type of men and boys who were in his Company. He was a gentleman alright, very kind but many years older than most of us. Regular Army instructors had probably thought that we were not gentlemen and any language was used to let us know, but I think that the C.O. knew all about us. I managed to escape with a caution.

Every man in the battalion had to declare his religion whether he had one or not because there were Sunday morning Church Parades. Those of no recognised denomination quickly found one or the Sergeant entered them as C. of E. (Church of England) because a good show was expected at that Church. I was a Wesleyan, graduating from the "tin chapel" of my early days. My school friend, Frank, whose father was a lay minister at the Great Thornton Street Wesleyan Church persuaded me to join his Church and I learned to type in the vestry there. Besides that, C.H. Hulbert, the minister there, corresponded with me, keeping in touch and sent me a New Testament. (Two of his relatives were well-known on the London stage).

How I recall the Sunday morning parades. The C.S.M. would call out: "Fall out the Atheists or any others who have not a religion." They were put on cookhouse fatigue – peeling potatoes, cleaning out the large dixies (especially the greasy ones). A lot depended what minister was to take the service at the Aldershot Church. If a Bishop was to give the sermon then all but Roman Catholics were made C. of E. for a very good muster.

In our own Company some nosey N.C.O. noticed that our hair was still very much civilian, that there was a parting and that some hair stood out at the back of our caps. Hence a few junior N.C.O.s formed nightly raiding parties, seized the long-haired men and "jail cropped" them. Some of us alerted to this press ganging and slipped into town to get our hair cut very short at the back and sides. Our caps hid the hair on the top and we were left alone.

Zeppelin raid alarms caused a stir and a little excitement. Whenever it was known that such enemy airships were approaching England we had to rise out of bed, dress in the dark and rush to the barrack square. No Zeppelin came near our part of the country and so we never knew what action we would take. All we did was to stand in Companies, as on parade, ready to march off if there were any danger. We stood there for two hours or more, gradually becoming annoyed at having been called out. On one occasion Mac Williams slept through the alarm but he was never missed as no roll was called. Another time when all were outside, an N.C.O. going round the barracks to see if anyone was still in bed, found me asleep. The Lance Corporal in charge of our section was so windy, not of the alarm but of being found out that I was still in bed, said nothing, just dragged me up and helped me to dress.

Then came the days when parades were from early morning till late at night with just breaks for meals. Reveille was at six o'clock when those who wanted it rushed down to the mess room for "gun fire" – weak but warm coffee and biscuits. This consideration for our welfare was good and very acceptable, especially on cold mornings and the biscuits were tasty and sweet. Some men did not bother to go for this appetiser, preferring a few extra minutes in bed, but I always went. This extra item on the daily menu was available for only a quarter of an hour, so I had to be very slick – others were too slow and missed the chance of a warmer. A short parade immediately followed, some physical jerks which also warmed us up; I thought the latter a very good idea because I always woke up cold – many years passed before I knew why: a skin deficiency). After breakfast the morning parades started at nine o'clock. Noon – dismissal for dinner. Afternoon – parades, tea. Still the days were not finished. Something was found for us to do from six until nine. One evening we practised and practised again the making of a tidy full valise. It was quite an art, folding the greatcoat so that it fitted perfectly into the pack and still left room for such articles as the body belt, cap comforter-cum-scarf, socks, housewife, spare shirt, towel, etc, to form a rectangular box-like container.

Another evening in the barrack room the C.S.M. took us for putting together our equipment – practice and practice again after taking it to pieces. Finally, "Let's see who can put the equipment together and put it on and stand to attention when finished." I won, much to my surprise. I was to know later that the C.S.M. duly noted it.

Strange how we did our best despite all the time taken up on extra parades. We groused more but still worked hard. Life seemed to be hard and monotonous and at one time felt it really was a dog's life. Some classed Aldershot with a very hot place and said that we were being made fed-up with England in order to be ready and willing to go out to France. We had evening barrack room rifle practice; loading and unloading with dummy clips of five, practice five rounds rapid fire. A parrot-like instructor described the service rifle, the Lee Enfield Mark III. He never paused, seemed hardly to take breath as he recited his story from butt to sight. I wonder what would have happened if one of us had interrupted him. Would he have fainted? Would he have become hysterical and blazed away at the interrupter? I wonder, but I'm sure he would have had to start all over again from butt to sight.

I was given the Lee Enfield rifle Mark III No. 8301 T and before I left England for France I realised that it was perfect, it had been perfectly sighted. As soon as it was considered that we each knew our own rifle we were given a scoring book in which to enter the results of a general course of musketry to be fired at the Ash Vale ranges. The weather on that morning of our musketry course was shocking, two or three inches of snow lay on the barrack square as we lined up. What a wait before setting off and then we marched a few miles to the ranges. Field kitchens accompanied us and were we glad for the hot meals between shoots! At my first shoot I managed a twelve inch ring and did fairly well in all the other shoots, gaining enough marks to be called a second class shot. My highest score was seventeen out of twenty but what I consider my best effort and the worst was a four hundred yards, five rounds from a trench. My first four shots were all bulls, so the Adjutant (Honey) and Eden in charge gathered round me with those who had already finished. They spurred me on but actually put me off with my fifth shot. The excitement was too much for me. They distracted me and that final shot was signalled by a red flag – I had missed the target, but put it in the bull of the target on my right where the man using it had already finished. So I really did score five bulls. I had not done quite as well at shorter distance targets. At moving targets I was a little slow, perhaps due to very cold fingers, but I did learn that my rifle, if aimed at six o'clock did score a bull, and even with bayonet fixed it behaved in the same way. I often wonder if the wearing of glasses was of great help in that, in aligning the two sights, I had only a small lens to look with.

"All work and no play makes Tommy a dull boy," if you let it. It was all graft now, excepting Saturday afternoons and Sundays when Mac and I, in walking-out dress wearing a belt and carrying a swagger stick, left the barracks behind and paid a visit to the town. Aldershot was alive with Military Police (M.P.s) who were very keen on watching Tommies on pass-out. We did not mind them much at first but they seemed to acquire a bad name. It was rumoured that they eyed everyone hoping to take someone in charge for "clink". Our walking-out appearance had to be absolutely correct, tunic buttons fastened, no hands in pockets, boots cleaned and polished bright, etc. Aldershot itself was a poor sort of place. There was nothing about it and I found it even difficult to find postcards to send home. All I could find was a set of *Daring Deeds*. These were pictures of soldiers winning the M.M. or D.C.M. In fact, I could not give anyone an idea of the layout of Aldershot, a sure sign that it was not a very pleasant place in which to spend an afternoon of leisure.

A little fed up with Saturday evening, I strolled through our lines to those of the Queen's and entered their wet canteen. A concert was in progress and a young lady was singing *Keep the Home Fires Burning*. I sat down and listened and forgot how fed up I was. We had sung that song in the evenings in the barrack room and marched to it, but that girl put something into it that touched her listeners. We felt forced to listen and no-one made the slightest noise. It struck some hidden chord in us and made us go back in time and made us daydream. She finished it, then there was a pause in which we pulled ourselves back into reality, then the applause was deafening. The next turn, a comic, did not receive the same respect. Some listened to him and enjoyed his quips, some half listened and joined in the laughs, and others paid him no attention whatever but talked and laughed among themselves. Yet at the end of the turn, they joined in the applause. The canteen was becoming very stuffy and full of tobacco smoke which made my eyes sting so I left.

By far the best relief from all the rush was a weekend visit to London. An old school pal called Frank Lancaster had gone to relatives in Charlton in order to recuperate after a severe illness, which he called double pneumonia. I had often visited him when he was ill and he had tried to teach me the game of chess in one lesson and beat me in three moves, so I had never played chess again. We had kept in touch when I joined up and I had no doubt that he would have joined with me if he had been well. He was staying with his aunt and uncle and invited me over for the weekend. From the Company Office I received my pass: "C/12747 Rfn. ... has permission to be absent from his quarters from 1 p.m. Saturday to 10 p.m. Sunday for the purpose of proceeding to London." With a light heart I set off and eventually reached Waterloo Station alright. There was no-one there to meet me, as I had expected. Not knowing London at all, I went outside the station and asked a policeman to direct me to Charlton. He did not know where it was, for London was such a big place that he knew only certain parts of it. I tried another policeman and he did not know, but suggested that I by asking someone else. I did at last find someone who could tell me which bus to use and where to find it. Consequently I did not reach Elliscombe Road until six o'clock and his aunt told me that both Frank and his uncle had gone to search for me. They did not return until seven o'clock. By the time we had had tea and talked a lot, it was too late to go out. Although there was no Reveille the next morning I awoke early but did not get up until ten o'clock. We had an early dinner and then left for the City. Frank showed me many of the well-known places which I had, of course, heard about, but never seen – the Houses of Parliament and St. Paul's. For the most part talk of old times at school together and news about the Army took up most of our time and interest. We had tea in one of the Lyons' cafés at some corner, but I do not remember its name.

Shortly afterwards I had to be making my way back to Waterloo Station; the weekend seemed to have been very short and I had not really done much in London, but the break from barracks was very welcome. I bid goodbye to Frank, whom I was never to see again, and at a few minutes to ten reported back to the battalion Guard Room – which I knew fairly well as I had done a turn on guard there, or rather I had been picked for guard duty but was judged to be the smartest man in the group and hence did the mess orderly duties for those who were not so lucky.

Keenness on parade led to the Sergeant-Major asking Mac and me if we would like to be Lance Corporals. We had watched the Lance-Jacks, as we called them, and noticed that they seemed to do all the work which was passed down from all of higher rank, and they got all the blame if anything went wrong and everybody knew too that some of those junior N.C.O.s, if not all, were not paid for their one stripe – they were acting unpaid provisional, but recipients of all the kicks. So Mac and I fought shy of the idea and said that we preferred to stay as we were, at least for the time being and that we would think about it We were however frightened that we would have to accept such promotion if the C.S.M. insisted, so we cast our eyes about with the idea of joining some specialist group. Suddenly one Monday morning at the nine o'clock parade, it was announced that some specialist sections were short of the required number of men. Bombers? No, we turned down the idea of preparing for suicide. Then, the Signal Section of the Company needed two more volunteers. Up went our hands like a flash and we were told to fall out and go and report to the Signal Sergeant in a hut not far away. He turned out to be that very smart N.C.O. we had seen in Helmsley market square. Though we did not know it then, that quick change on our part was one of the most sensible moves we ever made. We never regretted joining the Signals Section and were often thankful that no-one else volunteered for it that morning.

We were told to take off our equipment and take it back to the barrack room and then were put with two newcomers to the Section from each Company into the beginners' squad. Our first task was to learn the morse code, the Sergeant himself taking us. Without the Morse code alphabet we could not do any actual signalling. He sent out the Morse with the buzzer key of a D Mark III telephone and helped us to grasp the letters and their codes with long and short sounds corresponding to the sounds of the Morse. We had to remember the letter "c" with dash-dot-dash-dot, or "murder, murder"; the letter "f" by dot-dot-dash-dot, or "does it hurt you?", and so on. He emphasised the opposites: A and n; B and v; d and u; g and w; etc, then all the dots: e, l, s and h, all the dashes: t, m and o. I knew one of the dashes from Scout days. All good Scouts make a dash for tea. We soon picked up all the letters and in some cases their signalese pronunciation: ack for a, pip for p; vic for v; toc for t, and so on. The letters that had their special pronunciation were those that sounded much alike – b, p, t, c and v. The next step was to learn the use of some of the apparatus used in signalling: the telephone, the flag, the disc and lamp. There was only one way to hold the buzzer key when making the letters. If the flag was not held properly when sending morse, then blisters soon came on to the hands. All this work was very interesting; more so than ordinary company work and drills, etc. Soon Mac and I caught up with the others. Then came office work, the receiving and sending of messages, laying telephones, the care of the lines and station work. The evening work too, with the Lucas signalling, was of great interest. Practice followed practice – tests of six word groups – speed in sending and speed in receiving groups, aiming to get beyond ten words a minute and being able to qualify for a first in the forthcoming tests, and wear a first class badge on the lower sleeve of the tunic – a pair of crossed signal flags.

I put on one side my manuals of the different drills, formations, etc, and bought the Army Signalling Manual, Notes on Army Signalling and Hints on Signalling as did most of the others. We spent the little spare time we had studying those books, usually just after nine o'clock in the barrack room. The other company men heard us helping one another nick-named us the "Flagwaggers" and the "Iddy-Umptiers". (Iddy was the short, and umpty the long in saying to ourselves the letters: the letter A was iddy-umpty, the long in saying to ourselves the letters; the letter C was umpty-iddy-umpty-iddy, and so on). We also made up another sort of alphabet to help us in fixing, the letter with the morse code; we made the letter A with a dot on the cross stroke and then one line of the letter itself, the right hand one, and so we had λ for B one upright stroke and a dot at the top right, a dot in the middle and a dot at the bottom left, thus ╞ etc.

There was a lot of leg-pulling in the barrack room without any ill-feeling. What could be said of our barrack room could be said of the other companies – we were all good pals, on and off parade, and let nothing mar the good spirit of comradeship that was wonderful. Even Bob Faill, a farmer from the wilds of Rothbury in wildest Northumberland, threatened to shoot us in fun if we dared another iddy-umpty, and he pointed his rifle at us, laughing at his own idea of a joke. His blunt language with a distinct northern burr was beautiful to hear.

Old friends sought one another when parades were finished and when the time permitted it. Bram had joined the Bombers and he revealed that whilst he was on a bombing course a Mills bomb had exploded prematurely and wounded one man. The wound was a slight one, and that news of our first casualty hardly affected us – a nine day wonder, and then it was forgotten by us, but not by the Bombers who learned from its cause. I asked Bram how he came to be one of the Bombing Section and his explanation as to how the Section had been formed was quite amusing. On parade one morning in the good old Helmsley days a Sergeant had asked all cricketers, especially bowlers to step forward. A number of men, thinking that there was going to be a cricket match, stepped forward from the ranks and received the news. "You are now Bombers."

After pay day each week I sought an interview with C.Q.M.S. Woodward concerning the allotment I had made to my mother and the understood additional amount from the Army. Some weeks had passed and she had received only the amount deducted from my pay, no additional money. He had kept on saying that it had not come through, but finally he explained that, as I was not earning anything at the time I enlisted, no extra could be given, i.e I was not entitled to anymore. So much for the scrap of paper I had signed about allotments of pay. I was somewhat upset for I felt that I had been bluffed and now my mother would have to suffer. Just a few shillings saved, in my case, but I learned later when I got talking to other young boys and men who had joined up voluntarily that the same thing had happened to them. It made me, Mac, Mac W. and Jimmy and many others think that the "Prinnie" had been right in one way – we ought to have been laggards and waited to be called up. Then we should have been better off for our families' sakes. I don't suppose that Kitchener knew of this aspect of the volunteers who swelled his battalions. Like all the others, I soon got over this upset and knew that what was done could not be undone. It was better to grin and bear it. Besides, I had a feeling that I was somewhat of a fatalist.

So, no longer feeling sore, I did not let the matter deter me from preparing myself for the Brigade Signalling Test. I was very keen to get my crossed flags. With the other late Joiners of the Signal Section, I went across the parade ground to the Royal Engineers' Barracks and was put through a stiff examination in every branch of signalling and was then invited to tea – which included a banana, much to my great surprise. When the results came through we had all passed and were now first class signallers, at last privileged to wear crossed flags. As soon as possible we bought the crossed flags and sewed them on our left sleeves at the bottom. I wrote home and told my mother of a slight change in how she should in future address letters to me, "Signaller" not "Rifleman" any more. I was greatly amused for, in her very next letter to me, hopefully she said that she was glad to hear the news because she had been told that Signallers did not go into action. This idea was far different from that of a certain N.C.O. in 'C' Company. When his friend joined the Signal Section, he said, "You've done a nice thing. Signallers have to stand on the parapet of the trench and send back messages by flag. You've committed suicide, Perce." Perhaps he was leg-pulling or perhaps that is what a lot of people thought. In any case, I let my mother keep on believing that what she had heard was right.

The Signal Section was about thirty strong under 2nd Lt. T.E. Turner, whom we all liked. From one point of view he was as much an officer as we were soldiers. He was more like a gentleman in an officer's uniform, just as we were civilians in green-khaki. When our Sergeant reported, "All present and correct, sir", he showed that he felt ill at ease. The moment when he returned the Sergeant's salute seemed to be a hard one for him and he looked happier when it was over. Our number was just sufficient for the battalion's needs, so each Company was asked to provide four men more to be trained as reserve signallers. We soon got to know them but hoped that they would not have to be called upon, as they would be used when some of us – dreaded thought – would be prevented from carrying out our duties. One of those reserve signallers had earlier been caught by the Sergeant-Major shaving with his tunic on and had been brought up before his Company Officer for being "dirty". What had startled the "prisoner" when caught was a very hard voice that yelled out, "What a yer a-doing of?" A very serious crime, according to the S.M., who was a regular, his time being almost up.

One evening George Bramley brought into the barrack room a dummy Mills Bomb for him and his fellow members of the supposed "suicide club" to take to pieces and gain some knowledge of this type of bomb. I joined the party and learned as much as I could about it, for as a specialist signaller I should never have chance again to do so. I preferred to be occupied with something in the evenings when not busy with letter writing or reading my manuals. I tagged on to the machine gun section when possible and allowed to do so. Grayson of 'C' Company sometimes brought a Lewis gun into the room to discuss it, to handle it, to take it down, and I listened in. I was only too sorry that I did not get any handling practice – that was too much for me to expect as his section had prior call.

All the specialist sections spent most of the parades at their own particular work and thus missed much of the boring "jerks" and drills. Only occasionally did we, the Signallers, hear "In two ranks, fall in", "Number off", "Fall in", "Form fours", or when rushing at a sack with bayonet fixed: "Do you think you are pricking a sausage?" We did spend a day in mock trenches and took part in a mock battle. None of the Signallers was picked to learn to reverse arms and so attend a funeral party.

On route marches with the battalion we joined in the wonderful singing of the many songs we picked up. I felt sorry for the men near me, for I could make only the poorest of sounds. *You ought to join, you ought to join the King's Royal Rifles You ought to join the King's Royal Rifles: Six bob a week and nothing to eat: Damn great boots and blisters on your feet. We are Fred Karno's Army* (tune of Greenland's Icy Mountains) *Tipperary* and *Pack up your Troubles* were two very popular ones. *At the halt on the left form platoon Here we are – here we are The Farmer's Boy* was sung more often in the barrack rooms by the many men from the land, especially those from County Durham.

In mid-April the Sergeants invited the officers to their mess for an evening is entertairment. Many concoctions were brewed and drunk with very little effect. Captain Worsley, in Yorkshire dialect, told all of a poor little mouse which swam round and round a vat till it drowned – much pathos.

About the same time many of the other ranks began to think that "out there" could not be much worse than Aldershot, save the killing. The days were long and the parades non-stop and, in our ignorance of trench warfare and the real war, for all the spit and polish and boring training did not seem to be of much use, we were tempted to look forward to leaving Aldershot. Any move and change of scenery would be welcomed. Then we heard that there was to be a Divisional Inspection by the King, and when it took place on Laffan's plain on Wednesday, April 26th, we knew that the end of our stay was near. The review was almost the last straw when we saw how such inspections were carried out.

We all stayed in our barrack rooms on the Tuesday night and though we had no brass buttons to clean we did wipe over our black ones. We put together our equipment and packed our valises, not daring to substitute boxes for greatcoats. We cleaned our boots and saw that our rifle barrels were clean. All this so that there would be the minimum to do in the morning after the morning meal. We got down to sleep as soon as possible; we did not need "Lights out".

Reveille was sounded sometime about five thirty a.m. Breakfast was ready at six o'clock and we had to be out on the battalion parade ground at seven thirty a.m. prompt in full marching order. Once again, our valises were absolutely full and contained all the required Army kit. We set off for Laffan's plain some miles away and took up our fixed battalion positions, all present and correct, ready for those who had never to be kept waiting. Officers and N.C.O.s were the windiest of all the troops – would anything go wrong even at the last minute? Suddenly we were ordered to take off our packs and sit on them; we did so and watched the looks of anxiety on the faces of the higher-ups. Not long before mid-day there was quite a stir in the air, which seemed to whisper, "They're comin" – whoever "they" were, and perhaps scouts had been sent out to watch for their approach. All excitement – "Packs on", "Stand-at-ease" – to wait until the mysterious person or persons got nearer and nearer to our battalion. The weakest felt the strain for the wait was no short one. A few fainted, some almost fainted. All the "fallen" were taken away by our medical room staff (practice for the stretcher-bearers), as those unfortunate men had not to be seen – out of sight, out of mind. As "they" had reached our battalion, our Company, " ... Shun!" and finally our platoon. "Rear rank, one step back March!" Red tabs or brass hats and I know not what passed along glancing at us, or some of us, and talking to one another. Perhaps they were discussing, and perhaps not. Then "they" were gone. "Rear rank, one step forwards. March!" "Stand at ease." That part of the business that concerned our platoon was over, all in a few minutes. Did the breeze murmur as we gave a well-drawn out sigh? Another long wait. Another stir. "Yeoman Rifles!" and we all came to attention. "Battalion will move to the right in fours." We formed our fours then did right turn and the battalion moved off in Companies. The March Past had started. "Eyes right." A matter of six or more paces, "Eyes left". We marched away from a saluting base hearing a muffled whisper, "The King". It was all over and we set off to march back to our barracks, many of us very tired. We were very glad to get our equipment off and slowly make our way to the mess room. Tea was eaten leisurely and the drink of tea most welcome. By the time we left the mess room, darkness had fallen. The day had been very long – had we satisfied "them"?

We did not realise the significance of this inspection because a direct result of it was leave for all ranks of the battalion – we paid our own railway fares. We had the impression that on Final Leave a free travel warrant was given to all. I was one of a group that was given leave from April 14th to April 19th, 1916, and for this I had to raise twenty-four shillings and sixpence. Of course, each of us appeared on a special Pay Parade but, though I was given more than usual, I still had a struggle to raise the fare. Just a few days at home, not knowing that this leave was after all Last Leave. What a horrible word "last". Fortunately I did not grasp the fact and looked forward to a grand break from all the activities at Aldershot. So the leave followed the same pattern as the last one, calling on friends, walks with John Bell and many hours with my mother, who was happy, not knowing that I was on Last Leave in England. The hours passed very quickly and the time came for my return to Aldershot where, no sooner in the barracks than rumours began to fly around.

The call for more men "out there" was common knowledge. It was said that the 40th Division, the Bantam Division, had not completed its training and was not ready to fill the breach so we would be going out almost immediately. Once again, photographs became the order of the day. This time they were of each Company and of specialist sections to be taken more or less officially by F. Scovell of Aldershot. The Company photographs having about two hundred men on them could not have the names of the men, but our signallers' photo of some fiftyseven had the names put below the photo. Mess room forms were arranged in tiers against one of the walls of the barracks. Our signal officer, Tocky Turner, and the N.C.O.s sat on the front row and the rest of us, except two who missed the parade and were admonished later, stood behind them and made a fine compact group . I suppose the expert military and commercial photographer would hear rumours of our "going out" or perhaps had been invited to come and take photographs. We bought postcard size to send to our friends and an enlargement to send home. I do not know when my mother received the one

I had ordered for her and I do not know if its arrival suggested what she was afraid to learn about our moving abroad.

A few days of doubt, then days of rush, excitement and preparations. "Each man will hand in to his Quarter-Master his spare uniform and spare boots, keeping those in a better condition."

Those things such as books, brushes and oddments, which it was said that we would not need overseas, were to be put into a parcel addressed to be sent home. We had to keep only issue clothing and kit. We were short of nothing for we had never had to watch our property, it was always safe. It was a recognised fact that any man could leave anything in his locker, on his box or his bed or just lying about – whether it was personal property such as a fountain pen, a wristlet watch, a wallet, etc, or his Army kit. He could go to the mess room, the wash room or anywhere else and return to find any article there where he had left it. Parcels had been opened and things taken out whilst on their way to us, but no-one ever lost anything in the barrack room.

I sent a card home warning my mother that our departure for overseas was imminent. At the time I addressed another letter ready for when I knew the exact time of our going. Certain men who had been found unfit were put into an 'E' Company and were to be left behind and later sent to the 22nd (Reserve) Battalion up at Skipton. With them were a few very young boys, who had been found out to have given the wrong age when enlisting and a 'C' Company youth we nick-named Guisboro because he came from that north Yorkshire town.

We were a complete battalion, ready for the Western Front, well-trained at forming fours, good at section, company and battalion exercises, rifle drill, marching and a little trench digging. The Signallers knew their morse code and could send messages with one flag and with two flags use the semaphore code; they were fully conversant with the D Mark III telephone, message forms, receiving and sending wiring and signalling with the Lucas lamp. The Bombers knew their Mills bomb and the Lewis Gunners their machine gun. All other specialists were also fully trained.

Whereas at Helmsley we had known very few of the recruits, through being billeted in houses, we now knew very well indeed the men of our Section, our Platoon (64 of them) and Company and all the N.C.O.s too. We were all good friends and a great spirit of comradeship had developed. All were looking forward to going out to France – some boys of sixteen who had not yet been found out; more aged seventeen, also not yet found out; and very many eighteen year olds who made up the majority of the battalion. All were volunteers except a few who had been called up (registration R/..). and the regular Sergeant-Majors and Quarter-Masters. A few officers from the south had joined us to complete our numbers; they too were mostly young.

Each man was proud of his own Company and, though I ought to have been in 'A' Company with the men of the East Riding of Yorkshire, I was delighted to make such a lot of real friends with the lads of County Durham and Northumberland. Their twang was quite distinct and they were full of fun; to me they were the salt of the earth. Many were the numbers of brothers in the battalion. In 'C' Company one pair were Jim and Buller Barrass from County Durham whose favourite expression when amused was, "Ye bugger o'hell, man!" The brothers in 'A' Company were named Duggleby and Frank and Gordon Hickes from near Hovingham; those in 'B' Company were the Nicholsons, Ernest and ?

After twelve weeks' intensive training at Aldershot, the "featherbed" image had

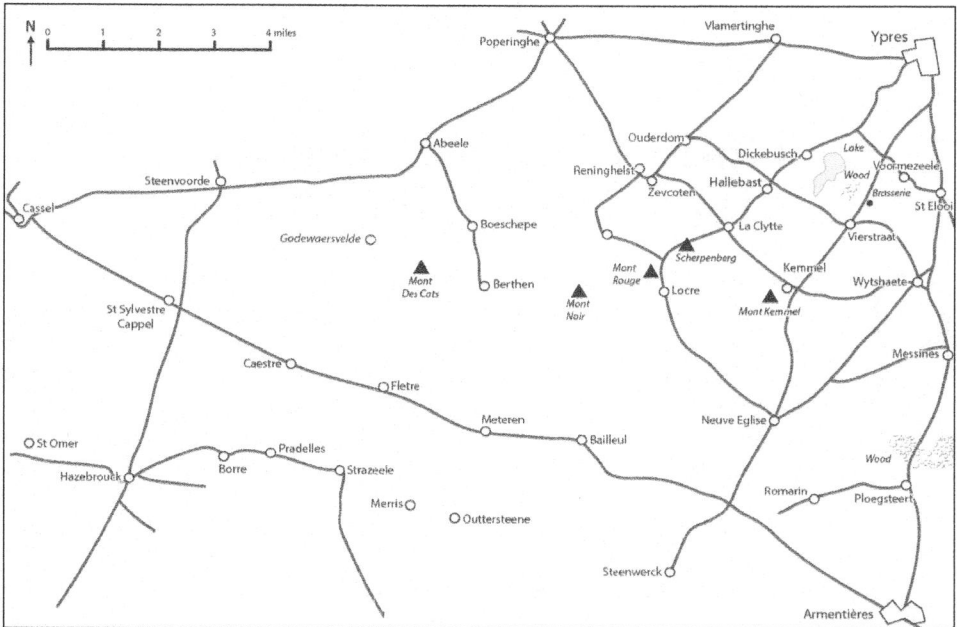

Map 1. Ypres, Armentières and vicinity

disappeared and we were all well-disciplined (self and Army). Now the Army, considerate of our welfare out there, gave us some advice. It was said that every man received a printed piece of paper from Kitchener warning him that care must be taken when drinking the wines for, being unaccustomed to them, he might easily become drunk. Be warned of the dangers of associating with a certain type of loose woman who would pester him out there as harmful diseases could be picked up from such. Very fatherly advice indeed, and I am not sure that all the recruits, particularly our youngest, understood what was behind the latter advice. Probably an English variety of that type of woman haunted the Aldershot area.

3

Outtersteene and Plugstreet – Preparation and Initiation

On Friday morning May 5th, 1916, the battalion assembled in full marching order outside the Barossa Barracks and then, without regret, its men left their training quarters. Carrying I know not what weight, we bid goodbye to Stanhope Lines. If our packs seemed unduly heavy, our hearts were light. I had prepared a letter addressed to my mother to let her know that I was going out to France. It was already stamped and I was looking for some means to get it into a pillar box. On to Farnborough where we entrained. All the way to Southampton Docks we were out of touch with civilians and I still had my letter.

Our train had not stopped anywhere, certainly not at a station where I had hoped to signal to someone to post it for me as I threw it out. We left the train and very slowly boarded a transport ship, 'A' and 'B' Companies went on board the *Marguarite*, and 'C' and 'D' Companies boarded the *Inventa*. One of these vessels was a recruited pleasure steamer from one of the Welsh coastal resorts. What a tight squeeze it was on board – talk about sardines in a tin, we felt like that. Most of us went down below and found places for our gear, on which we sat for a time. All the portholes were closed so that no lights shone out into the night. We were so packed together that there seemed to be little or no ventilation and soon there was a terrible fug.

Each one of us had to don a lifebelt. When I heard the sound of throbbing engines I went up on deck to get some fresh air and to see as much as I could of the disappearing warehouses, the dockside and Blighty. A slight drizzle fell but it did not last very long. I went down below again and tried to get some rest but it was impossible; sleep would not come. I was tired as were many others, but an innate excitement kept me awake. Back on deck again a moonless night with countless stars twinkled overhead, nothing to hear but a slight throb of engines. The thrill of looking about was to see all the other twinkling lights. A glance to the left or right revealed that signals were being flashed in morse code from destroyer to destroyer. We could not see these ships of war but realised that we were being escorted across the Channel. We were very safe, we were in the care of the British Navy. We were like chicks safely looked after by broody hens. Of course, there may have been German submarines lurking in the watery depths looking for suitable targets, and their commanders might think that a transport full of soldiers worth more to sink than a destroyer.

I was to make the Channel crossing five more times and only the last one of all, when I came home in order to be demobilised, was again by night. The other four were made during the hours of daylight. It had become to be deemed safer by day than by night for future transports, for hospital ships and leave boats. The shorter crossings were most used; Dover to Calais and the Folkestone-Boulogne and the reverse direction.

About six o'clock in the morning of Saturday, May 6th, all the men were a stir after a restless night and were now ready to stretch their legs and get moving about. The escort vessels were behind us as we went on deck and in front was a lighthouse and the entrance to the harbour of Le Havre.

Off went our life jackets and on went our pack; our best friend, the rifle, firmly held in hand. The *Inventa* was safely docked, the gangways were laid down and we slowly left the ship. We were shepherded along the long quayside and then formed into our platoons and companies until the battalion was ordered to stand at ease and we were told to take off our packs. At first we had seen very few French people as we stepped onto foreign soil, but gradually there appeared some women and many children. As soon as we were seated, the children advanced and came to talk to us, almost to possess us. A young French boy in a little black overall resembling a girl's pinafore and wearing a peaked cap came up to me and said, "Souvenir?", as no doubt he had done to many thousands who had taken this same route. I opened my haversack and took out of it a very small writing pad and he in return gave me a ten centimes piece. I could hear other boys calling out to their victims, "Pennies". I began to use my secondary school French and found out that, although I knew quite a lot of ordinary French words, my pronunciation of them left a lot to be desired and I had to ask him to speak more slowly when he replied to my questions. I found out that I could write down in that little writing pad the message I wished to convey far more easily and correctly.

The French women and a few men showed little emotion. To them, here were more English soldiers and the war was not at all near being finished. Perhaps they too had great thoughts of peace by last Christmas. Most of their menfolk were away and, to them, had been away a very long time. Yet they smiled at us and thought what?

At last our officers had received their orders and directions. They consulted the N.C.O.s and we were told to stand up, put on our packs and get into marching order. We took curious looks at the buildings on the dockside and the houses and mentally compared them with our own. Quite mechanically we obeyed our orders, but there was a slight difference in the first order now we were abroad. "By the Right, quick march," instead of "by the left".

Another thing we noticed as we stepped off, the feel of the road under our feet – the French cobblestones seemed harder on the soles of our feet and we were to march many, many hundreds of miles on these cobbled roads before the end of the war. We marched along the streets in Le Havre and all the houses were shuttered. Everything seemed so quiet that glorious Saturday morning. As was customary on route marches, we had a ten minutes' rest after fifty minutes' marching. More little children appeared from nowhere each time we rested and all wanted "souvenirs" and, to our astonishment some, when refused a gift, regaled us with a flow of unprintable English, unlike anything we had heard from youngsters in England. Over the months they had picked up the unsavoury language probably more easily than they would have learned the better English.

Up on our feet and ready again to continue our march, uphill we went leaving the town behind us, slowly tramping on at a pace nowhere near one hundred paces per minute. Then we reached No.1 Rest Camp where we were given three grand meals and the remainder of the time we did nothing – no drills even. Some took a nap to make up for lost sleep, others idled around. Our stay was for less than twenty-four hours but it could not have been less carefree. My worry was how I could let my mother know that I was in France and it looked as if there would not be an opportunity of getting my letter off until we were settled somewhere and now that letter would have to be opened and censored. I tore it up.

Whilst here we soon realised that we had money troubles. We had some English money but no francs. Mac and I went to the Y.M.C.A. hut and at the counter found an old sweat.

He helped us out of our difficulty by changing our money and, of course, we lost on the deal. He was a base wallah and took his chances to make a bit on the side.

Sunday morning, full pack after another grand breakfast and back to Le Havre railway station. All aboard Tommy's first class foreign carriages, cattle trucks, all plainly marked "40 hommes – 8 chevaux", and the wags amongst us began to neigh. We were now "hommes" and placed forty to a truck with no reckoning for kits. Up to that moment I had been unaware that one horse took up the room of five men. It did not seem to work out that way. Our truck was very full as all the Signal Section were together for travelling. On the way some of us dangled our legs in the large doorway on each side. Looking around, I was first struck by the odd looking cattle – to men of the towns, black and white headed cows were strange animals. Our first impressions of French soldiers was amusing. They looked shabby in their baggy blue trousers, darker tunics, peaked caps and long greatcoats fastened up at the back. As guards or sentries they lolled against posts at all level crossings and against walls or stations and tunnels. Their rifles were slung over one shoulder and their bayonets were so long that we opened our eyes in wonder. What strange level crossings – no gates but just two long poles with the end of each weighted. An old man, or even a woman or a young girl, worked them. They were raised when the line was clear and lowered at the approach of a train, which on our journey made frequent stops for briquets and water. The constant clanging of the engine's bell sounded and resounded as we went on, via Harfleur, Rouen, Abbeville and Hazebrouck to Steebecque where, after a tedious twenty-two hour journey, we detrained and had breakfast in a field. Then I was given a bicycle, and thought it a very heavy one. I was pleased for I took off my valise and put it on the carrier. I was to be one of four men who, along with an officer (Eden), formed a billeting party, and we set off ahead of the battalion. I was very thankful for the use of this all steel Raleigh bicycle because I had realised that I was not strong when carrying a full pack. The left brace pressed on my heart and I had become accustomed to holding it off my body with the thumb and index finger of my left hand. My mind went back to the medical inspection when I had enlisted and the additional words the M.O. had used after testing my heart; "You'll die in any case." Whenever we moved later I volunteered to be responsible for one of the Signal Section's two bicycles because of it proving an easier way to transport my pack.

We stayed one night in a barn at Renescure and left early the next morning a few hours before the battalion left. Although the cobbled roads were very bumpy for riding the cycle, I did not mind. We carried on till we came to Outtersteene and there we set about finding billets for the battalion. There were no featherbeds available on this occasion; in fact very few beds even for the officers, most of whom had to sleep in their roll up beds on bedroom floors. Billets were found in houses, cottages and at farms. The Signal Section (H.Q. Group) was put into a very large upper room of a largehouse on the left hand side of the road as we entered the village. Everything seemed to be very peaceful and we saw no signs of war. The village consisted of a main street, a church, an estaminet or two and a few scattered cottages and farms. We were to be thoroughly at home for some time here. The battalion arrived and we took the various sections to their billets. A meal was laid on and I learned how the battalion had fared after we of the billeting party had left.

A band had appeared to go in front of the battalion to ease the marching. When it resumed after a ten minutes' break for the hourly rest, the usual order came, "March at ease", and the men promptly transferred their rifles over their shoulders (slung), the band began to play the regimental march and their pace quickened in order to speed up to 140 steps a minute. This was a preliminary practice for, about half an hour later, the order came, "March to attention", and shortly afterwards, "Eyes right" and there, taking the salute, was General Plumer, rather short in stature but cheerful looking. This surprise inspection had not taken long and when all the battalion had passed him the battalion was brought to a halt. The Companies were told to close up and make a compact gathering and the General came up and addressed them.

"Men of the 21st King's Royal Rifles, you have no reputation to make. Your Regiment has already done that. All you have to do is to maintain it." The General and his party rode off and the men were rather pleased with the informal way the inspection had been carried out.

I spread out my waterproof sheet and got ready for bed. I was very tired for I had tramped from farm to farm, from house to house and I soon fell asleep. I was soon disturbed by someone shaking me and a voice said, "Come on, listen to the Sergeant with the orders for tomorrow." What a good job he woke me up, and what a shock I got. "The following Signallers will parade in full kit at nine in the morning to go up to the line for training." My name was read out along with three others. Immediately after breakfast on Wednesday, May 10th, forty of us representing all the various specialist sections and platoons of the battalion paraded and were inspected, our kit checked. We were to go on a fresh adventure and we wondered for what our Aldershot training had prepared us. We boarded an old Piccadilly London bus. It was rather badly knocked about but still showed the usual adverts in its dowdy interior. It was a double decker type and, after a glance inside, I changed my mind and went on top. It had no cover, just an open top and I would be able to see the sights. After a run of about twelve miles we came to the village of Romarin. No sooner had we passed through it than we were ordered to get out. Our conveyance could go no further because the road we were on was under enemy observation. We knew what that meant though we could see no signs of war. The fields around us were all green and an occasional civilian could be seen on the land. Everything was so peaceful that we wondered where the war was. Where were trenches and the guns? The officer in charge told us that we had to proceed along the right hand side of the road in Indian file, that is at intervals of ten feet; no marching, but to go along quietly and slowly. As we idled along we could not understand why these precautions. We passed a windmill and saw signs of life there as a Belgian busied himself round some out buildings. A few hundred yards further on we saw that we were approaching a village and from its crossroads we saw houses and other buildings in all four directions for short distances. Soon we were in a short street, then at the crossroads or the square, and there was Plugstreet. Across the space and to the right was the Church. We turned immediately left and went on. The house on the right looked rather forsaken and queer all its windows were shattered. An open space and a field; another little group of houses, all deserted, their immediate surroundings seemed to be under a spell, something seemed to breathe, "Keep away and do not stay". It was abnormally quiet and then we saw a shell hole here, a shell hole there, and a house that had recently been hit. The shell holes were only small ones, about a yard in diameter, but we knew we were getting nearer to the war. A few yards further on was a wood, the well-known Plugstreet Wood, the sector for beginners or learners. A turn to the right brought us to the western edge that ran parallel to the road. Before us was a duckboard track leading to the trees and beyond, "The Strand".

We stepped on to the wooden track and entered the wood. Pip, Mac, Fred and I were to be attached to the H.Q. and we went only a few yards. As the others passed us we noticed that a Scottish Lance Corporal took charge of them, whilst another led us to a barn where we dumped our packs. He told us that his battalion was the 8th Black Watch of the 9th Highland Division and their headquarters was at the farm called Creslow. The Signal Office was in another farm building and he showed us round. To our great surprise, there lived at the farm the Belgian civilians, the owners.

The sight of these people and the beautiful appearance of the trees, the bushes and the ferns gave us a feeling of safety. We could not be very near the front line, we thought, or there would not have been any natives there. Our first look round the immediate vicinity of our quarters revealed no signs of damage and so we settled down well. What a peaceful morning it was, so quiet that we could not realise that we were in touch with the war; up to that time we did not know how far away we were from it.

We visited the Signal Office, watching the Scot on duty and seeing how he worked the exchange and we asked questions about the lines of communications. With whom was he in touch? How many units/which units?

We learned that the companies were in huts in the wood, scattered about near other duckboard tracks, all with London names. The Black Watch were in support to the Royal Scots who were in the actual Front Line. Almost across the middle of the wood stretched a breastwork which separated the Front Line battalion from the support battalion. In it were narrow openings like doorways through which troops passed.

At this point we stopped asking questions about the line because we felt that the Jocks were getting greatly amused with it all. As for them, they had been out at the front about a year but they did not talk about any fighting they had done. In other words, they did not try to put the wind up us. What struck me most about them was what fine men they were. They were taller, broader and more manly looking than we were. They made us feel at ease, almost at home. We had dinner with them and what a novelty that first tinned, ready-cooked dinner was. That meal in a taller tin than a McConochie was called a Morton and contained similar fare; a piece of meat, some carrot, some potato etc. After it had been warmed up by dropping it into a bucket of water which was then put on a fire, and when it was considered hot enough, the tin was opened with the help of an Army jack-knife. I enjoyed mine and thought it was great. Having finished that meal we were free to roam about the wood, but we did not venture far from the barn. The chatter of the Belgian civilians made us gasp for they seemed to talk a sort of dialect very much like "broad' Yorkshire.

The war might have been far away instead of less than a mile that was the depth of the wood. The afternoon and evening passed without us hearing the sound of a gun. I slept well in our barn and needed a little rousing in the morning. Yet another quiet day, and with it perhaps a more carefree attitude as I ventured further into the wood where I saw some of the large tin huts with Jocks idling about. On the Friday we accompanied the Scots H.O. spare man and went to Nieppe where we had a bath. We left the wood, turned left and at the village of Plugstreet went straight across the crossroads and on until we came within sight of Armentiéres, but turned right before reaching that town. Not far from another forest we reached the baths.

The next day, Saturday, 13th, was very quiet until dusk when, just as we were thinking of bed, a terrific (to us) bombardment started. This was the very first time that we had heard gunfire. Pip and I went outside the barn and walked to the right hand edge of the wood. We could see gun flashes from beyond where we estimated our Front Line was and felt certain that our guns were not responsible for the terrific din. It looked as if the Royal Scots were being strafed. As we stepped back among the trees, the bombardment seemed to be far off and, although the shelling went on for about an hour, yet we did not feel at all ill at ease. The Jocks too did not seem to worry; no shells came anywhere near us and, of course, we did not know if any action was being taken by our guardians. Perhaps the Signallers had been busy and perhaps the Companies had been alerted. We had been completely left to our own devices, not that we imagined that we could have been of any use.

On the stroke of ten o'clock the bombardment ceased as suddenly as it had started. We returned to our barn and before we got to sleep news came through that the enemy had made a raid on the Royal Scots and had been driven back. We slept well and soundly, thanks to our hosts. In the morning (Sunday) the Black Watch proceeded to relieve the Royal Scots and when we reached Rifle House, the headquarters of the battalion in the Front Line, we heard more about the raid. According to one of the Royal Scots, the Germans had a few days earlier put up a board in their Front Line bearing the following message. "Welcome to the 41st Division". Our Division! Evidently our movements were known well enough by the enemy, even to our being on that front, but I hardly think that they would have known of the presence of our party of forty – or had we been observed approaching Plugstreet? Did the Germans think that all our battalion had come into the line and taken over part of the Front Line? Naturally they must have thought that fresh troops would be scared of a bombardment and, if a raid followed it up, then they might be fortunate in taking some prisoners. As it was, their artillery, having smashed our barbed wire, a party of about fifty Germans crossed "No Man's Land" and found the Royal Scots ready to receive them, not some newcomers to the art of war. It was said that the Germans leading the way were so astonished at seeing "Kilties" in our front line that they put their hands up as a sign of surrender, so the Scottish officer and his men lowered their arms. Unfortunately the Germans in the rear did not know of this state of affairs and began to throw grenades into the trench. A horrible slaughter began as both sides set to. The Scottish officer, the men nearest to him, and those of the enemy who had signalled their intention to surrender suffered the most, as we were to see.

The dead of both sides had been brought up to the little cemetery near the battalion headquarters. It was called the Rifle House Cemetery. We were requested to go and view the bodies. Why, I do not know. We felt that the request was really an order, so we went. That Sunday morning it was so peaceful and quiet, the only sound was from the twittering of a few birds, and there, just outside the rough fence of the cemetery, lay ten German dead and an equal number of Scottish dead. I stood there and counted then, but not in order to count the scores of each side, just to realise the cost of that raid in human lives. What a sight! What an initiation to the art of warfare! At least six of the Germans were fine strapping men, fair to look upon with blue eyes and almost like giants, not a little bit like the pictures of captured Germans seen in the newspapers at home. Two were mere boys, not more than seventeen years of age. Their uniforms were tattered and torn and their faces revealed that their deaths had not been without pain. Most of them had been bayonetted. It looked as if the bayonets had become stuck in and had been fastened and then turned round and round to get them out because the insides of those enemies were horrible to see. Blood was everywhere and a sticky mess. What they had been like when first picked up, possibly by Jock stretcher-bearers, I could not imagine. Their clothing was bereft of all buttons, souvenir hunters having done their work well. To think that in an hours madness men had become the very dogs of war, straining to tear one another to pieces.

In comparison the Scots looked noble in death and it was impossible to see in what manner they had met their deaths. After being told that we now knew the proper way to deal with the Germans, a digging party quickly set to work. Long before they had finished their sickly task we had left the cemetery. Would there be any gloating or boasting of such killings? No. Already those who had participated in it had forgotten what they had actually done in their temporary madness. The German General who organised the raid would be sitting comfortably in his clean and sumptuous quarters behind the line, making out his report. "We carried out a very successful raid on the enemy line (Plugstreet) last night. Our gallant troops entered the enemy line doing much damage and killing many of the enemy." Whereas the Royal Scot Commander would report. "We successfully repulsed last night's enemy raid; otherwise all quiet on the Western Front." An unforgettable scene. The memory of it will never be wiped away.

Not far from the cemetery was the huge high dug-out of the Signallers consisting of an office, sleeping quarters and orderly room. It might be called the nerve centre of the battalion. From here went lines, cables, to each company, to each battalion on left and right and to the Artillery. Pip and I were shown how the office worked and were allowed to have spells at the phone. Mac and Fred Johnson, Linemen, went with the Scots counterparts and learned the routes of all the lines and learned how to repair breaks. The next five days passed in peace, not even one enemy shell in all that time.

What impressions did that first spell in the Front Line leave with me? I was struck by the fine Spring-like weather; not a drop of rain and the sun's rays coming through the unscarred trees showing the light undergrowth and some wild flowers, the sweet songs of occasional birds overhead. The absolute quietness of the daylight hours except for now and again the faint sound of a shell bursting far to the left, over to Ypres. The starry nights and the trace of light paths from Very Lights sent up from the German lines.

The names of the "rides" or duckboard tracks in the rear half of the wood, with their signposts showed The Strand, Regent Street, Piccadilly Circus, Oxford Street, etc. The Jocks walked about with a complete air of nonchalance, they played cards, wrote letters, read newspapers and smoked innumerable "gaspers" as though there was nothing at hand to disturb them. Kilts were examined for "little friends" or "pilgrims of the night" as they were often referred to. Their fine chests were rubbed with "Harrisons", a preventative pomade to keep the "chats" at bay, race meetings were held with lice as the runners, so they said. Despite much poking, the races were not a success. One Jock most tenderly returned his runner to his kilt for the poor wee mite was getting "cauld". What was very startling to me was that nothing was worn under the kilt.

Great changes came at the end of daylight; there was furious activity with working parties coming up from reserve or support, reporting prowlings in "No Man's Land" and trench materials were lugged about. There was the rat-tat of the enemy machine guns and one in particular which seemed to have a certain rhythm, seven beats – rat-tat-a-tat-tat-tat-tat. The art of falling low – at night time bullets whizzed low through the trees and the sky flashed. There was nothing about this in the Aldershot text books on war.

The disturbing thought was that after twenty-one months of war, the Germans on this front could put up a notice board above their parapet welcoming the 41st Division. How had they got such information? Not from prisoners taken on a raid; surely not from "talk in England"; then how? It had been drilled into us that if taken prisoner all we were to divulge was our rank name and number.

The front line at the very front of the wood was a breastwork, open at the rear amidst broken trees. Dugouts were built into the breastwork and shelters were made up of corrugated iron sheets and one layer of sandbags all round them with an opening left for a doorway. They would stop bullets and bits of shrapnel, but not a shell. The doorways of such shelters were made up of two blankets.

My greatest realisation was that in England I had been taught very little about warfare on the Western Front and, except for knowing how to use a telephone and repair wires, the training did not prepare me for the trench conditions. So how was it that instructors at home knew so little of what it was like out here? Had none of them been out? And, what was more upsetting – how would our battalion have fared if it had been actually in the line for the German raid?

Back again at Outtersteene after ten days' absence, four in reserve and six in the very frontline (Saturday, May 20th). Days that had seemed long and drawn out. Of course our comrades crowded around us and asked what it was like. We told them what we had learned by hearsay and, because we were totally unable to paint the awful picture of the raid in its true colours, the horror of it was not driven home. We all but forgot it because we learners were basking in the sunshine of safety and the freedom from worry. In Outtersteene we signallers had a very fine billet and the old lady of the house treated us very well. She helped us in many ways, especially at meal times when she saw to the cooking of some of our food. Here I first tasted bread fried in bacon dip. Each of us received a full slice morning after morning. The little things she did for us were similar to those things done by other civilians for our comrades of other sections.

We were certainly well in at Outtersteene and having a fine easy time. Parades were few and fatigues never troubled the Signallers. Life here, let it be said, was much preferable to that at Aldershot. Footballs were obtained from somewhere, bought out of canteen profits or out of battalion funds, and intersection and inter-company matches were frequent. Many enjoyable games were played and witnessed, the civilians being as much interested as the Tommies. True we had not the best of grounds, an ordinary field was the only ground available, nor proper football kit – we played in what we had, Army boots and shorts. In the Signal Section we all played, all being given a turn and someone always dropping out. Walks into the country and to the neighbouring villages of Merris and Strazeele revealed the presence of other battalions of the division. Though Hazebrouck was only five miles away and the largest town in the district and worth a visit, very few of us bothered to go to it. Outtersteene, perhaps because troops had been billeted here before, perhaps ever since the war developed into trench warfare, could supply all our scanty needs. Besides, many of us would not have many francs to spend, having given up half or more of our weekly pay for our parents. My wants were very few because I did not drink or smoke. For the others, wines and beers were in demand in the evenings at the estaminets. I understood that the beer fell short in quality in comparison with English beer, so some men took to drinking wines, which went to their heads very quickly at first because they were not used to them. Later, as the men became accustomed to them, wines became more popular.

The village boasted an engraver who varied his trade to suit our needs. He made and sold wristlet identification discs, thin oval-shaped pieces of metal, similar in colour to and as light as aluminium with two small pieces of chain that fastened with a clasp. On each disc were the following particulars: rank number, battalion and religion. Many of us bought one such disc and did not mind always wearing it. On the other hand, we did not like wearing the two Army issue discs on a piece of strong string around the neck The string soon became dirty and clammy because we were often too lazy to remove them when washing our necks.

Perhaps too we did not like the idea of carrying them always with us, one red and round and the other green and almost octagonal (the corners being shorter than the sides), one to be buried with and the other to be sent to Records should the worst happen out there. Thus many of us carried the issue identification discs in our haversacks or in the valise and did not bother with them unless a special parade was held to see if we were wearing them. We were always warned beforehand if that was the purpose of a parade and so no one was ever caught without wearing his in the ordered place. Yet I often wondered how it was that some were not lost through being kept in such a careless way.

On the first Sunday after our party's return to the battalion, a special full C. of E. church parade was held. It took place in the open air in a large field and our Brigade C. of E. padre took the service. He was a gaunt man, well over six feet tall. All men except Roman Catholics and some on fatigues were ordered to attend.

The following Sunday a service for Wesleyans was held in the same field which was quite near the Signallers' billet. This was the first occasion that I saw the Reverend E. Sayer-Ellis and recognised that he was a padre of great zeal, determination, good heart and heavenly fervour. There was something about him that compelled our respect, he was no sham and reminded me very much of the Reverend C.H. Hulbert of Thornton Hall in my home town. The spirit of God flowed from them.

One of our signalling parades caused great amusement. The R.E. Signals had come to explain a lot about the laying of cables and had reached that branch of it that dealt with overhead lines. A telegraph pole was erected and we had to climb it with the help of leg irons to fasten wires to the crosspiece at the top. What fun! Most of us managed to climb about five feet up and then we would slip down to the ground. It was explained to us why this was – we had been trying to climb up with our legs too straight and had kept our bodies too near the pole. We did much better when we tried again and held our bodies not quite at arm's length from the pole, our hands around it, and our knees stuck out as if we were bow-legged. I and others succeeded after a few more attempts. Our hands suffered a little as the time went on and they caught the rough pieces of wood broken by the irons.

The days were exceptionally fine and the signallers did plenty of visual work out of doors with flags, shutters and lamps. Three men worked on a station: one sent messages, a second looked for acknowledgements and the other wrote down. Messages received were put down on a pink form and the messages sent out were on a white form. We began to use code letters. Our own battalion code was K.R.U. (K for King's; R for Royal; U for 21st). The three other battalions of our Brigade under General Clemson were the 26th Royal Fusiliers (Code R.F.Z.); 32nd Royal Fusiliers (Code R.F.C.B.); and the 10th West Surreys – known as the Queen's – (Code Q.U.J.). In other words, the initials of the units followed by a letter or letters of the alphabet to suit the number of the unit. Such simple codes could fool no one, especially not the Germans.

The signallers had to take part in the route marches, held perhaps once a week. Sometimes only our battalion took part but occasionally the whole Brigade would turn out. Order of seniority: 10th Queen's, 26th R.F., 32nd R.F. and we, the babes of the Brigade came last. Of course we had our own bands which helped us to step forward in an orderly manner. Much later when our Light Infantry band was formed we marched at one pace and the other battalions at another, and the poor unfortunate 32nd R.F.s just in front of us would be a little confused hearing two bands of different pace makers.

Only once in the next four weeks were we reminded of the war. One evening we were

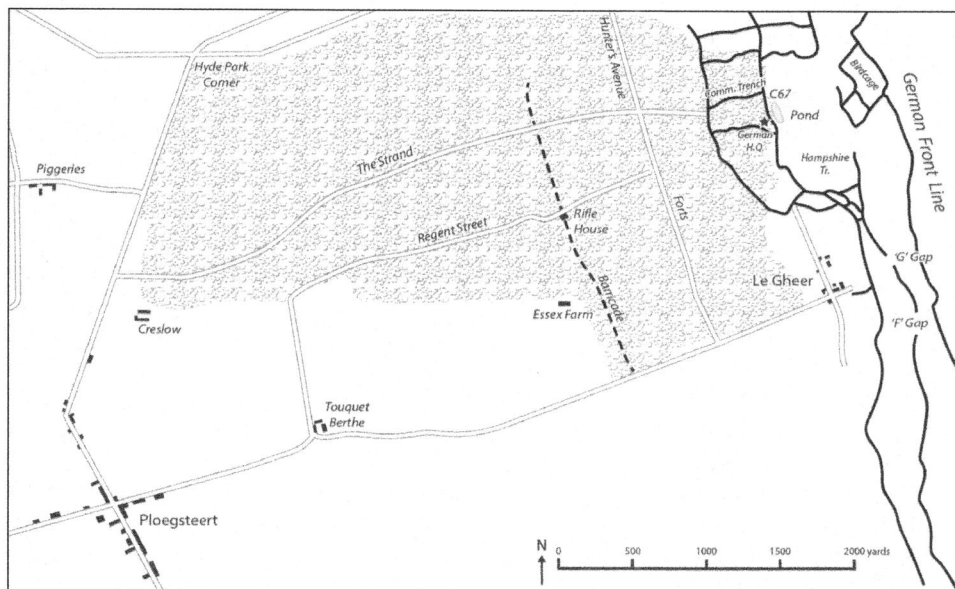

Map 2. Ploegsteert Wood

aware of a terrific bombardment taking place and we gathered in groups to look at the sky lit up with countless flashes and to hear loud explosions. We wondered if we would get the order to stand-to. We surmised that there was something doing between Ypres and Armentiéres. The next morning a special parade was held. It was for a surprise medical inspection and took only a few minutes as we went before the M.O. in sections. It was known as the "Short Arms" inspection, and we were all found to be clean.

The afternoon parade was the best of all parades, a pay parade. For we forty who had gone up the line the day after our arrival at Outtersteene, this was our first one out there. I drew ten francs, equal to eight shillings and four pence but with far less spending power. It was not much short of what I was entitled to – a shilling a day, less two pence a day for battalion funds and the allocation to my mother, which did not leave me much. As long as I could buy some writing materials and some picture postcards, I was alright though. I had started buying the picture postcards of places we knew around Outtersteene and sending them home. I wanted to build up as far as possible a pictorial record of our travels. We did not have to buy stamps for our letters as, by putting the letters B.E.F. on the top of the envelope, they went free. I eventually made good use of this privilege and gave the censoring officers quite a lot to do.

At Outtersteene all specialists, through their training together, missed some of the comradeship of the other men and what they thought of us later, when a Brigade Order stated that specialists could not be taken for fatigues, I do not know. So far I had never been on a cookhouse fatigue, peeling potatoes by the hundred, nor had to wash out the greasy dixies after meals, nor taken a turn as mess orderly serving out the food or tea. Occasionally the tea tasted like stew and we suspected that the dixies had not been washed out thoroughly, perhaps a shortage of hot water had meant that all the grease had not been washed off.

We were quite happy and contented and I had such a lot of spare time that I developed a habit that might later on cause my mother some anxiety. I used to write to her daily, sending home either a postcard, a silkcard, a letter or, very occasionally, a field card. I soon realised that such correspondence would not always be possible so I wrote home and said that I would write home twice in one week and then three times the next. What optimism! In my first letter home after a spell with the Jocks I confidently told my mother that, no matter how long the war lasted I should return safely. Owing to my quick trip up the line I had sent no one my address so it was some time before I heard from home or from friends. As for myself, I took a great dislike to field cards because they affected the recipient a little like a telegram did. They caused a few minutes' fear until read and grasped. The pale buff colouring was off-putting. Their news could be mostly good, but sometimes ill. The sender was either quite well, or sick or wounded, the words that did not apply being crossed out. Hence it was my preference to send other types of cards.

Once a very unfortunate incident marred these quickly passing happy days. It was said that one of the company men had been guilty of a most serious offence and, according to military regulations, had receive Field Punishment No.1. For two hours each day he was tied to a limber wheel in the transport lines, usually about midday and thus receiving the doubtful benefit of the sun's warmth. At first I did not know what the unfortunate man's crime was. I was not curious and did not go to see him. I had no wish to see a man suffering so much. Later I heard that he had been found asleep whilst on duty and the orderly officer for the day had reported the matter to the Colonel. This was a very serious crime indeed and, according to the Army authorities, needed drastic punishment. Our sympathy was with the man for it was not as if he were a regular soldier, nor even in the Front Line. We were not even in support or in reserve and thought that a severe warning would have been sufficient but, I suppose, here was a chance for the Army to make an example to a newly-formed battalion – shades of Oliver Cromwell. "Desperate ills need drastic remedies." From our point of view, it was very hard on one of "t'owd lads".

4

Plugstreet Wood – the thin edge of the wedge

S uch pleasant and carefree times could not last forever. About the end of May it became evident that we were to move and on Tuesday, May 30th at six in the evening in full pack we left Outtersteene and proceeded towards the line to take part in a Divisional Relief. The 41st Division relieved the Scottish 9th, which went south to the Somme. Our Brigade, the124, took over the Plugstreet Wood sector, the 26th Royal Fusilier Battalion going straight into the Front Line, whilst we, the 21st K.R.R., went behind them in the rear half of the wood. Thus began a sequence of moves that the four battalions of our Brigade were to follow in the next eleven weeks. Each battalion would spend five days in the Front Line, five days in support, five days in the line and finally five days in reserve. The latter period was sometimes called "Out at Rest". Too often it meant far less rest than was found on the Front Line. In this sector, the little place of rest was either Romarin or Papot.

Though I had been on headquarters all the time we were at Outtersteene, I went with 'D' Company into the wood where our billets were huts with canvas roofs near to Essex Farm. Such flimsy huts were no protection against shell fire or pieces of shrapnel, or even bullets, but they were pleasant sleeping quarters in pleasant surroundings for at this time of year the trees were a mass of foliage and resplendent in shades of green – a very cushy sector for beginners.

Quite suddenly within a few hours came the rude awakening of war. Just after nine o'clock on the morning of Thursday, June 1st, we heard the sound of shellfire not very far away. A few shells of high explosive had burst above the wood and shrapnel rained down on 'A' Company, part of which was having a rifle inspection with Second Lieutenant P. Grahame (Pansy) in charge. As quickly as possible the men flung themselves down onto the ground – no drill book had taught this movement, it had to be grasped when the time for it came. Sergeant Seward was one of those killed instantly and some men were wounded including Ernest Forster. Sergeant R Seward, Rifleman J.W. Collier and Rifleman V.G. Hickes were buried in Rifle House Cemetery in Plugstreet Wood.

When is a wound not a wound? A nose cap from an A.A. shell (anti-aircraft) landed sometime later on the top of the steel helmet of Fred Cordukes. It drove the hat over his ears and, despite the efforts of his pals, it could not be removed. He had to be taken to the Casualty Clearing Station where it was cut off, but not with a jack-knife. Fred (known as Arthur at home) Cordukes was a York resident who had worked at Rowntree's Cocoa Works before enlisting. The bad news spread through the battalion and what had been sunshine turned to gloom as we sustained our first casualties.

We lucky signallers always had a night's sleep whilst the non-specialists turned out almost all nights to do fatigues, carrying to the front lines such things as wire, 'A' frames, sandbags, pushing loads of materials on the light railway line, etc. All we had to do was a period of two hours on the phone during the night and a similar period during the daytime.

Any one of us could be the runner should a message come through.

The next time we were in these huts in support, Harry Dent of 'C' Company could not wake the man next to him at reveille. The ex-policeman was dead, he had died instantly when hit by a machine gun bullet as he had slept. The bullet had come through the flimsy hut and bounced off some metal and struck him. It had come from the machine gun of Duckboard Charlie, an enemy gunner who fired only at nights when it was thought this instrument of death came up from a camouflaged concrete emplacement. He it was who periodically poured streams of bullets across No Man's Land, just skimming the parapets and also sailing through the trees into all parts of the wood. It was more dangerous to move about the wood at night time than it was during the day. At night the low rat-tat-a-tat-tat, rat-tat was his trade mark, echoing through the wood with a distinctive staccato burst. Not far behind the German lines was a haystack-like contraption and this is where we thought the gun remained hidden in the daylight hours.

This rear part of the wood was really a very quiet place and very pleasant. I have walked in it in all directions admiring wild flowers and enjoying the small, sweet wild strawberries to be found in season. The breastwork across the middle of the wood was five to six feet high. To keep us on the alert an alarm was sounded occasionally to see how quickly we could man that breastwork in case of need. As we couldn't hear gunfire, we knew we were being tested to see how smart we were. We slept in our uniforms and never took our boots off so it was just a case of donning our gas masks, putting on our equipment and taking up our rifles before dashing to positions, first taking to the duckboard tracks and then stumbling through the undergrowth to spread out along the barrier. Any stumble brought forth a mild blast or damn-words that relieved the tension of what was always a false alam. Fear of the unknown and the darkness and the fact that we were certainly very raw soldiers affected our involuntary behaviour. We were at last trying to cover the men in the Front Line and, when our turn came to swap places, we too would be pleased to know that we were being covered.

Our very first spell of five days in support ended on Monday, June 5th when the battalion, fully equipped with all that was necessary, passed through the barrier in specialist sections, platoons and companies to go to their allocated positions in the Front Line. 'D' Company left behind the huts near Essex Farm, walked along part of Regent Street and, by way of Piccadilly Circus, reached a gap in the breastwork and entered the front or northern part of the wood. On the left was Leicester Lounge, reported to be the chattiest dugout on the Western Front, where nights were far from restful because of the hordes of lice which got into one's clothing and gave a great deal of irritation as soon as one got warm. On the right was Rifle House, the headquarters of the battalion in the line.

H.Q. personnel had high dugouts with doorways of at least five and a half feet high; there were some beds of wire netting an orderly room and dugouts for officers, signallers, sanitation staff, medical orderlies, runners, etc. 'D' Company continued on its way on a duckboard track to Hunter's Avenue where several dugouts at intervals housed support company. It ran more or less parallel to the Front Line, but we carried on for we were to occupy the left sector of the Front Line and left the duckboards to enter a communication trench built entirely of sandbags. Because of tree roots at the very edge of the wood, no trench digging had been possible so what was called the Front Line Trench was above ground and also built up of sandbags. It was nearly six feet high and hid from the enemy the last approach from the communication trench to the Front Line, which had bays with fire steps and dugouts built between every two bays. They were like igloos, not of snow but of sandbags, and without a tunnel. The doorway was rather low and about two feet square. Inside there was just room for the six signallers to sit upright and a corner for the telephone. It had many layers of sandbags on the top of it and was safe against bullets and small shells. The wires were brought out through the doorway, under the duckboard outside and across to the communication trench. That duckboard track ran the full length of the line. On the opposite side from the bays were many stumps of trees and very small areas of clear space. The taller trees behind them were shell marked, bare of leaves, withered and shattered, but did not affect the general appearance of the wood beyond. Almost as soon as 'D' Company reached the Front Line I fell out with the Signal Section for, because I had the experience with the Black Watch, I was put in charge. I had paid two short visits to this part of the line as part of my initial learning but did not stay the night, always turning to the Black Watch H.Q. I entered the signal dugout, had a short chat with the Jock (surnamed Martin) and took over after signing for a few articles which belonged to the station. It was soon done, I have no doubt that the Jocks were keen to get away. I was keen to allocate duties to my five signallers, make out the duty rota and set one man on duty straightaway. I did this, instructed him as regards the call signs and then showed him how to test each station – H.Q., each Company, the battalion on the left and the Artillery (eighteen pounders). I was now a Lance Corporal and could put up one stripe, which I bought and sewed myself, one on the upper arm of each sleeve. I was now an unpaid provisional acting N.C.O. of the lowest kind. Although I was a 'C' Company man I was in charge of the 'D' Company section which consisted of Burkill and Cooke, the latter was not yet seventeen years of age; Jim Machin, eighteen and Procter, nineteen – all four of 'D' Company; the other member of the section was Joe Stone, some twenty-six years of age and of 'A' Company. Joe was like a father figure, very quiet and thoughtful and a real stalwart. So we settled in and each man had to do two hours at the phone followed by two hours as runner, if needed. One great drawback was that a candle had to be alight all hours of the day. Our station call was C 67and that of H.Q. was E.W. One. Every quarter of an hour the man at the phone had to test every station; the four companies and the H.Q. were on the same line so we were able to hear all the testing the battalion on the left (the 20th Durham Light Infantry) was on the same line as the artillery. This continual testing would, at least, help to keep the man on duty awake during the night. In the meantime, the Company ration party delivered our six rations separately in a sandbag. They had to last twenty-four hours and consisted of bread – perhaps two loaves being a third of a loaf per man; a varying amount of butter and jam – because it was difficult for the Quarter-Master to cut up a tin of one or the other and manage to give a fair share for six; sometimes some bully beef if the cooks did not need a lot for stews etc.; two candles and a cigarette and pipe tobacco ration.

That evening and night were very quiet, just a faint noise when the company men manned the bays with rifles and bayonets fixed. This was stand-to, a critical time when it was known that the enemy sometimes raided. I went out of the dugout and looked towards the German lines. One of his sentries was doing his rounds and at a point here and there he sent up a Very Light. Much further to the left (north) an arc of brighter sky was illuminated by many Very Lights and gun flashes – Ypres (Wipers). Before "Stand-down" I retired to our dugout. The next morning our two youngsters said that they had found it very difficult to keep awake; the stuffiness of the dugout was no help. I made a bargain with them, if they would do double duties during daylight, I would do their night spells. They agreed and I was only too pleased to have this arrangement. It was better than risking them falling asleep on duty – they need only to have missed one quarter-hour check and someone would report our station being disconnected, the linesmen would be sent out and eventually arrive at our station and find what? I could make very good use of the time I spent at the phone at night.

About four weeks later these two youngsters were withdrawn from the line and sent to a base near Calais for under-age recruits. Their parents had claimed them, giving their correct ages and the War Office could not but accede to their request that the boys should be taken out of the line. Cooke never saw the line again. When he came of age he was posted to Marseilles; because of his knowledge of the French language he became an interpreter at the docks there.

Tuesday, about 7.30 am the cry came: "Breakfast up!" The Company mess orderlies had brought up from the wood and the company cookhouse a large dixie of tea and a dixie lid of bacon. Each of us received our own small dixie of tea and a small piece of bacon into its lid. I took one slice of my bread and ate it with my bacon and, if biscuits were plentiful, I ate a biscuit as well. I soon grasped the fact that by drawing my meals this way I had to clean both mess tin and lid. Grease in either of them was hard to remove because hot water was not often available. Often our mess tins were inspected by an officer to see if they were clean – for health reasons it was a crime to have a dirty one. As soon as possible I bought an enamel mug and enamel plate, which we referred to as tin, as they were more easily kept clean whilst my mess tin was always clean as I gave up using it.

After breakfast I cleaned my rifle and saw that the others cleaned theirs. The signal office was running smoothly so I left Joe Stone in charge and took a short stroll along the duckboards, a few yards in either direction. To the left as I faced the enemy line were the officers' dugout, the Sergeant-Major's dugout, and finally the first aid post with the stretcher-bearers' dugout. That was at the end of our sector and the beginning of that of the 20th Durham Light Infantry. Behind my back and almost at the edge of the wood proper was the company latrine. This had been constructed on a piece of ground a little lower than the ground round about so it could not be seen by the enemy. It consisted of a hole about six feet long, one foot wide and of varying depth because of the roots of trees. Around it was a canvas awning hiding three sides only; the open side faced the wood, and across the full length of the hole and supported on a trestle at each end was a pole which acted as the seat which was about two feet above the hole. This sanitary contraption was always approached with great care, the body held a slow as possible if the visit to it was in daylight hours. It was not much used in daylight, the fear being that a German sniper up a tree or on top of a ruined building might be on the look-out. When two or more men were at the latrine at the same time that pole was quite a seat of learning it was also an information centre where snippets of news of all companies could be heard. Above all it was the birthplace of countless rumours, where news of and from Blighty was disseminated. Here it was circulated that the Germans had suffered heavily at Verdun and that they were almost finished. In fact, if we saw the Germans across the ways end up three green Very Lights, one immediately after another, then that was the signal for the end of the war. We did not see them go up and eventually stopped looking.

I turned back, retraced my steps and passed by the office. Two bays further on I came to the snipers' post. Sam Benson showed me the fixed rifle and its periscopic attachment by which he could in safety watch the German Front Line. I had a look-see but saw no movement or German. As I was preparing to leave him and return we heard soft plops of anti-aircraft shells bursting and on looking up into the sky behind the enemy lines we saw lots of little puffy clouds of German Ack-Ack shells bursting in the blue sky. They were trying to bring down a loose observation balloon which was drifting towards our lines. They failed to hit it and as it drew near to our lines our own Ack-Ack batteries opened fire, but it passed over the wood and further away and out of sight. It was probably a German balloon which had broken away from its moorings. That was too simple an explanation and the latrine news was that it was a Russian balloon and had been blown all the way from the Eastern Front. No rumours explained what had finally happened to it.

Our gas sentries (another duty we were excused) and snipers had been alerted to keep an eye on the German lines in case gas was discharged, the wind being reported as favourable for the enemy to take advantage of it. Each gas sentry stood near an empty shell case suspended from a piece of wood, with a handy piece of metal nearby with which to strike the shell case and give the alam if necessary.

We signallers were left very much to ourselves and some little time passed before we knew the names of the 'D' Company officers, at least before Joe Stone and I did. Major Paget was in command and two of the junior officers were Second Lieutenants John Cole and Monty Cole, affectionately known as Darkie Cole and Ginger Cole from the colour of their hair. The former was stocky and short whilst the other was tall and slim. The Company Sergeant-Major was Gibson, an old soldier who had served in the Boer War. The two Coles were not related but they both came from London.

For dinner each man received a pint of stew and an "after". The stew consisted mainly of shredded bully beef and very few potatoes. Once a week we were supposed to have "fresh" meat but I do not remember ever having any. The "after" was either rice pudding made without sugar but with a few currants or sultanas added, or "Dundee" pudding made of ground up Army biscuits with sultanas added. Other regiments gave the same concoction other names.

Simple diets, the bare minimum of rations, but we thrived on them. I used to think what my mother used to say about meals: "Always leave the table knowing that you could eat more" – her warning against over-eating. There was no chance of over-eating out here, we were more likely to feel like Oliver Twist. A full dixie from the cook house held twenty pints of liquid and if twenty men drew a pint each there were no leftovers.

There was no doubt that this left sector of the battalion line was very cushy. I think that we were a little further off the Germans than the other company in the Front Line was. No Man's Land must have been wider in front of us. We had heard explosions to our immediate right on a few occasions, particularly at meal times. The grape vine at the latrine clarified our suspicions. Jerry was in the habit of giving the company on the right trench mortars for breakfast; horrid rifle grenades because they burst just above the parapet and took some dodging. Minnies or trench mortars did much damage to the trench. Whizz bangs, the smallest of the German shells, were unpleasant too. A sentry was posted to watch for minnies or trench mortars and when he saw one coming he would blow his whistle and shout, "Minnies to the left/right!"

Further along our sector to the right was the Hampshire T, a trench dug at right angles to our breastwork and going into No Man's Land. It was unmanned and both sides watched it. The German snipers had it taped and often had a machine gun trained on it. It was a very dangerous trench and a nuisance. Beyond it were the two gaps, G and F, also unmanned and unoccupied parts of our line. Here ended our sector and there began the sector of the battalion on the right of our Brigade front.

Just past the snipers' post was a very remarkable "tree". It was an artificial one, exactly like the partly shattered one that had stood on the same spot earlier. The Royal Engineers had removed the original one and erected in its place a hollow one. The work of substitution was accomplished fully one dark night, and quietly too so that the Germans had no idea of what was going on. Anyone wishing to observe the German line or beyond his line could enter it and look across No Man's Land, an excellent O.P. for the artillery spotting officer. It was given the name of German House. Almost in front of it, just beyond our barbed wire, was a large pond, fairly long and narrow. Its occupants were almost as good as sentries. The frogs, when disturbed by prowling raiders or patrols, croaked noisily and helped our sentries when it was known that we had no patrol out that night.

Glorious, flaming June. So far everything so quiet when unexpectedly a tragedy struck our section. In the afternoon of Wednesday, June 7th, in order to save the runner on duty from coming out of our dugout, I took along to the officers' billet a message for Major Paget and as I left him there came the welcome cry, "Tea up!" I proceeded to our bay where I had left my rations and mug, for we had decided to have tea there. I drew my tea and returned to the bay to take up the place where I usually sat. Young Machin was already there, standing at the bend of the bay. He was facing the enemy and leaning with his back against the sandbags at the rear of the bay. Just as I drew level with him, absolutely face to face, bodies touching as I was squeezing past with my face no further than six inches from his, something struck in his jugular vein. Blood gushed out, slightly splashing my tunic, and he silently dropped gradually down although I was trying to hold him with my arms underneath his armpits. He was dead as quickly as that. Jim Procter and I tried to lift him to see if anything could be done, while Cooke yelled out, "Stretcher-bearers!" and ran to the First Aid Post. Nothing could be done. The stretcher-bearers came and placed the body on a stretcher and took it up to Rifle House where he was buried in the cemetery there. I visited that grave on pilgrimage-cum-tour of the battlefields in 1928.

Jim Cooke and I were numbed; we couldn't speak. It was so hard to believe. Silently we drank our dixies of cold tea and got on with the remaining bread ration. Almost at the same time we all three began to speak how had it happened? No-one had heard a sound. Jim suggested that a piece of shrapnel had done "it". I felt sure that no whizz-bang had come over, nor had there been any ack-ack fire. I favoured the sniper's bullet. I thought that a German sharpshooter from an elevated post, perhaps watching the latrine or the path that led from the communication trench to the duckboard track, had suddenly seen a movement in our bay. I realised I had had a very lucky escape, a very, very narrow escape. If a bullet had killed Jim then it must have passed two or three inches to the right or left of my own head. Yet I had heard no sound. Perhaps Procter was correct in thinking that a piece of shrapnel caused the death. I was to think of this very sad affair when men used to say that a target never heard the shell or bullet that killed him. But who was to know? The dead man could not reveal that fact.

I felt very downcast and depressed and asked myself if I ought to have "ordered" him, when I entered the bay, to have sat down on the firestep. If he had done just that he would have been lower down and had his back to the breastwork. If ... if ... I felt so responsible and some time passed before I could dismiss any blame from myself. A quiet Lincolnshire lad was Machin, a mere youngster, a good-living lad who like many others in the battalion said his prayers nightly. He had not suffered, so we liked to think but his sudden death had brought the war very close indeed. I had to rearrange my roster of duties as no reserve signaller was available and our first day in the Front Line was nearly over. This task was easy enough because we were not at all overworked like the Company men. We were having quite a cushy time, but we could not help thinking of young Machin.

During the dark hours of the night our dugout doorway was covered by a blanket which was rolled up during the day and fixed above the opening. But for the candle light we might have kept the blanket up to save the dugout getting so stutff. During my turn on I sat with the headpiece of the phone strapped to my right ear, leaving my left hand for the telephone mouthpiece and my right hand free for writing anything down. During the intervals when I was not testing I wrote numerous letters to my mother and to many friends, so I often had post from kind friends who replied to my letters.

Every night between midnight and three in the morning the 'D' Company officer on night duty called at the Signal Office and asked me to put him through to the battery covering us. He would then give the operator our map reference and ask for a test round. He would time with his stop watch how many seconds it took for the blank shell to pass over us and land in No Man's Land. The gunners were always on the alert. It was gratifying to know that in the case of an S.O.S. from us the eighteen pounders would quickly come to our aid. Each of the four companies of our Brigade had its own covering battery of four guns quite close to the Front Line, the 183, 187, 189 and 190 R.A. Batteries for the 10th Queen's, the 26th R.F., the 32nd R.F. and the 21st K.R.R.s respectively. After his first testing of the covering battery, the officer used to call through the doorway and ask me to do the necessary. I would say "Through" as soon as the gunner operator answered my call and the officer would be outside the dugout listening for the shell coming over.

What of those letters I wrote to pass the time away? Sometimes I wrote seven a night. I discussed the weather, mentioned the trees, gave a bit of other news about the men who had joined up with me (especially Mac whom Mother knew), and of the tallest lad in 'C' Company, Willie Spence, who lived in the same street. We were not allowed to give place names or any information about the battalion, so there was a lot "all O.K." and weather terms.

I started to keep a diary and my friends used to smile when they saw me sit down and enter something in it every day without fail. That diary and subsequent diaries I always carried with me. The entries were small because there was only a small space allowed per day. Immediately on the left of each space I put the initials of anyone who wrote to me and I had received a letter that day. On the right I entered the initials of those to whom I replied that day. All letters were handed to the orderly corporal unsealed to be given to the officer on duty to be censored with his blue pencil. I always felt sorry for the men who never received any mail. I have seen them withdraw to a corner and look so pathetic. Mind you some of them did not like writing letters, like Willie Spence whose mother used to see my mother receive a letter from me and then slip across the road to ask her for news. Some men retired to a corner to look at photographs of loved ones to make up for no news. As for my diary, I kept it in my top left hand tunic pocket along with my pay book as an extra piece of packing above my heart. It could stop a piece of shrapnel or even a bullet. I had not got a cigarette case like some had.

Despite my double duty at night, I got very little sleep during the day and got used to that state of affairs. My life as a signaller was not a strenuous one, no hard physical work but just clerical work. The average Company man was very busy most of the night and had to carry rifle and gas helmet always, even when on a fatigue party. Some would have to go right back to the main road at the entrance to the wood to meet the transport limbers bearing the rations, reload them on to the light railway and push the trucks as far as possible towards the line. All rations were in sandbags, clearly marked by each Company's own Quarter-Master and all correctly allocated according to the numbers in a section, platoon, etc. Other Company men would be busy building up weak parts of the breastwork, cleaning drains and others did sentry work. Three men worked together on sentry duty. One stood upright on the fire-step watching over No Man's Land and the German Line, number two sat down near him and the third man rested, sleeping if possible. Each spent two hours at each stage of this important job. Number One was in danger all the time and had to keep perfectly still, not even moving his head. Thus he could not be seen as only movements drew an enemy's watchful eye. But Duckboard Charlie would now and again skim the top of the parapet with his machine gun, just hoping that one bullet would find a target. One's white face, partly shaded by a tin helmet, was hard to see. A nerve-racking job for beginners because there was a tendency to stare and then the eyes fancied things. A shadow, a remnant of a tree, a barbed wire post, all might seem to move and make one believe that an enemy was approaching. Imaginations could lead to alarms.

All workers, sentries, etc., looked forward to stand down in the morning when they could relax and eagerly await the coming up of the breakfast. The meal over and the cookhouse utensils cleaned and returned, all the men would clean their rifles, have a wash of sorts, and a shave if necessary, and have a quick inspection by the orderly. Only then could they call their time their own and get down to it for a nap. The trench would be almost deserted. Only the midday meal broke the stillness of the trench, except when Fritz gave us a splash of "hate". The afternoon was usually quiet and, but for the few minutes "hate" at meal times, it seemed to be a case of live and let live on both sides. Were not the Bavarians across the way said to be much like the English?

The Company men did find a little grouse to let fly at the signallers. In their comings and goings they often tripped over or caught our wires in their clothing or the slung rifles, especially in the communication trench. They were strung about five feet high on the sides of the trench and hung in loops and could number six cables. The loops seemed to catch anything especially in the case of men carrying stores and materials. Thus the wires were often broken or bared, which meant a leakage. It was drummed into us that Jerry had very acute listening apparatus which could pick up the faintest signals from a leaking wire so that any message of any importance was not sent by phone but by runner. I admired the runners, they did such a lot of our work and always smiled. We were great friends.

Although we had learned a lot about simple codes and could create our own, no-one in authority bothered to have messages put into code. It was known that clever Germans could crack the hardest of codes in next to no time. The code could have been changed every few hours so by the time the Germans had cracked it we would not be using the same code and the message sent, well it wouldn't matter by that time whether he knew it or not as it would be of no value to him. Even the Playfair Code could have been used for non-important messages.

On Thursday, June 8th, 'C' Company had Brown wounded and Spencer killed. The latter, who was one of Second Lieutenant Eden's platoon, was buried in the little cemetery near Essex Farm. At the weekend the 26th R.F.s known as the Bankers' Battalion relieved us and we returned to the rear half of the wood to be again the battalion in support. I was ordered to report to the headquarters so once more I was billeted at Creslow Farm. The spell here of five days was a very quiet one but for a serious gas alert when we stood-to most of the day and night, but no gas was sent over by the Germans. Whitsuntide passed uneventfully and the battalion went back into the Front Line. I was kept on the headquarters at Rifle House, the Sergeant being able to ring the changes because he had spare N.C.O.s. He had taken into consideration my upsetting time at the loss of Machin.

To remind us that there was a war on, Jerry gave 'B' Company on the Front Line a short sharp Minnie strafe at 7.30 a.m. on the second morning in and two men were killed. Every morning at nine o'clock the casualty return was sent to Brigade H.Q. and that morning the number was two. The H.Q. cooks used charcoal for their fires and so were able to supply us with warm stews and teas at the right meals. Occasionally we could see spirals of smoke rising through the trees; perhaps a little firewood had been used, and we wondered if the Germans would see the tell-tale signs. We owed a great deal to the cooks and to the transport as well. They never failed us.

Gas alarms were now more frequent as the wind blew more and more from the enemy lines. We signallers got quite used to the word "London" being received by phone. It was a safe code word to warn us to be on the alert for gas. "Sunloch" was a more welcome word because it meant that the wind had changed round and there was no longer any danger of a gas attack. Early in our trench duties all men carried a gas helmet, P.R. It was a bag about twelve inches long and ten inches wide. It had two goggles for the eye pieces, a contraption to nip on the nose and a mouthpiece to suck and it had been saturated with a chemical. As soon as the alarm was sounded each man undid the hook and the top button of his tunic, pulled the open end of the bag over his head and tucked the loose folds into the neck of his tunic before replacing both button and hook. The nipper was applied to the nose and this ensured that he breathed in through the mouthpiece. I was always a bit scared on these occasions because, as my glasses were of the rimless, pince-nez variety, I was frightened that in pulling the gas bag over my head I might knock them off. The nipper of the gas mask could dislodge the nipper of my glasses. I felt very lost in a gas mask and felt that I would have been useless. To keep the goggles clear and clean each of us had a tube of "anti-dim", very good stuff which was like grease and prevented the goggles from steaming up.

The powers that be decided that the Germans should be given a little dose of the medicine with which we were threatened when the wind was favourable. Some cylinders of our own gas were taken up into the Front Line, left sector. The Royal Engineers specialist group saw to them, they were known as P.O. or P.W. Special Section. To make sure that the conditions were absolutely safe to set off the gas, a phosphorous bomb was to be ignited and then thrown over the parapet into No Man's Land to see if the wind was in our favour, blowing from us to them. Unfortunately it did not clear the trench and Captain Burton and C.S.M. Gibson were sprayed with the contents. The officer, not too badly affected, made his way to the H.Q. and the medical room for attention and treatment whilst the Sergeant-Major ran along the duckboards with most of his clothing, face and hands glowing in the dark. The stretcher-bearers, with Darkie Cole helping bound him up with field dressings and "four-by-two". He got back to Blighty and made a splendid recovery and later greeted some of our Yeomen who had been transferred to the Machine Gun Corps and to his Company. The R.E.s removed their gas cylinders, to everyone's relief. I felt that they were not as clever as the Germans were with the sending over of gas.

It was a bad habit, as far as the battalions in the line were concerned, of Brigade Staff and other units in the rear to want information about the German units in front of them – who were they? What were the regiments? When we were in the Front Line our Colonel encouraged the officers in turn and after evening mess to go out into No Man's Land with one N.C.O. and see if they could "snaffle a Hun". It was a kind of sport like hounds going after a fox. Even our Signals Officer took a turn. He took Sig. Bell with him and in the course of prowling towards the enemy line was struck in the foot by a machine gun bullet. He was brought in, bandaged and sent back to hospital. We all thought, "What a lovely "Blighty"!" (ie wound), but it was not so. Back in England he died and had deemed that he had got a lucky hit. Many, many hours were spent crawling around No Man's Land but without success. Jerry had cut the grass very short this side of his wire for some yards in depth and it was thus impossible for our gallant adventurers to get near enough to catch a Hun before being seen. I do not know why it was, but the officers always referred to the Germans as "Huns" or "Beastly Huns", whilst the men used the terms "Jerry", "Fritz" or "Bosche". The cut grass allowed the enemy to have a good field of fire as well as a good view of any approach by us. We gained the impression that the Germans did not hold their Front Line with as many men as we did, but just placed one sentry or perhaps two and withdrew their men to the support line where they lived more comfortably and safely. They also had a machine gun here and there. It was rumoured that our officers wore their luminous wristwatches inside the wrist instead of on the outside so that the glow could not be seen by an alert German sentry. Was this rather a far-fetched idea, or was it just that it was easier to look at the watch on the inside of the wrist when crawling along on all fours?

On another occasion when I was at Rifle House on H.Q. Jerry brought up his "travelling circus". About half past seven in the morning as we were all up and thinking of breakfast, we could hear the sound of a railway engine coming from behind the Bosche line. Shortly after it had stopped a heavy gun went over about a dozen shells all around the headquarters. One burst just behind the sentry box, which was blown over by the burst, onto George Bramley, with whom I had enlisted. He was shaken but otherwise none the worse for his unusual experience. He had just left the bomb store where Eden had been examining a fresh box of Mills bombs. Shrapnel sprayed the wood all around the barricade and our tall dugouts and pieces of shell also hit the canvas roofs of some of the huts in the rear half of the wood. We got to expect that chug-chug of the railway engine but it came only twice more whilst we were there. As far as I know that effort resulted in no casualties, what a welcome waste!

Another rumour came into existence that whenever the crucifix in our line was shot down, then the victory in the war would go to our arms. It was shot down during our spell in that sector and the Colonel had it reverently buried, but the war went on. I felt sure that there were many crucifixes and that the same superstition prevailed.

The Signal Section had attached to it a "pigeon man". Wakeling, a very quiet person, looked after our birds which were for emergency use only. He had two pigeons and every morning at nine o'clock he freed one and it flew up into the sky from the slight clearing in the wood and usually flew around once or twice to get its bearings and then set off for the brigade pigeon loft. It had been kept unfed and so flew straight back. Not long afterwards a despatch rider brought up another one, fed before he had set off with it. The next morning the other one, by now hungry, was freed. If a message had to be sent, it was first made out in triplicate. One copy was kept in the Signal Office in the "sent out" tray and the other two copies were put into a very light aluminium container which had two soft catches attached to it, and these were put round the pigeon's leg. On two occasions, when he arrived from the brigade pigeon loft, the despatch rider reported that our pigeon had not arrived back at the loft. They had been sent and, as we discussed the matter and puzzled over it, someone recalled hearing a rifle shot shortly after the birds had been released. Could a German sniper be such a crack shot that he had been successful in hitting our birds as they circled above the trees before turning away from his lines? If so, where were the bodies? Why had not we, who watched it set off, noticed its fall? What was to have been a well-kept secret was later disclosed. It seemed that at a company mess one evening an officer had said in fun more than anything else to his cook batman, "Can't you do better than this with the bully beef?" The batman, who had been a game-keeper in civvy life, took the remark as a challenge. The next evening and the evening after that the officers' dinner was supplemented with pigeon pie, a rare delicacy and much enjoyed. However, after the second tasty dish, the batman's own officer gave him a hint that he had better not produce another tit-bit like those pies. Our pigeon service continued normally after that.

Our place of rest after two spells in the Line and one in support was Le Romarin, a small village about two miles from Plugstreet. It had a few houses, estaminets and many farms. We were billeted in the farm buildings. A very lazy life lay ahead for five days, for the signaller; who had less than normal duties to do and gained much sleep. Most company men did some nightly fatigues going up the Line. Though tee total I accompanied my friends each evening to an estaminet and had a coffee in a little basin. There we met men of other units, including artillery men, the gunners of our covering artillery. I casually mentioned how struck I was when we tested them. "Oh, you are the b ... fool who wastes a round of our ammo, are you?" they replied. It appeared that they could ill spare a single round of their ration of shells, which was seven per gun per day, because of the demands of the artillery on the Somme. They relied on saving up to have a good supply in hand in case of emergency. They had to economise with the minimum of shells allocated to them. Quite an alarming insight as to what was behind us. I was thinking how well we were covered, and now all I knew was that the covering was quick but for how long would that cover last? Everyone knew that Lloyd George was pressing for an increase in the shell out-put and many believed he was the man for the job. When news from home revealed that some munition workers were on strike for more money per week we felt that we ought to let them know that we could not strike, not even for more shells, let alone more money. Needless to say, we were all disgusted with them. They did not have to worry daily about their lives.

I got quite a surprise in one letter from my mother. She told me that Great Uncle with whom we lived had pinned a huge map of the Western Front on the kitchen wall and that he liked to put little flags in position showing the Front Line. He also put a larger flag where he thought I was. I had tried to let them know that I was in Plugstreet Wood; many times I had talked about the trees. Now Mother wrote to say that they thought that I was at Le Gheer, the broken down deserted group of houses just behind 'F' and 'G' gaps, almost in our lines near the unmanned trench. They had not exactly scored a bull's eye, just the edge of the wood near its right hand corner as we faced the enemy. I wondered what the censor of my letters would have thought if he had known or recognised my hints as to my whereabouts!

That map on our kitchen wall must have been on a very large scale to have shown a mere hamlet like Le Gheer, which was marked only on trench maps of a particular sector. Trench maps were usually one inch to the mile and specially printed to show the sectors in detail, and very many such maps would be needed for the whole Front.

In my reply I congratulated my Great Uncle and quite easily let him know that I was in the nearby wood. They soon knew when I was out at rest, and where.

Immediately after breakfast the first time we were out at Romarin, Mac and I hurried to the OrderlyRoom and asked the Sergeant, Arnold Rush, if we could have a pass-out for

Bailleul. We knew that there would be a rush by many others also keen on visiting that large town. We were the first applicants and had to wait for the N.C.O. to arrive. He gave each of us Army Form W.3105, a faded, buff coloured form on which we had to write our Army number, rank and name and state why we wanted a pass and the hours we wished to be absent from our unit, which was for the purpose of proceeding to Bailleul from 1 p.m. to 10 p.m. Arnold Rush told us to be at the Orderly Room at one o'clock. We then attended the Church Parade, had dinner and duly reported to the Orderly Room after making ourselves look as smart as possible. Our boots were specially cleaned for the occasion and we wore our walking-out belts. Mac had bought a lightbrown belt, a civvy belt, about two inches wide. This spare belt, light in weight, saved him the trouble of having to take his equipment to pieces which was a bit of a nuisance. The Orderly Officer for the day had signed our passes and we set off on our seven to eight miles' journey. At Papot we turned right onto the main Armentiéres – Nieppe-Bailleul road and for half the walk we were just on the French side of the Franco-Belgian border. At about three o'clock we strolled into Bailleul Place, the main square. What a great expanse it was. It seemed far too big for such a town, but yet I thought what a grand sight it would be on market day if it was filled with stalls. The square was paved with the familiar cobbles, or "kidney stones" as we often called them. We had marched on such a lot of roads paved with cobbles and if one's boot soles were getting thin one knew the feeling of these stones through to the feet. Many were the fine shops, cafes and estaminets, some of the latter with English looking names. After a tea of eggs, chips, bread and "cafe" (coffee), we had a further look round and saw many very fine old buildings, some of which reminded me of Spanish buildings. On our way to Bailleul we had seen for quite a while a prominent belfry and bell tower. We could tell that the Church was very old and not like many of the French churches. The Town Hall too was very old. We left the pleasant market place and town just after seven o'clock and leisurely strolled back, noticing that nearly all the fields were well cultivated and not shell marked. The farm buildings showed signs of prosperity.

We were back in Romarin before ten and, intact, in bed by that time. The many Red Caps (Military Police), dreaded because of their bad name, had not troubled us. They were the very first I had ever seen.

I never knew if the Wesleyan padre, the Reverend E Sayer-Ellis, was the Brigade or Division padre, but he never failed to visit us in the Line or out. He ministered to our spiritual needs with unflagging energy. He made one tour of the Front Line every time we were in. If he set his mind on the time of his visit, then no matter if there was enemy shelling he still came. He had a cheery word for all and we certainly felt his presence. When we were not in the Front Line he always managed to arrange a special service somewhere. If he could not use a hut in the wood, he found a small clearing. A small altar would be erected, sandbags and a sheet of corrugated iron, or a box on which he placed his case containing bread and wine. The quiet service of Holy Communion that followed was very impressive. He carried with him too a few hymn books and well-chosen hymns were reverently sung.

Each battalion of the brigade had its own police, called Regimental Police, and each wore an arm-band bearing the letters R.P. Whatever their duties were, they could not have been much. One day when I was near the Transport Lines I noticed a new recruit to their ranks, Charlie Hutton who was with 'D' Company on the first occasion I was a signaller in the line. He was, in a way, an embarrassment for, although he was one of the babes of the battalion, he was six feet two inches tall; taller than the breastwork and he must have been many times fed up with his comrades calling out, 'Keep your head down, Charlie.' Not only his head needed keeping low, but his shoulders as well. He was always in great danger of having to develop a stoop, as well as being seen by an enemy sniper and, of course, he could draw fire on his comrades. Darkie Cole discussed the matter with the Colonel who decided that Charlie had better be given a job on the Transport Lines. Thus he was made an R.P., a job he did not like; he missed the Company comradeship. (When he was transferred to the 2nd K.R.R.s on the disbanding of our Battalion in March, 1918, he did not receive the same consideration and became a Company man again).

We lived on rumours and we never knew who started them. A few that caused some airing of views were the following: One of the farm hands at Essex Farm used to signal to the German Observation balloon and give away some of our troop movements. A German Officer dressed as a Belgian and accompanied by a vicious looking dog with red, watery eyes roamed the wood. Some of us had seen a dog but never the supposed spy in a blue rig-out and peaked cap. When the troops at Romarin were setting off for the line, the sails of that windmill on the Plugstreet-Romarin Road were deliberately turned to show which route they were taking. There were three ways of reaching the wood: straight down that road; going so far and then cutting off the corner before the cross-roads; or a longer way round, not taking the main road past the windmill, but leaving Romarin by a different road passing the Piggeries and Hyde Park Corner.

All the men of the Bankers' Battalion were going back to Blighty to an O.T.C. to train as officers because of the shortage of commissioned men, due to heavy losses of such on the Somme. Before long it was said that we were going back for the same purpose, that the K.R.R.s were going to make a raid on the German lines with a view to snaffling a Hun. This was true and was common talk in the estaminets of Romarin and district. The Brigadier arrived at our headquarters one morning and said to the Colonel, "We want a Hun. We want to know what German troops are in front of us. Pick a dashing young officer and just a few men to rush into the German Front Line and grab a Hun." It was an order and nothing the Colonel could say could alter the request. To make the raid more of a surprise the artillery would not be asked to cut the enemy barbed wire as such preparation always gave the show away and Jerry replied by fixing a sited machine gun to cover the spot and wiping out the raiding party when it arrived. Instead the officer and his few men were to cross No Man's Land, cut the enemy wire with wire-cutters – two men to do the job, one holding the wire and the other cutting it so that no sound was made –

jump into the trench and capture the sentry. Young Eden led the raiding party, but failed to get a Hun. One man was wounded as the enemy were on the alert and raked the vicinity with machine-gun fire. I was on signal duty when the party returned. The Colonel was waiting and heard a full account of what had happened. When Eden heard that the wounded man, Sergeant Harrop, had not returned, he went back with an N.C.O. into No Man's Land and brought him in. The raiders, all with blackened faces and looking a little untidy, were then given a hot drink and hurried off to the Transport Lines for a clean-up and a well-earned rest.

On my second turn in the line I went with the 'A' Company Signallers as I/C. We went to the extreme right of the sector, the part of our line nearest to Jerry's Line. Here we suffered a great deal from his meal time "Hymns of Hate". Without fail, every morning at half past seven he sent over trench mortars; at dinnertime a few whizz-bangs; and at teatime some deadly rifle grenades. We soon learned that it was not safe to congregate in one place for our meals, but spread out in the bays. We were always on our guard because Jerry was so regular with his greetings and so our casualties were few. One morning though a mortar dropped directly on top of a dug-out and did great damage, wounding five of the men in it, but not the sixth, "Attie" Attenborough. He never was the same, becoming quite morose. He was dark in complexion. He very often said, "The luckiest man is the one who gets a cushy wound and gets back to Blighty." Probably the shock to his nerves was worse than a cushy wound.

Another morning after I had had my breakfast and moved into the bay a few yards from the Signal Office, perhaps I was a bit lazy for I leaned my back against the parapet instead of at the other side so that I could look towards the Bosche line. Then thud, a mortar had dropped between our wire and the parapet against which I was leaning. I was hurled to the duckboard floor; bits of parapet were flying in all directions. Fortunately I had been struck in the back by broken sandbags. I got up, felt myself and realised I had not been hit. I looked round and saw that part of the parapet was missing the top two layers. I had been caught unawares and all my own fault. I had not heard a thing and I ought to have been on the lookout, not listening. I was very shaken, in fact my hands trembled for some time. I was asked if I wanted to report to the H.Q. Medical Room, but I did not. So I lived and learned, it was rather easy to get out of the way of a mortar, to move two or three bays away directly its flight was observed, and we all knew that these little strafes were very localised and regular.

Not far behind the Front Line was a Support Line held by a Company and also used by the Front Line Company cooks. A little distance further behind was the Reserve Line. The latter was known as Hunters Avenue and it was not too far from Rifle House. It was probably an old "ride", the trees were not so dense, a duckboard track was laid along it and a series of "forts" constructed. Such dugouts were built up high of sand-bags and given names such as Rose Villa and Eel Pie Fort. My own 'C' Company was occupying this line and life was very carefree. One glorious day Jerry decided to give them a few shells. One shell made a direct hit on a fort which was being used only as a storehouse. Unfortunately Sergeant Jock Parkes had gone to obtain something and he was killed. He was a very popular N.C.O. and another shadow of gloom fell on the Company. (Jock Parkes had been engaged to a girl from Bond Gate, Helmsley). That Reserve Line hardly ever got shelled and we in the Front Line were amazed when we heard of the tragedy there. Our First Aid Post in the wood was aptly called Iodine Manor.

No matter which was your Company or specialist section, the spirit of comradeship was everywhere. It characterised the whole battalion, each one was most friendly to all others. It was a common saying that in the Army the motto was, "Number One first". How ironical this saying was to the men in the very Front Line. It was said that to keep one man in the Front Line, nine others were needed between the line and Blighty to see to all his wants and to keep him there. That motto must have been that of those nine men. I have seen many a man part with his last fag to someone dying for a whiff. Sometimes cigs were in short supply and to hear a man say, "Here, take it, I've plenty more", when he had not, was so self-sacrificing and so typical. We loved to oblige our comrades.

How welcome parcels were! Eats to supplement the sparse diet of Army food, which varied so little. Parcels were shared out as if at a party. No-one sat in a corner like Little Jack Horner. I recall when I was with the 'A' Company Signallers. "Scruff" (Jack Scaife) of Scarborough received a parcel of kippers packed in a Rowntree's sweet tin and looking absolutely fresh. What happened to those fish? Each man of the section was given one, and one for the cook for dealing with them. We did enjoy them; we hadn't had such a tasty dish for ages. One wag wondered if Jerry would catch the smell as the wind was favourable. Would he raid us to capture the fish course – he would have been too late in any case. It was thought better not to hang on to such delicacies until tomorrow; anything could happen in the meantime.

One mother's boy received a body shield for him to wear under his tunic, to be like a knight of old with protective armour guarding his chest and back. It was very awkward to put on and also much too large for him. No-one had anything like it for a swap, even if they had wanted to, so it was soon dumped.

Some of the clothing parcels caused great amusement. When a Tommy received a body belt from home, to keep his tummy warm, there were howls of laughter as he held it up for others to see. Each of us had been issued with a body belt so another one was not needed, not even to be washed as a spare. Goodness knows where there was anyone who liked his body belt! I never wore mine but it had to be taken care of in case of a kit inspection. It was always deep down in my valise. Lice loved them, they were "home sweet home" to them.

Socks were always welcome. I used quite a lot of them and, thanks to my Blighty friends; I always had pairs to spare. I used to wear two pairs at a time because I found out that by so doing I saved my feet from getting blistered, especially when we were on the march. On route marches I felt no discomfort at all. The parcel that brought forth the greatest roars of laughter was the one that contained a tin of bully beef. Except for the one day a week when we had fresh meat, so called, we lived on bully and relied on it for our main meal of the day – be it in stew, fried cutlets or just bully. Sometimes it was in great supply and we had a tin per day per man, but on some occasions the ration was a tin for four men. The latter case was when we were going into action. It was said at the latrine "news centre" that many of the paths in the wood were made of tins of bully. If so, they were better than slippery duckboard paths.

The dear ladies in their knitting circles and girlfriends really need not have bothered about scarves. Each of us had an issue cap-comforter-cum-scarf. It was a very useful and much appreciated article of clothing. Its dual purpose – at full length it was a comfortable scarf, and when tucked into itself twice it became a woolly cap and could be pulled down over the ears – was a blessing in winter. I had another use too for mine – I used to put it in my tin hat to make a softer pillow for my head.

In answer to appeals there came from Blighty in some parcels a tin of Harrison's pomade, the best concoction at the time for dealing with the lice which tormented us such a lot at night time. The tender parts of the body were smeared with the ointment and it did some good, but I believe that in time the little beasts got immune to it – mind you, there were hundreds and hundreds to cope with. Such evasive action with these body pests was not sufficient to wipe them out for they laid their eggs (nits) in all manner of places – in all seams of underpants, vests, cardigans, shirts and trousers. To strafe them we set about them when we were in the rear half of the wood; many men could be seen leaning against a tree, tunics, shirts and vests off and they would run a lit match or the flame of a candle along the seams to destroy these eggs. Some little scorching of the garments was bound to occur, but that did not worry us. Trousers were given similar treatment when the time was opportune. We had to feel sure that the enemy (human) would let us alone inpeace to get on with the job. This struggle to keep clean of "chats" was an uphill one. They were no respecters of persons, the officers could not be completely immune.

Twice, once from the rear of the wood and once from Papot, small parties of men went to the baths at Pont de Nieppe. Most of the route (between Plugstreet and Bizet) was under enemy observation, hence the small parties. Earlier in May, whilst the battalion was at Outtersteene, some of the Company men had been on fatigue there cleaning out huge tubs as used by the brewers there and installing hydraulic apparatus, under the supervision of the R.E.s, the usual task-masters. Then the baths, or vats, had been taken over by the R.A.M.C. (Royal Army Medical Corps). The French girls who had been helping when I went there with the Black Watch had been dispensed with, not because they were too shy but that the Army in its wisdom thought that our own troops should run the show. We stripped on a grassy lawn and ran eagerly to a tub and six of us enjoyed a real soaking and lathered ourselves time and time again. We did not want to leave off. However a whistle was blown and we went back to our clothes and dried ourselves on our towels and made our bodies glow. We had not shown any modesty, except a certain Sergeant who had gone as far as his tub with a towel draped around him. Did three stripes change a man and make him shy? When we had finished drying ourselves we were given clean shirts, shorts and underclothes. Goodbye to the old friendly lice and new laid eggs in return. So we were soon lousy again. There was a little time to spare after we got dressed and we were allowed half an hour in the nearby village where we made a few purchases. This was a welcome change and very relaxing.

The place Romarin makes me recall cheese. I had never seen so much, whole cheeses, half cheeses and quarter cheeses. The battalion was ready to go up the line when up came a half-limber from the Transport Lines, heavily laden with an extra-ordinary ration of cheese. Already burdened to capacity no-one wanted it. Hurriedly large pieces were thrust into anybody's hands, whether wanted or not. The Quarter-Master had to get rid of it and much was wasted and left by the road side. It had arrived at the lines too late to be included in the rations already given out in sandbags and tied on men's equipment. The men just did not want to untie them.

Romarin also recalls a great submission by the Transport. After many requests the Signallers had at last been given a half-limber in which to put all the apparatus wanted in the Line; telephones, flags, flappers, discs, lamps, lamp-stands and reels of wire. Previously, all these things had previous had to be carried by the signallers themselves in addition to their packs, rifles, etc.

From Romarin departed Tebb, a 'B' Company signaller, to Blighty for a commission, the first to leave for such a reason. In all the estaminets I visited I was always amused at the way the troops ordered wine; white wine was always referred to as "vin blanc" or "vin blonk", but red wine as "vang rouge", the latter a better effort in pronouncing the words correctly. Another popular wine was Grenadine. According to the troops, the biere there was not as good as English beer.

At Papot in our Transport Lines was a dry canteen from which we were able to buy some Blighty goods; Gold Flake cigs, Huntley and Palmer's biscuits, Peak Frean's Pat-a-Cake biscuits, Nestle's chocolate, H.P. sauce, writing materials, etc. The profits went into the Battalion Fund. For some unknown reason, signallers had not to carry an entrenching tool, only its case which hung by two straps from the back of the equipment belt, although it was wrong to think that signallers never had occasion to dig in after an attack. I made a special use of the empty case, putting in it one packet of biscuits and a bar of chocolate as supplementary rations for emergency use.

On two occasions when we were out at rest at Papot, Jerry shelled the Transport, once rather heavily and the other time just lightly. During the former shelling the women of the village were greatly scared and cleared off along the roads and returned when the shelling had finished. Captain Potter had ordered all the mules and horses to be taken away from the lines. They were brought back when the strafe was over. No direct hit was made and no damage done on either occasion.

Rest at Romarin and at Papet – yes for the signallers, but not for the Company men. They made up fatigues and working parties for up the line. They shovelled tons of French earth into sandbags, built up broken breastworks, carried miles of barbed wire, manipulated through the wood endless supplies of 'A' frames, lined the sides of trenches with sheets of corrugated iron, carried innumerable duckboards, all under the instructions of a Sapper who decided how man hours had to be spent on any task and left the troops to get on with the jobs and wait till they saw fit to return and let the troops go back to their billets.

Cigarettes and tobacco appeared in the rations and everyone was issued with a fair share. Probably the pipe smokers came off better for there were fewer of them to share the tins. At one period there was a glut of cigs: Beeswings, Flags, Ruby Queens, Red Hussars and Oro. Such a fine variety and plenty of them. The problem arose as to how to get rid of them. A few were smoked but some varieties could not have been liked for men began to gamble with them, hoping to lose, so fed up were they with the flavour. The stakes in brag, pontoon and whist were cigs, not francs or centimes. I kept my supplementary eats in my entrenching tool case, empty of its small spade-cum-pick, but I was astonished to see where some men kept their emergency fags. Every man had a field dressing which he kept in a little out of sight pocket on the inside of his tunic at the bottom left corner. Some men took their dressing out of it and put it in their haversacks or valises and put in its place a packet of cigs and a box of matches. They were the men who could not do without a smoke, the chain smokers. It amazed me too that a man would wake up two or three times a night, light up, have two or three puffs, dot the fag and then get down to sleep again. I did understand how a smoke was of use, that it eased the tension for some and helped them to soothe their frayed nerves. Men would thus put their minds onto their smoking and momentarily forget the horrors and conditions around them. The field dressings were made less than two hundred yards away from my home, at Smith and Nephew's in Neptune Street. I understood too why men gambled, it was not to make a fortune but to keep their minds off the war. It was better to have some outlet like that as a means of keeping thoughts off the sordid, rather than idling and thinking what might happen. I wrote many letters and even played a lot of patience. No difference in the result, one did what one liked according to taste.

In the Front Line and in support we did try to keep clean and, though water for that purpose was scarce, we tried to give our faces the once-over every morning. Fred Johnson, a 'C' Company signaller, successfully scrounged a canvas water bucket and would try to get some water from somewhere and we all had a wash and brush up, all in the same water. Those who had to shave took a little water out of their water bottles. I had never shaved as yet, but on parade at Romarin at the morning inspection, our officer Tocky Turner when examining me said to the Sergeant, "I think that this man should take some of the down off his face." It was an order for me to shave, so that night in the barn I lathered my cheeks and got ready to shave with the Army cut-throat razor. This was the type of razor I had so often seen my great uncle use. As a small boy I had watched him, yet I could not call that a lesson in the use of such a razor. I had started on the left side of my cheeks and was making quite a hash of things when

Mac came in. "What are you trying to do? Cut yourself to pieces?" Goodness knows how many cuts there were as I awkwardly used the weapon. Mac took over and finished the job for me. I was very thankful to him, and thankful too that many months had to pass before I had to shave again. One of our youngsters never shaved at all during his Army days, he used a pair of small scissors and just trimmed his "down".

An Army order about this time caused much laughter "All men will let their moustaches grow and frequent inspections will be made to see that this order is complied with." No penalties were mentioned if this order was not followed out. Why had we to do this laughable thing? Guesses were wild. Had we to look fierce? For what purpose and for whom? If all that most of us could do was to grow down, what a struggle we would have to grow a full moustache. "Football teams" and "Eleven-a-side" were now common remark; as we examined one another to see what growth had been made. The novelty wore off and the matter was forgotten. When our upper lips did begin to show some results and inspections were made, a man might be asked, "Have you been using nail scissors?" I never managed to grow one.

About the same time, another order forbade men to spread rumours. Anyone found doing so and proved guilty would be severely punished for "harming our war effort". It was no rumour when it was whispered that Lord Kitchener had been drowned in the early days of July. We, one of the last of his Divisions, were sorry to hear such grave news – the country had great faith in him and his loss was a great one.

We saw very little air activity and thought that this was due to our planes being required on the Somme Front. The antics of a German plane interested me. It came almost over our lines and from a fair height dropped hundreds of pamphlets. We watched them sail down majestically but they missed our line. It was later said that they were printed in English and were expected, when read, to cause unease in our troops. We did see two of our planes bring down two German observation balloons near Armentiéres and watch the observers jump out and land behind the German lines.

Lammas Day, when we were at Rifle House headquarters in the front half of the wood, was my birthday and I was rather pleased that I was not in the Front Line itself. There arrived for me right on the day a strong wooden box, twelve inches by twelve and eight inches deep. I borrowed an entrenching tool and prised off the lid. Inside was a luscious iced birthday cake. It had been made at the request of my mother by a baker and confectioner, the son-in-law of my great uncle. At tea-time with the help of a borrowed sharp knife I cut it into twelve pieces, one piece for each signaller and runner of H.Q. It was very rich and much enjoyed. "Eat, drink and be merry ... " and save nothing for the morrow. Two days afterwards we experienced a thunderstorm, the likes of which I had never seen before. The thunder rolled heavily for hours and sounded so terrific, probably because of the trees. It made more noise and was more deafening than any bombardment we had had up to then.

It had become widely known that Colonel Feversham would willingly recommend likely applicants for commissions, provided that they wished to become officers in the Regiment. Mac and I studied the question and considered the pros and cons. We realised that an officer's lot had its advantages, such as a better mess, a better dug-out, sleeping quarters and a batman, but held tremendous responsibility. News of great losses among young officers on the Somme, where it was said that few survived more than one attack, and that the expectancy of life of a young subaltern was reckoned to be about three months in

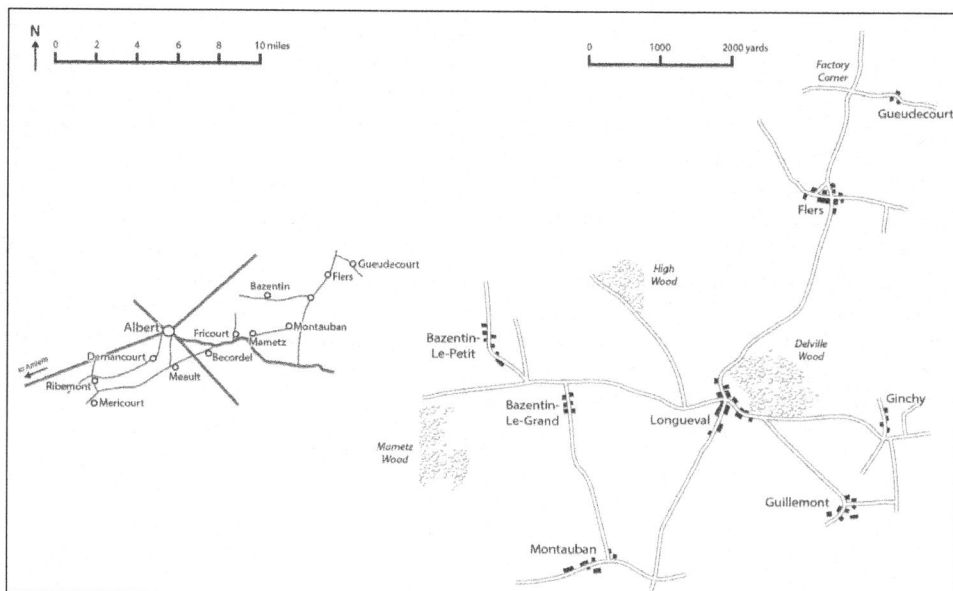

Map 3. Somme 1916

other sectors, so we decided to leave well alone.

In our early days many optimistic men hunted for and carried about souvenirs to take home with them on leave or when the war ended. Nose-caps, bits of shrapnel, Jerry bayonets, the little caps of the enemy, Prussian helmets, etc., besides silk cards and picture postcards, all eagerly collected at first. In time, as the war showed no signs of coming to an end, the more heavy specimens were dumped, especially when a move was imminent and it was desired to carry the least weight possible.

Our Plugstreet picnic was coming to an end; it was not a rumour this time. Our initiation into the arts of trench warfare affected us in different ways. Perhaps we were now not so happy-go-lucky as we had been at Helmsley. A grey shadow now hovered over us and influenced us indirectly. We were not all that miserable but just subdued or placid, as if we had no right to be gay because we had lost some good friends. Fortunately there was always a humorist somewhere, men who could create laughs, though forced laughs, at times. When the dixie of tea from the cooks in the Front Line was being carried up by Jack Thompson a stray Jerry bullet punctured it and he arrived at the waiting queue for "Tea up" with an empty container. Everybody there laughed.

We were due to leave the Plugstreet sector on August 16th, but at the last minute our relief was put off for twenty-four hours. On that extra day, which we had to spend in the Front Line, some men of the Transport Section came down into that line so that they could say that they had been in the very Front Line. We left the wood the next day and marched out to Papot where we stayed for one night. The Notts and Jocks had relieved us, the remnants of troops that had gone over the top on July 1st on the Somme. We tried to learn from them what that sector was like and all they could say was "wholesale slaughter". We wondered if they were exaggerating the horror, the losses, the shelling, the machine gun casualties, and the death rolls. They looked at our black buttons and said that Jerry would have no mercy on us, the black buttoned b … s whom he hated as much as he did the kilties.

The next day we went to Meteren where we were billeted in barns. There I bought a picture postcard of a well-known Cathedral, Albert with its "falling Madonna", and sent it home, first crossing out very lightly the name Albert and writing on the other side, "I am not at present looking at this Cathedral."

For some six days we had a very easy time. Our billets were clean and we spruced ourselves up a bit. We drilled, unnecessary for trench work, and had route marches during which we sang; *Tipperary, Rolling Home, Here we are: here we are again, One grasshopper jumped over another grasshopper's back* … and really let ourselves go. On Wednesday, August 23rd we left Meteren and were taken on Dennis lorries to Bailleul West Station. We left behind, further back under hallowed grassy mounds, each with a little cross with aluminium name plate, a few of our "originals". Goodbye to a training sector with its associations with Bruce Bairnsfather and his expressive cartoons.

5

The Somme/Flers – Blood, Mud, Heroes and All

The familiar cattle trucks awaited us at the railway station and "we happy band" of brothers scrambled aboard, quickly taking up positions we preferred – the far corners for a better rest at night. As soon as we moved off, the doors being still open, four of us dashed to the doorways on either side in order to sit there with our feet dangling outside in order to see the slowly changing scenery. On we crawled through Hazebrouck and St Omer to Calais. How near to Blighty we were! How we gazed in a make-believe way longingly across the Channel, beyond the lovely stretch of sand dunes and caught glimpses of the White Cliffs of Dover, apparently so near on this clear, sunny day, or did we imagine it because we wanted to? Perhaps a few of the less optimistic wondered if they would ever see them again.

Many hours later on Thursday about eight kilometres beyond Abbeville we de-trucked at Pont Remy on the River Somme after a sometimes jerky and sometimes very uncomfortable journey in the wake of thousands of others who had gone that way two months earlier, and very many of whom had not come back that way in cattle trucks or come back at all. We marched away from the river and, just before most of the battalion turned right for the old French village of Francieres, 'A' Company left us to be billeted in the farm buildings just off the road. 'C' Company men were found billets in the main street and I and a few more of the signallers were billeted in the house of a French widow. The 'C' Company Officers and some of the H.Q. Staff were put into the chateau, a very large building of many rooms, shut in by tall iron railings. The 'D' Company officers were found a home with the village priest. To the officers, clean beds and white sheets were indeed a welcome change from "flea bags" and ground sheets. Every one of us was made very comfortable in this peaceful and restful countryside.

We settled down and so learned that our stay in this delightful spot was a preface to mightier things and that soon we should be taking a part on the Somme battlefields, where thousands had already paid the price of war. We gleaned a little about the war and what was happening from the English newspapers sent out to us, but the reports were very scanty and were censored. A little more news was to be had from the French newspapers and some from the Notts. and Jocks who had experienced the Somme, but gave us a vague idea of the immensity of the task there. We were miles away from the realities of war and had reached the stage in our Army lives when we paid little attention to the morrow and what it might bring. This was partly due to the fact that the battalion had scarcely suffered at all at Plugstreet. We were not really heartless; it was just that we appeared to be just as strong now as when we came out from Blighty. The Bavarians in front of us in Plugstreet Wood had been friendly enemies in a way, they had not bothered us much, nor we them.

Serious training started almost immediately, training in open war-fare; we noted the open touch. We learned a lot about extended order, creeping barrages, zero hour, bombing and mopping up parties and morale. We practised all manner of manoeuvres both day and night. Waving flags represented moving barrages and this job was done by the signallers, stopping in one place when the supposed barrage was stationary, and moving forward slowly when the barrage was lifted and slowly moved on. Machine guns clicked out a dull rat-tat and umpires dashed here and there and said to some men, "You're dead" or "You're wounded". So we were being moulded into a mobile attacking force. All these practices looked as if we were playing at soldiers.

Specialist instructors were brought in to help, men who had tasted the Somme fighting. They explained that the enemy included vicious Prussians and Wurtembergers who were capable of any trick in close fighting. We had to be ready for hand-to-hand fighting and were reminded that the Bosche did not like cold steel – the sword or our bayonet. We were shown how to use the rifle in such close fighting, when firing it was impossible. A jab under the chin with the butt end was as good as a knock-out blow. "Trip up your enemy: if your sword-bayonet sticks, fire a round into him. Kick him or jab with your rifle in the weaker parts of his body."

These instructors had seen such unclean methods of fighting and taught us how to save ourselves and get the better of a clever foe. Certainly a beastly sort of preparation, but then we were told that we were dealing with beasts. We learned these dodges, it was better to be prepared. At the same time we certainly hoped that we would never have to use them. We were hardly the sort to be filled with a hymn of hate – not like Fritz. It was pointed out to us that in a case of self-defence, if you wanted to live then you would have to use such tactics as necessary.

Between our heavy field days we had a fair amount of leisure time and many of us went on pass to Abbeville for sight-seeing, purchasing souvenirs and seeing the type of premises common to French towns and shown by their own particularly coloured lamps.

One afternoon John Barker and I went into Pont Rémy to its only shop which was situated just across the bridge, and on the right hand side of the main street. Though its window looked very untidy we went inside to buy some chocolate, though we considered French chocolate to be like dried wood, and we also wanted some silk cards and views. A very young, cheeky looking girl attended to us. Her knowledge of English was quite extraordinary and some of her words most foul. She had quickly learned many English words that were not to be found in an ordinary dictionary. Quite a foul and crude vocabulary and I much doubt whether she knew the meanings of the words she flung at us. She laughed heartily and, probably seeing that we were shocked, rattled off her worst words. She asked us if we wanted "art" – photos, coffee, and did we wish to go through to the room at the rear of the shop. We did not take her upon the offer.

No baths being available, many of us went down to the River Somme on the outskirts of Pont Rémy and used the river there, splashing about in the nude and enjoying the fun, as did some of the Mademoiselles.

Early in September a full battalion parade took place. The Divisional General came down to inspect us and then he made a speech. He gave us a warning of what was in store for us. His remarks left no loophole for any doubts we might have had as to our battalion being very depleted after we had been sent into the "melting pot". The battalion was to have its chance to show what it could do. The best German was a dead one. No quarter was to be shown. His main theme was the morale of the troops and also the necessity of keeping close to the barrage. He doubly emphasised the latter.

So, on Thursday, September 7th, not unexpectedly, we bade goodbye to our hosts and donned our full packs, leaving Francieres and marching by way of Ailley de Haute, Cloche, Buigny, Vauchelles, Longuet, Long to Longpré to board cattle trucks once again. The railway station of Longpré was only six kilometres from Pont Rémy, but we had marched some twenty-four kilometres in a roundabout way. How the air sounded and resounded with the nine hundred and more voices giving full vent to "Tipperary", that particular tune and song and time I shall never forget.

We were on our first trail, not to Tipperary but to battle. How we could sing "We are the boys who make no noise" and all the other popular war songs! Through the French countryside we travelled, eagerly noticing the villages and farms apparently undisturbed by fateful happenings not many miles away. We listened to the latest battalion rumour; that a regular warrant officer and a sergeant had been in trouble and had been severely dealt with and sent back to base – I wonder if they knew how lucky they were in missing the stunt! We learned that the 'C' Company Quarter-Master's store had been at Pont Rémy and had been broken into one night. All that the thieves had taken were six wooden boxes each containing twelve bars of carbolic soap. What an odd haul! Lt. Eden posted a guard on the hut the next night and the culprits were caught red-handed. They belonged to an Eastern Labour battalion which was helping in the construction and repair of damaged roads. At their trial an interpreter disclosed that the soap was eaten as a sweet. Everyone to his own taste!

More than a mere rumour was the following story, which had a ring of truth in it. Back at Francieres the sergeants had their own mess and billets and spent a lot of their evenings together. However, they were somewhat annoyed with one of their own number who, on being offered a cigarette by any one of them always refused saying, "I smoke only Blighty Gold Flake, I don't touch canteen ones." So they sought the help of the Sergeant-Major's batman. When the offending sergeant, a specialist, was safely on parade, the batman substituted some canteen cigarettes for the Blighty ones in the sergeant's kit and used them for themselves. Regularly after that they were quite effusive in offering him one of his own Blighty cigarettes, but he firmly refused their offer and unknowingly smoked canteen ones, much to their hidden glee. Could he not tell the difference?

It was not until we had passed through Amiens that we got glimpses of activity. There were places where the railway line came quite close to the River Somme, on which sailed river barges carrying wounded men from the Front. The peaceful-looking River Somme, with a name that was to be linked with bloodshed, horror, destruction and colossal losses.

Part of the battalion detrained at Mericourt-Ribemont and the other part went further on to Dernencourt. The first thing I noticed as I left the cattle truck at Mericourt-Ribemont was a huge wire cage – a prisoner-of-war camp, full to over flowing. Most of our four hundred – odd men had never seen a German soldier before. We looked closely at their grey field uniforms and especially their little pill-box caps with button-like badges at the front of them. The prisoners were munching bread or sitting down and they really looked as if they were tired out and had not slept for days. Some were in a terrible state, they looked filthy, unwashed and unshaven, a growth of stubble round every chin. Poor blighters – our constant barrages had left their marks on their faces. Only a few wore the German type of tin hat of a different pattern from ours. Theirs were deeper and rounder and almost covered their heads, ears and much of their faces, reminding one of the fashion plate of ladies' cloche hats. However, these prisoners were finished with the war and I wondered what they thought of us, whether they pitied us going up to the Frontline?

Our half of the battalion set off and marched as far as Meaulte, where we were just due for our ten minutes rest. We took off our packs and had sat down on them when, just as we were relaxing, there came the order, "Stand to attention!" We scrambled up and began looking about to see if we could discover why this order had been given. A Tommy on horseback appeared carrying a pennant and he was followed by several Staff Officers. We knew then that somebody of importance was about to pass through Meaulte, but who? Salutes were exchanged, the brass hats had disappeared and we sat down again. A buzz of voices broke the silence as someone said, "That was the Prince of Wales in the centre of the group, returning from an early morning look at the Front." It was said that great care had to be taken to prevent him going too near the war.

Up and on again and there was Albert and the Hanging Madonna from the Cathedral top. Rumour had it that the French believed that if the Madonna fell, the war would go against them and they would lose, so they had it held up by steel cables. On the other hand, the British believed that if it fell then the war would be over in next to no time. As we passed through the outskirts of the city we saw ruins everywhere. Soon we reached our camping ground on a hillside. Around us was a conglomeration of every conceivable thing necessary to the art of war. What a spectacle; as far as the eye could see that undulating countryside was alive with teeming masses of men, horses, wagons, guns, motor lorries, dumps, sidings, tents, bivouacs, huts, ambulances, Field Dressing Stations, etc. Beyond our rise and camping ground, the next valley and hillside were peopled and equipped similarly. The saddest sight of all was that all those troops who had been through a battle and were on their way back to somewhere quieter looked worse than they really were because they were covered in dust; there was dust everywhere.

In the evening campfires showed up clearly all around us and we knew then that we were a good distance from the Front Line. Bivvies were made of all sorts of things – biscuit tins, old blankets, wooden doors, wood from ruined houses and waterproof sheets. Tommies of different regiments were milling around, stopping to talk and trying to glean news of the Front.

I heard that there was an East Yorkshire battalion nearby so Mac and I set off to find it, just in the hope that we could find someone from our own home town. We spoke to dozens of East Yorks. but did not manage to find anyone we knew. Khaki was a great leveller; we spoke to all and sundry. The khaki-green uniforms of our regiment made no difference.

What tales those who had been through "it" told! The Bosche had been living in underground palaces for two years. He had massive dugouts, thirty to forty feet deep and equipped with almost everything for his comfort – real beds, paintings on the walls, away in and a separate way out, real stairways. Some of the Tommies said that the Germans had their women folk with them. All such done because he believed that he would never have to leave these safe dugouts. Jerry had made his funk holes real homes from home.

In relays we were taken to Meaulte for a bath. We had washed or bathed in brewery vats, biscuit tins, rivers and canvas buckets, but this time we had showers of lovely hot water followed by cold water. With a good application of soap we got a very pleasant clean feeling, though we had to put on our lousy clothing. Elated on the way back we sang, "We are Fred Karno's Army, A lousy lot we are: We cannot fight, we cannot shoot: what blooming use are we?"

Tommy could always laugh, and always pull himself to pieces. Storm troopers to be? In no way could I picture myself, or us, as this. Back at the hillside I saw two games being played that I had never seen before. One was called "Housey-Housey". This game was run by two old soldiers, or possibly two non-infantry men. They gave out to each of their customers a rectangular card of three or four lines of squares, in some of which were numbers: four numbers on a line. One of the men had a bag containing numbers one to ninety-nine. He shook the bag and then took out one number, which he called out. If a customer had that number on his card he put on it a pebble, or a bit of match stick. If the game was for a single line, then the customer who had covered his numbers on one line first thus having four on a line, won the prize which was usually about two shillings. If the game was for a full house, then the customer who first covered three or four lines of four numbers was the winner and the prize about four shillings. To help him call the numbers out correctly to his listeners, the Caller would use a lingo of his own. Some I recall were Kelly's Eye (number one); Legs Eleven (eleven); and Clickety-click (sixty-six). This game helped to pass the time away and the charge was small, one penny or ten centimes per single line and two pence per full house. The caller liked to remind us that we would not want our pennies where we were going.

The other game was Crown and Anchor – a mug's game. In some hidden quiet corner, because the Army authorities did not permit this game, one man would unroll a canvas sheet on which were marked a crown, an anchor, a heart, a club, a diamond and a spade. The sucker put his money on which symbol he wished to back and then shook three dice, each dice had the same six symbols. The man who ran the game was called the banker and he never lost. Yes, a real mug's game: had we not, even in the elementary schools, taught permutations and combinations!

The troops near us who had survived a battalion's usual two attacks against the enemy gave no glowing description of the Somme Front. They were short of vivid words. The majority said: "It's Hell" or "It's Hell let loose" or "It's Hell with the lid off". They emphasised that only fragments of their units came back. Yet we failed to understand the significance of these terse reports. So we were not unduly alarmed. Ignorance is bliss.

We changed camp and moved a little further up towards the Line to near Becordel. To keep us occupied one afternoon Darkie Cole of 'D' Company obtained from somewhere a blackboard and easel and gave his section and some of the signallers a talk on the prismatic compass. He said that we ought to be able to take a bearing and be able to move in a given direction. Map reading was one of the subjects I liked very much.

Suddenly one day, most of our officers disappeared. They had been given a map reference and told to meet at a certain loop to view some strange objects of war, with which they had to become familiar. Not one of the officers had the slightest idea what he was going to see, except that whispered rumours connected the mysterious object with water tanks. Darkie Cole thought that he was going to see a new form of apparatus to deal with impure water, changing the latter into drinkable water without using the usual chlorine.

Within a short time of arriving at the rendezvous all were quickly disillusioned when they were introduced to H.M. Landships – both male and female (tanks). Each tank was a mass of steel and of a curious shape containing most marvellous contraptions of motors and gadgets. The male species had besides machine guns two pompoms mounted one on either side which fired a small shell. They could traverse a wide area. The female tank had machine guns only. There were little seats for the gunners, belts and boxes of ammunition, a nest of shells all packed neatly away yet handy for use, small slits for observation purposes, places for all the crew. They were awe-inspiring in their antics; they straddled across trenches, crushed barbed wire, went up and down the fields at acute angles and generally wallowed about. The din of the motors was terrific. The crew needed extra strong helmets. Such a tank was H.M.S. *Cyclops*. They looked to be wonderful weapons of destruction and it seemed that only a direct hit would put them out of action. Duly impressed, the officers returned to tell their men about the new weapon and, because the powers-that-be were doubtful as to what would happen if a tank got into difficulties, a party of six men had to accompany each tank, going in front of it as a form of cover and protection – another task for the infantry.

We were not restricted in any way and could stroll about anywhere. Watching all the movements along the busy roads was quite thrilling. Seething masses of fresh troops were moving up the line and battle-scarred heroes moved in the opposite direction, thankful to have left behind them the devastated regions in which they had been living and suffering. Not far away were huge craters made on the first day of the offensive. Chalk had been hurled upon either side of a deep valley. Thrown in all directions were masses of material. Dugouts which had been strongly built well below ground had been blown up and here and there were traces of their occupants in the shape of shattered bodies. What a mess!

Empty motor ambulances rushed to the Field Dressing Stations and full ones were returning with their loads of the maimed. Guns of all sizes were being shifted forward, some by horses and the heavier ones by tractors; scores of motor lorries in long lines were taking all kinds of material to the dumps nearer to the line. Nearing the camp I heard the swirling of the bag-pipes and came to an impressive sight. There was a funeral and full military honours were being paid to a member of a Scottish Regiment as his body was being taken to rest in the cemetery at Becordel. Above the constant din of all the traffic, the bag-pipes sent their wailing strains of *The Flowers of the Forest* resounding through the countryside. The memory of this sad occasion stuck in my thoughts when later I remembered the number of my own comrades, and others, who had not a proper resting place and certainly no military honours. There were too many of them.

A very important day to our battalion had to come, and it was on Wednesday, September 13th that the six hundred and sixty officers and other tanks who were destined to go "Over the Top" were selected. Who would be chosen to go forward and who would be left behind with the details at the camp? How was the choice to be made? Certainly not by lots. It looked as if the Second-in-Command of the battalion, the Second-in-Command of each Company, a junior officer from each Company, a few of the specialist N.C.O.s and some other ranks were detailed to stay behind to form a useful nucleus should a lot of officers and specialists not return. Captain Pitt of 'C' Company selected some of the youngsters of the company to remain behind; one keen young rifleman and a batman failed to convince him that he was eighteen. Did we think in terms of good or bad luck? The men kept their thoughts to themselves, perhaps the superstitious amongst them thought that the thirteenth boded ill.

Preparations were in full swing. Each man had to put into his valise for up the line all the unnecessary articles of clothing, his souvenirs, books, etc. and take it to the Transport Lines to be taken care of until he returned. The troops were to go over the top in battle order, equipment and haversack – the latter to be carried on the back where normally the valise was fixed. The weight of what had been discarded did not make up for what was to be carried in addition. Extra items were: two hundred extra rounds of ammunition besides that carried in the pouches (a bandolier over each shoulder). Some carried bags of Stokes shells, some flags, telephones, reels of Japanese tinned wire (for communications), petrol tins of water, a pick or a shovel, flares, drums of machine gun ammo, a large signalling panel plus call sign for making contact with aeroplanes, two Mills bombs, rations. To sum up, Tommy was referred to as "being dressed up as a Christmas Tree".

In the evening in a roofless barn of three broken down sides, the Reverend E. Sayer-Ellis held a service followed by Holy Communion. The stars twinkled above, an almost full moon shone down and distant thumps broke the stillness, but the service was most impressive. Of the two hymns sung on that occasion *Abide with Me* and *When I Survey the Wondrous Cross*, it is the latter that always brings back to me the picture of that special service and my comrades there. A very touching memory.

As I left that barn there drifted over to me the strains of music so I went to where it was being played. The band was that of the Royal Fusiliers, the Bankers' Battalion, and the bandsmen were playing all the popular war songs. Other Yeoman Rifles were there and we all enjoyed the welcome and pleasant distraction. Somewhat subdued and very thoughtful, the Yeomen crept into their bivvies to lie awake thinking of the morrow. Some hastily wrote short letters and handed them into the keeping of the details, asking friends to post them if needed, whilst the optimistic wanted theirs to be sent off as usual in the morning.

Meanwhile the officers were ready to be transformed into Tommies. Their officers' uniforms had to be put on one side for each had been issued with an ordinary private's uniform. Sam Browns, collars, ties, breeches, caps, etc. were replaced by ill-fitting tunics, trousers, puttees, cheese-cutters, and equipment like ours – haversacks and mess tins. Would such dress deceive the German sharp shooters and snipers? The enemy machine gunners would not waste time picking them out, all their bullets would pass along the lines of troops.

Thursday morning's breakfast was a normal one and after the mess tins had been cleaned the unexpended portion of the day's ration was put into it. Its khaki cover was placed over it and it was ready to be hung on the haversack and held by its two straps. The men for the Line "fell in" whilst the others looked on, perhaps anxiously and a little sad. Rifles were inspected, the puttees were seen to be two inches under the fold of the trousers, moustaches were examined to make sure that they had not been clipped. Our equipment was not of the regular Army webbing kind, but our braces, belt, frog, water bottle carrier and entrenching tool carrier were all of leather. It was considered to be make-shift equipment. Eventually all was ready. Silent handshakes had been made, quiet goodbyes said, and the moment of parting was at hand.

"Battalion will move to the right in fours" and off went the fighting troops with little idea of what they were in for. Soon came the order, "March at ease" – a difficult task to sling the rifle over a shoulder already burdened with a telephone case strap, an ammo belt, and a spade or a pick sticking up from behind the haversack. No comfort at least. After going a few kilometres from Becordel we met, coming in from the opposite direction, a tired and haggard-looking remnant of a battalion that had been over the top twice. Thanks to the band that led them they put on a brave show, though they looked at us with pitying eyes. They appeared almost as ill-looking as the German prisoners we had already seen. We were too ignorant to realise the full significance of what we saw; they knew, and they knew what we were in for and we did not.

The countryside was changing – we had arrived at the German line as it was on the first day of the Somme Battle on July 1st. Here had been a village of fewer than two hundred houses and not a wall, not a roof, nor a room remained standing. Here was a tumbled down mass of bricks, charred timber and near-by some German graves, recognised by their own particular kind of cross – a plain cross like ours but with a circle of wood round the cross pieces. By the roadside was a piece of wood about ten feet long and one foot broad on two short posts bearing the word "Fricourt". Away to the right were the mine craters, the chalk showing up very white towards the skyline. We started to move up a gradual slope and, looking about us, we could see the old trenches like twisted ribbands of white, stretching as far as the eye could see. Higher up were endless dusty white tracks, full of moving troops. It was a hot afternoon and we went along in easy stages, passing many ruins, debris dumps; destruction was everywhere.

The earth, churned up by constant shelling, seemed to have given up the ghost and refused to produce a single blade of grass.

At the sight of a wide break in the plateau someone muttered "Happy Valley" but, as we did not know this district or even where we were, we smiled and thought, "Valley of Desolation" would have been more appropriate. Near Montauban, in which town some walls were still standing, was a twelve inch Howitzer battery and beyond it the road started to descend and a halt was ordered. We had arrived at a dump and much was to be done here. Battalion mail had been brought up and given out by Eden, who wanted to join us, but he had to return to details. The contents of the many letters were eagerly devoured, as good a tonic as any man could wish for. The unexpended portion of the day's rations was eaten. During a pause after that meal had been taken, the officers and N.C.O.s got together and studied the orders for the morrow. These covered a dozen or more typed pages, foolscap size and included a small map. What a lot to study and take in and then explain everything to the men. As far as possible the map had to be memorised, noting with care the names of the trenches to be captured and the times at which such operations had to be done and, above all, to watch the creeping barrage put out by our batteries. The objectives to be gained were marked in colours. Green Line, Brown Line, Blue Line and Red Line. Those typed sheets of orders and the two additional ones about the artillery programme were then to be destroyed. We were to be nursed forward by our guns, in four and a half hours of action: the creeping barrage and the covering barrage would ensure that all went well. We were assured that the enemy defences would be destroyed, that his barbed wire would be shot to pieces, that his machine gunners were wiped out, his trenches would be levelled to the ground, his dugouts knocked in – there was nothing to worry about! Lovely war!

When we left that temporary resting place, we moved at a snail's pace as the roads were very poor, and I think deliberately because it was not intended that we should arrive too early near the Front Line. Towards dusk, as we were once again resting by the roadside, some strange figures loomed into view – not quite rectangular but with rounded ends and pushed out of shape. Those who knew what these strange vehicles were informed us that so many were going over the top with all the attacking divisions and that they were armoured tanks. At last, we entered a communication trench which brought us to Delville Wood and through it. The trees, mostly stumps, looked ghastly and ghostly in the semi-darkness, and when we dropped into a better trench which had been hastily dug at the edge of the wood, we found hanging from its sides many telephone wires. For a long time could be heard "wire overhead" or "mind the wire", or even "mind your head". The occasional curse as some unfortunate Tommy caught his equipment on a wire and struggled to free his impediments from the tentacles holding him broke the stillness and sounded too clearly. We wondered if Jerry could hear the pleas for help as others tried to free the man. Such an incident would cause frequent pauses and the men in the rear were gradually being left behind. So the head of the column waited and so got a breather, but those at the rear never had such luck – they were always trying to catch up. Along with two P.H. helmets, each man carried lachrymatory goggles. These were hastily donned and taken off three or four times because Jerry kept giving the approach roads a dose of gas shells. Some men were slow in getting their goggles on so some sneezed a lot, some coughed and many wept copiously. Really Jerry was too far away to hear these sounds and did not send over any ordinary shells.

Many, many days had been needed to capture Delville Wood. Many were our attacks on it and many were the German counter-attacks to get back what he had lost. Both sides had bombarded it several times and, at last after thousands of our troops (South Africans in particular) had sacrificed their lives, it was not in our hands. No wonder it was now referred to as "Devil's Wood". Most of the trees were now jagged stumps, torn by shell fire. Some were blown out of the ground and were lying at all angles or leaning against others. The wood had been well fortified by the Germans with wire entanglements, which the shells fired by us had made into tangled masses, very hard to pass. Dugouts were smashed in and many were the hastily-dug shallow trenches and slits. What a sight! Picturesque in a way, illuminated by an almost full moon, every part of it looked ghostlike and eerie. A German evidently coming out of his dugout or making a dash to get back to it had been a fraction of a second too late -one of our shells had burst, pinning him down in the small of his back by a part of the roof which had collapsed. In that position he died, his bespectacled eyes staring at the moon and his facial expression showing the agony in which he had died. During another slight pause in that communication trench, one of the men realised that he was standing on something very soft. It was a dead man, though of which side could not be recognised. The body had been lightly covered with earth and the troops passing that way, to and fro, had been treading it in.

After the next move forward, a longer pause occurred and some men tried to sleep; some managed it even though the sound of our guns was now continuous. Many a prayer was said, silently. A meal of sorts was attempted by those who still had a little of their rations left. Some had mixed feelings when at last the orders were whispered: "Move into position."

'C' and 'D' Companies were to be in the first waves and numbers ten and thirteen platoons were to provide a small section, each to guard or help with the new weapon, the tanks. A few signallers were a little late with their impromptu breakfast and were eating bread and pozzie a few minutes before zero hour – 6.20 a.m. on Friday. A muttered "dash!" came from one of them – he had decided to have a drink of water from his petrol tin and found it contained petrol! He threw it away.

The sinking moon came just at the right time and gave the troops a good opportunity of getting well into No Man's Land and extending their line the length of our sector. Watches had been synchronised with the Colonel's. The young Company Subaltern of 'D' Company set his compass and took the required bearing of the direction in which he had to move, 37 degrees. Flanks kept in touch with one another. All were more or less physically tired, having been on the move at least fifteen hours – the last six of which had been painfully slow and each was carrying at least sixty pounds weight under tiring conditions, yet all were mentally alert. Perhaps tension was at its highest when we waited in shell holes for zero hour. Nothing was said, each person busy with his own thoughts. Seconds seemed like minutes and minutes like hours, in what seemed an interminable wait. The greylight of dawn was appearing over the German lines and then we had a faint view of the first enemy trench to be taken, a Tea Support Trench.

We could vaguely make out the nature of the broken ground in front of us. The ground sloped away and then rose abruptly and on the top of what seemed like a ridge was the enemy trench. All round us were shell holes reeking of tear gas and fumes. One sudden burst from a German machine gun was a little disturbing. Had we been seen? Then three Germans were to be seen silhouetted against the skyline. They moved along the top of their trench and then disappeared. They were allowed to pursue their way without a shot being fired by us, we could not give anything away at this stage. Soon after this, a sound like that of a convoy of lorries without silencers and with the engines knocking their very innards, shook our ear drums. Whatever was this noise? Why did not someone stop it? We feared lest the show be given away. Then we remembered the talk about the new weapon of war which was going to do wonders. Before we had time to place the tank, zero hour had at last arrived and, as we moved forward we realised what "hell with the lid off" and "hell let loose" meant. It was our first experience with a barrage of such intensity, an awareness of the screeching of hundreds of shells, their bursting beyond us, the flames, the flashes, the acrid fumes, the clouds of smoke and the uplifting of tons of earth. All these conjured up a vision of awfulness, yet of tragic grandeur. Then a lot of the noise seemed to fade away as we jumped, or rather struggled, to our feet to get on with the job of going forward. With an air of almost indifference we literally marched forward at a slow pace towards our objectives. No sooner had we started on our way than the enemy had begun a very useful reply to our guns by dropping a barrage round the Tea Support Trench. One signaller, Drake, remained there with a D Mark III telephone from which other signallers ran out a line of Japanese enamelled wire from a reel. The other end was to be fixed to another phone when the first objective was attained. The tank seen earlier wallowed along, not fast enough for the keen troops who wanted to get on with the business quickly, and so it was left behind with its gallant infantry section protecting it.

In the meantime, before finally capturing that enemy trench, we lost some men. The stretcher-bearers were doing their best for our first casualties though some comrades were beyond their help. Actually one does not see much of what is happening to the right or left, one's eyes are forward, looking all the time. The German machine gunners were already very successful and our numbers were gradually being thinned. Any casual glance to the right or left sometimes gave the impression that one was the only soldier there. The creeping barrage moved on and, on time, the first objective, part of the Switch Line, was captured. A pause of some ten minutes or so here allowed some consolidation to be made in case of need and the moppers-up of the Tea Support Trench to catch us up. In some previous battles troops had captured trenches and left the German prisoners as they moved forward, only to learn later that those prisoners had taken up their weapons and shot our advancing troops in the back. Hence the moppers-up had to see that no such action occurred again.

On again as the rain of iron from our guns moved forward slowly. Heavy shells continued to sing overhead, more earth was being churned up and smoke slowly drifted in the wind. Although our main aim was to press on, we did look to the right and left occasionally in order to keep in line or keep in touch with our own groups, and on such occasions were sad to see one man stumble head foremost, another blown into the air, another collapse in a heap, one nearby with blood streaming from his face. All this time we had to keep on moving forward and not stop to help. Above us like birds of prey swooped any enemy plane that dare appear. The R.F.C. was master of the sky on our day. A very gratifying thought. Our lines were getting thinner and suddenly, near-by, shortly after an enemy shell explosion, a junior officer of 'D' Company was hit in the back but the piece of shell struck his mess tin, hanging from his haversack. He had been partly lifted into the air by the explosion and thrown to the ground. Gingerly he felt his back and expected to find blood, but the mess tin had saved his life. Lafer he managed to send that mess tin home, his most treasured possession. He got up and proceeded to move forward with his men, though badly shaken. A pause was then forced upon our little group in order to exchange rifle fire with a few Germans in a trench and they were quickly despatched. During this interchange of shots, a bullet from one of our rifles lifted the helmet off the top of a German's head. When we got to that German trench, that rifleman took a revolver off a dead German Officer, carried it about for some time, and then got fed up with it and presented it to his officer.

The Brown Line had nothing to do with our Corps and we proceeded to move forward and assault the Blue Line, over a thousand yards ahead. Two battalions of our 122 Brigade (the 18th K.R.Rs and the 10th Queen's) captured Flers and were the troops that followed a tank down the main street. Our battalion and the Royal Fusilier; kept to the west of that village and eventually, dead on time, reached Bull's Road. On the way 'B' Company's S.M. Huddlestone and his section came across a German field gun in a sunken road to the right of Flers. It was firing on our advancing troops. Rushing ahead of his six men the S.M. entered the gun pit alone and was confronted by six Huns and an officer. The men ran away as their officer shot at him and missed him. The S.M. shot the officer and captured the gun. He had earlier on put out of action two enemy machine guns in shell holes when our Lewis gun jammed. The miracle was that any of the party survived for, like the rest of the battalion, they were advancing through the waving corn and were easy targets for hidden Jerries.

Three lines of enemy defences had been taken and an advance of two to two and a half thousand yards made. We rested a while in shell holes waiting for our barrage to lift. German shells were dropping very close behind us and some of us wondered if we were ahead of our barrage and that the shells dropping behind us were our own – we seemed to be being shelled from all sides. Meanwhile the Colonel with the headquarters's party had also reached the same higher ground and could see to the left the much ruined village of Flers and to the front and slightly right the village of Gueudecourt, the final objective. The men were apparently restless and disturbed by the heavy German shelling, so they began to move about to find deeper and safer shell holes. The Colonel, on seeing these movements, borrowed a blue flag from a signaller and waved it about to draw their attention. No doubt his action was seen by the enemy, perhaps from an observation post in Gueudecourt, for the result was some heavier shelling of our positions. The Colonel of the Queen's with some of his men came up and discussed the position with our Colonel. Later a Brigade Major appeared and it was decided that a move should be made forward in order to capture the final objective.

The scanty remnants of two battalions drew intense machine gun fire and cannon fire and many fell amidst the standing corn. Our Colonel knelt down and, as he peered through his binoculars, he fell back dead. Signallers Baker and Gunson were wounded at the same time. The former had a very nasty wound in his neck. He was made comfortable in a shell hole which was deepened a little to give him extra protection. A liaison aeroplane appeared above us and the Queen's Colonel suggested that our signallers should attempt to send it a message. The battalion symbol, part of a white circle, was laid out and, with the shutter-panel, a Morse message was sent. It was acknowledged by an airman with his Klaxon horn, and heard by a few of the signallers, despite the din. An enemy shell dropped where the R.S.M., the Police Sergeant and the Pioneer Sergeant and Corporal lay. Two were wounded and two were killed; we learnt that Gunson had been hit in the leg. Immediately afterwards

Tockie Tunner, the Signal's Officer, was hit in the stomach and lay writhing in agony. The Intelligence Officer was killed and the Adjutant, who liked smart saluting on pay days, was hit in the eye. All these losses had occurred when Jerry had held up his intense fire and an advance up a slope was attempted; then he mowed them down. It was impossible to hold any position thereabouts and the depleted ranks fell back to the bottom of that slope amid a hail of machine gun bullets at knee height. There they dug in and soon dusk came, much to their relief, and no enemy counter-attack was made.

A young subaltern went to the left to see if we were in contact with the battalion on our left flank and he came on one of the tanks. Its officer had got out of it and, on being asked if he was in touch on the left, he said that he was very delighted with the work his tank had done. He was in a very merry mood and said that he would look around and report to any troops he met that our battalion had come thus far. Another tank was waddling along in the distance and I learned later that the two sections of our infantry guarding them had almost been wiped out because the new weapon had drawn much rifle fire. Our right flank seemed to be up in the air.

It was now evening and dusk was changing to night. Here and there small groups of men were busily digging-in, deepening shell holes and trying to join up with the others. Jerry, having apparently resisted some of his guns, decided to give us a quarter of an hour's real "hate" and he succeeded in making us change our positions. The temptation was to fall back for there was no-one to give orders, no-one took charge. We signallers tried to help in the trench digging work after having scrounged an entrenching tool or a spade.

Suddenly, at about eleven o'clock, other troops appeared on the scene – to our relief they were not Germans, but men of the Divisional Pioneer Battalion (Middlesex) to relieve our battalion who could now make their way back. Some of our battalion had already set off but Pip and Mac were ordered by an officer brandishing a revolver to stop there and help with the consolidation work. He kept them busy and some hours later he allowed them to go back.

What a weary and awesome trek back it was – hard work because there were no recognised tracks to follow. They followed their instinct and kept the enemy Very lights behind them. Much stumbling in and out of shell holes, jumping over low shell-battered trenches, trying to avoid patches of barbed wire, but sometimes being caught by a single strand and so having trousers or puttees torn. We passed scores of dead men, the wounded we tried to cheer by promising to send back a stretcher. We were in a frantic haste to leave behind the awful destruction and the horror of the day feeling that the job of work had been done and that we had now to get away from it.

Artillery men were digging new gun pits ready for guns that would be brought forward in order to keep up with the advance made. A G.S. wagon smashed to pieces, the dead horses stretched out beside it, dead men still lying about, both ours and theirs. Our own stretcher-bearers were now very busy and we saw fewer wounded lying about as we neared our remnants, who had had many hours start of us in coming out of the line.

Later Lance Corporal George Williams, a stretcher-bearer, told me of a little interesting experience he had had whilst he was going up the line for the attack. At the last ten minutes' pause before moving into assembly positions, he and a fellow stretcher-bearer, S.B.M., soaked to their skins, had left their bit of trench and wandered around. They came to what George, in darkness, thought was a "road engine", which was still warm, so they leaned against it to get their clothes dry. As they were enjoying this little bit of extra comfort, along came a

Sergeant of another unit, who asked them, "What are you two doing here, leaning against a tank?" "A tank my foot!" replied George. "It's a road repairing machine." All three laughed. George thought that the sergeant was pulling their legs. Did the sergeant wonder if his leg was being pulled? Until the next day George did not know anything about a tank and was quite serious when he thought that the machine was used for road repairs. Having dried out somewhat, George and his friend set off to return to their trench but in the darkness they got separated. At the end of the "show" S.B.M. was reported missing. Three months later George heard that he had been taken prisoner and he wondered if S.B.M. had wandered aimlessly into the enemy lines after they got separated.

In the meantime throughout the morning and afternoon of the 15th, our First Aid Post had been exceedingly busy. At first our popular Canadian Doctor Hart quickly dealt with the walking wounded, those men who had been able, under their own steam, to get to him when wounded. His augmented staff worked very hard and especially the helpers like the buglers, other bandsmen, pioneers and other specialists. The medical staff, standing in a narrow trench with scarcely any protection attended to the waiting casualties. Lying outside the trench were others who had been carried there by our own stretcher-bearers, all showing such wonderful patience as they waited to be seen by the M.O. Blood-stained tunics, trousers and puttees were being ripped off, shirts, pants and socks torn away with fevered haste to find the injuries. Iodine splashed on a field dressing was applied to a wound or a hastily contrived splint as required. A cheery word too, and then, "Next please". Those who could walk were told to find their way to the Dressing Station. Stretcher cases were made as comfortable as possible and laid down in what shelter could be found. Lt. Jones had been brought in, shot through both legs, and so had the Sergeant-Major of H.Q. whose face had been pitted with shrapnel. A thrilling sight to those men lying outside the aid post was an Artillery Battery coming forward and being wheeled into position not far away. One limber and team were caught in the enemy's fire, as Jerry searched the area for targets and some shells began to drop nearer and nearer to the aid post and the sound of the "crumps" was getting louder and louder. The Medical Officer, fearful for his patients, decided that a change in position must be made and a more suitable and safer one found, across the embankment underneath Tea Support Trench which was dead ground; it could not be hit. It was no easy task getting all the more seriously wounded moved because stretchers were in short supply, such had been the demand as the advance was made. In the course of moving, a heavy shell fell rather too close and bugler Hannah (one of my six friends on joining up) was himself seriously injured – eighteen pieces of shrapnel struck him and some months later he had to have a specially built-up boot for one foot. He was one of the extra helpers.

Towards the end of the afternoon the M.O. became increasingly worried about the number of serious casualties still at his post. Fortunately an ammunition limber arrived for the guns nearby and, as it was making its way back near the aid post, he stopped it and persuaded the driver to take back with him two or three walking cases. After this piece of luck each returning limber took wounded men back with it and so helped to reduce the number of wounded lying about. Only one case, a man with a leg wound, very unhappy and "windy" because he had seen a shell blow up a limber, man and horses, did not like the idea. He was so miserable that he kept saying that he would never get back. However, by pointing out that the sooner he got further away from all danger, the better he would feel and by a cheery promise from the gunner that he only bid to hold on tight to him and he would be alright he was lifted up and, before he had time to collect his thoughts, the horses were galloped away. Those gunners did a wonderful job and helped to safety many a cargo of maimed men.

Great joy was shown when a little later a Ford ambulance bumped up to the aid post and a few of the worst cases were got away. A shuttle service followed and soon most of our severe cases were taken to the Field Dressing Station. No praise would be too great for the way which the "doc", his staff and his stretcher-bearers worked that day and night. The one wounded German brought in was extremely docile and very patient, a lamb in the lions' den. The look in his eyes revealed he was wondering about what sort of treatment he would get: the best, to be sure.

During the early hours of the morning of Saturday, 16th September, the remnants of our battalion and of some other units arrived back at Green Dump, just behind Delville Wood. First, tired eyes looked round for pals, friends and other comrades, but could not see many of them. Some men sprawled about awaiting collection by their own officers, wherever they were. Others lay down and took a welcome rest. The earliest of arrivals had found any old spot in which to sleep: beside a broken ammo box, against a smashed limber, in a shell hole or in part of a trench. Rain began to fall and all felt cold. The Transport men had been making some preparations and came round with tea and slices of bread and jam. At last the Yeoman Rifles were gathered together and quickly exchanged experiences. Only one Junior Officer, Darkie Cole, was there of all the commissioned that went over, the only survivor. He had been more or less blown up twice and had suffered severe pains in his back from a blow from a lump of shell.

Major Foljambe, our former Second in Command, now our new C.O. came up with a reserve of officers and some men from the details. On an informal sort of parade a roll call was taken. Unshaven and unwashed, dirty and haggard-looking, the tired survivors answered their names. The horrors of the attack had left their marks on some of them. They looked around unbelievingly – where was their platoon? Where the Company? The Company was now only as big as a platoon and the battalion little more than the size of a Company. It was estimated that just over a third of the battalion had returned. Such a lot of names were not answered and how pathetic were some of the comments: "Wounded, sir", or "Killed, sir", and the others? "Missing" because no-one had seen what had happened to most of them. Our Division, the 41st and the last of Kitchener's battalions, had lost on that day just over three and three-quarters of a thousand men.

According to rumour, the battalion had come out to the wrong position, so rest was not forthcoming and we were again given extra ammo and bombs and taken back through Delville Wood to occupy a position not far from where we went over the top. We were to hold that position and be ready in support in case Jerry counterattacked. However, this position was also found to be wrong and we made another move, but not too far away. Some German shelling disturbed us, the enemy knowing full well that our troops would be occupying old trenches of his. Fortunately we were not wanted and during the night moved back into Delville Wood. Later we left it, that awful shell-swept place, slowly returning with mingled feelings of joy and sadness: joy because we were really being relieved, and sad because of our much-depleted ranks. We were a motley-looking crowd. A few needed a shave. We were leaving behind the rumble of the guns. We, in our turn, passed by those going "up", all clean and spick and span and laden with all their implements of war. In the evening we passed Montauban, Pommieres Redoubt (once a German strong point), and reached our details where those left behind were waiting to hear our news and what had happened to friends. They had to wait, for men who had scarcely had any rest for forty-eight hours only wanted to drop off their equipment and fall down beside it to sleep, without even waiting for anything to eat and drink.

And what had happened at the details? On that memorable Friday morning when the battalion had received its first baptism of fire many of the details had risen early, but not at 5.20 a.m. (zero hour for their comrades), but yet not much later and before breakfast had left their bivvies and gone to the road that ran near the camp to watch for any activity. Already prisoners were passing by, under smiling guards. One of our enterprising pals counted them, 1241, and thought that the Yeoman Rifles must be doing well, forgetting that other units were taking part

in the battle. "That's the stuff to give 'em," someone declared laughingly.

Farther away where the fighting and the line was considered to be, another man counted thirty-three of our observation balloons curving in a large flattened arc, and "That's the stuff to give the troops," someone else said. Suddenly we noticed behind those balloons of ours one solitary Jerry balloon rising into the sky, but no sooner had it risen a few feet than it was quickly taken down for our planes were about to swoop down on it. "We must be winning," another voice broke in. The men at the details were now in a very happy mood and rushed back for breakfast which they hurried as they did not wish to miss a thing. However, barely had the meal been eaten when an order came to fall in. They were instructed to go and get on their equipment (skeleton) and rifles and parade as quickly as possible in order to go to the line and help in stretcher work. They followed the footsteps that the battalion had followed the day before, but only so far. They too passed through what had been the village of Fricourt noticing the ruins and destruction on either side of the road. In fact, they too entered a different world, a man-made wilderness dotted with wrecked transport vehicles, dead horses, man's building efforts destroyed and many other signs of the success of the "god of war".

Beyond Mametz Wood and Montauban they went into a chalky valley in which was situated an Advanced Dressing Station, well protected by the high cliff on the right. The left side was less hilly and many of our guns thereabouts were firing non-stop. The sergeant of the R.A.M.C. to whom they reported told them to go over the chalky top and work forward bringing in any wounded, or carry the wounded to the nearest roadway where the ambulances could reach them. They were kept very busy but felt satisfied that they were doing good work, which was made harder owing to their rifles having to be slung over their shoulders. Really the rifles were not needed and were a nuisance, but if the Germans had succeeded in a counter-attack then they would have been of use in fighting them. The sight of a low-flying German plane distracted attention for some moments. Its observer was intent on seeing what was going on our side, but it did not last long as, like a flash of lightning, one of our planes swooped down towards it, rat-tat-a-tat went its machine gun, and the enemy plane sank lower and lower, seeming to come down almost at the front line – perhaps it managed to escape, but certainly our planes were masters of the air.

Every time they saw a wounded man they thought of our battalion and wondered if they would come across some of them. One of them did find one of the thirteen with whom he had enlisted from the same county village of Spennymoor. He'd had both his legs blown off. Another helped his own company officer; a heart-breaking job at any time. Many were the tin hats put on rifles whose bayonets were stuck in the ground to serve as landmarks to those who were detailed to bring in the dead. There were far more dead than wounded.

Needing help was a seriously wounded German, an old man of about fifty-five with dark grey hair. He had been temporarily, like our own men, a battalion stretcher-bearer; so he was put on a stretcher. His eyes spoke volumes as he tried to stem his signs of pain. He began to speak in French and asked if he could have something with which to prop up his head. A couple of great coats were scrounged, folded and made into a pillow for his head. He smiled his thanks and in a well-toned voice said, "Germany kaput. You British will win. Your artillery is great and terrible. By November the war will be over," He really meant it and must have suffered a lot from our continuous bombardments. He was a Bavarian and it looked as if our boys were once again in front of Germans of that race.

"Over by November" was a month earlier than our usual, "Over by Christmas". So the ordinary German soldier too was guilty of wishful thinking. The wounded German was passed onto be dealt with in his turn, just as if he were one of our men. The details continued with what seemed an endless task. Some of the wounded died as they were being helped and a glance at some of the faces and bodies showed that they had suffered much; some faces contorted, some bodies twisting in pain, their fingers clenched. Other bodies were completely mutilated and obviously their owners had known nothing about being hit from almost direct hits. What a long spell of help it seemed, the day seemed endless. The many times a journey was made from out in that open space to the Dressing Station or to the road. Many other fatigues had been done in the past and perhaps less fatiguing, but no-one groused on this occasion. The number of times the wounded asked for a puff at a gasper was countless, but a puff eased the tension and helped tattered or shattered nerves. Inside the Dressing Station working at a tremendous pace were the doctors and the Royal Air Medical Corps orderlies. Each case was being dealt with with as much skill as possible in order to relieve suffering quickly and make room for the next one. In by one entrance, labelled and docketed, and moved out through another. Sad cases indeed were those where something had snapped mentally and for a short period they seemed to be wrecks of humanity. In most cases a few sharp stern words had the effect of pulling them back to reality. Only a rest from the line would cure the very worst of such cases. Grand work being done – all praise to the staff and to the stretcher-bearers who did such a lot of the donkey work, being the go-betweens between the fighting areas and the first aid or Dressing Posts.

Back at the details the rest of the men at the camp were full of gloom, upset by the awful rumours that reached them. Bad news had travelled quickly. The Colonel had been killed, scores of Yeomen had been killed or wounded, surely it couldn't be true? Almost all the officers had been put out of action. Gone were the thoughts of glory, the cost was too great. When, early on Sunday, the remnants joined the details, the truth was seen. The rumours had been true and only when we all looked around could we calculate who had not returned.

I was made orderly corporal for the day, which started off very badly for me. I was in trouble because I had allowed my two great friends, Pip and Mac, to sleep in. The latter and I had been at the same school for five years and I took it very hard when my sergeant ordered me to "run them in". How can one "crime" one's great friends under such circumstances? The sergeant had been at the details all the time. I failed to do as ordered and in the heat of the moment and with a feeling of dumbness following the attack, I said to him, "If having one stripe, unpaid, provisional, acting, means doing that then you had better have the stripe and give it to someone else." The sergeant was upset too and I was reported. Three days later, in battalion orders, I was once again a rifleman and, worst of all, transferred from 'C' Company into 'D' Company. I believe that I ought to have asked to see an officer about the latter half of the punishment. I do not think that the Colonel would have permitted a man to be taken away from his own special comrades. Perhaps it was better that I left things as they had been ordered. The irony of it is that the stripe went to Mac!

I did all the duties of the orderly corporal that Sunday and one additional job was helping Bugler Sergeant Wilcox with the mail. When he, the battalion postie, called out a name on a letter and it wasn't claimed, he asked for news of the man from practically the whole of the remnants gathered round him. If someone shouted out "wounded", he asked, "Did you see him?" If the answer was "Yes" then he wrote "wounded" on the envelope. "Killed" was also checked, and when he learned nothing at all, he wrote "missing". It was a sad gathering, especially for Ernest Nicholson of 'B' Company who had to say "killed" when the name of his older brother was called. Very few mistakes were made but one concerned me. Of the three surnamed Dennis in 'C' Company, one was missing, one wounded and one present (P., C. and G. respectively). One of the college girls to whom I had written had her reply to me returned to her marked "wounded". She went along to my home to see my mother, who was fortunately able to assure her that I was alright as one of the first things I did after the attack was to write home and say that I was safe. However, in the same letter I had said, "I am afraid that the worst has happened to Willie (Spence)". He lived in the same street as I did, across the other side some forty yards down. It appeared that mother was in the habit of standing at our front gate many times a week, waiting fot the postman to see if there was any news from me. Willie scarcely ever wrote home so his mother also stood at her gate watching to see if the postman called at our house. When she saw that he left a letter she came across and asked for news for I occasionally mentioned him; we were in the same platoon. That awful morning she came across as usual and mother, not waiting for the usual question, handed her the letter so that she could read for herself. A few days later I was called to the Orderly Room and handed a telegram which read. "What has happened to Willie?" It was from Mrs Spence. I wrote to her and told her what I had been told by Solly Temple who was next to him as they got up at zero hour out of a trench. Willie was immediately hit in the head by a machine gun bullet and he died at once. I showed the telegram to our padre, the Reverend Sayer-Ellis, and he too wrote a letter of sympathy.

Our Company Officer and all four platoon officers were wounded that day. The padres and a few surviving officers wrote nearly three hundred such letters; a tremendous job and a very sad one – wondering what words to use to the loved ones of the killed and wounded. Newspapers were being received and we were keen to see what had been reported of the glorious(?) victory: three lines of enemy defences captured, the greatest depth ever reached in the enemy lines, the tanks a great success, much credit given to the Guards who did not capture Flers, and little mention of some Northern units involved. We felt disappointed but of course, only the barest account of the attack would be given to the press – details of all units and their participation could not possibly be given. Someone called Gibbs had been a special reporter on our front, perhaps from an observation balloon.

At the camp I was astonished to see two men crying. One was our beloved Wesleyan Padre, down whose face the tears rolled non-stop. The other was our popular 'C' Company Sergeant-Major, a regular soldier whose time of service was nearly up. He had served in the Boer War in South Africa and had seen nothing like the Somme. They just could not believe and the lads, their lads as they often called them, had gone. The junior platoon officers who had been left behind at the details were greatly upset too. To live among, work with, look after and share privations with sixty men for nine months and then to find almost two-thirds killed, wounded or missing under such terrible conditions had meant such a lot to them. Was it for this they had helped to create a wonderful spirit of comradeship?

For special work done on September 15th, the battalion was awarded three Military Crosses and sixteen Military Medals. Three of the latter went to runners, very well deserved for they did not pause to take shelter in a shell hole when sent with messages when the telephones were not in working order, they went straight through the shells and bullets without stopping. One of the Military Cross winners also received the Silver Medal for Bravery from H.M. the King of Montenegro. He was that 'B' Company Sergeant-Major, Acting R.S.M. Huddlestone who captured the German gun.

After breakfast on Monday, the 18th, we were on the move again, back to civilisation. The weather broke and the rain poured down in torrents and we were soaked through. Our boots and puttees became so wet that we felt as if we were paddling along. The mid-day meal, such as it was, was no picnic as even the food was soaked. When we were a few miles from Albert, we were marched into a stubble field which was ankle deep in mud and water. Tarpaulin sheets were issued, three to each six men. I was with Jim Procter, a signaller, and four other 'D' Company men. Our little party laid one sheet on the soaked stubble and erected the other two sheets to form a bivvy, support sticks had been provided. No-one bothered about the alignment of the bivvies, which were scattered all over the field. I for one was delighted to get inside the bivvy and lie down, my clothes saturated and uncomfortable. Every tooth in my head seemed to be aching. I felt very much off-colour, dispirited and my limbs were shaking. Suddenly outside came a loud shout, "Rum up! Bring your mugs and dixies." Someone had "won" a few gallons of rum (S.R.D.) and had made it into a hot brew with boiling water and sugar. A good ration was being given to all who wanted it, or needed it as "medicine" before turning in for the night. It countered the damaging effects of the sodden clothing and horrible conditions. A staunch teetotaller, I remained shivering in our bivvy. However, Jim told Darkie Cole that Dennis had neuralgia and would not take a rum ration. Along he came with a mug almost full of rum in his hand and proffered it to me, saying, "Orders is orders, this time, so drink this." Though I knew that I could refuse to obey him, I did not like to do so and I drank the stuff. What a horrible taste it had, nevertheless I quickly fell into a deep sleep. The next morning all my aches and pains had gone and I felt very much better.

It rained heavily all the next day, which I could not forget for the following reason. When the rations were dished out, the bread ration was one loaf to sixteen men, but there was an extra issue of army biscuits to help out. It was not possible to cut a loaf into sixteen equal parts so we decided to draw lots, eight to win and eight to lose. I was one of the losers. How this small, inadequate ration of bread came to be was difficult to tell. Rumour had it that the number of losses on the day of battle had been underestimated and too little bread had been on the Quarter-Master's indent. The matter was put right for the next day's issue.

During the fortnight that we remained at this camp Summer Time finished at the end of September. We trained in the morning, drills, etc., the signallers, snipers, machine gunners and other specialists having their own parades. In the evenings, bonfires of empty ammunition boxes of which there were hundreds and hundreds lying around and of wood scrounged from nearby dumps were made and around them the men would sit or stand and sing. The harmonies were really splendid; plantation songs – *The Farmer's Boy* was a great favourite, *Blaydon Races* from the County Durham men, *Keep the Home Fires Burning*, very suitable around the campfires, but later the order appeared that this practice had to cease –

not the singing, but the fire-making. Hardly a day passed but Jerry sent over a few heavies into the town of Albert, but the Madonna did not topple down, she still looked down on the ruins below.

6

The Somme – A Sacrifice Attack?

I had been ten months in 'C' Company before I was suddenly transferred to 'D' Company, many of whom I already knew by sight but not by name. I missed the men of the Northern Counties and found myself with men from South of the Humber. Being a specialist did not help me to get known as quickly as I would have liked. I saw them only at meal times, at lights out and at Reveille. Were we to have a second go on the Somme like most of the other battalions that had been that way? Yes, we learned on October 1st that we were to go over in support to the two Fusilier Battalions, that 'B' and 'D' Companies would advance from their trenches and that 'A' and 'C' Companies would be held in reserve.

The next afternoon, John Barker, a signaller of 'C' Company and a great friend of mine, asked me to take a stroll with him. He was six feet tall, very broad shouldered and somewhat awkward in movement. He was a few years older than I was and had started teaching. I shall never forget our chat – not because of the scenery of shell holes, broken down limbers, the dumps of materials and the destruction all around us, but because of the topics. He began to talk about music and his association with Thirsk Church where he was the organist. Then he turned to English Literature and began to quote from poems by many English poets. We ambled around, having to pick out steps with care. Suddenly he began to talk about his home life and told me that he lived with his parents in the village of Thirkleby, between Thirsk and Easingwold, and that their house was not far from the large entrance gates on the main road, the entrance to a large estate. He told me the name of the owner, but I have forgotten it. Now and then, as he talked, he put his right hand towards his tunic pockets. Only then did he come to the point, why he had wanted me to walk along with him for a private chat. All his meandering on this topic and that was for the purpose of calming himself down, he was a bit on edge wondering how he could put forward what he wanted to emphasise so that I could understand. He appeared somewhat worried how to begin, but then he got going. He had had a most vivid presentiment, a most startling dream, only a few hours earlier during the night. He was going to be killed in the next stunt and wanted me to do him a favour. Before listening to his request, I pointed out to him that it was almost impossible for him to be killed as 'C' Company was being held in reserve. That did not convince him at all and he proceeded, "I want you to take charge of these three green envelopes and post them for me when you come out of the action." To this I replied that there was more chance of my being killed than there was of his death. He was adamant and handed to me the three letters: one was addressed to his parents, one to his girlfriend and the third to the Vicar of the Thirsk Church at which he played the organ. I put them in my top left tunic pocket – more padding above my heart. Then he said, "Here's my Gillette safety razor, you'll have to start shaving some day and it is better than a cut-throat." I took it and put it in my right lower tunic pocket. He was always sincere and an honest-to-goodness sort of friend. I failed to cheer him up and I could not get him to change his mind, yet he was not miserable or even scared. We strolled back to camp, each to our own Company.

Green envelopes were a special concession to the troops, who could write letters of a private nature on subjects they did not wish their own officers to read – a Tommy's feelings towards his girlfriend and his affection for her, or perhaps family matters of some importance. When written, such intimate letters would be put into a green envelope and at once sealed. The writer addressed the envelope and also signed his name, etc. declaring that the letter contained no military information. It could be opened at the base if it was thought necessary or perhaps it might be the one in a hundred that was opened just to test the honesty of the sender. As for myself, I never used one and was content to let anyone have my ration, not that I got many – they were nearly as scarce as leave passes. Besides, I had found the means of letting my mother know where I was.

One lovely afternoon my platoon officer, No. 13, Darkie Cole, and another one of 'D' Company were detailed to go to a certain map reference where they would find the headquarters of the New Zealanders. Lieutenant (later to become Captain) Potter of the Transport Section lent them a couple of nags, usually used as pack animals, and they rode off in great style. They jogged along and followed divers and sundry roads and tracks until they found the New Zealanders between Longueval and Delville Wood. They were kindly received and given all the information that they sought: the best possible routes to the line ready for when our Division relieved one of theirs for a second stunt.

On October 2nd, in full pack for we had drawn our valises from the dump at the last camp, we were on the move towards the line. We stopped at a maze of trenches, now battered about and known as Pommiers Redoubt – a German position which had taken over an hour to capture on July 1st. Some of the officers were put into tents, where the debris had been cleared away.

Whilst here a draft of new K.R.R.s arrived from Blighty and we originals felt very sorry for them, reaching us without trench experience just as we were going forward for another stunt. In the valley, below this commanding point on the Montauban-Mametz road, some engineers were constructing a railroad. They were making good headway: trucks full of rails and sleepers were being brought up, the sleepers put down and the rails hastily placed on them and then the truck was pushed along the newly-laid piece of line, and so on thus making a track towards the dump further on. The new draft was not to go any further on but stayed there, as details, with men chosen to remain behind and included was Darkie Cole, my new platoon officer, because he had been in the first stunt and had been the only one to come through. He deserved a rest. Before we others left to go up the line, he came round and asked if anyone had a letter he wished to send off – a farewell letter? He promised that he would censor any such letters straight away and send them off. He would also deal with a lot of letters he still had to send off to loved ones whose boys or men had been killed or wounded earlier on. Our "farewell" letters were of three types: those of a cheery nature with the writer hiding from his loved ones any idea of coming shadows, those that boldly stated that they were going to take part in a stunt and that when they got back there was no prospect of leave to Blighty and a grand time at home, and those who wrote from a heart full of presentiment and that his letter was the last anyone would receive from him. What a variety of thoughts, what optimism, what sadness. As I had written so many times to my mother all I wrote was "In the pink – all's O.K." When someone asked him about his letters of sympathy, Darkie Cole said, "It is all worth doing when some mother writes to me and says she was so pleased to get my letter because it seems so hard to receive only the cold printed notification from the War Office."

The next day fewer than two hundred of us moved up nearer to the line, going about

Wood Lane

three miles in the footsteps of all who went that way on September 15th. The trenches we occupied were known as Wood Lane and they ran from the top corner of Delville Wood to the left. They were very shallow and seemed to run in all directions. At eight o'clock in the evening I was put on a fatigue to go to a dump at Flers. What a journey! The night was pitch black as the heavy clouds were low in the sky and the gale force winds blew in all directions. The route took us through the wood. Here the going was very hard, the ground full of shell holes and bits of trenches and fallen tree trunks and branches had to be dodged all the time. It was very difficult to keep in touch with the man in front. Our guide took us to the dump to the left of the village and we queued up outside a hut. Although we did not have to wait long, the time seemed to pass ever so slowly as many shells were dropping in the village and we were standing out in the open near an ammunition dump. Eventually we received our boxes of Mills bombs and scores of bandoliers of rifle ammo. Quickly we hurried back to our quarters for the night as if fear and the unknown added wings to our feet. What a mysterious place our resting spot was. I spent there one of the most uncomfortable nights I ever experienced. There were so many criss-cross shallow trenches and Jim Procter and I would choose what we thought was a suitable bit of trench and scoop out holes in its side. We tried to rest and even sleep, but the wind howled and blew in all directions, the rain striking our faces. We changed trenches and tried another spot. We seemed to have no luck at all, wherever we moved the conditions were all the same – unkind and persistently bad.

We were glad when morning came. The only news that day was that our second stunt, which was to have started on Wednesday, October 4th, had been postponed to Saturday the 7th because of the shocking weather conditions.

Back at the details on that Wednesday a special fatigue party of twelve men had to proceed to a certain map reference to join other small parties from other units of the division. Their task was to bury the many, many dead bodies still lying about behind and forward of Flers. Most of our twelve men consisted of the new men who were issued with rations for the day. In the evening only six returned and we learned what had happened to the other six. Shortly after noon the officer in charge had told them to break off and rest after the morning's heavy work and assemble in a large shell hole to eat some of their rations. A heavy shell landed there and killed or wounded the six. The corporal with them was one of the originals and he was killed; heart-breaking news that some of them, whilst performing a last rite for gallant dead, were blown up and either killed or wounded.

This was the second burial party we had sent out since coming down to the Somme. Shortly after the remnants from the first stunt returned to the base camp, a very small party of four men had been sent down the line to find our dead Colonel's body, but they were unsuccessful. This was quite understandable for the night was a very dark one, there was no recognised line of trenches, and not one of the party could pick out the spot where he had fallen amidst the corn in the fields. The men returned very disappointed that they could not find the body.

On the Thursday, the battalion moved up to the Switch Line, the first objective on the fifteenth of the last month. It was rather a wide trench with huge, high dugouts on the right hand side – when in German hands; they had stood with their backs to our line. With the great amount of earth piled up on them and behind them, they were very strong and very safe for the Germans. They were ten or twelve feet high, but now in our hands they were weak for their doorways faced the enemy who, of course, knew their exact position. I with another 'D' Company signaller shared one of them. His name was Nug Weston and he was a student from Leeds. Because we were going over the top as riflemen we had been issued with entrenching tools. We settled down for the night in this winding trench and I slept very well indeed. Jerry did not trouble us at all.

After breakfast the next morning we were told to put in to our valises all the articles and clothing that we did not need for the time being: greatcoats, soft caps, body belts (unless you wished to wear it), spare socks, etc. All we needed was our equipment, bayonet, bayonet pouches with ammo and our haversack with its usual contents, plus "iron rations". The latter consisted of a tin of bully and some small biscuits, if you could get them, or the normal larger type of Army biscuits. We kept these in a white cloth bag with string run through the top with which to fasten it. This was food to be used only in an emergency and on the orders of an officer. I preferred the small oval-shaped biscuits; they tasted better than the others and were so soft compared with the larger ones.

It was obvious that a stunt was in the offing, but what it was all about I did not know, or even the details of what I had to do. Nug was in the same predicament and I think that we must have been in signals parade when the detailed orders were given out and we were told of our part in the "do". When the valises were ready and had been collected, they had to be taken to Flers dump. It was the custom, as in this case, for two men to toss up to see which one should do the carrying. As I had never won the toss-up on any previous occasion, I told Nug that I would go on the carrying fatigue. We set off along the trench and soon the leader of the party decided to take a short cut by getting out of the trench and going across the open. The Jerry plane overhead possibly saw our string of men making our way to Flers, almost a mile away. Before we reached the end of our journey we heard shell fire some distance behind us but took no special heed of it. On our return, we found that our part of the Switch Line had received a severe battering; Jerry knew its range, of course. Perhaps we ought to have dug another trench in different ground, but why should we with a ready-made trench available? There had been many direct hits and amongst the dugouts blown in was mine. Nug Weston was very severely wounded in the thigh – a grand Blighty one? When I set off with his valise and mine, I almost said that the lucky ones stayed behind, so I wondered who was the lucky one and who were the unlucky ones! A young lieutenant of 'A' Company, who had been slightly wounded on the 15th, had rejoined us the night before with a few other ranks who thought that they were lucky to get back to the Yeoman Rifles. He had been hit by a shell and, when the emergency party were ordered to bury the dead, his head bid to be found – it had been severed from his body and blown many yards away. There were other casualties too – Nug Weston did not survive his wound, it hadn't turned out to be a grand Blighty one.

During the afternoon we were dished out with extras: each man was given two Mills bombs, two flares, two hundred extra rounds of ammo for his rifle, and could choose a pick-axe or a spade (I chose a spade). I had also to carry one of the platoon's tins of water. I should have both hands in use – one for the water tin and the other for my rifle. 'D' Company, which twenty-four days ago had consisted of at least nine officers and over two hundred other ranks, now had three officers (the C.O. Captain Sheardown, Monty (Ginger) Cole and Lt. Beechman), and sixty-one other ranks. (These figures did not include those left behind with the details at the camp).

After dinner we set off following the Switch Trench for quite a distance then passing into several others whose names I didn't know (for the German defences had been a mass of lines criss-crossing one another in many directions), coming into the open just after dusk. Having crossed the open we entered a raised trench (Turk Lane) a fine piece of work and a great protection, built by New Zealand troops, mainly the Maori Pioneer Battalion whom we had relieved. This trench was the only way in and out and was a great benefit to all. In-going men, outgoing men, stretcher bearers and walking wounded all used it. It seemed to be endless, possibly because it was now completely dark and also because the passage through it was so slow. When the cry "stretchers!" went up, we others all stopped and flattened ourselves against the sides of the trench so that the bearers could move along as quickly as possible with their burdens. The only fast-moving troops were those who were leaving the line, having been relieved, and in small groups they scurried past. Continuous "mind the wire!" reminded us of old times and, because of all the difficulties in the trench, a few brave souls got out of it and walked on the top, so wide was its sandbag walls. Finally we debouched and passed into an open space where those who had led our party waited for the slow-coaches to catch us up. On again into shallow trenches, only knee high, which had been dug by our advancing troops when consolidating. On the right we could just discern the faint outlines of a damaged tank, and further on a trench full of dead soldiers and we recognised khaki uniforms. We had just time to wonder what had happened there when a few yards further on was a trench full of dead Germans. We had no answer to our questioning thoughts, nor to the one that came more frequently, "Where are we?" We did not know what those lines of dead were, or where we were, in support or in the Front Line, if there was one. Everything seemed to be swathed in mystery. The strings of bits of trenches ended and we walked out of them and in a few minutes came a whispered order, "Line up along here and dig in." We extended our line, just as if on parade, took off our equipment and "extras", put them all in a line and then set to work. My working partner wielded his pick-axe on the chalky earth and when he had got quite a lot of earth loosened I took my spade and shovelled it up and threw it in front of us. Other pairs were doing likewise and soon we had got down a few inches. Gradually we made a trench, joining up with the pairs on either side.

Ahead, to our front and ever so far away, so it seemed, we could see Very Lights shooting up into the air at intervals. We knew that they belonged to Jerry. Shells passed high over us and burst well behind our lines, so we assumed. At first we had dug hastily, as if our lives depended on what we did and, though the night was weird it was so quiet immediately around us that we began to take our time with the job as apparently there was no danger. By day-break the trench was finished and those who felt like it settled down for a nap. Some of us ate a little of our rations.

At about ten o'clock the silence was broken by the sound of a low-flying aeroplane and we looked upwards, contrary to the advice always to keep our heads down, and saw a German plane flying parallel to our line. Then it turned suddenly and went back over its own line. If our faces had not shown up, or the tops of our shiny steel helms, then the fresh white chalk would give our position away.

Suddenly, squeezing his way along the trench to join us was our Platoon Officer, Darkie Cole, whom we had left behind with the details. He told us that at about midnight he and another officer had been aroused from their sleep by a Brigade runner with a message telling them to report to Brigade Headquarters as soon as possible. Hurriedly dressing and making a hasty toilet and accompanied by two sleepy batmen, they set off. Deep down in the bowels of the earth they found the Brigadier and his Staff and were given an excellent breakfast. A guide was provided to take them to the Advanced Brigade H.Q., which was also in a large captured German dugout. From there a K.R.R. runner took them up to our battalion and when they reported to our C.O. he sent the other officer up to 'A' Company and, of course, Darkie to his own platoon. He could not understand why he had been sent up the line when the Company already had three officers there, yet he was the only officer I saw during the forthcoming engagement. He had been given a small map to show what the battalion had to do, but it was just a rough outline on a small piece of paper and did not extend to show any places of importance, but as we were to follow the Fusiliers that did not matter. He was not in the least impressed that the stunt was to be a daylight one. Most of us could not understand why the Generals running the war could not think of any better time than between dinner and tea to have a stunt. No. 13 Platoon was to take the left flank.

About one o'clock we thought it time to have another bite to eat and the one man with the possie opened the tin and we ate our Army biscuits almost smothered in the jam. We ate slowly and chatted about this and that. We heard the sound of much machine gun fire and also realised that shells were dropping forward of our position and also behind us. Within a few moments a sergeant, with his helmet at a saucy angle, his face flushed and his eyes sparkling, shouted, "Jump to it!" A slight pause, as if he was pondering what to say next, then, "Out you get!" We did so and he told us to get our things on and fix bayonets. "We're going over now!" My friend pushed my spade down my back and I did likewise for him with his pick-axe. I forgot my tin of water as, in extended line with rifles at the port, we moved slowly ahead. I glanced behind me and realised that we had dug in in "No Man's Land". I could see no other troops ahead and then I suddenly knew why. The ground on which we were advancing sloped down away from the trench for nearly fifty yards and then rose again. The night before we had been digging in "Dead Ground". The enemy could not have seen us in daylight, let alone at night, nor possibly hear us. Hence, we had been undisturbed. He had no idea where we were, or indeed that there were any troops in this dead ground.

Most of us had not noticed that, because of the configuration of the ground, the Fusiliers had topped the first rise, four waves of men in the fine extended order and had been mown down like so much corn under a sickle by deadly machine gun fire. We followed in their steps and, as we topped that rise, we met a similar greeting, just as deadly. Shortly after topping the rise and trying to keep in line, I felt something very heavy hit my left ankle and at the same time I realised that something much smaller had hit my glasses. I went on a few yards and then dropped in to a shell hole to examine my foot. I found that nothing had pierced it and there was no sign of blood, so I concluded that a large piece of earth or the flat-side of a lump of shrapnel had hit it. I took off my rimless glasses and saw that a small piece of the right lens had been broken off and the rest of it was hanging loosely. I put them in my glasses case. I got out of the shell hole and moved forward, but could not see anyone in khaki. All the time there was the throbbing sound of an enemy machine gun, sometimes faint, then gradually getting louder, then to its loudest and gradually becoming fainter again. The gunner was obviously swinging his gun from right to left and back again all along our advancing troops. I quickly grasped the fact that the bullets were only dangerous when the sound was loudest. I shall never forget the swish-swish-swish of that German machine gun fire, not exactly musical but so thrilling and so frightening. I set off again, seeing no-one and when I heard that loud sound again I dropped into a shell hole, a very large one. In it were three senior N.C.O.s including Jack Palframan and Walter Foster, both signallers. There was no friendly greeting but the senior sergeant ordered, after pointing out that if a shell struck there it would get six victims, "Off you go, you signallers!" No sooner had he given the order and like a flash Fossie (Foster) said, "Foggie", and Palframan almost as quickly "Seggie", and that left slow me to be the last to get out. Out went Fossie and as Palframan rose up above the lip of the shell hole, swish, a machine gun bullet hit him right in the middle of his forehead and he fell back right into my arms.

"Leave him, he's dead – we'll see to him. Clear off!" kindly ordered another sergeant. I got up and went on, again seeing no-one on my right or my left. I kept repeating my usual tactics according to the sound of the bullets, down in a shell hole when the swish was loudest and up and on again all the time the sound was faint. Still I saw no-one and, just as I dropped once again into a shell hole, I saw in front of me a dull, reddish flash, varying in intensity as it moved from right to left. I took my glasses out of their case and put them on, watching as the dull flash now appeared brighter. Only the top of my head and my eyes above the shell hole, and there was the German machine gun, the destroyer of so many lives. What was I to do? What should I do? What could I do? I was a very good shot with a rifle but the broken right lens of my glasses might impair my shooting and aim. One shot from me would easily draw return fire or, worse still, an egg bomb (this type of German bomb with its long handle got its name because of its shape and could be thrown, thanks to the handle, with great accuracy up to fifty yards, and I was no more than fifteen yards off). I thought the better idea would be to use one of my Mills bombs. If it landed on the target it could do more damage. I had been a slow bowler at cricket and I felt sure that I could lob it very well. At that moment I got quite a shock as I heard a voice breaking into my thoughts, which had not taken many seconds.

"What the ... do you reckon you are doing here? You've come too far, and too far to the left. We are digging in thirty yards back and Darkie has sent me to order back that silly ... fool, you. Give me ten to fifteen minutes start and then you crawl back and report to him – half left." My problem was solved but I did not know whether to be thankful or not. It was already dusk after a lovely sunny morning and afternoon when we ought to have been playing football and not "skittles" by the enemy. I doubt whether I gave Bill Todd as much as ten minutes start but I set off and did not like the idea of going back – what if I were shot in the back! I heard many groans and feeble cries as I crawled half left, and to my great surprise I eventually came face to face with Darkie Cole, who greeted me with, "You're very lucky to be still alive. You had your orders – advance into No Man's Lane three hundred yards and then form strong points in support of the Fusiliers." What could I say? That I had not received any orders, which I hadn't and get told off for missing them, or say nothing. I did not defend myself, but knew why I had kept going on and on. I was frightened that I was lagging behind, not seeing anyone because of my weak eyesight.

We spread out and all set to, digging to build a strong point of trenches. What a thrilling experience! Because Jerry was still firing at us we lay down on our tummies and picked at the earth and then shovelled some soil and chalk in front of us, gradually deepening a shallow trench into a deeper one, by which time we could work in pairs, one with a pick-axe and one with a spade. A parapet was gradually built up. From working with our heads down we were able after a time to stand in the shallow trench and work standing up until we had a good protection. Those German machine gunners had had a picnic, squatting there in the open they had had sitting targets. They were to claim further victims.

Our Officer had gone along the line and counted up how many of us were left; twenty-six. After consulting the other platoon officer he decided to send word back to H.Q. for reinforcements because we had not enough men to hold our position should the Germans decide to attack. In reply, some of 'C' Company were sent up to help 'D' Company and after

Captain Brooksbank with 'B' Company had sent back Corporal Frank (Dusty) Miller twice to ask for reinforcements, some 'A' Company men were sent to him. As the 'C' Company men topped the rise, as we had done early in the afternoon, the Germans concentrated their machine guns on them and some of us rose up and called out, "Crawl! Get your heads down!" Whether they heard us or not or whether they got the message too late to comprehend, some of them fell, killed or wounded. One of those 'C' Company men struck and killed was John Barker, whose three green envelopes were in my top left tunic pocket and his safety razor in another pocket. Incredible and tragic that it had happened as he had dreamt.

Miller, the runner was again sent back with an urgent message, one that really should not have been necessary. The unexpected always caused the greatest worry. In the orders for the day's stunt a battery of our eighteen pounders was to move forward as we did and cover us when we had reached our new positions. From their new gun site their shells fell short – on us! Tommy did not mind the enemy fire and put up with it; he could not do otherwise, but to have to suffer from our own shells, to be wounded by them or even killed, that was a different matter. Such a mistake was very alarming and very unwelcome. This was something to grouse about, and we did. Of course, the message got through and the offending batteries obliged by letting Jerry have some medicine.

Darkie sent out Frank Berry to the left to find who was on that flank and he found no other troops for quite a distance when he found an officer of the Hants. (122 Brigade) and some men in shell holes. He told him where we were and gave him our position. Another scout sent to the right had found a few survivors of the Royal Fusiliers who then began to dig a trench in our direction. We of thirteen platoon under Darkie Cole began to dig another trench to the left; same procedure with entrenching tools at first as we lay on our tummies and then at the right time using our pick-axes and spades. Forward scouts reported that two other German machine guns were near the top of the rise and easy to be seen, whereas we were lower down and harder to see. At twilight a party of Fusilier reserves passed through us and along the ridge. Poor blighters. We tried to warn them about the enemy machine gunners, but they went on with their battalion's objective, the Rainbow Trench which had not been captured, and they hoped to be more successful at the second attempt.

The Bosche gunners spat and spat again and again and put many of them out of action. The rest got below the skyline and remained doggo. A Brigadier came up and complimented us on our work for we had established a strong point exactly where ordered. This work on consolidation had kept us warm as the evening was very cold. Having completed our task, and night having fallen, we began to think of the men lying in front wounded. Ginger Cole had been badly wounded and had already been taken back. Some of the wounded, those that could, had started to crawl back to us.

The sergeant who had given the order, "Jump to it!" was groaning and calling out and trying to get on to his feet. His loud voice was well-known and we did not want his shouts to be heard and to draw fire, so we threw clods of earth at him till he rolled back into a shell hole. Volunteers went out with a stretcher to bring him in – Sergeants Picken and Tiller, two small men, were half of them. The sergeant had apparently been shot through the neck. They rolled him onto a stretcher and made a very slow journey back, not daring to stand up fully and having difficulty in carrying it over the rough, pock-marked ground. It was thought that the rum which the sergeant had drunk helped his body to keep out the cold of the evening. He had had more than one ration for he had gone over in the afternoon with his water bottle full of rum. I think that he had had a few swigs before coming to order us out of our assembly positions in the afternoon. After all, that "medicine" probably saved his life. The two small

N.C.O.s who brought him in were afterwards made up to sergeants from corporals.

As far as I knew there had not been an issue of rum for the occasion. Alas, many of the men lying out there did not need the help of the company stretcher-bearers or the volunteers. The former were very much admired by the rest of us for their job was one of going out to help, coming back, and returning again to help, thus facing danger and death many times over. When they had done the most hazardous job and brought in the wounded, then and only then did the R.A.M.C. carry on with the good work where they had left off to return to further danger. The battalion stretcher-bearers wore an armlet bearing the letters S.B., which meant nothing to the enemy – they were looked on as combatants as much as the ordinary Tommy was. They had rifles and more often than not they carried them and so could be shot at or sniped, and they were. Bullets and shrapnel could not distinguish one enemy from another. Along with the runners, they were always very heroic.

I do not remember the position of our H.Q. that day but our runners found it. They were somewhere in the open between the Gird Trench and the dead ground from which we advanced, probably in some similar kind of ground. Later on, perhaps late Saturday or early Sunday morning, they relieved the New Zealanders H.Q. at Sugar Factory Corner, situated at some cross roads about two thousand yards north of Flers, towards Bapaume. Here the Germans had constructed, under some buildings now in ruins, a very deep dug out with a stairway leading down to the rooms below. It had been captured by the N.Z.s who erected at the corner a large wooden cross to the memory of their men lost in the fighting. Jerry never let us forget that we had taken something from him and, as he knew the exact map reference of the spot and other places, he never failed to send over from time to time some five-nines. In a way, the vicinity of Sugar Factory Corner was just as dangerous as the front line and perhaps more so. Runners and guides had to time their exits and their entrances to the second in order to avoid being caught by shell fire. One runner misjudged his timing and the next shell burst at his feet. He was lifted bodily up some fifteen feet and fell apart in fragments. Ghastly! The best procedure to follow was to lie flat on the stomach as soon as a shell was heard, wait a few seconds till it exploded, and then move on, repeating these actions and be thankful when stumbling down the roughly hewn steps of the dugout to get your breath back.

All was very quiet at our strong-point on the Sunday morning and we no longer felt isolated because the Pioneers had connected our trenches with the dead ground we had left behind, so that any troops coming to our position would be undercover. A runner came along with the message that our platoon commander had to go back and report to H.Q. and added his own personal message, "You are going to be relieved soon." When Darkie got to the H.Q. he was told to proceed to the Brigade H.Q. to arrange about the guides for the relieving division, some of which arrived back with him. We were very glad to be leaving this spot, which could be difficult to hold if attacked because we had advanced some three hundred yards ahead of the troops on our flanks. All the thrills and excitement over, I became a kind of walking casualty as soon as we started to move off. I found that I had difficulty in walking my left foot was in great pain and I could hardly put it on the ground. It seemed to be very heavy as if a weight was attached to it. I had to be helped along as we went along one of the new communication trenches to the dead ground and past the two trenches of dead to the beginning of the Turk Lane Trench. We rested there for a short time and wasn't I glad to get off my feet. There, in a small slit trench off the main one, was the Reverend

E. Sayer-Ellis, his only other protection was a sheet of corrugated iron held in position by a few sand bags. What was he doing there, of all places? As each wounded man passed by, walking or on a stretchet, he took his name and address if possible, and filled up a Field Post Card to send to his home. Some Cheshires and Hampshires passed us in the trench and we eyed one another and wondered. They did not know that all twenty-six of our 'D' Company represented all that were left after two stunts, not counting those left behind with the details. They were young like we used to be, for now we were "old" soldiers. I do not remember if any of the London draft joined us later on, or joined us for the stunt. Perhaps some of them came up with the reinforcements with 'A' and 'C' Companies, and had had a taste of German machine gun fire. Only an occasional shell dropped near us as we made our way safely through the trench, and no-one caught a "late packet". After what seemed a long time, we were told to fall out and rest near a dump, Thistle Dump I think. We seemed to be lost so Capt. Meysey-Thompson went and reported to Brigade H.Q. He was told that we had come too far back that we ought to have stopped at the Gird Trench which we had occupied the day before the attack. We were allowed to rest and stay there long enough to have a bit of something to eat.

Young True was very upset as he had had no news of how seriously his brother had been wounded on Tank Day. I was aware of the thoughts of some of the men; they had been through it and now they were expected to back-up. Uncertainty and lack of information always created doubts. Their disappointment, after being keyed up for some days and just beginning to relax at the thought of getting away from the Somme was clearly shown. They felt like grousing and, as one Geordie put it "They don't half bugger you about!" expressing everyone's annoyance; one needs to hear the deep throated dialect of a North Countryman to enjoy that expression of disgust.

With heavy steps we set off back and seemed to take a long time before we eventually reached the Gird Trench where we remained in reserve for just one night. There was a nasty spell of enemy shelling during the night, but we had no casualties. Before dawn we were relieved by fresh troops and found the way back heavy going because rain had made the ground very muddy, but with our backs to the enemy we felt in a better mood. Quite suddenly my feet seemed as heavy as lead. The hum of battle, the zip-zip of bullets and the excitement of the time over, my left foot seemed unbearable. It became worse and worse and once again I had to be helped along. When we reached Thistle Dump again a welcome sight was our transport. I was lifted on to a half limber and carried back to the Transport Lines, and there awaited the rest of the company. My journey was a bumpy one because of the state of the roads and yet I slept. When the tired out remnants arrived, they were informed that they had to go a further mile to a new rail head down in the valley near Mametz. They did not need much urging, although extremely tired, for they like the sound of "railway"'. I was lucky enough to be taken there by transport limber.

At the railhead we all rested and stayed the night and entrucked the next morning, slowly covering the journey back past Fricourt. A pleasant enough journey, for we all felt that at last we had done with the Somme and did not mind, after leaving the train, the route march to Suire-sur-l'Ancre for a short rest in a camp there. Some of the battalion were put into civvy billets.

Thanks were due to the R.E.s railway section (R.O.D.) for that lift by train, for they had laid the railroad track and the French had provided some de-luxe wagons, not the usual cattle trucks. The wagons were made of steel and had the ordinary type of door, as cattle trucks had sliding ones. Even some of the Brigade Staff were travelling on it. The journey was a very slow one and the stops were many. During one stop some alert Tommies took the opportunity to leave the wagon and "win" some bricks and wood from the wayside. There was plenty of both, if wanted. The bricks were needed to make a hearth in the middle of the wagon floor and the fire was made on them. Someone produced some Oxo cubes and, with water from our bottles, a good brew was soon forthcoming and the hot drink much appreciated. Of course, the smoke from the fire was much trouble but with the sliding doors partly open we saved ourselves from being smoke-dried. At stopping places we were able to pass along to some of the men on the Brigade and staff a Tommy's dixie of Oxo and they were very thankful for it. Our fuel supply gave out and, as darkness had fallen, we closed the door and endeavoured to keep warm, huddled together mostly in the four corners of the wagon. Nobody had a candle, so we remained in the dark, smoking and talking. It was almost impossible to sleep, dead as we were, firstly because the night was bitterly cold, secondly the wagon was very uncomfortable, and thirdly because the noise of our steel transport was sometimes overbearing, especially when the train got up a little extra speed.

During our little talks, I asked about the various friends I had made as I wanted to know what had happened to them. Ted, one of the college nine of 'A' Company, who so often wished for a Blighty one, had been hit in the arm and was not at all pleased with it. He was a good sportsman and played many games. After the war he played football and billiards, but not tennis. I never did get any information as to what happened to Frank Markham, another one of our college group, who was in 'C' Company and who came from Lincolnshire. Six of us had survived so far, probably because we were spread out in different companies, whereas the thirteen boys from Spennymoor who were all in my old company had suffered badly.

I had missed the second roll call after the action. It had not taken long to check on 'D' Company's survivors; as near as makes no matter two-fifths answered their names out of a very depleted company. This check yielded results no different from those of the other companies. A very keen frost showed itself all over the countryside as we left our steel wagons – not by any means "wagons-lit". I did not go "sick" as there was a full battalion parade ordered for Sunday, an inspection by Divisional General Lawton, affectionately known as "Swanky". The battalion was drawn up in a hollow square, an easy formation as we were so few in numbers and as we awaited patiently for his appearance. By and by he arrived on a lovely charger, beautifully turned out from head to toe. The General looked the picture of good health: his moustache, Sam Browne, tunic, breeches and boots were all just so and the usual little cane rested on his thigh. With him were his henchmen "betabbed in red" and his spick and span orderly with lance and pennant. We were brought to attention and the General proceeded to address us – what we looked like to that cavalcade one can only wonder. "Officer, non-commissioned officers and men of the … er, … er, … er, 21st Battalion, the King's Royal Rifle Corps. It gives me great pleasure to come here today to say how pleased I am with your efforts of the past three weeks … your work in dealing with the Hun … your splendid morale … " etc. What a lot of eye-wash! We were the babes of the Division and most probably the other eleven battalions had had these very same words of praise before we had them. As he spoke to us, did he recall how four weeks before he had addressed five times as many Yeoman Rifles? When he said, "Soon you will be fighting the Hun … " We had done so, and I think we would rather have been spared the day's speech.

Then followed the presentation of awards, awards of medals to those men who had earned them on September 15th and were still with us. I think all the men were heroes.

When they had gone, those "high ups" whom we blamed for everything in our bouts of grousing, we were dismissed and I reported "sick", not at the words we had heard but because of my left foot. I had not had my boots off for more than thirty days and the lace of my left boot had to be cut away so that it could be taken off. My left foot was black and blue, very sore and very painful. When it had been examined and my sock replaced, the boot would not go on – it seemed too small. An old slipper was found for it and a stick was given to me to help me with my walking. There was no sign of blood, no cut, just a severe bruising. I was marked, "No duty". The next day, Monday, we left Suire-sur-l'Ancre by train at 2 p.m. and reached Arraines at 6 a.m. the next morning. Then we marched to Allery sur Somme where we were again put into civvy billets. I travelled from the train to Allery on a limber.

Having no duty meant I had plenty of time on my hands, and I made great friends with a Monsieur and Madame Wattebled who had adopted two orphan brothers left when their parents were killed by bombs in Albert. A very quiet family and their source of earnings were from a cottage loom at which for most hours of the day one or the other worked at weaving cloth. I saw little of the battalion and I did not know what they did, but I spent my mornings and afternoons with the French family, learning how to work the loom and chatting and I had quite a few conversations with the two boys.

I had ample time to hold my own inquest on our visit to the Somme. The 21st Battalion of the King's Royal Rifles was practically finished; most of our losses were unnecessary and unwarranted. Yet all the Divisions that took part in the battles there, especially the Aussies, the New Zealanders, the South Africans and the Canadians (the Anzacs) suffered more than we did. From July 1st to mid-October, nothing seemed to have been thought but as to how to comb at the German machine gunner. For sure our artillery did not knock them out. They were always ready, sitting pretty, waiting for sitting targets. The Generals further back than Divisional Staffs had no idea how to master the problem and the young subalterns, killed in the attacks and the only ones likely to understand the menace, could not give their views. They saw the damage done by those machine guns, but did not live to tell the tale.

How it could be expected that the Fusiliers could advance some three to four hundred yards across a wide No Man's Land and take some machine guns at the Rainbow Trench in broad daylight, I don't know! Especially when the enemy positions had not been flattened by our artillery. In any case, the Germans would just have retired and made another wide No Man's Land and placed their machine gunners at suitable points. I believe that the French liked daylight attacks but they were always well supported by very good artillery fire from the seventy-fives – excellent guns.

Our 'D' Company gained its objectives but its orders did not include that machine gun I faced because it was not in our sector. I was in the wrong in going to the left of our set path. I think that we could have tackled it, yet it was not in our orders. Initiative? I learned at Allery that when our H.Q. was at Sugar Factory Corner an R.E. Officer reported that he had seen a body of a battalion commander lying in a cornfield now behind our front line. From his further description, our new commanding officer recognised that it must be the body of our original Colonel Feversham. This second time that a small party went to find it was successful and they buried the body in the cornfield where he had fallen. After the war, timber from the Earl's estate was sent there and a wooden cross was made and a sort of lynch gate put over the grave. Later still a bell from a church in the district of his home was used there as a flower vase.

Rumours of sadness were now prevalent: that the relatives of a soldier buried in an Army blanket had to pay seven shillings and sixpence for it; that a trooper who lost his horse had thirty pounds deducted from his pay – these were just two outpourings of the troubled minds of our remnants, quite excusable bitterness. Of the twelve Officers and three hundred and fifty Other Ranks who went up to the line for the October 7th stunt, just six Officers and a hundred and seventy Other Ranks returned – roughly about half of the battalion strength. For the stunt we received three Military Crosses and ten Military Medals. There was a nasty suspicion that the French sometimes let us down, occasionally failing to take part in a combined operation at the last minute. We blamed them for the daylight operation, because we felt that our own commanders preferred the early dawn time.

Two remarkable incidents were related to me later. Train, a Hull lad of 'C' Company, was wounded and could not use his right knee. At the base hospital, after much searching by a specialist a slightly curved bullet was found behind that knee. Two years after the end of the war he joined his Old School's Rugby Team and at half-time of one game he complained of a sore right arm; a bandage was put round it. At the end of the game when he took off his jersey, the bandage slipped off and in it was a machine gun bullet. The other incident related to Johnnie Hirst of 'D' Company. He had knelt down behind a bit of a bank to fire at a German soldier some fifty yards away. Immediately after pulling the trigger of his rifle, it gave quite a heavy recoil. He slid down behind the bank and pulled back his rifle bolt and the empty cartridge case had in it a German bullet which had passed down the barrel of his rifle till it came to a stop in his own empty bullet case. Lucky Johnnie Hirst of Harrogate.

The inhabitants of those small villages behind the Somme front yet near the river itself must have seen and welcomed many English battalions on their way up the line and returning from it. On the one side they would throw open their homes to many hundreds of a battalion, and on the other side show sympathy in their own way to depleted ranks of returning battalions. Most of the other ranks were in houses and some in farm buildings. The 'D' Company officers had a very fine billet. They were quartered in a fine house, whose owner was very considerate for their comfort. They had beds with white sheets, acetylene gas light in the rooms, carpets on the floor and beautiful furniture. Such comfort and luxury seemed extra-ordinary after dugouts and trenches. All of us had pleasant memories of those French people in the rear villages, who were doing their best to make things brighter for those who passed through them.

I remember quite clearly a conversation with the Wattebled family as we sat with the boys, Marcel and Maurice, enjoying a coffee. Madame asked me how long I had been in the trenches (not France). When I replied that I had been in the Front Line for nearly six weeks, she said. "Ce n'est pas beaucoup, mais c'est trop!" (It isn't much, but it's too much). It applied to all the Front-Liners, whether they had spent less or more than six weeks. I appreciated her deep meaning of sympathy. Such a deep understanding, simply expressed by my new friends in the Rue de Quayer, Allery.

My Army friends attended parades, whilst I led a life of ease. They were kept busy; indirectly a good thing, for it helped to take their minds away from the Somme and partially heal their mental wounds and stress. On their short route marches they did not yet sing their favourite songs as they had done five weeks earlier. The complete rest brought my left foot back to normal size, just in time for our next move. The battalion and, of course, the whole of the 41st Division, was transferred to the Second Army, and were we not glad to be leaving the Fourth Army of the XV Corps.

Most of our own thirty-six pairs of stretcher-bearers had been killed or wounded. One of a pair from 'C' Company, the very second he rose to go over the top, received a machine gun bullet which split the crown of his head, making a groove or furrow which never really healed. He suffered terribly and every three months had to be taken into hospital to give his wife a rest. He went quite grey in just a few months after the wound was inflicted.

7

Trench Warfare – The Brasserie Sector (The Salient – Ypres)

The rest and keeping off my feet helped the swelling of my left foot to disappear and, with the aid of liniments at the Medical Room the coloured bruises also cleared up and I was once again fit for the next move. I had been frightened that I would have to leave the battalion and was very gratified that the M.O. had been able to cure my disability without my having to go to hospital, from which I may not have been returned to the Yeoman Rifles, short numbered as they were.

A few minutes after midnight on Friday, October 20th, the battalion departed from Allery without the band to help us keep in step or to cheer us up, and marched to Longpre at which railway station just six weeks ago we had boarded cattle trucks in a light and gay manner to take us down to the Somme. This time we entered third class carriages and had wooden seats to sit on and we were going the other way. Because of our low numbers we did not need such a long train this time. At 5.30 a.m. we left the station and proceeded through Abbeville, with Crecy Wood away on our right, and very slowly made our way through Etaples ("Eat Apples"), Boulogne, Calais, near which we gazed more longingly across the Channel hoping to see the white cliffs of Dover, the gateway to Blighty. On to St. Omer then Caestre and at 1 p.m. on the Saturday afternoon we reached the end of our long railway journey. We were glad to leave our carriages, to stretch our legs and don our full packs.

We marched through Fletre to Meteren enjoying the old countryside of hedgerows and tall, undamaged trees, even though it was now chilly autumn and not leafy spring. We took in our stride the undulating road to Mont de Cats and Boeschepe, crossing the border between France and Belgium and arriving at Victoria Camp near Westoutre. Our one night there was a very wet one and many of us suffered from dampness from the leaking covers of the tents.

The Sunday morning proved to be fine and after breakfast and the drawing of our daily rations, we dressed up and set off for the Front Line. We marched through Zevecoten and took the road that led to La Clytte. On the way we passed some transport lines and then a large camp of round Nissen huts. At the crossroads, instead of going straight to Kemmel, we turned left and took a road towards Dickebusch. We passed a few dwellings called Mille Kruis and at Hallepast Corner, instead of proceeding to Dickebusche, we turned off right towards Vierstraat. Up to this point we had marched with platoons some fifty yards apart, but now we split up into sections with a much greater distance between each two. In this sector of the Front, reliefs could be carried out in daylight. We carried on until we came to a light railway which ran beside a stream and near which were a few cottages called Bardenburg. We turned left and walked parallel to the railway and entered Ridge Wood. On either side of the path through the wood we could see many low sandbagged dugouts and, at the left hand corner of the end of the path in the wood, a hut, not much larger than a sentry box. This belonged to the Church Army, two of whose members made hot drinks of cocoa in the evenings for the troops. Here we halted and were told that from this point we had to proceed in single file because we would be under enemy observation, if he had an observation up. We turned left and went along a road parallel to the front edge of the wood for about sixty yards and then turned right and, keeping close to the hedge on the right of a short road of some fifty yards, came to the Vierstraat-Ypres Road which we had to cross. This road joined the main Messines Road to Ypres some two miles to the left. We doubled straight across and came to the Brasserie – no longer a brewery but a First Aid Post. We proceeded along a third class road to the right of the building hidden from enemy eyes by a large canvas screen drawn right across it. On the left were a few battered cottages and trees, which also gave us some cover. A few yards further on, on the right in a straight line at right angles to our path, were some taller erections like high dugouts. I later found out that they were the headquarters of the battalion in the line. Then came a trench, off to the right, the M. and N. trench, which was used by the company going to the extreme right part of our sector. We, my new Company 'D', eventually entered a wide communication trench, zig-zagging for about a thousand yards through Bois Confluent at the end of which we came to a little wooden bridge over the Diependaal beck into the Front Line. This communication trench was known as the P. and O.

Some time passed before all the company was at the end of this communication trench because we had become well stretched out – the distance between each two men having become greater as the single file stretched from front to rear. The many looping telephone wires had to be avoided and heads had to be kept down where the trench had been hit. Guides awaited us and the men were taken to their proper dugouts, and then we realised that we were relieving the Australians who, although very good fighters and very fine fellows, were not so great in trench tidiness as was expected from us. True they could not do much with the water-logged trenches for it was well-nigh impossible to make them look tidy or comfortable.

The Aussies showed us round explaining the whereabouts of the stores, ammunition, bombs, gas gongs, cookhouse, latrines and – last but not least – the enemy. The officer in charge got his "chit" signed for the items handed over, had a final whiskey and departed into the gloaming. Jim Proctor, now Lance Corporal in charge of 'D' Company Signals Section, took over from the Aussie signaller after being shown the various telephone lines, station call signs, etc. and being given some small pieces of candle.

Our Company had only three officers, Captain Sheardown who had been awarded the M.C. for the strong point work on October 7th, Darkie Cole, and Lt. Beechman. Their dugout was near the end of the communication trench and was a simple sandbag erection in the parapet. All that could be said about it was that it was a shelter and that it could stop a bullet but not anything in the nature of a direct hit by a shell. Two Army blankets served as a door – the space between them was called a "gas trap". Inside were the usual furnishings: a wooden table, a couple of beds (i.e. wire netting nailed to wooden frames), a box or two to sit on, a few nails here and there to hang things on, the guttering candle, a tin of Gold Flake, a bottle of whiskey and a bottle of water and mugs.

The signal dugout, whose station call was E.W.21, was very similar to the officers' except that it was not built into the parapet and was at the other side of the duckboard track. Thus it faced the other way, the wrong way. Its double blanked doorway had to be used very carefully so as we signallers entered the shelter we lifted the outer blanket, stepped inside the space, lowered it as perfectly as we could, then lifted the second blanket down into position.

We followed this procedure so that there was not the slightest chance of a gleam from our lighted candle, always lit, escaping outside. Jerry might have been able to spot the flicker of a light, especially at night. Our furniture consisted of two beds between the six of us and two boxes, on one of which the telephone, candle, message forms, etc were kept, and the other one served as a seat for the operator on duty. Two men slept in the bed and the others on the floor, one close to the operator so that he could be roused if necessary (for example, to take a message to the officers' dugout). Corrugated iron and sandbags had been used in the making of this shelter, only one layer of the latter all round, except the doorway and on the top. It was high enough to stand up in. Sometimes only four signallers made up the section, for quite a number of trained ones had been lost on the Somme. The draft of London boys contained some signallers but, as yet, they had no training in trenchwork in fact they had not been sorted out yet because, since their arrival, there had not been any settled time in which to train them. We did not worry about our flimsy protection, not even after knowing of the deep concrete dugouts that sheltered German troops on the Somme. If a whizz-bang or a Jack Johnson or a coal box hit it, we would not know anything about it. So we felt safe enough and developed a useful coolness. It did not matter whether we were in a British dugout, out in the open or in a shell hole. We did not know of 'a better hole' than the one we were in. We felt that we could understand why Jerry, after many hours of safety in a deep dugout, was pictured as saying "Kamerad" as he came out of it and put up his hands.

At "stand-to" that evening I did a little tour of our new surroundings as I was off duty and, as a signaller, I did not have to do company tasks. Only every other bay was manned by three men as the company had not enough men to do otherwise. The enemy seemed to have chosen a very good position and from the higher ground at Piccadilly Farm and thereabouts all our movements could be seen by him. We were right at the bottom of the ridge. The whole trench works were Flanders soil packed into sandbags and piled up to form a trench and, owing to the passage of time and the poor weather, the parapet had sunk sufficiently for our tin hats to be seen quite clearly. I noticed two of our snipers posts, each in separate bays. I was told that less than a mile away on the left was St Eloi.

The sanitary man had prepared a new latrine and bucket. The back and two sides were hidden from the enemy by camouflaged sacking. I was reminded of my old Company's sanitary man, the cool, solid Scottie Simpson who on all route marches had carried his yellow flag and a spade with which to dig a hole to be used as a urinal when we halted for the ten minutes every hour. Before we resumed marching he filled in the hole. After the war he immigrated to Canada.

The company men's dugouts were on ground level in the parapet. The doorways were just high enough to allow them to crawl in, and inside the low roofs just allowed them to sit up. Each held four men and there was just enough room for them to lie down like pigs in a sty. Each day the men were dog tired after being up all night on various tasks and it was remarkable that they could sleep in such crowded and uncomfortable positions. The cookhouse was also a sandbag construction, riot too substantial, and in it was a coke fire burning day and night. Its roughly made table and a few boxes were covered with a sooty grime. There was very little ventilation and the fumes from the coke were appalling, especially when the wind was the wrong way. Yet these company cooks managed to provide all the necessary meals and many a cup or mug of tea or cocoa was provided by them for callers at night, for patrols returning from No Man's Land.

We soon realised that rats were in abundance all along the trench, such well-fed rats and such a size. The duckboards were very broken in parts; unlucky was the man who carelessly failed to dodge broken slats and in consequence found his feet in a foot or so of slimy water. The Aussies had told us that the German line was not far away and kept very quiet; that part of their line was unoccupied except for an occasional patrol; that their wire was not very good; that they relied on two or three machine guns, which could enfilade the whole of our sector in front of them; and that some of our wire needed replacing. It seemed to be another instance of "live and let live". I thought that the Germans perhaps knew that the Aussies had been in front of them and so they had better be quiet and try no raids or give any trouble, or they would soon know about it. The Aussies did not stand any nonsense from any Bosche.

In No Man's Land were many shell holes full of water and also a pond surrounded by pollarded willows, which caused no end of scares because, until they got used to this landscape, our night time sentries often imagined that the dwarf trees were men, the enemy, and at times they seemed to be justified in their imaginings . Fritz would send up a Very Light which would silhouette the trees and, as the light dropped down to earth, those trees took various shadowy shapes and appeared to move. The light would die out near to our line and all would then be black. Before their eyes could get used to the darkness the trees would seem to move again and the sentries would be tempted to blaze away at imaginary Germans approaching the line.

No sooner were we settled in then we had visitors with the result that the troops had very little spare time. The C.O. came up daily to make suggestions and officers of the Royal Engineers made recommendations for improving the line. Periscopes were frequently used to look at the state of our wire and the conclusion arrived at was that it would not stop anyone or anything. Indents had to be made out for screw pickets and plenty of barbed wire and much corrugated iron, many 'A' frames, duckboards and sandbags. All this material meant extra work during both day and night and consequently also meant very little rest. Rifles had to be kept clean and were inspected daily; other fatigues had to be done for rations, as mess orderlies; a very full programme to be got through. However some work was done in clearing away the mud and rebuilding the inside of the trench. We did a good deal of cleaning up and there was a distinct improvement in the general aspect of this part of the line by the end of our first tour in the new sector. The Fusiliers, the Bankers, would carry on with the good work when they relieved us. I was amused by the notice put up. "Keep your trench tidy", and by the sandbags hung up for the bits of paper, match sticks, fag ends, brown paper from parcels and the packing, etc. Much discussion followed when the question came of heightening the parapet. It was not advisable to put new sandbags of earth on top of the existing ones, no matter how much they were camouflaged. So what was to be done? Someone suggested digging a little lower into the mud and trying to insert new 'A' frames; an impracticable idea, but our time was up before any chance was taken to try out the idea.

Our 124 Infantry Brigade's Trench Standing Order stated: "The best security against attack is active patrolling." I wondered how it knew. So, of course, it was the duty of the Front Line Company to find and send out the necessary patrols each night. The O.C. 'D' Company detailed officer "B.M." for the first effort. He had joined us on the Somme with the London draft and had not had any previous experience of crawling about in No Man's Land. The night was dark, dampish after much rain, a bit windy, and rather cold. B.M. had chosen his

N.C.O. and two other ranks, received his instructions as to the usual mode of procedure, the direction and the length of his stay out in front. Chits had to be sent to the right and left companies that a patrol of one officer and three other ranks would be going out at such a time p.m., and work to the right and would return at whatever time

a.m. Complete for the part with revolver and two Mills bombs in his pocket, he went out by way of the sap in our first bay. How far that patrol got could only be guessed for before the time was up a little wet figure appeared in the officers' mess. Apparently No Man's Land was not so simple a place to wander in as it looked from the trenches, for B.M. had fallen head over heels into a shell hole which contained a good deal of water and the inevitable mud. He was a pathetic sight, wet through and his breeches, field boots, hand and revolver all covered with mud. His batman had a very busy time getting all his clothing and the revolver cleaned up.

Our stay in the left section of the Front Line was a short one, for on Tuesday, October 24th, the Fusiliers took over and we proceeded to Ridge Wood in support positions. Our huts were well covered with sandbags and some were quite substantial, being made of elephant cupolas. To be enclosed in a steel shell gave us a sense of security from most missiles except a direct hit. There were no proper trenches, but here and there, especially near the roadway, were holes which could be occupied in an emergency. At the back of the wood was a little cemetery.

Its rows of little wooden crosses, each with an aluminium name place, was evidence that some of the troops that had lived in the wood had gone beyond.

Nearly every night all companies had to find an officer and fifty men for various fatigues; ration parties, and working parties, would disappear into the night. The carrying party would go to the Engineers' Dry Dump and then, having been handed sheets of corrugated iron, 'A' frames, duckboards, coils of barbed wire, etc., would proceed to the Front Line. Thus loaded and laden with rifle and gas helmet, the "pack animals" would wend their way slowly to the required destination. The ration party would go slithering down the light railway track to meet our transport and then return with the good things needed to fill the ever hungry and also bring with it the most welcome postbag of letters, papers, etc.

Even during the daytime, some men were required to do some digging for the signallers' cables and for the artillery. This work generally consisted of digging a trench and burying miles of armoured cable six feet deep so that most of the enemy shell fire would not break the wires. We did not have much spare time in the wood and no doubt all the extra work was good for us, but if the rosters were fairly made out then each one of us would have at least one full night's rest. We were occasionally shelled, but nothing serious happened except to the exit towards the Brasserie where we had a few casualties from time to time. This spot was well marked by the enemy because it could easily be seen from his high ground. Obviously he would have a gun trained on the spot. One morning we saw one of our planes brought down. The Germans seemed to have a fighter plane much superior to our observation or spotter planes; it was faster and had darted like a hawk on ours. An unpleasant sight, seeing one of our planes crashing to the ground and the pilot standing no chance of saving it or his life.

The first stay in Ridge Wood soon passed and on Saturday the 28th we went back, away from the line, to that large camp we had seen on our way into this sector – Murrumbidgee Camp between La Clytte and Reninghelst – the name was surely Australian. It was a large camp of many Nissen huts arranged in lines, and it also had a large Y.M.C.A. hut complete with a canteen and piano.

The joy of payday! I had missed one and had drawn nothing since early September, so now I had ten francs. Actually the Somme area had not been the best of places to spend money, so I had not had need of any. Now, flushed with wealth, I looked around for delicacies more palatable than bully beef and stews. Eggs and chips at a cost of one franc were a most appetising dish, with a small basin of coffee as an extra. The drinkers found out that even the Belgian beer tasted better than the petrolised water we had on the Somme, or the chlorinated vintage from our water carts. However, this rest camp was to prove no different from the one at Romarin, of Plugstreet days, even for the signallers.

A similar routine was to be followed in this sector as we had followed in our first trench warfare days: six days in the Front Line; six days in support in Ridge Wood; six days in the Front Line again; and lastly six days back in reserve at Murrumbidgee Camp, and so on. Whilst there was a big stunt on at any part of the line like that of the Somme, we felt sure that it would be a case of "live and let live" in the new sector away from the battles, to come away and lick our wounds in a quiet sector. Probably the enemy followed a similar programme. So we wondered if the German troops in front of us had been on the Somme too. Would our generals, living a life of luxury well behind the danger zones, be satisfied with letting sleeping dogs lie, or would their curiosity get the better of them? Would they pass a message down from Army to Corps, from Corps to Division, from Division to Brigade, and from Brigade down to Battalions: "We are very anxious to know what German troops are opposite to you in the Brasserie sector. The Commander-in-Chief would be awfully pleased to know. Organise, dear boy, a small raiding party. It should be quite easy." Then some small empty space on a gigantic map of the front could be filled in: Bavarians, Württemburgers, Prussians, and everyone would be happy there.

The luck of the signallers was out. On Monday, October 30th, Brigade notified our H.Q. that signallers off duty in rest camps could be used for fatigues. This rule applied to most of the company signallers for there were no company stations whilst out of the line, only the men on the headquarters would be exempt. The Sergeant-Majors who had to find men for working parties were delighted and I expect some of the company men were too. To most of the latter, the signals seemed to have a cushy time; it was their turn to laugh. Every opportunity was taken to order so many signallers to turn out. No rest camp for all of us now. That very evening L/Cpl. Jim Proctor of the signallers took twelve other signallers the one and a half miles to the Brasserie, each of us carrying our rifle, gas mask and a pair of thigh-length gum boots. At the Brasserie an R.E. sapper led us down towards the line, into the

P. and O. trench and just past our New Reserve Line turned right out of the trench and stopped us by the side of Ballaartbeck (the stream that joined the Diependaalbeck at the other side of the P. and O. trench). Jim received his instructions. a fair length of that beck had to be cleaned out and the mud thrown forward towards Bois Confluent and away from the New Reserve Line. We had donned our thigh boots at the R.E. dump at the Brasserie and left our own Army boots hidden under some sheets of corrugated iron – a friendly sapper would see that they were safe.

The beck meandered and ran between three hundred and four hundred yards behind our Front Line and an extra two hundred yards from Jerry's Front Line. We worked as quietly as we could so as not to be a nuisance to our own troops. The sapper disappeared to wherever sappers went to, after setting the "ants" to work. We got on with the job, aware of the Bosche's many Very Lights and did not wish to stay there longer than necessary but, when the task was finished, we still had to stay put until the sapper arrived and gave the order for us to return. We got a move on – this was the time to make haste and get away.

We called at the Brasserie and took off our thigh boots to replace our own as it was not allowed to march or walk in gum boots on the roads. The worst part of this fatigue was the idling and waiting at the end of the job. We groused as the waiting time seemed so long and we hadn't a kind word for sappers – where did they spend their time? We knew that our small party plus the many others out that night swelled the numbers of troops in and about the Front Line who would be there to help in case of a raid. Did we risk too many men for nothing? We knew that Jerry did not pack his Front Line with men either at night or in the daytime, and that they had safer quarters.

We arrived back at the camp just in time for breakfast. After rifle inspection we rested in the huts and had the afternoon for leisure. If we went out of the camp we had to wear a belt and this meant stripping down our equipment. It was worth it in order to look round La Clytte. Thus refreshed we awaited the next evening's fatigue. On this second occasion I went with a larger party to the light railway this side of Kleine Vierstraat to help the R.E.s who were working on a sap. Whilst they kept in the sap we loaded on to small trucks at the beginning of the light railway all the materials they needed – rations, cement, slabs of concrete, etc. We made many journeys and I felt more tired than I had on the previous night, my feet dragged as I made my way back to the camp. I got very little sleep those days because I could not sleep in daylight.

I was not on any other fatigue that spell at the camp so I had a lot of leisure time, and I explored the district, walking in the four directions from the La Clytte-Peninghelst crossroads. My own special friends were on headquarters and had to do spells of duty at the phone and so I did my walking on my own. The cottages and houses in La Clytte were intact but along the roads leading to and from the village were many very poor Belgian homes, probably those of the many refugees who'd had to flee from homes near the line. Some homes were made of Army biscuit tins, old boards, corrugated iron, etc. The Belgians who had lost their real homes just managed to exist, eking out a poor living. At any one of these humble houses, Tommy could buy wine or coffee. The latter was served in a little basin and the sugar was like a little slab of stone and did not sweeten the drink sufficiently for some of us. Some civilians sold chocolate, poor stuff though it was, and silk cards. The Belgians had found out that Tommy was sentimental and that little souvenirs like silk cards and handkerchiefs with appropriate wording, such as "To my mother", "I'm thinking of you", "Friendship", "Birthday greetings", "Flowers of France", "Home Sweet Home", "Gathered for You" appealed to us. Perhaps by this means they helped us to keep in touch with Blighty and helped us not to forget the people of our other lives.

Other civilians made a living by taking in Tommies' washing, for quite a lot of us preferred to have our own shirts. Some of us sported khaki or fancy shirts and, of course, a spare one so that we had not to change a shirt at the baths. By this means we kept ourselves a little cleaner and rather more free from the creeping terrors commonly called "chats", the real pilgrims of the night. Somewhere near Ouderdom were the divisional baths, shower baths of hot water followed by a cold douche. On our few visits to them no shyness was now visible for we had lost that. If the Army shirt provided in exchange for one's dirty one appeared free from movement at first glance, usually it was full of eggs ready to be hatched by the warmth of one's body. Even in Plugstreet Wood we had begun to keep such lively visitors as chats and, if one desired to keep easy, one had to have periodical and regular strafes of all clothing – shirts, vests, underpants, trousers, tunics, cardigans and sometimes socks. There were more of them in this sector and they were everywhere. The means of easing their attacks on the body were various. The flames of candles or matches were run along all the seams and fingers were sometimes used. It is remarkable that no articles of clothing ever dropped to pieces or were scorched or burnt away. My private laundry was in the other direction, on the road to Kemmel, on the left hand side of the road but not far from La Clytte.

I should think that I have drunk coffee in every one of those houses and estaminets. The cafe tasted like poison most of the time, but one had to buy some drink or other and it was only ten centimes a drink. Our French was poor and our vocabulary small, the Tommies' lazy attitude to a foreign language. Sometimes he said "promenez" for promenadez, "boco" for beaucoup, "voulez-vous", "tut sweet" for toute de suite and "ce soir". Singsongs were much welcomed and the biére helped to drive away dull care. We were all miniature volcanoes always ready to give vent to our pent up feelings and so forgot much. It was better than grousing, always blooming well grousing. At the watch we were not really experts, just trying out the real soldiers' privilege. Yet we did grouse, but often it was only when we had nothing else to do. Tommy's nature to a T, and then we smiled when there was some work to keep us occupied.

On Wednesday, November 1st, four days after the battalion came back to Murrumbidgee Camp after its first spell in the Front Line, some of the signallers were sent on a refresher course to Brigade Headquarters in La Clytte. I was one of the lucky ones and, along with some others, I did not mind the fire alarm during the night. We stayed at the estaminet at the corner of the crossroads of the village and slept upstairs over the room of drinks. Madame was very fiery and she seemed to think that we ought to move about like angels, not that we were noisy. Fortunately her rapid mutterings were not understood, she could rattle off at us so quickly that we did not "compree". Our little concerts upstairs annoyed her but we had some real cards with us. Some of the new signallers were with us and one of the Cockney lads gave us jolly good imitations of George Robey, Albert Chevalier and Mark Sheridan. We heard for the first time My Old Dutch, The Old Kent Road and *Oh, Mr Porter*. He was familiar with the London Palladium and other music halls and, of course, saw and heard the best comedians and singers who kept to London halls and hardly ever came north. They were the stars of the day and could stay in London all the year round.

During the day we flag-wagged, did station work and flag drill in the field behind the estaminet and on the road to Kemmel. We had not practised in it before Jerry spotted us and sent over a few shells. The R.E. sergeant, a Jock, told us to disperse and that ended our work in that direction. No shells hit the village, yet it was advisable not to draw further attention to it because of the inhabitants and, more especially, for the sake of the Brigade Staff. The Brigade Signal Office was in La Clytte, on the left hand side of the road that led to Locre, and almost opposite the old Church. We were given instruction on the large telephone exchange and took turns in working on it. It was our first experience of such a huge exchange. It was kept very busy because of its connections in all directions and to all manner of units: to Divisional Headquarters, to the four battalions of the Brigade, to the other three Brigade Headquarters and to all the batteries in the Division. We were now more in touch with the Brigade Staff, especially with the Staff Captain and the Brigade Major, for each had his own line and was greatly in demand. They had, above all others it might be said, their fingers on every aspect of the working of the Brigade. An odd situation used to arise concerning the procedure to be used whenever anyone wanted to speak to either of them. It was to be recognised that we always obtained the battalion officer at the other end of the line before troubling the Staff Captain or the Brigade Major, either of them had never to be kept waiting till someone else had to come to see the phone. Naturally the battalion signaller at this end wanted all fixed at the other end before he called his officer to the phone, his officer not liking to be kept waiting. Hence, when we were learning the proper procedure at Brigade

H.Q. and doing the job properly, the Battalion Officer would ask the signaller if he was the Staff Captain, only to be greeted with "Just a minute, sir ... You're through" because the Brigade end never gave way, or we should have known about it. We enjoyed our stay at Brigade Headquarters, not only because the meals were better and the sleeping quarters better, but because we had practised more interesting work. The Brigade Signal Call was F.C.2.

One fine afternoon when not one of us was on duty and we were at liberty to go anywhere within reason, L/Cpl. Mac, Pip and I left the Murrumbidgee Camp, turned right and at the crossroads of La Clytte went straight across, past the field where we had been shelled for flag waggling past my laundry and strolled along to Kemmel, not a sound was to be heard. What a surprise when we reached Kemmel. How different it was from La Clytte. We saw no civilians whatever. All the houses were barricaded and those at the street corners had machine gun posts in the cellars. The guns behind the long and narrow slits covered all the approaches. We saw very few Tommies, and they looked at us as if we had no right to be strolling around. What we did not know at the time was that, owing to an inward curve in the British Line from St. Eloi to Neuve, in fact the headquarters of the battalion to the right of our sector were in the fine looking moated château on the left just as we entered the village. We did not stay long because we were obviously in the wrong place for a friendly afternoon visit. Kemmel Hill stood out well and we were given to understand that there was an observation post near the top. On our way back we saw to the left Scherpenberg Molen which, though we did not know then, was more easily reached straight through La Clytte. The places behind the latter village were not as familiar to us as those between it and the Line.

Shortly after this walk and during my turn on H.Q. the signallers had a short route march towards Reninghelst. As a Regimental Sergeant-Major approached us on horseback we were given "Eyes left" after "March to attention". Our N.C.O. soon realised his mistake and quickly ordered "Eyes front – march easy" much to our amusement, for this particular N.C.O. was a bit of a dandy and a know-all. He himself wore a non-regulation cap, shirt and tie, breeches and non-regulation puttees. The only change in his uniform the average Tommy dare risk was bribing the tailor to alter the neck of his tunic which otherwise hung badly.

On Friday, November 3rd, we left the Rest Camp and made our way to the Front Line. I was posted to 'D' Company Signallers with Jim as Lance Corporal in charge. Besides the usual full pack I carried the telephone. It was a daylight relief and after passing right at Hallebast Corner I noticed the end of Dickebusche Lake and then Gordon Farm with a Belgian battery nearby. We went through Ridge Wood, as usual, and then in single file hurried the rest of the way to the Brasserie. As 'D' Company were going to the right sector of the Front Line, we veered right halfway between the Brasserie and the entrance to the P. and O. trench, along another trench called M. and N. which went across a field and eventually brought us to Chicory Lane – the communication trench leading down to the Front Line. It went through Bois Carre not far from Western Redoubt and Sleepy Hollow. This part of the Front Line consisted of a conglomeration of trenches and sandbags built up to form a breastwork: there were dugouts of various kinds and dumps of material. But, strange to relate, there was a rather well-constructed machine gun emplacement which was evidently built to stand a good deal of knocking about. Here too was a Russian sap, a tunnel a few feet under the ground which went from our Front Line under the German Line. Of course, it was very "secret" and its occupants used to listen to see if the Germans were tunnelling too, and of course "Jerry knew nothing about it" though, of course, his plane observers could see the huge dump of sandbags full of blue clay which were piled a few yards from the sap entrance. Fritz had the place well taped as we knew by his occasional reminders in the form of minnies, rum-jars and pineapples, all of which fell perilously near.

At this part of the line the Germans were only eighty yards away so we were always on the alert. Two lengthy gaps in the line were rather worrying and there was a road leading across No Man's Land lower than the surrounding country, which afforded cover in the event of an enemy raid. The Signal Office was not too far from the end of Chicory Lane and near the officers' quarters. Our battalion's thousand yards of breastworks was nearer to the Germans at each end and in each case curved further away and then came unevenly to the shortest distance from them exactly halfway. The German trench (Obit) was more straight and opposite to Chicory Lane, passed through Bois Quarante, and ended at the road that crossed No Man's Land.

The days of our sojourn in this part of the line were very quiet. We kept out of sight, being at the bottom of a ridge on either side. We were very active during the night hours, quite a lot of men being engaged in doing jobs, whereas the Germans' front line was almost empty with an occasional visit by a man to send up Very Lights. As far as I know, we had no casualties that spell. The enemy shells that passed over about ten o'clock were aimed at the roads beyond in an effort to catch our transport.

On the Thursday, we trekked back to the huts in Ridge Wood, to the far corner, as before. I had quite a lot of free time, no signal duties and no fatigues. I took the opportunity to stroll out of the wood and explore that part of Belgium hidden by the trees. I went as far as Hallebast Corner, saw the Advanced Brigade Headquarters and signals, F.F.I. I called at the farmhouse where Madeleine lived with her parents. This became a regular port of call, not to pay our respects to the R.E. signallers, but to sup coffee in the farmhouse kitchen. We all got to know Madeleine and she welcomed us all, favouring no-one in particular. Really it was not the coffee we sought, but a change of air and to hear the cheerful conversation of mademoiselle.

Much nearer to Hallebast Farm was Gordon Farm. This was occupied by a Belgian Family of four – father, mother, son and daughter. They had come from near Ypres. This farm was also the billet of the artillery men of the Belgian Field Battery which was positioned in a field more to the left, and that field was very green with luscious grass standing out in marked contrast to the rest of the fields in the district. Tommies called there also for a drink. The farmer made much money out of the troops by selling tins of fruit, eggs, butter and other delicacies. We referred to the Belgian guns as "Spit Fires", they seemed to spit when fired and the explosion of the shells was heard almost immediately. Our equivalent type were the eighteen pounders and Jerry's Whizz-Bangs – whizzing as the shells left the gun and banging as almost immediately they exploded. They were always the guns nearest to the line and, if spotted by the enemy, received many a severe hammering and often were the recipients of hundreds of gas shells.

Our own reserve line for the companies in support ran from the beginning of Chicory Lane more or less parallel to the Front Line as far as the junction of the two becks, Diependaal and Ballaart. It was a very deep trench or breastwork and the Bois Confluent sheltered it at the P. and O. trench end, but Bois Carre was behind it at the other end. The Ballaartbeck meandered in front of it all the way past Chicory Lane and then it joined the Wytschaetebeck. Quite a number of yards behind the middle of the reserve line was Strong Point 7, a redoubt capable of holding almost a platoon. A similar redoubt was in Bois Carre and in a small wood between the latter wood and Ridge Wood, called Sleepy Hollow. It contained a few dugouts of a sort and it was none too dry . It was very isolated. The two redoubts had emergency stores, ammo, water, etc.

It sometimes happened that a company signaller was given a turn of duty on headquarters though we all realised that one N.C.O. there had never had a turn with a company section, nor had he ever been nearer the line than headquarters, he had never seen a firing-step, nor a trench bay, nor a communication trench, and certainly not the barbed wire. My turn on H.Q. came near the end of November. The Headquarters Line was not far from the Brasserie Corner and on the right of the roadway towards the P. and O. trench. The dugouts, though all above ground were fairly substantially built, i.e. the sleeping quarters. The orderly room and other offices were of the light type – sheets of corrugated iron covered with sandbags and blanket doorways. They were all very roomy and we could easily stand up in them. The Signal Office was in the orderly room and had quite an elaborate switchboard. Never did Jerry ever strafe this line of dugouts and huts and we were told that our aircraft could not spot them and on an aerial photograph they looked like a rubbish dump – unused and deserted.

I thoroughly enjoyed each turn of duty at the switchboard, the work of Cp. Ted Coulson. The lines had to be tested regularly, especially at night time when we called up stations, or they called us up, every quarter of an hour. Company signallers were responsible for their lines back as far as H.Q. and the H.Q. linesmen (Mac and Fred) were responsible for the lines back to Brigade and/or Advanced Brigade if there was one. At nine o'clock each morning we synchronised our signal watch with that of Brigade – we could have done similarly each evening when Jerry tried to strafe the transport bringing up the rations and other necessities. Regularly at half past ten we heard the shells whizz, seeming to pass just over our dugouts on their way to the roads beyond.

Out at Murrumbidgee Camp for rest, I was again with 'D' Company. I was never called upon to do fatigues this time and there were many signal parades. At this time I met some of the Cockneys because Turner, Bett, Hemingway, Russell (a Londoner) and the two Hammond brothers (also Londoners) were in the signals. Our dialects were quite different; when Russell said his name it sounded to us like "Rassell", and they used in almost every sentence two words which we had hardly heard before and which we found quite shocking. This habit eased off as the Cockneys got used to us Northern foreigners. They were very entertaining and knew many popular songs. They enjoyed On Ilkla Moor bart'at, Blaydon Races, A Farmer's Boy and other Northern songs. One afternoon when many of us were gathered in the huge Y.M.C.A., someone called out "Anyone play the piano?" Rifleman

M.R. came forward and started to play Home Sweet Home but he never completed it for he was affectionately seized and bundled outside. The Hammond brother Ted who wore the old type of pince-nez with rims became the signallers' barber; for a few centimes he saw that our hair did not get too long. He would charge 3d. for a haircut and eventually retired to Bournemouth – he had "all the swank imaginable". (G.V.D., 1992)

Our battalion was very fortunate in being at the far side of St. Eloi away from Ypres and the real hot spots of that salient. Clinging to the low-lying bulge, instead of retiring to the canal, meant a heavy toll of lives daily. We were in a very cushy part and that is why, no doubt, we had a surprise visit from the Corps Staff. I always thought that no-one beyond Brigade cared about the P.B.I. and knew very little of daily life in the trenches. A General with his various satellites beautifully groomed, tabbed with red and complete with armlets arrived when 'D' Company were in the left section of the Front Line. Darkie, on duty, greeted them. He was their guide and general information bureau for 'D' Company's section of the line, answering many questions and listening to several comments and brainy "armchair" suggestions thought out way back in some chateau where the war was fought and planned on maps. When the General insisted that more sump holes could be dug underneath the duckboards he was asked to move along and see the result of our efforts – when the trenches were dry enough. "Good work. Carry on with it."

At a suitable moment, Darkie pointed out that, owing to the parapets being low all day, movements could be seen by the enemy at Piccadilly Farm some short distance up the higher ground held by Jerry; the inspecting party thought it time to move on to the right section. Bodies were no longer straight and upward, but bent so as to keep out of sight. Unfortunately one young Sub, with finely polished boots and leggings stepped through a broken duckboard, not repaired the night before. He remained very placid and stamped off as much mud as he could. There was no parados between the two company sections and it was suggested that they should keep low, spread out a little and hurry to the next company where, no doubt, they received a similar welcome. We would have liked to know what kind of a report (or reports) they handed in. We suspected that to the C.-in-C. of the British Armies they would say that the men were in very good spirits, that the trenches and dugouts were quite satisfactory and, above all, that the men were eager to have another go at the enemy. But forward to the Divisional H.Q. and subsequently to the Brigade H.Q. they would report that much repair work must be done to the breastworks and the duckboards, that nothing is known of the enemy facing them and that, owing to a lack of aggressive spirit, the sector is far too quiet.

Late in the evening of every day, the ration party of our company handed in to the signal office a sandbag of supplies. Candles were always needed and were always there. Usually for six of us there would be one loaf of bread, a few Army biscuits in addition, part of a tin of butter, sometimes a little cheese and, every other day, a tin of pozzy (jam). A new make appeared, IXL made in Australia, and it was quite tasty consisting of melon and ginger. Very seldom did we get a pound and a quarter of bread per day (reduced to one pound 1.11.1917), so the biscuits made up for the shortage. Most of the ration of bread was eaten at breakfast time and the remainder at tea time. The cooks always provided a little bacon each morning and always a stew at dinner time (made of bully beef and some potatoes. It was very satisfying because it was always hot. Sometimes fresh meat was used. We felt sure that the further away a soldier was from the base supplies, the more he suffered the reduced ration. We could not picture any one on the lines of communication being in short supply. The Y.M.C.A. canteens and our own divisional canteens were well patronised, but I have known our own canteen be short on many occasions.

Our N.C.O. in charge heaved a sigh of relief when he had dished out the rations, for then each man was responsible for his share and had to take certain precautions to make sure that his bread and cheese were there in the morning. The wily rat had to be outwitted – a greater nuisance than Jerry in these peaceful days. It was a very hungry animal as there were no scraps to be had, nor were there any corpses to feed on. If Jim had just left the section's rations in the sandbag till the next morning the rats would have got them. The safest place was each man's mess tin, the only thing a rat could not do was lever the lid off. It could gnaw through the haversack or valise and even crawl along a beam and carefully descend a rope at the end of which hung the bag containing rations, if we did this. It could nose out chocolate, cheese, biscuits and the contents of food parcels sent from Blighty. A direct result of the activities of this crafty pest was the organised rat-strafe each morning (company level) when men would use some of the powder from cartridges and a little ingenuity and try to scare the rats out of their holes, near which stood men with entrenching tool handles, sword-bayonets and pick-axe handles. Competitions could have been arranged between companies, battalions or brigades and some form of award (a certificate or ration medal) made to the group making the most kills.

The smart instructors at Aldershot had drilled into us that the soldiers best friend was his rifle. So far we had not realised this fact. But for frequent rifle inspections, the breeches of our rifles would have rusted away. Perhaps the sword-bayonet was our second best friend because it served many purposes: sergeants wore them on their belts when out walking in the villages and towns; it was almost as useful as the Army jack-knife; it was an ideal toasting fork for the hard Army biscuits which we held against a fire to soften them; it was a very handy and satisfactory wood chopper when additional fuel was required for our small braziers; a small mirror fixed on the point at an angle and held above the breastwork acted as a temporary periscope to observe what Jerry might be up to (many such a spying glass was shattered by an enemy sniper); and lastly it could be used to open tins when other means failed (sometimes the keys of the bully beef tins failed to do their work). All old soldiers who had to resort to their Army jack-knives on such occasions could be recognised by a scar left just above the left thumb knuckle. The left hand held the tin and the right hand used the jack-knife, which invariably slipped and gashed the left thumb. Such wounds were not recognised by the Army.

On Sunday, December 3rd, we returned to Ridge Wood and to the front right corner dugouts. Brigade Signals of the R.E.'s ordered that Tuesday was to be a Visual Day when, except in case of emergency, no telephones had to be used but that all messages both in and out were to be dealt with by some visual means, either flags or lamps. Three of us were sent on loan to the advanced Brigade H.Q. near Hallebast Corner. Sergeant Mac of the R.E. had reconnoitred and along the road to Dickebusch had found a deserted house which had the roof and part of the back bedroom blown off by shellfire. The front of the house was intact and the stairway alright and, from what was left of the back bedroom, a good view of the rear of Ridge Wood could be observed. We reported to him at half past eight with a Lucas lamp and flags and he posted us in that room. We aligned the lamp and we could see the battalion signals just to the rear of the wood. We gave the call up sign using one flag and Morse and quickly got in touch, our white flag showing up well with the dark wall behind it. The morning was very quiet and only a few messages were dealt with. Just after midday the peace was interrupted by the sound of exploding shells a little to our left. We finished receiving a message and, as about a dozen shells had straddled the position, we lay low. Sergeant Mac did not wish to invite too much attention to that part of the road near which advanced H.Q. were situated so he told us to clear out and stay away for at least an hour. After a walk along the Hallebast-La Clytte road, we returned and made contact again with Ridge Wood by white flag. We did not have to wait long for the next salvo of shells, so we gave the code letters. N. A., i.e. we were prepared to receive only D. D. messages, that is those that needed no answers, each group of words being sent twice to make sure we got the message satisfactorily. Jerry had either spotted us from his observation balloon or from the high ridge. We were to have used the lamp after dusk had fallen but Sgt. Mac decided that the experiment should end, so we sent the closing down sign and left the deserted ruin.

On our way back to Ridge Wood we had just got as far as the remains of Bardenburg when we heard the sound of marching feet approaching. We stopped by the roadside and then realised that a small party of Yeoman Rifles was on its way to the battalion. All of them had been wounded at Flers and a sergeant in charge proved to be a 'C' Company man, Danny Wood. All were delighted at returning to the old batt. and we joined their ranks. Danny was a very popular N.C.O., very dapper and a smart soldier. We marched along together and I gave him news of the boys. I think he was a County Durham lad. (In 1919 I was crossing a large square in Hull in the East Riding of Yorkshire and I ran into Danny Wood, who had been commissioned in the artillery, and was not surprised at his warm greeting; "Let's go somewhere and have a drink. You know the city, don't you?" I did; but I was not acquainted with the public houses. We went to one called The Manchester and, to our great surprise, there sat two more of the old 'C' Company, Jack and Duggie, both of whom had been contemporary sergeants with Danny, Jack later becoming the C.S.M. What a natter we had about the old battalion. Duggie was a great cartoonist and many were the magnificent sketches he did of "our war").

Two mornings later, as Jim and I waited for the rest of the sigs. section to parade in the open space at the rear of the wood, we heard a sudden whizzing sound as if a shell was on its way. Each of us did a dive to the earth, heard a thud and realised that there had been no explosion. We got to our feet and saw, partly buried in the earth between us, a nose cap from a shell. Jim took out his Army jack-knife and dug it out and kindly offered it to me. I refused it as I had now dropped the idea of collecting souvenirs, at least those that would be heavy. There was a sale of such souvenirs to soldiers behind the line, but I gave that idea not a thought. I had got myself a very fine German dagger, double edged and very sharp, on September 15th on the Somme, but someone "won" it from my pack, which I took to Flers dump in early October.

After the next six days in the Front Line we went back to Murrumbidgee Camp where we suffered a real disappointment. We had heard that one of Lena Ashwell's Acting Parties was in Reninghelst and was coming to our camp to entertain us in the Y.M.C.A. hut. We spruced ourselves up and got early in the queue so that we could have seats near the front. To our surprise and disappointment, the cast was an all-male one. However, they gave a jolly good show and we enjoyed it immensely. We had fully expected to see some Blighty girls in the cast, it seemed ages since we had seen any. The men, all of military age, were unfit for service and had volunteered to entertain troops at the front.

I had started to buy in the villages any picture postcard of the district. I had already sent my mother a view of Albert, followed by one of the chateau at Francieres. Next to be sent were one of La Clytte Church and of the chateau and lake of Kemmel. I was very lucky in that I received at least two letters a day and these I answered as soon as possible so as to have regular correspondence as replies came. Old school friends, college friends and relatives all wrote. A college group of six girls sent me a photo and called themselves the "Bunnies" because of the style of their hair, done up in a bun at the back. Two younger old sixth formers had now joined up and kept in touch with me. Though I did not know just then, both were following in my steps, out in France. All letters were very, very welcome and

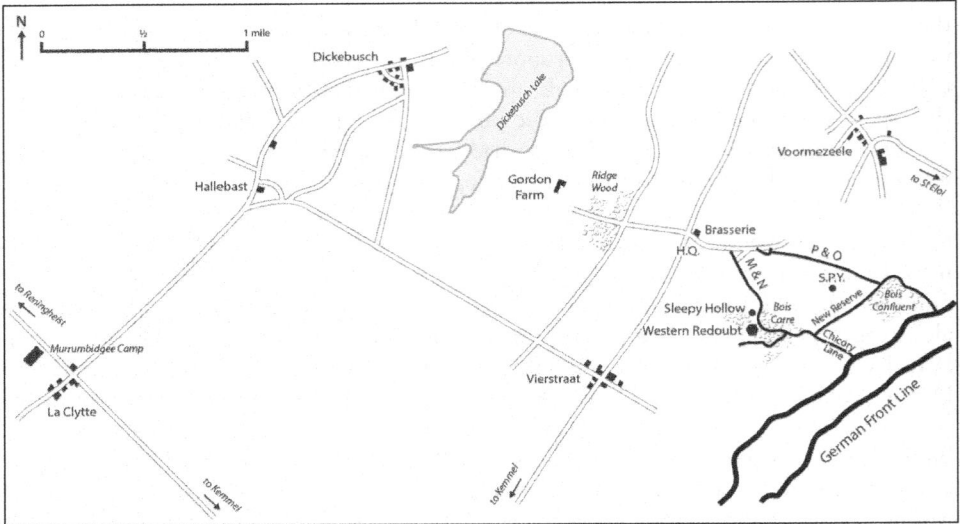

Map 4. Brasserie Sector 1916–17

I took great pleasure in replying to them all. I always kept the officer-censors busy and I had a suspicion that all my letters were not read by them, but signed knowing that I never gave any direct Army information. Also they were probably influenced by the fact that I did not put my address on my letters home. As for the picture postcards, if I sent one by itself, the name of the place was scored out – why, I don't really know because no unit was shown. When I sent a view in a letter the name was sometimes not crossed out.

After the monthly pay parade at which I received ten francs, I asked to see the Quarter-Master Sergeant of 'C' Company for the purpose of solving why my mother had not received the additional allowance as promised when I joined up. He said that he could not understand why the matter of the allowance had not gone through and that he had reported the matter to Winchester, asking the Pay Department to settle it with the Pay Office. Nothing ever came of it, and many months passed before I learned that dozens of us never received the expected allowance for parents. Evidently it was because we were not working when we volunteered and so were not entitled to any additional help, not even to a widow from her only son – one cheap way of running an Army, but very paltry. This economy was on a par with the payment, or rather the non-payment, of N.C.O.s; very few Lance Corporals were paid for their one stripe, they had extra responsibility but no extra pay. At one time I was a full Corporal (two stripes), but paid only as a rifleman. Yet none of the N.C.O.s grumbled, they carried on doing their extra duties quite willingly.

Soldiers' lives were just as cheap, not to loved ones at home, but to battle planners. A notice outside the orderly room showed that Christmas cards were on sale at a few coppers each. A thin piece of card, about five inches by six and a half, had printed near the top of one side "Xmas 1916 from the 41st Divn."; the first part was in a circle and the second part in a scroll. Near the bottom was the greeting: "Hoping you will 'capture' all the Season's Pleasure". In between, the picture showed a Tommy with his "capture", a Bosche. The latter wore very baggy trousers, gum boots, a massive tunic, a tight belt across the middle, a very round and uncouth face capped with a pork-pie hat. Tommy was just as rough looking with baggy trousers, very thin putteed legs, rifle at the slope, webbing equipment, box respirator, scabbard and cap. A broad grin spread across his face. It was a very good likeness of a Tommy – not at all smart. The picture frame was supported on either side by a rifle and an eighteen pounder shell. The card was designed by G.C. Benson. Many hundreds were sold, the men being very keen to enter the spirit of the occasion and be able to send Christmas cards to their loved ones.

One thing we had learned about French money – the five franc and ten franc notes could be spent anywhere in France, but the local smaller denominations like five centime notes could be spent only in the district in which you were billeted or served. If you were not on the alert when you knew that your battalion was about to move out of that area, you could be left with some tatty pieces of paper, about two inches by three, which could not be spent in any other area. "Ville de Lille – Bon Communal 5 centimes" could not be spent in, say, Pop, or Bailleul or St. Omer. Such a note is one of my souvenirs.

We heard by way of the orderly room and the runners that the Front Line had received another visit from the Brass Hats, but only a small party of six. They had not gone to suggest this or that, but to observe. Each carried a cylindrical periscope about twelve inches long and covered very nearly with a canvas or sacking piece of camouflage so that it would be hard to see by the enemy when very cautiously pushed up above the breastwork. They examined No Man's Land, Jerry's wire and his trenches and were not spotted. Their stay was not a very long one, and we began to wonder why this interest in our part of the line?

Once every spell at Murrumbidgee Camp, all of us had a foot inspection. Darkie and a sergeant would hold an indoor parade in a hut and we had to have our boots and socks off. At the time I did not know the object of the inspection, if it could be called an inspection. Each of us was asked, "Are your feet all right?" or "Are the soles of your feet all right?" and the usual answer was "Yes, sir" and that was that. Later I realised that the inspection was to detect if any man had trench foot, when the soles of the feet became milky white.

The weather that winter was shocking, for snow had fallen heavily and the frosts were very severe. The earth was frozen to some depth and ditches, drains and streams were entirely frozen, the ice being anything from ten to eighteen inches in thickness. Shaving water froze before the task was finished. The pint of hot to warm tea we received each morning froze almost immediately if it was not drunk straight away. Water was scarce and it was a difficult job getting any for washing purposes. We shared out the little we got, sometimes from a shell hole. Dirty as it was, we all used it, six or eight of us of the signal section. I have known that same number wash in a cigarette tin of water and even shave with it before throwing it away. Of course, the first one to use it had the cleanest water and then, the more that used it, the dirtier it became. Before the last one of us used it, it had quite a scum on it. We called that procedure the shaving brush wash. Could it be said that we were very dirty, carrying on in this way?

No, we would do anything to keep as clean as possible, and the morning lick-and-a-promise seemed to be very refreshing. When we had to resort to the shell holes for water, Fred Johnson produced the water bucket, a canvas bucket he had "won". He carried it everywhere and it was a very useful friend.

I recall that we felt the cold most on one of the occasion when we were in reserve. When we arrived at the Murrumbidgee huts for the monthly rest, we found that the men of the battalion we relieved had torn up the floor boards of the huts for fire wood, so we had to lie on the bare ground and keep warm the best we could. Our groundsheets felt very cold indeed and the one issue blanket was hardly enough covering so two men would kip together and so share two blankets. Every week mother sent out to me two newspapers which I read to see how the war was progressing and to note in particular what the war reporters said. When I had read them I saved them to use as bed sheets, placing them on top of my ground sheet and they absorbed the initial cold feeling. I was following the old saying that one should have as much warm material under one as over one. It worked very well.

The rats were very, very daring on account of the cold and their resulting hunger. At night they came out of their holes in dozens and it was strange to see how we disliked their ticks, and some of us showed fear of them, the more well-built and sturdy ones. They bit our knuckles and hands, sucked at our noses and even pulled our hair so that we were only too pleased to cover ourselves completely without blankets and leave no parts of our bodies for them to get at. They were whoppers, twelve inches long and they were not in the least frightened of us, even when we stirred, and too often did we see their glowing eyes in the darkness. We had to take extra care of our rations and leather equipment or we should have found the one missing and the other chewed up.

The fatigue that I clicked during this same rest was typical of Army red tape. Fifty of us had to go to the M and N trench and repair some damage, which was only slight, because the earth was frozen so hard that shells made no impression on it and had not even made any shell holes. Each man carried a pick or shovel, and his rifle, so that there were twenty-five of each tool. When we got there and were given our orders by the R.E. sapper, who quickly disappeared, we could not find any loose earth with which to fill the sandbags that we needed to build up the trench. Those with picks began to strike at the earth with unfortunate results; some were immediately broken, and so were some of the shovels when used to pick up after shifting clods of earth. It was impossible to do the job and no repair work was done. We could not blame the sapper, he had followed orders. Someone had examined the trench and found the damage, but when? By the time the divisional maintenance officer received the report about the damage, the frost had done its work and the fatigue was a wash-out. Why couldn't the sapper have used his initiative and cancelled the job when he saw the conditions? – he was not there to think only to obey his orders. We had to wait until he returned some six hours later, when the job should have been completed, for him to dismiss us. No doubt the sapper had a comfortable rest and a cup of cocoa to warm him up during that six hour period. We arrived back to our billets about five o'clock in the morning just before dawn, and just in good time for breakfast. Such was the lot of a working party – P.B.I.

We were in the line for Christmas and, just before that day of peace and goodwill to all men, the battalion received a message from well in the rear that there had to be no fraternising with the enemy on Christmas Day. Jerries and Tommies had not to meet in No Man's Land as on previous Christmas Days, no shaking of hands, no exchanging gifts or souvenirs, no spirit of goodwill to all men. Such friendliness of other Christmases was not to be. The message also stated that there would be an early morning strafe at eight o'clock precisely, with trench mortars or stokes for half an hour only. This stunt had the desired effect from the Red Tabs' point of view – there was no friendliness shown to the enemy and the rest of the day was very quiet indeed. We, the Tommies, would have have minded fraternising as had been done the previous two years, for in a way the opponents on each side of No Man's Land were kindred spirits. We did not hate one another; we were both P.B.O. and should have liked to have stood up between our respective barbed wire, without danger, and shaken hands with our counterparts. And why not?

I was one of the signallers from 'D' Company in quite a decent dugout in Western Redoubt near the new Battle H.Q. and Sleepy Hollow. The office was across the way in a taller dugout. Our sleeping quarters had a very low entrance, about two feet square, and we had room to sit up and just room to lie down to sleep. It was always dark inside and we had to keep a candle alight whilst we were inside. Because of the extreme cold we had a small charcoal fire in a brazier and in consequence the interior of the dugout was always very stuffy. We ate our meals outside, when the weather was dry, and on this particular Christmas Day it was. The orderlies brought up the dinner, warmed up Maconochies, but no sign of pudding. After eating mine I was very sick and I don't think that the meal was the cause, more likely the charcoal fumes. We had been warned that charcoal fumes had affected the occupants of some dugouts in the Front Line and that on two occasions men had just been dragged out in time, having been gassed in a way as they rested or slept after their duties were finished. Men had even succumbed from the same cause.

A spell in Ridge Wood immediately followed our Christmas stay in the Front Line. On New Year's Eve our beloved Wesleyan padre held a Watch Night Service in the drying shed among the trees. As on previous occasions he improvised an altar with empty boxes. His theme was "When two or more are gathered together in my name … " *Abide with Me* was the hymn and Holy Communion followed the short service. As we dispersed one enemy shell burst in the wood a few yards from the shed. A strange New Year greeting from the Bosche, who was reminding us that the war was still on, as we had let him know on Christmas morning.

I was again on H.Q. for the next tour of the Front Line and noticed a different type of telephone was being used, the Fullerphone, which was larger than the old D Mark III. A wooden box about eight inches cubic, instead of a leather case, held the phone, which had a very advantageous property over the old phone – any message sent on it by Morse could not be tapped by the enemy. Only a similar instrument at the other end of the line could change what passed along the line into Morse. We were ordered to use this instrument only for Morse messages, but we found out that we could speak with it and often we held private little conversations with our friends, particularly at night. What we spoke about was never of any value to the enemy if he did listen for any leakage.

The signals office-cum-orderly room was often very busy and much frequented by runners, specialists, company officers, the adjutant (the "Boy" of 'C' Company) and the C.O. On one occasion I overheard a friendly argument between the Adjutant and the C.O. concerning the New Battle Headquarters that had been built near Sleepy Hollow and not far from the Western Redoubt. "I'll bet you that the Hun knows nothing about it," said the C.O. Taken," replied Adjutant Eden, "and we'll have to wait and see." The amount of the bet was settled, though I never knew the outcome of it. The front hereabouts was really very quiet, though what happened about a month later may have served to answer the question.

Early one morning just before dawn a German soldier had crawled out of his trench and under his barbed wire. He proceeded under the cover of the road that ran across No Man's Land and then under our wire at the weakest part of our line just to the right of our sector. Cautiously he moved between the breastwork and the wire until he came to a bay where one of our sentries stood. "Kamerad, Kamerad," he whispered, and he was helped into our trench and so had given himself up. We had a "prisoner of war". A Yeoman with rifle and bayonet-sword fixed led the way, then followed the German soldier who immediately lit up a very fine cigar, and finally a second lieutenant holding his revolver almost in the middle of the German's back. The troops who witnessed this trio passing up Chicory Lane, along the M. and N. trench to our H.Q. were tickled pink. In between puffing his cigar, the German's face was showing a huge happy grin, as he probably thought that he had finished with the war, and no doubt he had. His escort looked very grim and at last they came into the orderly room. What a stir and buzz. Brigade was informed and finally the very happy prisoner was on his way to be interrogated – lucky blighter! My thoughts went back to the Divisional Christmas card which seemed to have looked into the future.

The P.H. gas helmets (phenate-hypo), smelly and consisting of one thickness of flannel or flannelette and not proof against all gases were called in and the troops were issued with a new type, the box respirator. It consisted of a mouthpiece, a nose clip, goggles and a mask which was connected by a breathing tube to the filter box containing charcoal and granules, and was a complete protection against the different gases likely to be met. These parts fitted into a canvas case about ten inches long, ten inches broad and two inches wide. It had a long sling so that it could be carried over the shoulder. This sling could be shortened by hole and stud so that the respirator could be carried in an alert position, resting on the chest. A piece of string could be taken from the bottom right corner round the body and tied to the bottom left corner to help to hold it securely. When in this position the top flap was pulled off two press studs and put back so that the mask could be taken out very quickly and put on the face. To help to keep the eyepieces clean and clear, a tube of Anti-dim was provided. They were very, very slightly smeared with the paste and then wiped with a piece of clean four-by-two, and thus when the mask was worn the eyepieces did not steam up. I used to treat the lenses of my own glasses in a similar way.

Seeing that the battalion headquarters was quite a distance from the Front Line, the H.Q. stretcher-bearers were accommodated nearer and were housed in a dugout in Sleepy Hollow. One afternoon, L/Cpl. George Bramley was busy "big game hunting" and had for that purpose removed his gas helmet, equipment and tunic. As he was busy strafing the lice in the latter he saw someone pass the doorway with whom he wanted to talk. Quickly he donned his tunic and ran after the man. On his return he met, to his great surprise, the Divisional General, the Brigadier General and a few of their staff.

You are not properly dressed, Corporal," said the D.G. L/Cpl. George explained what he had been doing and the D.G. replied, "Well, if you want to be gassed, it is all right by me."

I had many talks with the stretcher-bearers before I realised how dedicated they were to their specialised job, even though they had not had the chance to volunteer for it. We all recall how a sergeant-major would say on parade how he wanted volunteers for whatever, followed very quickly by, "You, you and you"! They tackled this important job with the true Yeoman spirit. They gained early experience when disaster struck 'A' Company on its rifle inspection in Plugstreet Wood on June 1st, 1916. Without fail they always sewed each of our dead into a blanket and buried them with deep respect. Not far from Plugstreet Church were the remains of a few houses and at the rear were the gardens, which had been little disturbed by shell fire and the flowers looked out of place. Our stretcher-bearers would go and collect some of them for the graves of their comrades. It was no picnic bringing three or four dead from the line using the trolley on the light railway, for the track was broken in places. The bodies had to be taken off the trolley so that it could be lifted back onto the rails and the bodies brought up to one or other of the cemeteries nearby.

The winter turned colder and colder, the very sandbags of the breastwork of the Front Line and of the communication trenches became as solid as marble. Shells only chipped pieces out of them and no longer could repair work be done. The troops were warned not to hold the trigger or breech of their rifles without hand protection. Mittens were issued, either of leather or some other skin. The hands were fastened to a long leather thong which passed round the neck and hung loose when not in use. To help to ward off the danger of trench foot, each man was issued with some whale oil with which to rub the feet daily. Empty round cigarette tins served as containers.

The dixie lids holding the morning's bacon rations, said to be American bacon and of poor quality, were affected insomuch that the dip soon froze. Daily foot inspections became the order of the day, and it was a crime not to apply whale oil to the feet. I found it more comfortable and easier on the feet to wear boots a shade too large and so wear two pairs of socks at once. After foot inspection, I turned the inside pair inside out and replaced them first; the next time I placed the outer pair nearer to the feet; the next time I turned that pair inside out, and so on. Such a procedure helped to keep the feet warm and in fair condition.

Snow fell often and for many days. It froze and No Man's Land was more dangerous than ever; crawling about in it was a ticklish job, yet a fresh order from Brigade stated that we had to be the masters of it and frequent patrolling had to be done nightly. This order was rigidly followed and never an enemy appeared to dispute our superiority there. Out at La Clytte busy times lay ahead. In addition to the usual working parties to the line, all troops had to undergo general training during the day, short route marches which enabled us to become familiar with the seven hills of the district, short sharp rushes over fields, rifle drill, etc. In the midst of such training we lost our Colonel, our C.O. Lt.Col. the Honourable G. Foljambe, who had taken over command of the battalion on September 16th after the Somme battle in which the Earl of Feversham was killed. He took up an appointment at Aldershot to instruct at a school for Commanding Officers. All were sorry to see him go as he was very popular, a thorough gentleman and a model of smartness. He was a real leader. Our temporary Commanding Officer was Captain E. Worsley who came up to the H.Q. from 'A' Company and he held that post till January 26th when Lt.Col Talbot Jarvis of the 10th Royal West Surreys, (the Queens), assumed command of the battalion, just eleven days after the previous commanding officer departed. We were to find out that we had got another very fine C.O., so kind, considerate, pleasant, jolly and well-built.

Another peculiar sight on the La Clytte-Kemmel road one morning was a native leading a horse which was pulling a framework of shafts and wheels on which stood a huge barrel, at least eight feet long. It rested on its side and was six feet in diameter. The bung hole was in the middle of the top and the smell all around it was overwhelming for the Belgian had been round most of the houses in the district collecting the contents of the earthen closets. He was taking his precious load to his fields to be used as fertiliser. He must have been used to the smell -we were not!

The next time we were in the Front Line Brigade R.E. Signals ordered another visual day for our signallers. The sigs. on H.Q. had to find a suitable "station" – a site out of view of the enemy yet able to be seen by a Company Station in the Front Line. Just forward of our H.Q. dugout line and a few yards to the right of the P. and O. communication trench was Beggars Rest. This was an old farm building which had been shelled by the enemy many times before we came to that sector. Now all that was left standing were two adjacent walls. Grass grew among the rubble and the building was derelict. On the day fixed for visual communications only, Mac and I crawled from the comm. trench to the ruin. Just a foot from the right corner of it we fixed and aligned our telescope on a spot about halfway along our Front Line sector.

There the company signallers had fixed on to the breastwork a shutter, about fifteen inches by nine inches. It showed green till the connecting strings at the bottom of it were pulled, and then it showed white. Thus Morse letters could be sent. As on the previous "visual" day, no-answer messages were sent. We were able to read them quite easily, and the trial was a success. We had to keep very low and were somewhat cramped as we dare not move and give the position away. The Company sigs. could have used the disc, a smaller piece of apparatus, showing black when not being in use and white as the front was pulled down to make the letters. The operation ceased at dusk and the Lucas Signalling Lamp was not tried. There would have been a difficulty, the Company sigs. could not have aligned it on us for we could not reply to their call.

The Royal Flying Corps, of which we infantry men knew very little, were very anxious to improve methods of communicating with the infantry in attack the Somme battle had shown up some weaknesses. So the order came through that infantry signallers, in turn, should go to some aerodrome and be taken up in a plane that patrolled up and down the German Front Line. The idea was that our signaller would see the difficulty the observer had in looking at our signals when he was on the turn – there were always some seconds during which he had to take his eyes off our signals. Our linesman Fred was the first one sent; he was thrilled and emphasised the difficulty in keeping the eyes on the signals because, he said, the German ack-ack guns were firing all the time and the white puffs of smoke from the exploding shells were distracting. Unfortunately the scheme was dropped and no-one else had a chance to go up. We knew only from hearsay of pusher planes and tractor planes, D.H. Scouts, Bristols and the commander's streamers. In fact for the most of the winter we hardly ever saw a plane.

Quite an exciting day of sport followed the visual day. Someone on the Brigade Staff owned a couple of ferrets, Popsy and Wopsy. Our officers borrowed them for the day and they were brought to our H.Q. by the N.C.O. in charge of ferrets, who put one down a rat hole and then the other down another some distance away. Armed with borrowed entrenching tool handles, pick-axe handles and, of course, revolvers as a last resort, our officers stood by and bagged the rats as they left their holes. A good morning's sport was had and the good work was continued in the afternoon until, alas, Popsy failed to appear after no little time. The official war against the German had to mark time while all men at hand helped in the search for the missing ferret. When it was finally found, the "meet" dispersed; the rats were glad for there was no close season for them, or lice for that matter, and the N.C.O. in charge of the ferrets too was happy. Back at the Brigade H.Q., would he have had to face a charge of neglect, loss of rat warfare weapons, or failure to return to stores the animals in his care? What a lovely war! Tallyho!

Most of the officers' dugouts, whether they were in the Front Line, reserve or support, had pinned on the walls some form of picture. Some favourites were the front covers of *La Vie Parisienne* and sometimes early cartoons of Bruce Bairnsfather were on view. A second-lieutenant of the Scottish Rifles attached to our battalion was wounded during a trench-mortar shoot on the enemy's wire. Jerry, who had come out of his winter sleep and was a bit touchy, had retaliated very quickly with a few rounds from his whizz-bangs. A few days later whilst we were in Ridge Wood he had pasted the 20th Durhams of the 123 Brigade positioned in the adjoining sector on our left, causing many casualties and doing great damage to the Front Line, support line and communication trench. Revenge was demanded and preparations were made to give it. I was strolling about a few yards away from

Battalion H.Q. in the wood at about six in the evening when I heard Sgt. Jim Dale calling out, "On parade all headquarters!" I could easily have remained in the dim recesses of the wood but I decided to go on parade. We were ordered to put on our equipment, put our gas masks at the alert and sling our rifles. A special fatigue was in the offing. We were taken to a trench, a mortar dump, and each of us was given a sixty pound mortar with iron carrying bar. The going was good as far as the Brasserie, from which we followed the usual way to the P. and O. trench. It was harder work now as we followed that trench, dodging the telephone wires, keeping the slung rifle in position and watching our footsteps where the duckboards were anything but whole. Suddenly we came to a large hole in the trench and realised that forward of it much damage had been done. Our leader gave the order to get out on top and leave the shelter of what remained of the comm. trench. It was almost dark by now as we struggled along over broken ground to the Durham's support trench, where we dumped our burdens. We returned the same way but more quickly and how we were not seen by Jerry I do not know. The next morning at eight o'clock Jerry received a dose of his own medicine but I do not think that his P.B.I. suffered much in consequence, for they would be safe in better dugouts than ours, and probably further back than the Front Line.

During that same spell in the wood the telephone line to Advanced Brigade Headquarters went "dis" and it was our responsibility to repair it. L/Cpl. Mac, Fossie (Walter Foster) and I set off to see to it. Every twenty yards we tested the line and had almost reached the ruined buildings at Bardenburg when we found the break. After repairing it and checking with both Advanced Brigade and our own battalion signals, we strolled round the ruins. I found there a light brown hafted knite complete with hook, corkscrew, blades, etc. No-one claimed it and I put it in my pocket. Not many days passed before I realised that I had lost it I suspected that someone had "won" it for, a month later, when needing a knife, one of the new draft handed me one just like the one I had lost except for the initials "J.R." printed on the haft, to which he drew my attention with a disarming smile. Was it the knife I had found and had now lost?

Our numbers in the companies had been increased by the drafts we received from Sheerness and also by some of the originals who had served on the transport. When our numbers were very low immediately after our great losses on the Somme, it had been decided that instead of having one man per horse or mule on the transport, one man should look after two animals and the odd man out be returned to his company for duties with it. We felt sorry for them because they now had to learn much that had not been taught them on the square at Aldershot. Life was not so cushy for them now, we all looked forward to a cushy job, not a less cushy one. A very pleasing change the next time out at La Clytte was to see a football match. Though the ground of a field near Reninghelst was almost solid due to the cold weather, an enjoyable game took place between the sergeants and the officers, who won by the only goal scored.

February saw our lives mostly taken up with fatigues, route marching and training for we did not know what just then. There was little choice of routes for the marches: La Clytte-Reninghelst-Westoutre-Locre – passing through those places in that order but occasionally in the reverse order. These were main roads and sometimes we went a short way along second class roads and saw some of the well-known hills of the district – Mont Rouge, Mont Noir and Scherpenberg. We always proceeded away from the line and never went by way of Kemmel. The band would accompany us and play appropriate fast marches but our singing was not as happy, cheerful or rousing as it had been going up for the Somme Battle. Perhaps the songs were of a sadder type: *I want to go Home, Old soldiers never die, When this lousy war is over, If you want the old Battalion, Take me back to dear Old Blighty* and *Grousing, grousing, always blooming well grousing.* We were not fed up nor down hearted but disillusioned at not seeing the end of the war. Both sides had received a battering and it looked as if numbers and stamina would triumph in the end, but for which side? In our leisure time perhaps the most humorous discussion centred around the evergreen question, 'How long are you in for?' Someone would say "five years" and someone else, "ten years". The questioner would thereupon reply, "Lucky blighter, I'm in for the duration." Other questions were: "What did you do in the Great War, grandad – what will you answer to that?" With no ill-feeling whatever, the question: "When did you join up?" would be asked, and the usual replies shouted out: "Before you came up" or "Before you were ... " and the rest of the remark was left to the imagination. When the leg-pulling had ceased the men turned to playing games like brag, pontoon and even patience. The stakes when the two former were played were always low for nobody was wealthy. If funds were very low the games were still played – for love. Many were the sing-songs which I enjoyed as a listener, for I could not sing a note. At suitable moments the more quiet ones would turn to letter writing and perhaps draw out from the top left pocket of the tunic a photo of a dear one being thought of. Perhaps a more conscientious one would try to beg some oil and a bit of four-by-two to give his best friend (his rifle) a clean-up.

Towards the end of the second week in February, when the companies were occupied a great deal in working parties and fatigues both night and day, I had a very restless and painful night. Darkie insisted that I joined the sick parade in the morning and at nine o'clock an N.C.O. took me and four others to the sick hut near H.Q. In the meantime, most of the others had set off on fatigue, leaving behind mess orderlies and a few specialists. A high temperature gained me two days excused duty. On my return to that right hand corner of the wood where 'D' Company stayed I found that Jerry had sent over a few whizz-bangs – too late to catch many men – and had wounded one mess orderly. It was the only part of the wood that caught any shelling and I often wondered if his observers must have spotted some movement, or even the smoke from the cook house. I considered that I was lucky again to miss the danger, and more lucky still for, because of my being off colour, I was put on H.Q. for the next tour of the line. This was immediately after breakfast on Saturday, February 17th when we relieved the 26th Royal Fusilier (the Bankers), a very quiet relief without incident.

For the first time during our winter trench positions we had the 18th K.R.R.s immediately on our right with the roadway between us and a short piece of unoccupied trench. That particular Saturday morning just after eleven o'clock, Sammy Benson, a sniper of 'D' Company, was on duty at a periscope in a bay near the end of the P. and O. trench. The breastwork curved a little and Sammy could see a stretch of No Man's Land and a part of the German trench well to the right. Just at the moment he heard a shell explode near our reserve trench he saw a Jerry pop his head up above his trench and observe the shell explode. This happened a second time but Sam could do nothing about it because his fixed rifle was wrongly sighted as regards the Jerry. So he left his pal at the periscope and moved along the trench as far right as he thought would be almost opposite to the German. In that bay were two brothers of 'A' Company and they had seen nothing. Sam waited till the next shell came over and, sure enough, up popped the head of the Jerry, who was seen to be wearing a soft hat with a green band around it – an artillery officer? He was quickly down again below his parapet, but Sam noticed the spot and put his rifle carefully over the top and waited for the next shell and the consequent head of the enemy popping up. The next shell never came! The head did not pop up again – the registering was complete.

Sam returned to his own bay and at noon he and his pal were relieved. He made out his report of the incident and took it to the sniping officer who was in a dugout at H.Q. When he had got something to eat and had rested a while, the sniping officer came to him and said, "Come on, Benson. We'll seek the help of the Stokes Gun Section and go to the bay and give the Hun a few Stokes shells in return." However the retaliatory little shoot was never carried out for, just as the party reached the reserve trench, Jerry opened out, prompt at three o'clock. The snipers and the Stokes Gun party took refuge in a very deep dugout. The terrific bombardment struck part of the Front Line, Chicory Lane, the Redoubts, the M. and N. communication trench and that part of the 18th K.R.R. line adjoining ours. I was on duty at the telephone and switchboard in the orderly room at H.Q., rather thankful that I was there. The noise was terrific and slight earth tremors could be felt all the time of the strafe. Every kind of German battery gave us a sample of its fireworks, hour after hour without a break. We seemed to be the recipients of a Corps strafing. Every German battery of more than one front seemed to be directed on to us. Over came ten-point twos, five-nines, whizz-bangs, trench mortars, minnies, rifle grenades, etc, and so a ring of steel or fire was put round our sector except for our H.Qrs. and the P. and O. comm. trench. Such was the bombardment that we at H.Q. were cut off from all companies except the one of the left – 'D' Company – and it was not long before we found that all the telephone lines were "dis", ie. disconnected, having been smashed by shell fire. For four hours the murderous fire was kept up and how so many Yeomen in it came through was a miracle, fortunately every bullet and every piece of shrapnel did not find a billet. All heads in the area strafed were kept low and as many men as possible sought the refuge of dugouts or succeeded in moving to a safer area – the left sector. Fred Johnson, our lines man, happened to be wiring near the Front Line when the muck began to fly over Chicory Lane end. He dived into a fresh shell hole and lay flat through the whole bombardment. He saw a minnie land not far away and lift a lump of the trench away. In the orderly room some runners and I sat and hoped for the best for our comrades, for little news came through to us. The din was deafening and alarming and stray shells, few in number, dropped between us and the comm. trench, bursting at a safe distance. At five o'clock the Adjutant, the boy subaltern Eden, asked me to put him through to the Brigade Major. He was a little agitated and much concerned for the men and waited impatiently whilst the brigade signaller brought the B.M. to the phone (not till the Boy was already on the phone). He asked if it were possible to have some retaliation, for the men had already been subject to two hours' strafing; he asked if something could be done if only it meant a battery of eighteen pounders being used. The B.M. emphasised that no retaliation could be given and he could not give the reason for this apparent lack of feeling. Again, at six o'clock our young adjutant appealed to the B.M. for some retaliation. His language was more forceful this time, but it was to no avail – nothing could be done about it but a runner would be sent down next morning with a message explaining why no help could be given. Not much of a consolation. Although I had my headpiece on and overheard all the conversation, which I knew I had to keep secret, the others in the orderly room had a very good idea of the outcome of the talk between our Adjutant and the B.M. When our officer left the room we discussed the matter among ourselves and tried to reason why no help was to be given. We thought we knew that our divisional artillery could not be called upon to retaliate on German batteries outside their area, but that did not explain why our own divisional guns could not fire on to the Germans facing us. Whatever the reason our men had to grim and bear it. (P.B.I.).

Only three messages came through from Brigade and they were not important: one concerned a return that had not been sent in; a second was a reminder that empty cardboard butter containers had to be collected and sent in by way of the quartermaster's stores; the third was a reminder too that casualty returns were to be sent in at nine o'clock each morning. I was thankful that I was still at the phone on H.Q. and not with a company section.

Then, quite suddenly, at seven o'clock, the strafe ceased and the silence was uncanny. Our sergeant sent out all available signallers to help with the repair of the telephone lines under Linesman L/Cpl. MacGahey. The party took with them extra reels of wire, sticky tape and telephones for testing. I was told to stay on duty at the phone there in the orderly room. Runners began to come in with news. Tremendous damage had been done to breastworks and trenches, and repairs to them had already started. Gaps and holes were so large that much building up had to be done during the hours of darkness so that the enemy snipers would have no chance of bagging victims unable to have adequate protection. Work of all kinds went on all night and gradually, after many, many testings by the linesmen, I was through to all companies. Apparently, thanks to a heavy mist and the approach of dusk a party of Germans had crossed No Man's Land, undetected, by way of that road that crossed it to the very right of our sector, and captured five of the crew of the somewhat isolated machine gun. The sergeant, Frank, had set off for

H.Q. by request at two o'clock and had been delayed there and did not set off back till after the strafe started. He found he could not get through by Chicory Lane, had turned back and attempted to return to his gun by the P. and O. trench and the Front Line. He never got back and so was not taken prisoner with his crew. Of that crew, Frank Clarke lost two fingers before being captured and then marvelled that the Germans took him and his pals back across No Man's Land and down the German trenches without having to fear any shell fire from us.

Just after eight o'clock the next morning the promised runner came from the Brigade and I was still there and heard the C.O. and the Adjutant read the message. I gathered that no retaliation had been possible because of great changes in gun positions and the digging of many more gun sites; it was considered very important that the enemy had no idea of these changes, not only on our front but on a very broad front. The P.B.I. that felt the ferocity of the Bosche strafe would not know this as the sound of the enemy shells drowned any other sounds, even if any of ours had been passing over. The men on our eighteen pounders and those on the Belgian spit-fires must have wondered why they were not called upon to do anything. My thoughts went back to Plugstreet days when I had the authority to test our covering guns and learned that a shell for that purpose could not be spared, I wondered what the answer would have been if an officer had asked for retaliation, if we could have got through that night.

The Colonel and the Boy (Eden, now Adjutant) then discussed the bet they had made about our new Battle H.Q. near Sleepy Hollow. They decided that the Hun had not attempted to shell it and that the Boy had won the bet. Occasionally both the Royal Fusiliers and our Battalion had lit very small fires in an old disused support trench to draw Jerry's attention from where the new H.Q. was being built.

The casualty report was late in being sent off that morning. Only the "other ranks" suffered: seven killed, fourteen wounded and five missing. We did not know then, but the

18th K.R.Rs had twenty-one casualties. These numbers were incredibly small considering the hundreds of shells that must have fallen in such a comparatively small area. Two dud enemy heavies (ten-point twos) were found in our Front Line. The arrival of such shells there was a very unusual event because absolute accurate firing of them was impossible. There was always the danger of their falling short and landing in one's own lines. Fancy being "gun fodder" for a shell of that size! What were the thoughts of our lads during this strafe? Was it a Blighty one this time? Is it my turn at last? Has this shell got my number on it? Yet, some wag would come out with the well-known saying, "Where did that one go?" or "Ours or theirs?" but the shells that time had been all theirs.

Only those boys and men who lay cowering behind some sandbag erection or waited in the flimsy dugouts, expecting a direct hit, knew what thoughts passed through their minds. The optimist would be thinking, "Jerry's getting a similar pasting – or even more than he's giving us". The cheerful, happy grumbler at all times, probably a Geordie, would mutter aloud, "Where the h ... are our guns?" They're always b ... ... missing when they are wanted most." No panic at all. Fear, not terrifying fear, but just the worry of keeping one's body safe from being hit. The British Tommy had the innate characteristic of being able to stick it, no matter what the odds against him.

During the strafe the Reverend E. Sayer-Ellis had arrived at the headquarters, post haste from Brigade H.Q. and asked for a runner to be provided to take him to where the shelling was the worst. The Colonel said that he would not do such a thing and begged him to wait till all the shelling was over. His face showed deep signs of distress as he made his way into the Officers' Mess. As soon as the shelling ceased he went down the line to see his boys, to comfort the wounded and get their names and addresses so that he could write home for them. This Wesleyan padre of ours was a true Christian Soldier.

I was still on duty when the senior N.C.O. of the orderly room staff came in and ticked me off. I had let L/ Cpl. MacWilliam sleep through all the shelling when he, though he had not been given any orders, ought to have gone out on the lines of communication. Such a sound sleeper was he that he had not heard a single shell explode or been aware of the terrible din. Shortly afterwards he left us, transferred to the Royal Engineers Signal Section.

In January he had been sent to Brigade on a power buzzer course. This apparatus, new to us, was a kind of one-way telephone. It consisted of a sealed metal case in which were the batteries and coils. On the top of it were two terminals and a tapping key. It was used in the very Front Line, quite close to No Man's Land. To each terminal was fixed a wire, both of them earth wires, instead of one earth wire and one aerial wire. These wires were run into No Man's Land and their pins driven into the earth. In case of an emergency such as an enemy raid or an attack the S.O.S. signal was tapped out and Brigade picked it up. Evidently Mac, whilst on the course, asked the officer in charge if he could be transferred to the R.E. Signals and so, with his permission, the necessary application form was filled in. The stratagem worked and Mac (MacGahey) departed with our good wishes for we all knew that he would not have been permitted to apply to our Colonel and try for a transfer from our end. Eight months later I went on a signals course and had a far better chance of working that dodge, but I failed to take the opportunity.

At noon that Sunday I was relieved by L/Cpl. MacWilliam for he was the only signaller who had had any rest. I had done a spell of twenty-one hours at the orderly telephone and had been very busy all the time, testing and trying to get through to companies, and yet I did not feel tired. The work I had been doing was nothing like as tiring as the work the other signallers had been doing; following the lines (cables) in the dark, groping for breaks, climbing overbroken trenches. L/Cpl. MacGahey told me later that he had used up all his adhesive tape and that he had to use ordinary pieces of paper to insulate some of the joints of the repaired telephone lines.

On February 22nd, the battalion was relieved by the 26th R.F.s and withdrew to Chippewa Camp where we rested a lot, did some training, did only a few working parties, and so we had more rest in more comfortable quarters than usual. Yet I cannot recollect exactly whereabouts this camp was. From it we went to the Ouderdom baths, quite a luxury, with a hot shower followed by a cold douche. Clean underclothing was given out, but as usual this was a doubtful blessing because of the eggs of our insect pests in the seams.

We continued to change and change about with the Bankers and during an early March spell in the line we concentrated on rebuilding the Front Line to the right of Chicory Lane. When in Ridge Wood we provided working parties. The enemy was very quiet and so were we. Whilst snow was falling heavily on Spring Day, we left the line and marched to Steenvoorde where we were billeted in the various farm houses round about. The fortnight here was very pleasant and carefree. The men did a lot of training by companies and the signallers joined them on the days when an attack in open formation was practised over specially marked-out trenches. The Army commander inspected us on the 24th, the usual kind words, which we suspected had a hidden meaning the sort of parade we never did enjoy. We would sooner have done a route march or some other sort of training. We did enjoy the games that were laid on, joining in if we were competent enough or watching others compete. The 124 Brigade sports were held in the first week of April and the Yeomen did very well: three firsts for the relay runners, the cross country race, and the obstacle race. Our football team won the Brigade Tournament when it beat the 32nd Royal Fusiliers by 5 goals to 3 in the final.

Evenings were free and most men went into the town to the estaminets, cafés and even houses where eggs and chips could be purchased. On one of my visits, I bought a picture postcard of Steenvoorde showing the market place and the band stand. I wrote on it, after addressing it to my mother, "This is the market place of the town from which I am not far." Unfortunately on this occasion the name was cut off. How it came to be censored by an 'A' Company officer I do not know. In January he had been the temporary C.O. Perhaps the officers were all helping one another, perhaps there was a glut of letters to be seen to. (Captain E. Worsley of 'A' Company was now the temporary C.O.).

In our leisure hours in our billets, especially just before retiring for the night, many were the topics discussed and many were the rumours. Was it true that the Belgian battery fired a salvo when a relief was taking place? At night time when men were moving about behind Ridge Wood, were mysterious shots fired at them? Did some of the civilians lock up their water pumps and refuse to let Tommy have any water? These rumours were never taken seriously, unlike the superstition that something would befall the third man to light his cigarette from the same match.

We were all a bit sentimental and when someone said that from Cassel Hill top the white cliffs of Dover could be seen on any bright day, quite a number of us strolled the five miles there to see if it were true. We never did see the Silver Streak between France and Belgium and our own country, not even in our imaginations, but it was pleasant to think that Blighty was not so far off and we could gaze towards it and think what we liked. My mother wrote to tell me that on three occasions someone else had written "On Active

Service" on postcards I had sent and occasionally someone had inserted dots in the angles of the crosses I added at the end of my greetings. Tit-for-tat, we played about with field cards and some censor of our cards played about with them.

Rifleman Gerald Dennis, Aldershot
December 1915. (Source: Richard Frost)

Corporal Gerald V. Dennis
(C/12747), autumn 1917.
(Source: Richard Frost)

Duncombe Park (Source: Richard Frost)

Helmsley, North Yorkshire (Source: Richard Frost)

Sergeants' Mess, Aldershot 1916, Lieutenant-Colonel The Earl
of Feversham left centre. (Source: KRRC Association)

Second Lieutenant Anthony Eden
1916. (Source: KRRC Association).

'A' Company 21st K.R.R.C., Aldershot 1916. (Source: KRRC Association)

Rifleman Norman Carmichael.
(Source: Richard Frost)

Riflemen Herbert 'Bert' Rowsby
and Herbert 'Tom' Hore 1917.
(Source: Richard Frost)

Private Gerald V. Dennis (No. 50517) in his Cameron Highlanders uniform 1918. (Source: Richard Frost)

Anthony Eden during the unveiling of the Yeoman Rifle memorial plaque at Helmsley Visitor Centre 1935. (Source: Helmsley Visitor Centre)

Yeoman Rifles' Association Reunion, York 7 May 1949: Programme cartoons and caricatures. (Source: KRRC Association)

The Riley High School under twelve-and-a-half 'A' football team 1953–54.
Gerald Dennis is seated at the far right. (Source: Richard Frost)

Riley High School teaching staff c. 1960. Gerald Dennis is standing
in the back row, sixth from left. (Source: Richard Frost)

Helmsley 1991. L to R: Gerald Dennis, Lieutenant General Sir David House, Colonel Christopher Consett and Captain Sandy Fletcher. (Source: Richard Frost)

The King's Royal Rifle Corps
(THE YEOMAN RIFLES)

(Raised and commanded by the late
Lt. Col. the Earl of Feversham)

SERVICE of THANKSGIVING and COMMEMORATION

for the lives of all Yeoman Riflemen
(from the first who gave their lives on
1st June 1916 at Ploegsteert Wood, Flanders

C/12966 Rfmn J.W.Collier, Helmsley
C/12300 Rfmn V.G.Hickes, Scackleton
R/15612 Sgt R.Seward, Birkenhead

to the last, Gerald V.Dennis, who died at Hull,
5th December 1993, aged 98, and whose ashes
have this day been scattered in
Duncombe Park)

To be held in

All Saints' Church, Helmsley

at 3 pm

Sunday, 18th September 1994

Gerald Dennis memorial programme 1994. (Source: Richard Frost)

137

A moving Last Post tribute to the late Gerald Dennis at Hull's
Northern Cemetery. (Source: Richard Frost)

As per his wishes, Gerald's ashes are deposited at Duncombe Park. (Source: Richard Frost)

8

Messines Ridge – Preparation for, and attack

O n April 6th, 1917, which was Good Friday, the Battalion paraded in the cobbled square of Steenvoorde, marched off towards the line and arrived at Dickebusch, where we went into billets being in reserve to the 122 Brigade which was holding the St. Eloi sector. Their main communication trenches were Middlesex Lane and Crater Lane. On the way up an interesting piece of news spread from 'A' Company leading through 'B' and 'C' Companies to 'D' Company – that the United States of America had declared war on Germany the previous day. Just a buzz of wonder and surprise, certainly not pleasure, stirred the ranks. What had caused the President and his followers to change heart, for many of us thought the Yanks did not like us.

Every day and night the battalion provided over four hundred men for working parties repairing trenches, digging trenches for telephone cables, replacing damaged duckboards, etc., all work and some sleep for six days. Then our brigade took over that St. Eloi sector, but only our three other battalions went into the Front Line trenches – we still carried on with the working parties from Dickebusch till the end of the month. A railway line now ran as far as Dickebusch Lake and on three occasions at dusk a train drew up with a heavy gun on an extended waggon. It was a naval gun manned by some Royal Marines. We loved to watch the barrel rise into the air and a shell leave the barrel for the enemy lines – backward areas. No more than fifteen shells were fired in an evening and then off went the train. We marvelled that during our stay in the neighbourhood no retaliation came 'A' Company and 'B' Company remained at Dickebusch for a further three days and the other two companies moved to Micmac Camp, situated down the road that ran from near Hallebast Corner to Ouderdom. Opposite to it, civilian women still lived in the few scattered houses.

Two officers, wounded earlier, returned to the battalion – Captain Patch W. and 2nd L/t.Waldy, a popular 'C' Company sub. I did no fatigues at Micmac Camp because I was on H.Q. and doing signalling duties, and thus had a fair amount of spare time. I decided to do something about my broken rimless glasses, damaged on the Somme. I had not gone "sick" because of them, for I did not want to leave the old battalion. As it was obvious that we were leaving the line I took the chance of packing them up, wrapped in four-by-two and in a strong piece of brown paper I saw my Company Officer and explained to him that nothing of information about the battalion was included, only my name and address and a request for the repair to be done. I had also included either ten or five francs, I have forgotten which, for the cost of repair and postage. A week later I received the repaired glasses together with my change, a one shilling postal order. I wrote and thanked the opticians, Prouts from my home city, and gave them my custom after the war.

Lazing one very fine afternoon outside the signallers' tent on my groundsheet, I gazed upwards at a very blue sky dotted with lovely white, fluffy-looking clouds. In the distance beyond the line the German observation balloons were up and suddenly out of one cloud dashed an R.F.C. plane. The enemy balloon went up in flames and our plane flew into another cloud. Out it darted again, and another balloon went up in flames. Seven times in all did this brave R.F.C. pilot destroy enemy balloons before flying back across our lines to safety. It looked so easy and the Germans had done nothing to prevent it. I wondered why. Within twenty-four hours I got the answer, for the very next afternoon a German plane did exactly the same to the same number of our balloons, and got away with it. Why no evasive action was taken by either side, I do not know.

Many of the men started a new hobby, a souvenir collecting of a different kind. They obtained a cloth belt about three inches broad and fixed in it different cap badges from other units. The belt was worn immediately above the trousers. It became a mania with some of them as they tried to see who would be the first to get his belt completely covered with badges. All Front Line Tommies were very friendly towards one another and this idea helped all to recognise a man's unit by his badge.

After dinner, for which I had volunteered to be the mess orderly, I could not help pondering on the events of the last twenty-four hours. Had the support battalion in Ridge Wood "stood to" and had the reserve battalion at Murrumbidgee Camp at La Clytte been ordered to be ready in case Jerry over ran our Front Line? Only nine days earlier when the battalion was in the Front Line and I was with the left company I had sent a message to H.Q. reporting for the sniper section that a party of Jerries was working out in the open near Wytschaete – at least fifty of them as seen by sniper-observer Sammy Benson. Nothing was done although the message was sent on to the artillery. The next morning I sent a similar message and it was not till the third report that four shells were sent over and the party scattered. But there was no comparison between that incident and the strafe we had suffered without any retaliation. Our guns had not been able to oblige the request for help. For a few months, I was baffled.

Between our H.Q.s and Sleepy Hollow could be seen a wire strung across some trees and another wire leading down from it to a hut half hidden by trees. L/Cpl. MacGahey and I ventured that way one night pretending that we were following our telephones and testing them. We found three R.E.s in the hut with a wireless set and they let us see how they worked the set. We were thrilled and wished that we had joined such a section.

Our smartest in appearance signaller and very quick at visual work was a real old soldier who had joined us in the latest draft. He had been in the 1st Battalion and had seen service in India and was very precise in all he did. He had been wounded three times – a Mons man. His parents had been killed in one of the first bombing raids on London and Blighty seemed to have no home for him. He was one of the unfortunates that never received any mail. He was an expert at signalling and a good soldier in general. We all liked him, except the N.C.O. who had not as yet seen the line. Someone finally got him a transfer to the R.E. signals, though I doubt whether he wanted to leave the K.R.R.s.

Four days of perfect peace followed on our front; the only shells we heard were the German ones each evening trying to find the transport as it brought the rations up, and the only signs of war were the Very Lights that our opponents sent up at frequent intervals during the night. There always seemed something doing Ypres way and Armentiéres way.

Our dugout was near the beginning of the H.Q. line and its doorway faced the line, a duckboard track separating it from the breastwork protection. It was fairly roomy and a mere shelter against the elements but had no strength against shell fire. Our regular meals were cooked by Dick Pallister and Bricky in a cook house some distance away. They did their best for us, concocting dishes out of bully beef, biscuits, pork and beans. The meals were never heavy and the mess orderly for the day always found it hard to share out fairly what there was amongst us; there was never any spare. The man at the end of the queue and the mess orderly shared the dip in the morning bacon dixie. The dishes sometimes had fancy names like rissoles, but we knew their contents to be bully beef and biscuits. "Afters" at dinner time could be made from treacle and biscuits, crushed biscuits and raisins boiled in a cloth or may be rice with floating raisins. We enjoyed the meals for we were nearly all young some still growing and, thanks to the fresh air, we had keen appetites. When the tea tasted like poison, we knew that it had been dosed with salts and that the cooks had obeyed orders in doing so. Actually we lived on very little as the rations were never excessive.

When time hung a little too heavily on our hands, we used to see who could play about with a field card, make up the strangest message on it by crossing out words or letters here and there. On one of these occasions, unknown to most of us, one signaller sent a field card to his pal. It was handed in, perhaps censored, and gassed through the usual channels and duly arrived back to the battalion and the pal. The recipient's leg was pulled perhaps by someone asking him, "Have you received your registered card yet, there's a piano in it." Really there was very little to write about when we wrote to Blighty, except about the weather, but men would sit down, take up pencil and paper and pretend to be writing home and reading out what they had written. "Dear Mother, it's a b … ." (a north countryman), or "Dear Mother, I am sending you five shillings, but not this week. Please send me ten." They raised a laugh and so the fun was worth it.

From Micmac Camp we went further back to Alberta Camp on the road between Reninghelst and Westoutre, already known to us. On May 6th, to celebrate the anniversary of the arrival of the battalion in France, a tea, a concert and a play were given in the large Y.M.C.A. concert hall in Reninghelst. For the tea, a substantial one and more like the old Blighty teas, we paid the equivalent of six pence and then queued early for the enjoyment that was to follow. The concert hall was shaped like a large capital letter 'T'. The top cross piece was the refreshment room and the longer down piece the concert hall. Our very own Divisional Concert Party provided the entertainment and it was called "The Crumps". All Tommies knew the sound of enemy shells exploding. Each shell, whether known as a coal-box, a black Maria, a woolly bear, a Jack Johnson or just a nine-point five, seemed to say "cr … ump". The party had at least thirteen members, including two officers, five N.C.O.s, four privates, one gunner and Private Purkiss, the feminine lead, all of the 41st Division. Each of them was doing his bit in a splendid way and probably thought they were very lucky to have what seemed a jammy job. In an emergency they could be called upon to do stretcher-bearer duties. They were dressed somewhat like the pierrots at the seaside before the war – black caps, ruffs, jackets with wide cuffs and three large white pompoms where the buttons would be, wide trousers and a large black pom-pom on each shoe. The girl wore a dark skirt and blouse with similar pompoms. The programme was of the musical variety, a mixture of songs, jokes and a play, usually starting off with the dance and song and ending with the party's special farewell number.

One of the great hits of the evening was a duet between a boy and "the girl" called "If you were the only girl in the world". It had great appeal to all of us. It may not have had the setting of The Bing Boys with George Robey and Violet Loraine, but it deserved and received rapturous applause. The farce that followed *A Sister to Assister* had us in stitches. At the end of the programme, the hall resounded with the cheers from hundreds of Tommies who had not had such a relaxed time for ages. At each performance The Crumps gave a different playor sketch from their repertoire: *Telling the Tale* (one officer and an N.C.O.), *Glad Eyes* (an officer, four other ranks and, of course, the "girl"), *A Seaside Burlesque* (three other ranks and the "girl") – two scenes, *Some Girl* (Miss V. de Vierstraate, the "girl"), *The Drums of Oude* – a dramatic Indian episode given in three scenes; *The Attempted Murder, The Farewell* and *United at Last*.(2 officers, 3 other ranks and the "girl"), *On the Staff or How Temporary-Major Harry Tate Won the D.S.O.* (featuring two officers, three other ranks and the "girl") in two scenes: *The Arrival of a Lady Upsets the Major* and *The Manor Captures a Hun Spy and wins the D.S.O.* Some of the audience managed to get a programme entitled *"The Crumps Play Pictorial", a souvenir of the 41st Divisional Concert Party.* (Instead of "41st", the Divisional sign, a square divided diagonally top left corner to bottom right corner. The Foreword read:

"Trench Magazines" we know: regimental journals we have heard of: but here we believe is the pioneer "Play Pictorial" of the Just-behind-the Front area. In this edition "The Crumps" record their initial successes: we have already made great preparations for the binding of subsequent numbers into volumes. Have we not the tip straight from Captain Bairnsfather, that the first seven years of this wonderful war are going to be the worst, and after that every fourteenth? Be patient then, O Public! For if, during the next four years, the appearance of this pioneer among periodicals is spasmodic, we can at least promise a more steady stream through the following thirteen. And what choicer souvenir of the Great War could one wish to possess than serried row on serried row of volumes, crammed full of pleasurable memories?

We are fully aware of the magnitude of our venture, and are equally sure of its success. With great foresight therefore we have made huge contracts with the R.E.s for the manufacture of bookshelves to contain this mass of pictorial enjoyment. The bookshelves will in themselves be a souvenir, for frames and biscuit boxes play a prominent part in their unique design. It has also been suggested that bully beef tins could be used with effect as a border decoration. Orders will receive immediate attention. ORDER EARLY AND AVOID THE CRUSH. THE EDITOR."

During our fourteen days' stay at Alberta Camp, 'A' and 'B' Companies went on working parties to the line whilst 'C' and 'D' Companies did training exercises. The next day the companies changed over, and so on. At long last, how wonderful it was to be able to sleep without one's boots on, night after night. Whale oil treatment had ended but a few men suffered from trench feet and left the battalion. Again, I missed all the working parties because all the signallers were either learning to use the new type of signalling panel for liaison with aeroplanes or moving in front of advancing company men to represent a creeping barrage; at times stationary until an imaginary barrage lifted.

On Thursday, May 17th, the 10th Royal West Kents of the 123 Brigade relieved us and we marched to a site quite near to Poperinghe and slept the night in bivvies. The next morning we entrained at "Pop" and after a four hour journey we detrained at Watten, from where we marched to Eperlecques, a beautiful, unspoilt village in lovely surroundings with not a sign or any sound of war. My billet was on the very outskirts in a pretty lane at the bottom of a slope. A farm building nearby was the signal office and outside was a visual station in touch with Brigade H.Q., in a chateau at the top of the hill. Our telescope was aligned so that we could observe signals, flag or lamp by day and sometimes lamp by night. All around us were valleys, hills, woods, etc, excellent ground for training for battle.

As it was deemed that we may have become rusty in the use of our rifles, all men were marched to a rifle range on the first Sunday to do some firing and grenade practice. All specialists – signallers, bombers, machine gunners, stretcher-bearers and transport men – had to join their companies and take part. I was in the first group of five 'D' Company men to get down to fire and scored five bulls straightaway. When I fell out to the rear, other men asked to borrow my rifle, my trusted 8381 T. I lent it out on the condition that the borrower gave it a pull-through at once after using it. That was done and our company had some good shots, there being no doubt that my rifle was perfect, with or without sword-bayonet attached. I had similar good results in all the shoots that day. Tragedy did strike in another corner of the range. A party of men were practising with a new type of rifle grenade. They were lying on the ground and firing up some rising ground. Some stretcher-bearers were taking cover at the side of a sunken road about two hundred yards to the rear. Whilst the firing was going on some French girls from the village were advancing towards the firing party and getting too close as they tried to sell the men some apples. The stretcher-bearers rose up and came forward to get the girls to come away from the danger when suddenly a grenade exploded prematurely. It had gone straight up into the air and dropped straight down onto the party. One man was killed and an officer and eight other ranks were wounded. No harm befell the fruit sellers.

For the next ten weekdays, all the battalion except the transport men turned out to take part in offensive training for battle. The ground practised on consisted for five or six fields completely devoid of crops and rising from a low valley. Everytime about six hours were taken in moving from the dip up to the rising ground. Every movement was timed as the signallers led the way waving flags and representing a barrage. Men were "wounded" or "killed" and stretcher-bearers saw to them We had no doubt now that some part of the Salient was to be attacked – we were going to take some of that high ground that Jerry had held and looked down on us from. Actually, maps showing the section that the 41st Division, and of course other divisions, had already been printed on May 5th. Three mornings not long after midnight we paraded and set off for the practice ground and started our "attack" before dawn. Everything was done to make us perfect and to understand the nature of the task. It would be up to us. The second Sunday at Eperlecques was free from all work for the company men. As many as could asked for a passout to St. Omer, to where scores of eager Tommies set off straight after dinner, fit and able to walk the five miles or thereabouts each way. Of course, some signallers had to do afternoon and evening duty so I offered to do the two hours on for any of my pals who wished to go to St. Omer. Two accepted my offer with the result that I did a spell of six hours, two for myself and four for them. It was a light task as we had merely to man the visual station in case of a call. I had bought some picture postcards in Eperlecques and spent some of my time with my correspondence. I sent three views of St. Omer home: one of the New Bridge and the railway station – front view; one of the Cattle Market – a large cobbled space with chains on posts round it; and the New Bridge – side-view with tow path.

My two friends had enjoyed themselves very much. They had arrived at the park in St Omer just as a band began to play and stayed some time listening to them, as did many civilians. It reminded them very much of the Thursday nights in a part in their own home city when a local band played waltzes, marches and the latest jazz music. After tea in one of the many cafes they went to investigate the "red lamp". Curiosity drove them and the others to see for themselves what sort of an establishment it was. Near the cathedral they found

MESSAGE

.... Division
(Map reference or Mark on
Map at Back.)

1. My Company has reached ....
   Platoon
2. My Company is at .... and is consolidating
   Platoon
3. My Company is at .... and has consolidated
   Platoon
4. Am held up by M.G. at ....

Legend

5. I need:– Amunition   NN   Machine Gun ....
            Bombs   XX   Anti Tank Empt ....
            Rifle Grenades GG   Strong Point ....
            Water   WW   Wire ....
            Very Lights   VV   (in red)
            Stokes Shells YY

6. Counter attack forming up at ....

                                                        Right
7. I am in touch with .... on   at ....
                                                        Left

8. I am not in touch with .... on

                                                        Right
9. I am being shelled from ....
                                                        Left

10. I estimate my present strength at .... rifles

                Battery   ....
11. Hostile   Machine Gun   active at   ....
                Trench Mortar   ....

    Time .... m.   Name   ....
    Date ....   Platoon   ....
                                   Company ....
                                   Battalion   ....

No. 4. Its ground floor was an estaminet so they entered and bought a drink, at the same time noticing what they could. They spotted "madame" at the far end, seated at a counter against a door near some stairs. Clients went that way but my friends and two others of their own company came away as soon as they had finished their drinks. They made a lot of fun out of their visit, hadn't we all heard of such places, but had never been near one.

The good time was coming to an end: the carefree days, the peaceful surroundings, the relaxation and freedom from strain had banished the lines from our faces and made us forget the war, even though we now knew that battle lay ahead. The company men especially deserved the rest they got. They, and in particular the younger members of the battalion, had for many months done work to which they were not accustomed – using pick-axes and shovels, hugging duckboards and 'A' frames about, rebuilding trenches and dugouts, and all in good spirits. They had benefited from the change and even resumed singing on the marches to and from the battle area – rousing, cheerful songs; the sad ones back in the background.

On Thursday the last day of May, we left the quiet of Eperlecques in full pack and marched by way of Watten to Ameke. We did about three miles an hour with the usual ten minutes break per hour and a longer break at about five o'clock in order to eat the rest of our daily rations. The next morning we entrained and went by way of St. Omer to "Pop", crossing the Franco-Belgium border just south of Abeele. The march to Micmac Camp was somewhat tiring but the welcoming dinner prepared by the cooks in their field kitchens was much appreciated. Poor company men – working parties to the line started immediately and continued every day for the next three days. I, fortunately, was on H.Q. on signalling duty and had a much easier time. Off duty I had a good look round the district because it was obvious that some changes had taken place. I strolled in the direction of Ouderdom and beyond to Vlamertinghe on the main Pop-Ypres road: because of increased activity all round and heavy shelling I hastened back. The civilian houses opposite the camp were deserted and I gathered that all such civilians within two miles of the line had been evacuated to other parts further from the front. The Belgian battery near Gordon Farm had been replaced by one of our eighteen pounder batteries, and the green field was no longer like a lawn but was already dotted with shell holes. A large trench mortar dump not so far away from the farm had gone up into the air and a tremendous hole was left in its place. The occupants of Gordon Farm, too, had gone and this, together with the change in the green field and the dump of trench mortars being exploded, gave rise to more serious rumours.

It was said that the parents had been in touch with the Germans all the time and were spies, that the father and son had been shot – a fate they appeared to have deserved – but the mother and daughter had been spared because of the help they had given to the Canadian troops who suffered so much during the first gas attack Ypres way.

More and more military traffic was using the roads and railways at Reninghelst and the Crumps were still giving their concerts, for no shells had landed on the town. Just a year and two weeks later when I was a kilted Jock and my new battalion was marching through Wallon Cappel I saw high on a wall a poster for the Crumps. Three days later from the camp where we were billeted I got a pass-out to Wallon Cappel and there I saw seven of t'owd lads; runner Bob Iley and signallers Bruce, Wakeling, Rhodes, Ramsden, Scruff and Atti. What a long natter we had and how they laughed at my new rig-out!

Two companies at a time were marched to Locre to see a large scale model of Messines Ridge and the section that our division was to attack was pointed out to us and the various physical features explained. We saw the resemblance between it and the ground that we had been practising on at Eperlecques, but on the model were shown: machine gun emplacements, strong points, wire and anti-tank emplacements. Such features as a sunken road, farm buildings, estaminets, woods, and a signal station, in fact anything enemy was shown. No wonder a lot of civilians had been moved further back from the front.

At mid-morning on the Tuesday the expected move forward took place. Two of our companies relieved the 23rd Middlesex Bn. in the St. Eloi sector taking over the front and reserve lines – the communication trenches were Crater Lane and Middlesex Lane. I was allocated to H.Q. whilst my company and 'C' Company went in to General Reserve near Ridge Wood.

Our Headquarters occupied a Canadian sap in which I believe was the support line and to enter it we had to descend quite a number of steps, which brought us into a fairly high passageway. The signal office was down here, temporarily given a corner off the passage – the safest office I had ever been in so far. There was just room for two men to do the duty spell, and the rest of us spent our time towards the top, with some of the staff at the top as an extra guard for the sap head.

The next day, Wednesday, our artillery really bombarded Jerry very heavily both morning and afternoon but he did not retaliate then, despite the terrific hammering he was getting. That night it was our turn to be heavily thrashed, so much so that S.O.S. rockets were fired in the Front Line and our protective barrage prevented the Germans reaching our Front Line. Although some of our two companies there had been withdrawn into deep St. Eloi dugouts, we suffered ten casualties, of which one officer and two other ranks were killed. Fortunately this enemy activity, due to his having the wind up, probably suspicious that something was brewing on our side of the line, ceased before midnight. During the strafe the signallers had received their orders and were split into two groups – one party with the signals officer and a corporal and six signallers were to form upon the extreme right of the battalion, and the other party, with a sergeant, two lance-corporals and five signallers, were to go over the top on the extreme left. I was in the latter party and had volunteered with Bill Drake to take charge of the signalling panel for communicating with our aircraft. Someone else offered to carry the large white semi-circle, which denoted that we were a battalion and he was to keep close to me. The Brigade positional sign was a large three-quarters of a circle made from canvas. I also carried my two flags, one blue and the other white with blue diagonal stripe tied to my rifle. Others had telephones, reels of Japanese wire, earth pins, etc. There came into my possession one of the special maps of the Front Lines as far as the 41st Division was concerned; of the thirteen inches by eight inches of map, only a small area three and a half inches by nine was devoted to showing the lines either side of St. Eloi. The position of four old craters and the mound in No Man's Land in front of St Eloi were shown. All the rest of the map showed every trench, all the wire, farms, roads, etc. of the German sector. I noticed that all the enemy trenches began with the letter 'O'. A real work of art and the result of aeroplane photography. It was dated 15-5-17, 41st Division and was printed by No.2 Advanced Section A.P. @ S.S. 8/5. Half of the other side was for use of an officer wishing to send back information about the attack and its progress. Probably each officer had a number of these maps and would send back a runner with the necessary information about the stages of the attack. Such particulars filled in on the map front would be easier for the officer.

We were told about the barrages, their movings and their pauses, quite understood by the signallers who with their flags waving had acted as barrages up at Eperlecques. The new information we got was that the first pause would be at the red line and the second at the blue line, followed later in the day at the black line. Then we dressed up, loading ourselves with two hundred extra rounds of ammunition, rifle, etc, spades or shovels and telephone gear. We rubbed the goggles of our respirators with anti-dim and put the respirators on at the alert position and waited outside the sap. We waited and those minutes seemed like hours. The time dragged as we did not realise why we stood there. Then at last at about one in the morning guides appeared to lead us to our assembly positions. The officers' section of signallers went off to the right to Middlesex Lane whilst our party went left down Crater Lane. A few yards before we reached the Front Line we were led over the top of the communication trench and spaced out in the open, parallel and just behind our own Front Line. All had gone according to plan – we were in our assembly positions by 2 a.m., just an hour and ten minutes to wait for zero hour. This waiting period was the worst time of all. Where possible, we each occupied a shell hole, we all kept low and quiet. A whisper was possible, but most of us did not want to give anything away. Next to me was the one of the originals who had never ventured thus far and who had never been over the top. I kept wondering how he felt because in action under these circumstances could be scaring. At intervals one of Jerry's sentries would send up a Very Light and on only one occasion a salvo of Jerry shells flew over on the right. Then the stillness was broken as someone touched me on the shoulder and said, "Rum ration up. Dish it out." It ought to have come up before midnight but the shelling by the enemy of the back areas had delayed our transport. I suppose someone thought it should still be issued to help us to keep the cold out. What a joke, that I should be handed a jar of rum, S.R.D. I took the cork out and the pop seemed to be like the explosion of a shell. I crawled to the man on my left and started to pour his ration into his mug-whether it was his hand shaking whilst holding his mug to the neck of the jar, or my hand shaking as I held the jar, I failed to know, but with many of the men not bothering and the awkwardness of the job, I packed in, replacing the cork and I dumped the jar. This was the only occasion so far that the rum ration had come up so late just before an attack. That little interlude had helped to pass some time and distracted our minds from the business in hand; it was now a few minutes before three o'clock.

The darkness was not so intense now and was giving way to the approach of the dawn. Many anxious glances were given to watches and also towards Jerry's lines. More coloured lights sailed into the air. Did he suspect, or was he just windy? We really did not need to check with our watches for at 3.10 a.m. our senses of sight and hearing were suddenly assailed with the most terrific din and a glorious spectacle. Our bodies rolled like snakes' as the earth shook and we stumbled to our feet. This was it. Not far to our left two great flashes of light and flame split the air and the flashes from our guns rivalled the Northern Lights. It was said that if all the guns on this front were put together they would be wheel to wheel for nine miles. Eighteen mines went off together on this front, one a few seconds later. "That's the stuff to give 'em," thought our troops.

Shells of all sizes were screaming over simultaneously; in parts the sky was a vivid red for a few seconds as the mines went up. We were moving, Bill Drake and I hugging the aeroplane signalling panel. The noise was deafening, so much so that if the enemy were retaliating it was impossible to pick out his shells and, to my great surprise, I did not hear the old rat-tat-a-tat of the German machine guns. Had the answer been found at last how to silence them? Then it seemed to me, having become accustomed to the din, that there was no noise – I was so busy getting on with the job at hand. It was a bit awkward getting across our own Front Line with the panel and my attention was diverted to the man unfamiliar with the trenches. He thought that we had reached the German front line. I quickly pointed out to him the way the fire-step faced and then explained to him that we had two lots of wire to cross before reaching Jerry's front line. Both lots of wire proved no obstacle, they were flattened – the shell holes were more of a problem. My "learner' would have it that we had reached the first objective and I had to point out to him that we hadn't captured much and that we had to gain his support and reserve lines plus a bit more. I gave up wasting my time and pressed on, after casting a glance at two square openings some few feet apart, expecting some Jerries to come out. So far there was an absence of them.

We moved forward just as slowly as we had been shown when practising for the stunt, the barrage in front of us leading the way. We passed the support line and did see some pale grey figures hurrying through our ranks with their hands up. As we neared the enemy reserve line I felt the panel drop and so I looked to my left to see Bill holding one hand and saying "I'm hit." I dropped my end of the panel, examined Bill's hand, which was bleeding profusely, took his field dressing out of its little pocket at the inside corner of his tunic and applied it to his injured hand.

"Lucky blighter," were my words to him as he set off back to find a first aid post or a field dressing station. I don't suppose any of us heard the enemy shell that did the damage, though someone might have seen an explosion, or perhaps we had got rather too near our own barrage and a piece of shrapnel had come our way. I doubt it. On reaching the enemy reserve line more of the enemy appeared with their hands up and looking very scared indeed. They had known what heavy shelling was for some time and the long wait for our attack had left its mark on them and no doubt also they had felt the tremor of the earth when the mines went up . We did not worry about them for our moppers-up would take them in hand. Our first pause came shortly afterwards, and another signaller and I laid out the panel and a third one put down our battalion sign, just in case an aeroplane came to investigate our progress so far.

All had gone well, according to plan and right on time. Much to my surprise we had reached the Red Line, just where a disabled tank lay, so I had moved away from it when the panel was set up. I knew that the tank would probably draw fire so it was better to give it a miss and get away from it. Besides, I knew also that, if Jerry observers spotted our battalion sign and panel, we would draw some fire. I was glad that at this stage we did not have to use it, for I was to be the one, standing up, who would have to send the message without any cover whatever. Company men spent their time digging in and making a strong point, consolidating our gains. Two signallers had safely run out a line of enamelled wire, joined up the phone and fixed a piece of wire from "earth" to the earth pin in the ground. We were through to the Advanced Brigade Section, which consisted of two R.E.s, one a sergeant, and mostly of Battalion signallers on loan; one of these was Pip. At this stage we learned that we had taken eighty prisoners.

The barrage lifted and moved on so we moved forward. Right on eight o'clock as planned, the Blue Line was captured without any opposition. Our shells had pulverised all the enemy lines, and there was evidence that these had been numerous. Our lines of defence were paltry compared with the German ones. Obviously the Germans, conquerors of that part of Belgium, took whatever land they needed and dug scores of trenches in depth, whilst we, in consideration for the native farmers, used the least we could. Nevertheless the shelling had been so intense that trenches, roads, buildings, etc. had all disappeared. On the left the

26th Royal Fusiliers had captured the well-defended sunken road called the Dammstrasse, without opposition.

Again we dug in and made strong points. I had understood that at ten o'clock another battalion would pass through us and continue with the attack. I was wrong but evidently our guns, or some of them, were moving forward whilst other guns continued to keep up the barrage. We stood up and looked towards the enemy and became very frustrated because we saw at about a thousand yards ahead some Jerries bringing forward horses in order to take away some light guns just at the front edge of a small wood. I was ordered to send back a message by Bag. We seemed to be on top of a ridge then the ground sloped a little downwards before rising again to the wood. I was on the skyline so I used my blue flag and sent in morse "H H". I lowered the flag then raised it again and sent once more "H H" and proceeded thus quite a number of times. The code letters meant "lengthen your range", and the message would, we hoped, be transmitted to the artillery. This signalling action must have been a fine sight to the signallers at Brigade H.Q.rs. because it would be a very uncommon sight: a visual success without interruption from the enemy in the midst of a battle. To make sure that the message had got through I was sent back to our telephone in the Red Line with two purposes; one to send the H H message by phone, and secondly, having done that, to see to a line being brought forward to the Blue Line and the phone set up there. Nothing was done about those enemy guns, to our great disappointment.

Not long after my return to this last position, the other section of signallers joined up with us. We sat down and had a bite to eat. The enemy was recovering from the shock he had received and we became aware of some activity near an estaminet. At half-past three we advanced to deal with it and, thanks to very good work by our own machine gunners on the flanks, the enemy fled and the Black Line was captured and some fifty prisoners taken. Our machine gunners continued to harass the fleeing Germans and they had many casualties. Except for digging in again, our work was done. Everything had been done for the infantry that could be done to ease the task and, above all, to save casualties. How different from the Somme! We now realised why we had been unable to have retaliation some fifteen weeks ago when we had been severely strafed – besides keeping our gun positions a secret, our observers had been taping the position of the enemy guns. What splendid work had been done by the miners of our own country and the tunnellers of Australia, Canada and New Zealand.

With my mind being concentrated on what I had to do, I did not realise that we had some casualties, except Bill Drake. Our losses were indeed light, one officer and six other ranks killed and one officer and sixty-three other ranks wounded. The excitement had died down. Inaction followed the tremendous activity of the many hours earlier in the day; a feeling of light-heartedness took the place of our recent seriousness. Sentries were posted, machine guns at the ready and we waited for any counter-attack that may develop, but Jerry did not seem up to it – he had no eyes to see what our positions were and it was getting too late for him to do so. Those of us that had any left-over rations had a bite and a drink from our water bottles. The hours were dragging and darkness descended on the scene.

It was three o'clock in the morning when we were relieved. Only then did we realise how tired we were for we hadn't had any sleep for at least ninety hours and facing us was a weary trudge back of over two miles. The battalion had advanced more than a mile and a half. The ridge was a mass of shell holes, in fact every square yard had been struck by some size of shell. A tank officer came to our rescue for it was known that there was no real way back. He had

had laid down a very long stretch of white tape, along the crests of hundreds of shell holes, and we followed it back to where roads and old trenches of ours were recognisable.

We crossed the old front line near Crater Lane, skirted Voormezeele, crossed the road and stopped at Scottish Wood. Here was a camp that had been used regularly by the 123 Brigade. It lay in a similar position to Ridge Wood, being off the road that ran between the Brasserie and Ypres. We took off all our gear and were quite pleased to receive a warm welcome from our details and the battalion cooks – and what a spread awaited us, rather late in the day. Hot tea, plenty of bread and butter and ham! We watched in amazement as the waiters for the occasion cut slices of huge hams, Yorkshire hams without a doubt. Whilst this al fresco meal was being enjoyed, Red Cap P. and D. staff officers appeared on the scene and signified that we had to carry on with our meal. Only when we had finished and were still sitting down, quietly at last, did the senior general proclaim the usual words of thanks and appreciation of what we had done in the battle. Again, the usual hints of things to come. They departed to carry on their good work elsewhere and we rested quite a while. Later, the wag of the company translated for us the general's speech like this:

> Men of the Yeoman Rifles. You have done well and I know when the time comes again for you to extinguish yourselves, you will do so with the same determination and courage.

Loud applause, yet we spoke of General Plumer, the architect of the battle and the co-ordinator of all the services involved, with admiration and respect. He was of the infantry, not of the cavalry, nor the gunners, nor the R.E.s, and fully understood the trials of the P.B.I., for whom he had showed great concern; he was a soldier of great common sense so we gave the praise to him.

Later that evening one of my own friends, Johnny Watson, appeared on the scene after he had been missing for some hours. He was a machine gunner and, fed up with the inactivity the previous night, he had had a stroll round the Jerry lines and examined some of their dugouts, strong erections of concrete. Thus his pockets and haversack were laden with souvenirs such as photographs, German black bread, enemy soft caps, etc. He gave me a German Field Card which was about the same size as ours. On the reverse side, where the German soldier wrote his message, was a straight line almost as long as the card marked off in nine centimetres. What this was for I do not know. Also there was a dotted line for the date. On the reverse side on the right was the address to whom sent, lodgings, street and house number, and a circle for delivery time. On the left hand side was the senders military rank and name, dotted lines for battalion, company, division, battery, squadron and other particulars. How different from ours.

Fred Johnson, our linesman, had entered a German signal office and taken possession of a signalling lamp. Its box was about fifteen inches long, eight inches broad and eight inches deep. On the top were numerous keys and at the back many holes through which showed various coloured lamps. Any number of variations of coloured signals could be sent, a very useful instrument by which the pressing of one or more keys some coded message in coloured lights could be sent. The box also contained the batteries for working the lamp. It was too bulky a souvenir for me.

Leave. A most mysterious word. Perhaps because I was in a specialist section, I scarcely heard the word. We had been out in France thirteen months and all I knew was that one of

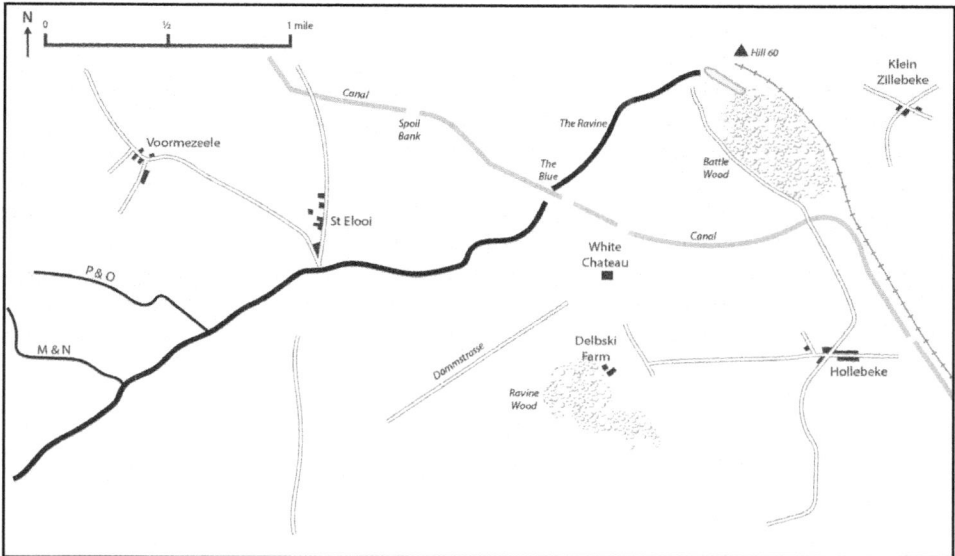

Map 5. Messines 1917

'C' Company, Jack Ward (whose home was in Fairfield Road, Bricknell Avenue in Hull) had been granted compassionate leave because of the serious illness of his father. He had been with the company a short time and then had been transferred to the Transport Section as saddler. Sometimes there was a whisper, "So-and-so is sweating on leave", and that was all.

As a result of our twelve months service out there, our originals now wore a blue chevron near the bottom of the left sleeve of their tunics. Pip P. had rejoined us from duty with Advanced Brigade signals and told us how he had read the message "H H" that I had sent by flag. He had sent off to his girl a field card just before the attack. On the address side of the field service post card was a warning: The address only to be written on this side. If anything else is added, the postcard will be destroyed. At the top of the other side were these words:

Nothing is to be written on this side except the date and signature of the sender. Sentences not required may be erased. If anything else is added the postcard will be destroyed.

> I am quite well.
> I have been admitted into hospital. erased
> sick and am going on well. erased
> letter dated 2nd June.
> I have received your telegram. erased
> parcel. erased Letter follows at the first opportunity.
> I have received no letter from you. erased
> lately. erased
> for a long time erased
> Signature only ... ...
> Date 7 erased 6th June, 1917
> 8 p.m. (added).

The field card was duly received by his girl and the date and time noted.

The last time that I had been on duty in the orderly room when on H.Q. a message came from Brigade stating that ten Military Medals would be awarded to our battalion for the forthcoming stunt. "Please have recommendations ready immediately afterwards." I pondered about this message as I kept it to myself. There was a saying "Medals come up with the rations." At last I could see the reason for this unfortunate saying. If, as on the Somme, we lost every officer but one in the action, how could a man be recommended? Only an officer could do so after seeing the brave action, and many a brave deed did go unrewarded, but an officer could bring to the notice of the C.O. any particular worthy action during the periods between battles, like bringing in a wounded man from No Man's Land, taking messages through shell fire, etc. Thus a man's award need not necessarily be for bravery during a battle.

9

Messines Ridge – Ours now – Consolidation

From the other side of Scottish Wood away from the camp we could now stand and stare without keeping our heads down. We could safely look down to our old line and up at Piccadilly Farm (if it had still been there) and gaze at will. Just a weekend's rest, during which we cleaned ourselves up and then up to the new line. Again I was on H.Qrs. and it was positioned at the Dammstrasse, the sunken road which ran from the St. Eloi-Oosttaverne Road to some hundred yards short of the canal. It led to a white chateau, of which there were many. The enemy had built dugouts into that side of the road that used to face us and now, of course, their doors faced Jerry and were therefore weak. The companies proceeded to Ravine Wood to the left of Denys Wood. It had been heavily fortified with many concrete dugouts and much wire. Many trees had been blown down and now hampered whoever occupied it yet most were still leafy and the home of birds clinging to their natural habitat. This made Tom Liddell remark to "Tiger" Pratt, "How can a bird sing in a dump like this?" The dump, such as it was, was a veritable death trap, a maze of destruction. The stretcher-bearers' dugout was in a concrete erection some three hundred yards back. The concrete dugout had been Jerry's answer to the problem of erecting something that beat the Flanders' mud.

Quite a number of the Dammstrasse dugouts were still intact and the headquarters staff placed themselves at intervals along the road. The other side had suffered far more from our shelling and, in consequence, was lower than it used to be and so was less protective to us. Our dugout was situated some ten yards short of three quarters of its length from the chateau end, and next to it was the old German bread store. Not far away was a dugout occupied by an artillery officer on observation duty, and his batman or runner. Jerry was recovering fast and, as was his custom, he decided to blast us out of the positions we had gained. At two o'clock on the Saturday afternoon he started a most systematic strafing of the sunken road. At the same time he hammered Ravine Wood. He used four guns on the sunken road: one at the chateau end, one a quarter of the way, the third gun halfway and the fourth three-quarters of the way – that was just past our dugout. So for four hours each gun worked its way systematically along its allocated target) yard by yard, never changing its set piece. Eight signallers were rather cramped in their dugout. Dally was on duty when the strafe began and I was due to relieve him at five o'clock. We were quite aware of the shelling as the fourth gun was dropping its shells quite close to us, but moving away as time went on. MacGahey, Pip, Cpl. Ted Coulson, Ted the barber, Fred the linesman and Wakeling first discussed a topic started by Fred, who insisted that a shell hole was a far better place to be in than a dugout when a severe strafe was in progress. Four began after that to play cards, and we others looked on. Five o'clock came and I went on duty at the phone, not without some thoughts as to what I should have to do when matters got worse. At five thirty Dally (who hailed from Cottingham and was a "chemistry spiv") suggested that we ought to be moving as the last shell of the third gun dropped fairly close. Someone said, "Just another game and then it will be time to leave the position." A shell dropped just behind the dugout and Cpl. Ted warned us to be ready to quit The next shell fell just in front of the doorway and the door jambs gave way a little at the top and the doorway itself became smaller. We called out numbers as we left the dugout and I was given number seven. On reaching the doorway the hooks in my tunic caught in the woodwork and I was slightly delayed, but a kick from behind by Ted Coulson helped to get me through, and we all ran a few yards towards the chateau end and entered a dugout; we were undamaged and safe again. Here we stayed some twenty minutes and then returned to our signal dugout which had sustained no further damage. The only casualties were the artillery observation officer and his runner who had been on the top of a dugout trying to locate the enemy guns and inform their own battery of the positions. All our lines to the companies and even to Brigade were broken, but our repair man quickly set to work to repair the latter, but the damage to the company lines was much further forward near Ravine Wood, into which the Germans poured countless shells, far more concentrated than on the Dammstrasse. Very little help could be given to those who were wounded for some hours. Friends and the stretcher-bearers from their distant dugout attended to them on the spot, but there was no chance of getting them away. The stretcher-bearers were lucky to get through to the wood, but the carrying of stretcher cases through the inferno was out of the question. The wounded had to wait for the lull in the shelling and the agony of waiting was terrible. Scores and scores of men needed help and when the strafe ceased all helped to get the wounded away. The task was made harder by the debris that was everywhere – stunted trees and broken down trees over which the stretchers had to be lifted. It was dark before the job was done and then efforts could be made to improve the after-effects of the damage. We had got off lightly in the attack but now we had paid dearly, very dearly, as our casualties numbered about two hundred. Jerry was great at shelling what he had lost and had probably foreseen that this part of the new line was slightly less ahead than the flanks. On this occasion our casualties had been easy cannon fodder, a change from being victims of the deadly machine gun. Nevertheless two days later when the battalion on our left made an advance and captured one of Jerry's lines, our forward company moved forward and established posts two hundred yards in front of the line they had been holding, thus securing their flanks. Jerry still peppered the wood we were in all the time, and still at quiet moments from shell fire that blackbird carefully picked its notes and refused to be driven away.

In the meantime, Fred Johnson our linesman, left the Dammsbasse and made his way to repair the line to Advanced Brigade H.Q. and then foward to our front line. He restored conmunications with all the companies. Fearless Fred had been awarded the M.M. for such previous work and richly deserved the award. Communication was very important and two runners had gained similar awards at the same time.

On the 16th the Bankers relieved us and wearily and sadly we made our way back to the support line where the roll call took quite a time. We were having to get used to losing such a lot of the old originals who had become very dear to us. We spent some time in resting, cleaning up, training and letter writing. Six days out soon passed and we returned to the very same sector, but this time H.Q. was at Delbski Farm a few yards in front of Ravine Wood. Jerry had fortified the farm and built near it a huge dressing station. This huge erection was many yards long and consisted of many cells or separate dugouts. These cells opened out on to a concrete pathway and the whole front was built up like a verandah supported by concrete pillars. When Jerry had it, it must have been abnormally safe for its back wall was of concrete nearly two feet thick. Now, in our hands, it would not be quite as safe, an enemy shell might drop into the verandah or though the concrete pillars. What struck me as a great coincidence was the inscription on the name plate inserted in the middle of the front, which read: "Built by the 124 Inf. Bde." and we were of the 124 Brigade. The numerous cells were occupied by most of our H.Q. – orderly room, officers' sleeping quarters, signal office, runners quarters, first aid post, R.S.M.'s quarters, etc. Because there was not enough room for all the signallers to be accommodated there, three of us were allocated a pill box, some sixty yards to the front left. It had a narrow doorway, facing Jerry of course, and no other opening unless previous troops had filled in the low slit for a machine gun in the opposite wall from the door. It was always dark inside and a candle was very often lit all day and night. Mac G, Pip and myself were placed here.

Hollebeke lay directly in front of us about a mile away and was visible as the trees of two small woods in between had been much shelled and were now stunted. The Front Line was about half way between Hollebeke and Delbski Farm, as our H.Q. was called. There were no regular paths to and from it, and runners and others who had to call had to follow a zig-zag course as they meandered round the many craters of shell holes. Only a short shallow trench was at each end of the H.Q. building, to be used so that no visitors came directly to the front of it as it was under enemy observation all the hours of daylight. Traffic was cut to a minimum throughout the day.

The signal office was in the far left cell (as seen by Jerry) and the phone wires came out through the open doorway and straight round the corner and then branched off backwards to Brigade and forward to the line companies. The latter had no sheltered office but just a shell hole behind some broken-down tree or building. When MacG. or Pip or I came from our pill box to do our spell at the phone we approached behind the cells and dropped into the little trench on the left and reported for duty. Because the cell was small we did not do any night duty, the other signallers did it. An N.C.O. and a signaller on duty would be in the cell and the others outside in the corridor. The sixty yards between our pill box and the H.Q. we did at the double. It did not pay to loiter for naturally Jerry had the H.Q. under observation. He would know for sure that we would use such a fine strong shelter. On my way to duty one day I ran into Bram and we loitered to have a chat, but not for long – we soon heard the familiar sound of an approaching shell and immediately doubled off to our respective duties – Bram had been to see the bombing officer about supplies of Mills Bombs. The shell burst not far from where we had paused.

Jerry was in the habit of sniping with shells at anything that he saw, and one of his favourite efforts was to try to hit our pillbox and others. Regularly a shell would land on the top of the pill box, explode and the candle inside would be blown out. Pip and Mac G., the smokers, were getting short of matches, so often had they to relight the candle. Such luck, as Jerry tried to drop the shell in the door way but never managed it. There were other pillboxes scattered about, some damaged by our shells, others tilted where our gunners had been fortunate to hit them at the base with heavies. Such a feeling of safety in the dugout made us apprehensive when we came out of it.

Bad news travels quickly and we were very down hearted to hear that on 10th July the Germans had almost wiped out the 2nd Battalion, the K.R.R.s in the coastal defence sector. That battalion had been trapped on the enemy side of a river, the bridges used by them had been destroyed and only nineteen men had been able to swim their way to safety. Rumour had it that the enemy had forestalled any attempt by our forces to turn his flank in support of the attacks made in the Ypres Salient. I wondered what had happened to one of the college "nonet". Don Wardell (whose parents kept a confectionery shop at the corner of Fountain Road and Brunswick Avenue in Hull) had gone as a batman with an officer transferred from our battalion to the second. Many months later he wrote to me saying that he and the officer had been on a course at the time and so they missed the battle.

The luck of the H.Qrs. held out, but only just. On the night of our relief we had got nicely away from Delbski Farm and the oncoming battalion H.Qrs. had settled in when an enemy shell dropped straight into the veranda doing terrific damage and killing and wounding many men. We three of the pill box were far away when it happened and we did not know of it until the others, somewhat late in catching us up, told us they had gone back to give assistance. The place was a shambles. It was quite dark and no unnecessary lights would be on view.

For three days and nights we stayed at the old familiar camp of Murrumbidgee at La Clytte. Here we rested and had an easy time. One afternoon I was in the Y.M.C.A. hut reading when there was a very loud knock on the door which was pushed open and a voice called out "Is there anyone called Dennis in here?" I went to the door and, to my great surprise, there stood Cabby (George Henry Westfield Parkin of Alexandra Road, Hull, a school pal of the old secondary school). Good old Cabby, we had been staunch friends right up to the last week at school when, one evening we were at the playing field. Two or more matches had been played and I had been an umpire for the tennis games. During a pause when a few of us stood together, George had taken a tennis ball and served it a practice shot, in a way. It had struck me very hard in the face, smashing my glasses and bruising my face. Always rather serious, I told him off, as I could be of no further help in the tournament. The school year ended and we had separated. I had enlisted and was out in France before George joined the artillery and was commissioned. He wrote to me and we forgot the unpleasant incident. It seemed that in my letter to him he got a very good idea whereabouts I was at the front. He told me that he had followed, roughly, my travels – Plugstreet – Somme – and back the Salient and that his battery had taken part in the Messines Ridge stunt. I took him to our signal office to meet MacG. who had also been at the same school. Cabby asked if the two of us could be given permission to go with him for the afternoon and evening to his battery. I was due on duty at four o'clock but Mac was free, and off they went. If Cabby had seen the Boy Eden, our adjutant I have no doubt that I would have been given permission to join him. The N.C.O. in charge of the signal office would not think of finding a substitute. Mac was given a great welcome at the battery and all the officers beated him as one of them and, of course, encouraged him to tell of his experiences in battle.

Goodbye to La Clytte and Murrummbidgee Camp: on July 1st we marched further away from the line. Scherpenberg Hill on our left, then Mont Noir on our right through Locre to Bailleul and on to Meteren where we stayed for seventeen days in barns in the neighbourhood. An enterprising photographer came to see us with the result that many various groups were taken. The surviving original signallers, eighteen out of fifty-three were on one group – Wood, Carter, Pip Porter, Attenborough, Ingell, Stone, Fawcett Proctor, Brantingham, Fossie, Brewer, "Coalie" Ted Coulson, Mac, Vickers, Morley, Johnson, Womersley and myself, the last two holding a white flag each. Not many of us to carry on with, so volunteers were called for and the new section had its photo taken with all of us on it. We numbered sixty-four plus the signalling officer. The C.O. too was on the photo, which I no longer have, unfortunately. 'C' Company showed eighty originals including two officers (Lt. Eden and Lt. Waldy, who was wounded on the Somme and returned to us). 'D' Company showed fifty-three originals including just one junior officer. Each of those two companies, of course, had been over two hundred strong when we came out fourteen months earlier. Some of both companies, wounded on the Somme, had come back to us.

I sent home copies of those photographs: A view of the church and school of Meteren, the children, all girls, in two groups, one at each side of the street; and two more views of St. Omer – an open park scene and a view of the steps leading up to the Basilique, Notre Dame – all at different dates. What happy days; a little light training with the companies but mostly helping with the training of the new members of the signals. Many walks in the district, including a visit to our early happy days village of Outtersteene to renew old acquaintances. Hazebrouck and Bailleul were visited too, after pay day. Our own canteen was opened up and there was plenty to spend our money on, besides egg and chips.

Most of the original signallers were billeted at a farm in a huge barn, along with other specialist sections. One end of the barn needed a ladder to mount to a boarded space of some six feet high; four of us, as soon as we were dismissed and shown our billet, made a dash for this particular spot.We cleared all the straw and dirt off it and chose the place for our kit. Certainly we slept on the bareboards instead of on straw, but it was worth it because it was cleaner and probably free from chats.

Pip and I bought a tin of custard powder from the canteen and after every dinner we also purchased from the farmer about a pint of milk. Then at the cookhouse we boiled the milk in one of our dixies and made custard to drink. It was grand and refreshing.

During our evening visits to the Meteren estaminets we met some of the Aussie tunnellers and found them very generous and light-hearted. Their presence in the neighbourhood had pushed up the prices of some things, or so we thought. An Aussie's pay per day was more than ours for a week. Often with the Aussies was a Tommy, to whom I often spoke, and, to my great astonishment he told me that he belonged to my own home town of Hull. I asked him what he was doing with the Aussies. "In 1914 I joined the R.A.M.C. and, having completed my training, I was waiting for a posting. When one day volunteers were called for to help the Australian R.A.M.C. who were about to arrive in France, I immediately said that I would be willing to go and soon I was in France. When I report to the R.A.M.C. officer in a tent, he said, on my saluting him. 'We don't do that here, mate. What's your name?' When I told him it was Miller, he replied that I would be known as "Dusty", that he was Jack and the sergeant was Bill. The latter greeted me with a 'Hi there' and got me a mug of cocoa and some bread and butter. When I appeared before the officer on the next pay parade he asked how much I wanted. When I said I wanted ten francs if possible as I had been without pay for some weeks, they gave me a hundred and I have been drawing francs on that scale ever since – goodness knows how much I am in debt! They are a rum lot and a grand lot.

Last year near the coast five Aussies and I went into a town to find that all the estaminets were out of bounds to Australian troops. It meant nothing to them; they walked into an estaminet and ordered six drinks. They waited and demanded to be served, and they got served. Within minutes the Red Caps arrived and ordered them to leave, and they refused. One Red Cap seized my cap and that was the signal for a real set-to. Everything would have been peaceful if the Military Police had not intervened. So there was a scrap; my cap was retrieved and the Red Caps left". The Aussies here in Meteren seemed quiet enough, but we all knew that they had their own sort of discipline. Many years later I met Frank Miller at a cricket match.

The 21st Btn, the K.R.R.C.   (The Yeoman Rifles)

The TRANSPORT SECTION of the above BATTALION will hold a

GYMKHANA

in the CRICKET FIELD on MONDAY, JULY 16th, 1917

(By Kind permission of FRITZ, weather permitting, etc., and so forth.)

PROGRAMME OF EVENTS

Commencing at THREE pip emma

1.   Wheelbarrow Race

2.   Wrestling on horseback (semi-finals)

3.   Bolster and Bar

4.   Tug-o'-War, mounted (semi-finals)

5.   100 yards Flat Race

6.   Tug-o'-War, mounted (Final)

7.   Subalterns' Rade – on other than RIDE horses

8.   Blindfold Race, teams of three

9.   Jumping, individual

10.   Wrestling on horseback (Final)

11.   Machine Gun Race

12.   Mule Derby, owners up

13.   Five-legged race

14.   Surprise Race – open to W.O.s and N.C.O.s of the Bn, who can ride.
                Entries limited to 3 per Coy.

15.   Variety Race

16.   Tug-o'-War, Transport Section only

MEMO FOR SPECTATORS

I   The officers, N.C.O.s and men of the Transport Section will be "at home" on the ground. An alfresco tea will be served on the Lawn during the interval, according to the capacity of the kitchens — Travelling Mark U4. All ranks should bring their own drinking mugs

II   The order of the Programme is subject to alteration

III   This show is being run regardless of the cost, and for that reason the value of the prizes has not been divulged on the programme. Prizes will not be distributed on the ground but will be credited to the winners' accounts until the end of the war

IV   No betting will be allowed on the ground

V   All fat rendered down from competitors will be placed in the credit account of the Dripping Fund

VI   A band will be in attendance

The very happy relaxed days at our farm billet on the right hand side of the road from Meteren to Westoutre were nearly at an end. The muck midden around which the farm buildings were arranged was fortunately empty and the cobbled paths were clean. Many kit inspections had been held and our iron rations checked. Even our clothing was examined. Some of us had hopes of a new tunic or a pair of trousers, for we still wore those we had come out to the front in, but to get anything new with the quarter-master's approval was like getting blood out of a stone. Tunic or trousers had to be much torn on the wire, or really filthy before a change was granted. Probably senior N.C.O.s had a pull and got better treatment. What a great surprise we got at nine o'clock parade one morning! All men, including specialists, had to parade in the afternoon and then be marched to an unknown destination for the purpose of witnessing an afternoon of sport. It was a very memorable show giving a great amount of pleasure to all; there was plenty of fun, many falls from the horses, and especially from the mules. A carefree afternoon, all were at peace and the war could have been a thousand miles away – like our thoughts.

The field in which the show was held had been called the cricket field just simply because it was all green with no shell holes! To explain the Dripping Fund; for some time the mess orderlies at breakfast time had had orders not to let any man take the dip from the dixie lid. The dip, when it had cooled, had to be scraped off the lid and put with any other fat into a container and returned to base, from which it would be sent back to Blighty to help in the war effort there.

Two days later we again packed up and we marched in the early morning to Ascot Camp near Westoutre, a familiar training ground for that is what it was to be: training for attack by the companies and the training of many more signallers. The numbers of the latter were low as far as fully trained signallers went: the eighteen surviving original signallers, a few more that came with the earlier drafts, no more than ten, thus leaving the section much below strength. Though there was much lacking in the usefulness of signallers in attack we carried on with the work of training twenty or more. We never seemed to train in conjunction with the companies and their work. We had a far easier time and much more spare time.

I took the opportunity to return to the Reverend C.M. Hulbert (of the same family as Jack and

Claud Hulbert, actors) of Thornton Hall, the copy of Bunyan's *A Pilgrim's Progress* which he had sent out to me and which I had read. I let him know that I was going through the New Testament that he had given me on my enlisting. One of the large parcel of books sent to me by an old school pal, I passed on to one of the sigs. after reading it – *The Four Just Men*.

Everybody knew that the humble rabbit once introduced into Australia had become a pest. Twice in the next fortnight the British troops were thankful for this. Instead of having bully, bully beef stew, or bully beef rissoles or any other such concoction, for dinner we had rabbit. Crates of them had arrived at the quarter-master's stores. There was no stinting the ration per man, the battalion strength being very low, it might have been said that there was too much, but Tommy did not let the cooks down; none was returned. Our own trench pest could not be so utilised.

As Mac and I relaxed after one such meal we gazed up into the sky and far away saw about six triplanes; ours or theirs we did not know. We had never heard of such planes and never saw them again, and we wondered if either side used such innovations. We were told on our own specialist parades that greater attention had to be paid to possible liaison with aircraft in the next stunt. If the plane released a white Very Light this meant, "Where are you?" The observer would look out for our battalion sign and our call sign sent with the panel. There was a slight variation in the two letter codes which had to be learned. They were: N N = short of ammo; Y Y = short of bombs; O O = short of barrage; H H = lengthen range; X X = held up by M.G.s; Z Z = held up by wire; F F = enemy resistance; B B = enemy retiring; J J = raise barrage; P P = reinforcements; and W W = short of water. I was surprised to see the last one so put, as normally W W signified wash-out.

Our dry canteen was very well stocked and after the pay parade queues formed up and a roaring trade was done in such eatables as biscuits, chocolates, tinned fruits and sweets; HP sauce had become popular for it helped down the bully beef; Blighty cigarettes were in great demand for they were a lot better than the issue gaspers. ate up my reserve chocolate and biscuits that I kept in my entrenching-tool case and bought a fresh supply in its place. It always lasted me a long time for I ate sparingly of it, only touching it when I was really famished. We had all become very light eaters because rations were light and we had got used to their being so. On July 26th we left Westoutre and marched by way of Scherpenberg Hill and La Clytte to the familiar Ridge Wood: the last stage but one before another stunt.

10

The Third Battle of Ypres
– Gas, rain and mud

Almost eight weeks had passed since the capture of Messines Ridge and, but for some slight nibbles at the German line and some straightening in places, no major attack had been made. Jerry had had plenty of time in which to reorganise his battalions and defences. In the next three days we were fitted out with all we needed and were given our final instructions. Some men were being left behind as details and very few words were now spoken at partings as the battalion set off from Ridge Wood on the cloudy evening of July 30th. We passed through Voormezeele and followed a mule track. We were struck by the abundance of artillery ammunition – guns and shells seemed to be everywhere and small dumps of shells were all along the track. Many mules were using the track as well, carrying panniers of shells, one pannier on each side. Suddenly a shell burst not far in front of the leading mule, which stopped dead in its tracks and was refusing to go any further. It wanted to turn tail, as did the others, upset by the shell burst. "Stubborn as a mule" I thought, and no wonder, poor beasts, having to suffer so much. Whether they did move on eventually I did not see, as we passed them and plodded on, getting a move on as much as we could for obviously Jerry knew this track and shelled it heavily. As we got further on, some shells gave a different sound as they exploded. They seemed to approach with a nasty whistle or hiss and then go "phht" – duds, we thought. However, we were ordered to halt and take shelter in a dyke and put our gas masks on – the box respirators. In the next half hour we had to take cover twice; on the second occasion a badly wounded gunner came to us from a dugout not far away and told us that his battery had been very heavily shelled with H.E. and gas shells and that practically all the crews had become casualties except for a sergeant artificer who had had to go along with a surviving officer to work the guns on their own.

At long last we reached our assembly positions; we were to go over the top in support to the 123 Brigade which was to attack the enemy trenches near the road to Klein Zillebeke. Sometime during the approach to our assembly position, or at the position, we lost our Captain, "Patch" Watson. Some said that because, he had been transferred to the new 22nd K.R.R.s as its Commanding Officer, he had decided to pay a last call on his old company ('B') and against wishes made the fatal visit; some said that he had brought up some mail just to see the old company; others said that he grew impatient with the slow progress forward and had got out of a trench and whilst on the top of it Jerry had seen him and a salvo of shells was sent over and he was hit. Not far from where he fell the battalion M.O. and Lance-jack George Williams had set up a medical aid post and so were very quickly on the scene and found that Patch was beyond help. The force of the shell explosion had knocked the patch off his eye. He was buried at La Clytte Cemetery on August 6th. The Colonel and George with Claude Hey and others of the burial party all saluted in turn at the edge of the grave. Patch had associations with Bishopthorpe Church, in the church yard of which, whilst on one of his leaves, he planted an acorn picked up in France. It has grown into a large oak tree.

(Incidentally, Claude Hey was living in Bishopthorpe in the 1980s).

For some time we had seen walking wounded passing us, some men almost staggering along. The latter had been affected by gas, because they had removed their box respirators from time to time so that they could see better to follow the men in front of them. During these interludes the gas had done its deadly work, though some hours had elapsed before the damage was realised. This new type of enemy gas, known as mustard gas, was really lethal and it had a burning effect on the lungs, eyes and skins. As long as the respirator was being worn, eyes and lungs were safe, but not the skin. Pip realised that his back was hurting him and when he squatted down and rested it against a trench side it pained him very much. He opened his tunic and slid his hand under his shirt. Under his arm he felt a huge blister. Further probing made him realise that he had many such blisters, especially under the other arm and at the tops of his thighs; the weak, tender parts of his skin. His tunic and trousers showed no signs of anything being abnormal. Pip had been closer to the gas shells than I had been and I had kept my gas helmet on longer. Many men were affected still more and their eyes became matted with a kind of sticky matter, some developed a racking cough. George Bramley, with whom I had enlisted, was very unfortunate that a gas shell dropped straight in front of him and very close. He collapsed and remembered nothing till he came round in a hospital in Hastings. The less affected cases made their way to our transport lines and were directed to a dressing station near Locre where they received some treatment. The worst cases passed through a Clearing Station and the others sent back to the battalion details and were told to rest. When Pip reached the details, a sergeant, thinking there was nothing wrong with him, ordered him to go up the line and re-join the battalion. Pip explained and the N.C.O. found him a dugout in which to rest along with others who began to appear, suffering similarly from blisters.

At 3.50 a.m. on the morning of July 31st, the 123rd Brigade moved forward to attack the enemy and we followed in close support. The going was very heavy; water-filled shell holes, slippery craters, slimy mud – all made it hard work lifting one's feet to progress, little by little. Yet the troops went forward and, despite the cloudy day with its threat of rain, the tasks set to the brigade were overcome satisfactorily though with many casualties. A successful mission was achieved, though we did not realise it. We, in support, were now occupying some waterlogged trenches, well over the ankles in mud. We struggled to keep our rifles clean, it was a problem finding somewhere to rest them that was not wet through. A drizzle had been falling for some time and was getting more like showers By four o'clock the showers had turned to heavy rain, almost torrential. What ground and little there was of it, that had not been churned up by our bombardment was fast becoming a quagmire – not a jot of help to us, but helping the enemy to reorganise and reinforce his defeated troops. Some of Jerry's pillboxes had been uprooted and some damaged, but many more were still serviceable. They were hard to see because of the poor visibility – cloudy skies and the muddy surroundings acting like camouflage. The Durhams in particular and the other units of the 123rd Bde. had had to fight hard to capture them and their machine gun crews.

About seven o'clock we saw the Germans massing for a counter-attack. They were coming over a ridge on the other side of the valley and two of our companies were sent forward to help to meet this counter-attack. The foward British troops sent up red Very Lights as a signal that the enemy were about to attack. Then our artillery and sections of machine guns opened fire – trees were uprooted, fountains of water and mud rose into the air as the enemy began to retire after suffering heavy losses. The German guns ceased to fire and our covering fire ended and things quietened down. Our two companies waited till darkness fell before returning to their support positions, not an easy task for the area was now just a sea of mud. If guns had to be moved forward, what a difficult job it must have been for the gunners.

What a night it was. Did I get any sleep? I do not remember. The bed and the pillow were soft enough, and very watery, as I tried to find comfort in a shell hole. Luckier ones managed to find a piece of trench to rest in. I used my spade frequently to throw out water as I wanted to curl round the hole and keep my feet out of the water at the bottom. I had become accustomed to manage on a few hours' sleep and no doubt had a few naps. Like the others, I had eaten sparingly, a little bread and a thin slice of bully. Water was precious and I drank but a little. The crawl out to an unoccupied shell hole to use as a latrine was a frightening effort, not to be made unless absolutely necessary.

A very wet morning saw the 123 Brigade make another attack and successfully gain ground towards the Klein Zillebeke road and we were in support again. It was very difficult to move forward as we slithered more than walked or ran over the boggy ground. It was a really remarkable feat by the other brigade to reach and hold their objectives. We settled down again as best we could and only then had I time to reflect and remember that this Lammas Day was my birthday, so I celebrated by eating a little of my own special emergency rations – some Nestlé's chocolate and a few small sweet Blighty biscuits.

Any orders we received came by company runners who worked very hard and did wonders, finding their way from group to group. They had a canny instinct of knowing the correct direction to take and seemed to be untiring for they had such a lot of calls to make. They came round in good time to warn us that we would be relieving the Durhams later that night. I received a very welcome order I had to report to H.Q. while my company were to proceed to the Front Line. We expected this change for we had been very fortunate in being in support of the attacking battalions, who deserved a really good rest. There were no trenches in the Front Line and the conditions of the area made it impossible to dig them – water, slime and mud predominated everywhere.

Our not-so-tired men – only two companies had had to go really forward – did much work in helping with the many wounded in the neighbourhood of the Front Line and carried many such back to the support line. Then they set about consolidating the new position as best they could by making several strong points. Headquarters took over the Caterpillar – a huge, long and high mound. Whether it was German – made or natural, I never knew. Its entrance was at the side at ground level and it led into a tunnelled corridor from which branched shorter tunnels and little rooms. About halfway along a staircase had been made and some fifty steps led to the top and a small trench about six feet long, four feet deep and two feet wide. It was widened at the top and right hand side so that there was a kind of ledge, covered with a dark-coloured waterproof sheet. Down inside a smell of damp clay always prevailed. There were enough rooms to satisfy the needs of all sections of the H.Q. staff: offices, sleeping quarters and orderly room. In the signal office was both a Fuller phone and a power buzzer.

The air was so stuffy at all times that I volunteered for night work up on the top. Corps H.Q., which loaned us a prismatic compass, requested that we take bearings of all guns fired by the Germans. These bearings of gun flashes were passed on to the artillery and we were commended for our good work in this direction. In practically all the hours of darkness Jerry had many batteries sending over gas shells. H.E. shells and what we called armour-piercing shells, especially towards the Caterpillar. They kept me busy and I always had scores of bearings to hand into the office each morning.

Though the air was much fresher up at the top there was a funny smell and when I investigated by lifting up the black waterproof sheet I found that a dead German had been almost totally built into the side of the small trench. Only one knee and a leg stuck out and when they had been covered by the sheet I had rested my elbows on them as I looked through the binoculars or held the prismatic compass steady: in order to take a good bearing. A gentle breeze or a strong wind used to waft the corner of the waterproof sheet and show the knee of the dead man and in time, due to our resting our elbows there, the cloth wore and the knee became uncovered.

On the brighter days the view from this point the highest round about, was depressing – a watery wilderness, a polar waste without the snow, debris of all sorts, hardly a sign of any of our troops, just an occasional tin hat as its owner shuffled in his shell hole or tried to stretch his legs in his bit of trench. I raised the binoculars and looked towards Jerry's line but saw no movement. A little further off lay Zanvoorde; red tiles of houses, the cemetery and a large chateau-like building all showing up quite clearly. How tall some factory chimneys seemed to be and how natural the surroundings were – as Mother Nature should be. Further still to the left was the larger town of Gheluvelt. I swung the binoculars back to Zanvoorde and I could not believe my eyes. Near the cemetery a large party of about fifty Germans were working in groups of twos and threes, digging and shovelling. I sent the other signaller down to the signal officer to report this target and before long our shells dropped thereabouts and the working party of Jerries cleared off. Much to my surprise, the party turned up again the next morning and received the similar greetings from our batteries. They did not try a third time, having suffered some casualties on each occasion. We had often taken similar risks on working parties or signalling stunts and had had to disperse.

One evening when I was on phone duty downstairs in the office a call came through from the transport lines and I was asked by a C.S.M. if he could have a few words with the H.Q. Staff N.C.O. I sent for him and overheard the following: "Congratulations Sarge, in the Divisional order today you have been awarded the D.C.M." Knowing the latter, I wondered what on earth for. "Do me a favour, Sergeant-Major. See the tailor and ask him to let me have a new tunic with the ribbon up, ready for my going on leave in two weeks' time." The C.S.M. promised to do so and the conversation ended. The Sarge. strutted about and swaggered more than ever whilst I pondered and tried to think how he had earned that decoration. He had been very favoured when the lads went over the top. He must have written home immediately for within a week he showed me a reply from his mother: "Darling Phyll, Congratulations galore ... " That was the first time I had seen the word "galore". A very pet name was used instead of "Phyll". Of course, a mistake had been made, not in the Divisional Orders but in the reading of them. A sergeant of the same surname and of the K.R.R.s had been awarded the D.C.M. but the list had not given the initials or which battalion of the K.R.R.s and the recipient was in the 18th Battalion. I was glad that I had not divulged the conversation but the gist of it came back to us by way of the transport section.

The men of the transport section used to boast, quite rightly and in a friendly spirit that they never failed to deliver the goods that they always managed to get water and food to their friends in the Front Line. That task was now well-nigh impossible because of the state of the ground for there was very little solid earth anywhere from the transport lines even to our H.Qrs. The use of limbers was out of the question and the carrying of supplies part of the way fell upon the faithful mules for part of the journey and then the goods had to be man-handled. Eager company men would wait safely in the shelter of the Caterpillar for their rations, cut down to the minimum and then set off, as human mules, to trudge back to the Front Line using the one single track, slippery and dangerous, heads down, sandbags of supplies on their backs in addition to rifles and box respirators at the alert. No hot food was brought up and though water was scarce (never enough for washing purposes) we did try to brew up a warm drink. We had been supplied with Tommy Cookers, a small kind of stove consisting of a container, circular and about two inches deep. On it fitted a framework support for a dixie. In the container was a sort of methylated substance which we lit and its heat very slowly boiled the wafer in the dixie. When the wax showed signs of running low we put into the container match sticks, candle grease, old pieces of four-by-two that were still oily but of no further use as a pull-through for the rifle, and any other odds and ends that would burn. Most of us had had sent from home tablets of tea, coffee, cocoa or cafe-au-lait six in a box. They all contained sugar and were not a bad "sweet" when we wanted a chew. After what seemed an hour, the reward was something wet and warm – the dixie would be passed round and the section would enjoy a few sips each.

Spells in the line were of less duration and one night our friends the Bankers relieved us and we moved back to the old German line. The boys came out to join us and they looked the worst I had ever seen them. They were mostly caked with half-dried mud, very weary, unshaven and bedraggled. The conditions had been a worse enemy than the Germans and they sank down where they were and fell asleep. The next day, after hours of cleaning their uniforms, they were in great form, knowing what they had left behind. When they heard the official communiqué of the battle that "all objectives were taken on a fifteen mile front", they were astounded. They had thought it had been a wash-out, just like the weather.

Two nights later the 11th Queen's relieved us and we went further back to the familiar camp at Scottish Wood where we were in reserve to the 123 Brigade. We were reorganised and refitted out and so prepared to receive another visit from the red-capped staff of the Division and, of course, the parrot-like words of appreciation were delivered. Any one of us, by now, could have made the well-worn speech of appreciation, and probably have made them sound a little more humane. We all put a brave face on things but what a pity that Staff did not pay us a visit some few days earlier.

The day after the inspection we moved to a position we had never used before. It was called Wiltshire Farm and was further to the right of the old Ridge Wood – probably it had been the support line or reserve line of the brigade on our left when we were at the Brasserie. There was the usual type of long trench with low dugouts and to the left of it a huge sandbag erection which was our Headquarters. It was about twelve feet high and many sandbags thick and housed the officers and H.Q. staff and separate off-shoots for the orderly room and signals' and runners' office.

The weather was so fine and sunny for once that the signal office was for that day in a bivouac in front of the dugout in a clearing. Many trees, untouched by the war, were behind this small tent and to the rear of it. Quite a pleasant change of surroundings. One signaller was on duty at the phone and we others walked about aimlessly or sat around talking. Suddenly, at about half past three in the afternoon, the peaceful atmosphere was broken by the sound of a shell exploding. Two of our own batteries were not far away. Shortly afterwards another shell arrived and fell away to our right. At four o'clock the enemy strafe started and many shells were dropping on or very near our own trench, to which we were ready to go as a better shelter than the open space in which the bivvy was. We realised that the shells were dropping nearer and nearer to the signal office, so some of the section moved back towards the trees. At this moment I remembered that I was in charge of the day's rations which I had left in a dugout in the trench some twenty or thirty yards down. I rushed back along the trench to our dugout just beyond the fifth bay, bent down and seized the sandbag of rations and set off back. No sooner had I got on to my feet then came a heavy crump – something big had dropped quite close and a lump of something, earth or shell, struck my tin hat in which I later found a large dint. Another huge crump as a shell dropped in the trench some yards away from me. Something struck me a heavy blow to the back of my neck that caused me to stumble as I made an effort to dive onto the duckboard. I lay flat, waiting for the next shell to burst. It was further away so I stood up and most gingerly felt the back of my neck. My hand showed no blood, so I was alright; I proceeded on my way to the clearing. The last shell had knocked in the dugout occupied by two signallers, Woodie and Fossie. The former lost one hundred cigarettes and Fossie, a worse loss, his brand new safety-razor. Quite a number of company men and others had stood with their backs to the H.Q. dugout and were safe enough, for no shell fell near it or, fortunately, near the signallers' bivvy, their office. I displayed my rescued goods – two loaves, some pozzie and half a tin of butter. Shortly afterwards tea was up and our rations disappeared in quick time. We could not help noticing that there were no rats in this part of the reserve line, and wondered where had they gone? We learned that twelve Military Medals had been awarded to the battalion for the July 31st stunt – the mud bath. They went to four sergeants, three lance-corporals and five riflemen. One officer was awarded a Military Cross.

We spent only one night at the position called Wiltshire Farm and then set off in the early evening of the next day on a much longer trek back to the Front Line where H.Q. was in the mound called the Caterpillar. I was with my company ('D') for that spell. The going was easy for the first two hours because parts of our old support and reserve lines and paths had dried out somewhat and it was not till we reached the old German line near St. Eloi that our pace had to slacken. Whilst we had been away from the line for a week the Royal Engineers had done marvellous work, with the help of our Pioneer Battalion, the Middlesex, in laying duckboards, planks and railway sleepers in many parts of the recent battleground, both for the benefit of the moving artillery and for the infantry. It was hard to believe that so much mud had apparently gone and that so much water had disappeared hereabouts. As we reached these welcome tracks, we trudged along with rifles at the march-easy position, box respirators at the alert and our thumbs in our equipment braces to ease the loads we were carrying – and all the time with our eyes down carefully stepping along where the track was occasionally slippery. It was not so much the thoughts of the Germans that troubled us as the time it would take us to reach the Front Line and get settled in. The going was hard and wearying. The stars were shining overhead, but we saw them not.

In single file we saw only the man in front when we lifted our eyes off the duckboards. There may have been landmarks, though I doubt it. The track became wider than the usual duckboard track and we realised that we had reached the area of nothing but shell holes and craters. We hurried across a sunken road and the H.Qrs. party left us and we went on into the night feeling more and more alone in a wilderness and we got more and more strung out. Not till we reached the Front Lines did we see some other troops who hurried off without a greeting so glad were they to be relieved. Actually there was no real Front Line but here and there an occasional shallow trench – three or four of such forming a strong point and others took up their positions in shell holes. I was fortunate to be with Sam in a bit of a trench. Jerry for once had let us off lightly as we carried out the relief, very few gas shells and no other shelling. The hours of darkness allowed us to move about, to arrange things to the best of our liking and to settle in. We knew that we were to be cramped all the daytime and that we should have to keep our heads down.

The next morning we got a most unusual greeting from the enemy. I had crawled out to another bit of trench some twenty yards to the rear and left when I heard a terrific roaring sound. I looked around to see what the noise meant and saw, very close indeed, a brilliant red aeroplane plunging down to almost ground level and letting fly at us with its machine gun. The bullets were striking the wet earth just forward of the trench. Of all the cheek and how daring! Of course, we immediately wanted to know where the R.F.C. were, allowing this to happen to us! One other similar plane followed the first and also fired at us. They were two planes of the celebrated Baron Richthofen's Red Devils of Arras, or Circus. Along with others of 'D' Company, I waited the next morning to see if he would repeat his tactics – he did and we tried to bring him down, but failed – we did not know how to do the job properly. His aim was better on the second occasion for we were better targets as we tried to shoot him. Some of his bullets phutted perilously close.

I realised how lucky I had been at the Caterpillar with its freedom of movement, clean conditions and good opportunities to sleep. Further forward the two companies in the very Front Line and the two in very close support had no such comforts. A water bottle full had to last some days, so had a tin of bully between six and each of us had our own supply of Army biscuits – the main food after we had eaten the last of a small bread supply. The thoughtless man who had quickly drunk his supply of water would crawl to a shell hole and drink from its dirty, discoloured contents, containing goodness knows what. How we carried on a conversation in a whisper! Why? There was no need really, but we seemed to be overcome by the weird surroundings. How cautiously the smokers indulged in a few puffs!

All messages were brought by or sent by runners as there were no telephone communications. One such message resulted in an attempted raid by us being made one morning on some enemy pillboxes. It failed simply because we could not get going fast enough. The mud held us back – it was well-nigh impossible to keep on lifting the feet to progress to the objective. The ground, more than the enemy machine guns, prevented us from succeeding. Realising this, an officer blew his whistle and made signs that we should retire to our trenches and shell holes. We did so with only slight losses. We were able to carry back those wounded or killed later in the day.

Some changes were made as the two companies in the Front Line changed places with those in close support. I now had to live in a shell hole; it was not too wet. It was not as good a living place as a piece of trench, particularly during the day when I had to curl round its slope, keep my head down and see if I could keep my feet clear of the damper bottom. The daily hours were very long before I could stretch myself when darkness came. Wherever I raised my head to have a look round I saw no-one, our khaki-green uniforms blended well with the mud.

On the whole, Jerry left us alone, but reserved most of his continuous shelling for the back areas until very late on the night after our attempted raid. We had safely brought in our wounded and the dead and our sector was becoming active as a Wiltshire battalion arrived to relieve us when suddenly Jerry opened up. A very large party of Germans were advancing towards us in close formation. Whether this was a raid in retaliation or a counter-attack made no difference, for with the help of the Wiltshires the enemy was successfully driven off. When things calmed down, we began to depart. I shall never forget the trek out of the line – the Wiltshires were not of our division so we were fortified by the implication that we were going out for a rest, even if that were to be followed by preparation for another stunt. Quietly we were guided to the plank track and in single file at intervals of thirty yards we set off, backs to the enemy and to the discomforts of the last few days. As I slithered forward on this track I felt as if my head was up in the clouds and my feet in water, as if I were on a strange planet. I felt naked in so far as I felt unprotected should Jerry open fire on us. What would I do if a shell fell close? Would I dive on to the planks? I could not dive to the right or left, for that would land me into a shell hole which would probably be full of water and I could drown. Ahead, who was that ghost-like figure? Was it Fossie, Woodie or Sam? I did not know. Did this area now look like the Siberian Steppes or the Canadian Barren Lands or Tundra after the Spring thaw? Was it true that the High Command had sent a submarine up to find out where we were? Had a naval officer reported to the O/C 'D' Company a few nights ago? Had some marines surprised a sentry by saying, "Alright Tommy, the Navy's here". How long did this part of the nightmare last? After an hour's footslog I realised that a dark blur on the left was what was left of Battle Wood and that soon I should be near the Caterpillar and a change in the pattern of the wilderness.

The haunting fear of the unknown passed by as we approached the battalion H.Q. and the danger from shell fire and gas shells now started. We hurried on, impatient when we had to halt and put on our box respirators – gas shells far outnumbered the H.E. shells. Someone would lift up his mask and sniff the air and call "All clear!" Some attempted coughings, some sneezings and some splutterings could be heard as men tried to clear their throats. I hated donning the respirator for I had to be slow because of my rimless glasses and the fear that my eyepieces would get steamed up. Whisperings of Spoil Bank (on the right of us) and the canal – we knew the awful trek was nearly over and that we would soon be seeing a natural countryside and reaching almost perfect safety. Tired and much relieved we reached Wiltshire Farm. A very good meal awaited us and there and then most of us set to immediately to clean ourselves up. Our trousers were very wet and muddy and our tunics patched with areas of mud. The mud had begun to dry and we took out our jack-knives and scraped away at the worst parts. Boots and puttees, which we were glad to take off, were in a terrible state.

Relaxed again we could smile and even wonder what was going to happen to us next. We had not long to wait for the next move. Shortly after tea that very day buses drew up nearby and we were taken by way of Kemmel, La Clytte, Locre, Bailleul, Meteren and Caestre to Thieushouk, a hamlet near which were many camps of tents. We were billeted in one such camp. Here two days later we were inspected by Corps and Army Commanders, the latter thanking us for our recent efforts at the front.

We had noticed that round the outside walls of each tent was a sandbag protection against enemy bombs, but we paid no attention to this precaution till the 18th when in the evening Jerry decided to let us know that there was still a war on. About an hour before lights out as we stood in groups around the field, we heard the unmistakable throbbing of enemy planes – the drone of Bosche aero engines was quite different from ours. I leaned my back against a large tree that grew a few yards from my tent and looked towards the sound of the aircraft. Our anti-aircraft guns were busy when suddenly I heard a crash as a bomb burst some five fields away. Crash, crash, crash as other bombs exploded nearer and nearer to our field. Before the last crash some of the men had flung themselves into their tents and lay flat whilst I remained standing against the tree so that it stood between me and the bombs. Many more bombs dropped near the camps around Thieushouk and I saw the Dashes quite clearly. The raid was over and before I retired to my tent I heard the sound of a horse galloping quickly towards our field. Colonel Jarvis, our C.O., who had been having late dinner with his brother officers of the Queen's, had dashed back to see if his new battalion was alright. The Queen's camp had been hit but many more were the casualties of other battalions of our division in the neighbourhood. Jerry would, at least know that many troops would be in the back areas resting after the various stunts. He might even have flown over in recent weeks and spotted lights in the fields and concluded that troops were there. Had we not heard, "Put that light out …. Jerry up" or, as the wind-up increased, "Put that d … light out, you silly b … !" There was always some who were foolishly brave, or those who did not like to think that they had the wind up. We had been very lucky not to have any casualties that evening.

All the men had an easy time for a few days during which there were short route marches, battalion training and specialist training. Some paid a visit to Outtersteene, only six miles away, to renew acquaintances with the first French people who had taken us in last May. The countryside was beautiful and many walks were enjoyed in the free evenings. Just before the end of the month before the battalion moved, six of the signallers got a pleasant shock; they were to go on a six week course to the X Corps School at Boeschepe. The request must have come by runner, it certainly did not come by phone or a signaller on duty would have known and told the rest of us. We did not know who had been chosen until the very last minute. We learned afterwards that there had been two suggestions as to which signallers were to be picked for the course. Some said that six learner signallers of recent drafts should be sent and someone else thought that six signallers who had been through such a lot and had had no leave should be chosen. The orderly room staff, when asked their opinion, thought the latter idea the better and in consequence six original signallers were chosen. They were Jim Proctor, Pip, Mac, Vic, Dally and myself. I was absolutely dumbfounded when the N.C.O. came to see me at nine o'clock that Monday evening and said, "Be ready to go on a course after breakfast in the morning, it will give you a rest." As soon as he left me I went round the section to find out who the other lucky ones were. I had been with Mac and Pip in the 'C' Company sigs. and with Jim in 'D' Coy. sigs. but had never been in the same group as Vic and Dally. I knew them, of course, and the latter was known as a fine pianist and carried copies of music in his pack so he could play whenever he had the chance. We six were very excited and longing for the morning and a little selfish in our anxiety to be on our way because we did not believe in anything until we got it. There could be a slip and the course could still be cancelled, like leave, when the battalion was due for action. Nothing did happen to stop us and on the 29th we set off, our packs seeming very light as we walked slowly the four or five miles to our destination. Walking in the hills on the second half of the trip was much enjoyed as we looked forward to a very pleasant interlude. Thoughts of happy times to come brought forgetfulness of war in their train and we quickly realised that we were to know cleanliness, orderly meals and peaceful times for six whole weeks.

In the meantime the battalion was inspected by the Divisional General on the 29th, the usual words of appreciation for work done in the early days of August were spoken, and within forty-eight hours the men were on their way to Tatinghem, a long straggling village some three miles the far side of St. Omer and about five miles south of Eperleques (where the battalion had trained for the Battle of Messines Ridge). The land around Tatinghem, in our divisional training area, was very much like the hilly ground around and beyond Shrewsbury Forest, the area of the battalion's next attack. Many hours in the next fortnight were spent in training and practice attacks with signallers acting tis the barrage action of our artillery. The troops were to pause three times and during these halts the barrage would lift and then return before the men moved on again. The objectives were again named by colour – the Red Line and the Blue Line.

The battalion returned to Ridge Wood and were fitted out with the necessary materials for the forthcoming attack at the Forest, to which it moved on September 18th. The next day was fine and bright but later on a drizzle set in and finally heavy rain fell for a short time. A thick mist allowed the men to take up their assembly positions without any casualties, the German runners for once losing their targets. For four mornings our artillery had sent over practice barrages to fool the enemy as to the real attack and they had suffered a great deal of destruction as the enemy gunners retaliated, but, thanks to the very same thick mist, the enemy gunners had eased up and so allowed our artillery to make some reorganisation and be ready for the morrow. Runner Buller Barrass had time to go back to get details for the pigeons, which a signaller had forgotten to carry with him.

Promptly at 5.40 a.m. on the morning of the 20th the troops moved forward. It was not so light as expected because the mist still prevailed. Five minutes elapsed before the Germans realised that the attack had started and then very heavy machine gun fire came from the dugouts in the German front line – they had not been damaged or destroyed by the British gunfire during the preliminary bombardments. The advance was checked temporarily as many officers, N.C.O.s and other ranks fell and the men began to lose touch with the flanks which seemed to be able to make more progress. The Colonel (Lt/Col. Jarvis) rallied the men and the advance continued and gradually the men captured the German dugouts. Many were the casualties: the Colonel was wounded, the signalling officer received a few bullets and had to go back, Captain E. Worsley who was in support came forward and he too was wounded, and many other officers. Sergeant Ted Coulson who had started off with twenty signallers found at the first objective that he had only six left, including himself. Sad it was that the other fourteen were all newcomers to the battalion and for a few it was the first time over the top. The signallers carrying the aeroplane liaison strip, the battalion sign and the aero signalling panel had all been wounded or killed. When the contact plane flew over the enemy front line calling K.RU. – K.R.U. it was impossible to reply to it and the plane flew away to the left.

Because of the battalion's heavy losses, especially in officers, some reorganising took place before the advance could continue. Word was got through to Brigade of the state of affairs and the 124 Brigadier came up in person – a wonderful sight for he was minus his tunic and carried a machine gun. The Yeomen went forward and soon the German dugouts and the Red Line were captured. Fred Johnson, the fearless linesman, advanced alone at one point watched by another signaller, Tom C., and got round an enemy dugout and captured it. Most of the Germans who came out of their dugouts with their arms up shouted: "Kamerad" and wore Red Cross Brassards on their arms. They were taken prisoner and our men knew that they had been the machine gunners of earlier on.

Immediately the men got busy consolidating the position. The signallers needed an office and Ted and his survivors entered a pillbox and found in it many German wounded and a Tommy on the scrounge. He was Otto, who said that he was delighted to see them as he thought that he was the last of the British Army. This impression had not prevented his having a good look round for souvenirs. Just as Ted Coulson had set about organising some form of office there, a large shell burst in the doorway and caused havoc, wounding many men and the dugout was a shambles. One youngster had his arm blown off and Ted did his best to stop the bleeding with the help of a fork and a handkerchief. At that moment a machine gun officer appeared and chased out the signallers and made it his headquarters. Another pillbox was found and the office set up.

During the consolidation it was seen that the Royal Fusiliers, Queen's and K.R.R.s were all mixed up but they all worked well together to make a sound line. About six o'clock they noticed that Jerry was pounding the area behind them and suddenly he launched a counter-attack which was easily driven off by rifle fire, machine gun fire and artillery fire. Shortly afterwards the advance was continued and the Blue Line was taken without much opposition. More and more digging-in followed and another counter-attack driven off. There was heavy shelling most of the night as the Germans tried to blast the troops out of the captured positions.

The next morning, just as the troops were thinking of something to eat, a further counter-attack was launched but it was beaten off. Tired men worked hard improving the position and in the late evening were relieved by a Cambridge regiment. Heavy enemy shelling seemed to follow them all the way out and as they were passing a battery line Jerry lobbed a shell into the ammunition dump and things looked very unhealthy, so they went across country and struck a road further down. Eventually they arrived at Ridge Wood where the battalion cookers awaited them and seemed to have far more food than was required for the few that came out.

After that very welcome repast and a short rest the survivors of the battalion were marched to Ouderdom – a loosening up march after many, many hours of stiffness and wet conditions and nearly reaching the light infantry pace. A train of cattle trucks awaited the boys and they were taken to Caestre. From here a march of just over a mile brought them to Le Peuplier which could hardly be called a village because it was made up of several houses scattered along a road and side road and many farms in the open countryside. The billets were clean and comfortable and Hazebrouck was only four to five miles away and worth a visit. Some light training was done each day and just before the end of the month motor buses took the battalion via Hazebrouck, Steenvoorde and Bergues into the Ghyvelde area where billets were found for it in a small village. The next day the Divisional General paid it the usual visit and spoke his usual words of appreciation.

At long last, after almost a year in the well-known Salient of Ypres, the Yeoman Rifles left the sector – but not all of them. Many were in the cemeteries of La Clytte, Reninghelst, Vierstraat and Ridge Wood; many too were in unknown graves and some blown to pieces. Our casualties for the whole of August were three officers and twenty-six other ranks killed; ten officers and 253 other ranks wounded and nine other ranks missing. In the September attack from the night of the 19th-20th to the relief on the night of 22nd-23rd September, the battalion casualties were: two officers killed and thirteen wounded (of these the two killed and six of the wounded were 2nd/Lts. and I did not know them for they were newcomers); other ranks 45 killed, 192 wounded and 40 missing. Medals awarded: one bar to D.S.O.; one bar to M.C.; four M.C.s and fifteen Military Medals to other ranks. When so many officers are wounded or killed, many brave deeds go unnoticed.

On October 6th the battalion marched from the village in Ghyvelde area to Les Pannes Baines, good billets in a very pleasant town. Shortly afterwards the medals were given out.

Two of our companies relieved a Manchester battalion and took over coast duty until the 15th when we relieved the 18th K.R.R.s at Middlesex Camp, the position of the battalion in support. Just over a week later we relieved the Bankers in the Front Line. To our great surprise, a Scottish Battalion of the 9th Division took our places and we went out to St. Idesbalde and from there to Teteghem by motor bus – was a change of sector imminent? In between times during October, many hours were spent in training. A move to Wormhoudt – a march of twelve miles – took place on Sunday, November 4th, and the training continued.

11

Boeschepe – The Signalling Course

We lucky six signallers of the original section arrived at the X Corps School in the late afternoon. It was situated in a field on the right hand side of the road from Mont des Cats before it joined the main Berthen-Boeschepe road. It was sheltered by many trees: the wooden huts of the staff and the stores were at the beginning of the field, and the camouflaged tents for the men taking the course were strung along the left hand side, rising all the way. A duckboard track lay to the right and a thick, high hedge lay between the tents and the road. Boeschepe was about eighty feet above sea level and the camp from ninety to one hundred and forty. The last tent of all was at the highest point in the districk, at about one hundred and fifty feet. From it one could get an excellent view of the countryside to Godewaersvelde and the railway to Abeele, further north and the aerodrome. We six, after reporting, were put in a tent about halfway up the hill and in the other tents were groups of six from each of the other battalions of the division, about a hundred altogether. At the bottom of the field was the farm and the usual outbuildings and a huge walnut tree grew at the front of it – the first tree of that kind I had ever seen.

The officer in charge of the school was a Jock, Lieutenant K. MacDonald, and the instructors were S.M. Green and other N.C.O.s of the Royal Engineers. Fat faced, happy always and very pleasant at all times to us, S.M. Green was a good sport and did his best to give us a good time both on parade and off parade. He had always been in the R.E.s and on the Corps staff and thus appreciated the fact that we were from the line. At first he rather puzzled us because he always addressed us as "soldiers". We quickly found out that he was not being funny, as he used that word only to the infantrymen. Occasionally he arranged concerts for our amusement and his share came in singing hits from the latest musical comedies in Blighty – particularly *If You Were the Only Girl* from the Bing Boys; *They Didn't Believe Me* from *Tonight's the Night* and *Every Little Girl Can Teach You Something New*. All such musical evenings were held in the concert hall. Nearby was the camp's own canteen, always well-stocked and much patronised by us. Another large hut constituted the lecture room, used mostly on wet days for talks on the Signalling Manual, D Mark III telephone, Fullerphones, ringing telephones, telephone exchanges, jointing cables, labelling, elementary theory of electricity, cable laying, office control, station discipline and testing and maintenance of lines. Here out of the ordinary schemes were arranged and carried out outside on the finer days. We got plenty of practice in sending and receiving morse with the buzzer, the small flag, with the large flag, the shutter and the lamp and semaphore with two flags, increasing our speeds daily. The ultimate aim was to win either a second class certificate or a first class one, or better still an assistant instructor's certificate. We were all very keen and, whether it was because we were having a change from the humdrum training or whether it was because we were out of the line, we enjoyed the regularity of parading. There was now something decent to think about, a striving worth the effort and a goal to be reached without any killing. Nature round about us was as it should be – a clean world.

A piece of signalling apparatus with which we were not acquainted was introduced to us. It was a heliograph, by which the sun's rays could be reflected to a great distance by a movable mirror. Without a very important part called the standard arm, the apparatus could not be aligned on to a distant station. After receiving much instruction in it, it was decided on every sunny afternoon to see what we could do with it. One group of three was ordered to set up a station at the top of the hill in the camp and I was told to go with two others and find a suitable spot on the road towards Abeele. We had bicycles, a heliograph and a Lucas signalling lamp. Freewheeling down into Boeschepe, we went through the town, turned left and found a suitable spot. When we came to setting up our station we found to our dismay that the standard arm was missing, so we set up the lamp, got in touch with the camp station and asked for the missing part to be sent urgently. This was done and we had a successful first exercise with the heliograph. When we had returned to camp the S.M. congratulated us on having got over an awkward situation and quietly pointed out that all the equipment that we had taken with us should have been checked. I ought to have known what to do for I had learned that lesson at Aldershot and had always checked telephones, lamps, etc.

Only occasionally was there an evening parade to brush up our lamp signalling. Otherwise, we were free immediately after tea. When no concert was laid on we sauntered down into Boeschepe, which was only ten minutes away down the hill. If we could afford it we indulged in the now familiar eggs and chips and, after a pay parade, perhaps two eggs and chips: a Tommy's pay had been increased by three pence per day. We met more Aussies than before and enjoyed their company. They were very popular with everybody, especially with the owners of the estaminets. One egg and chips, a small piece of bread and a small cup of coffee now cost the equivalent of one day's pay. When an Aussie with a pal ordered "two eggs and chips for two twice", the look on the m'selle's face was wonderful to see. She just stared or flung her arms up in the air and muttered goodness knows what Such an order had her beaten. After much gesticulating and pointing to one another, the Aussies at last managed to get the message through. Many of the houses also supplied such a meal and wines or bieres could be readily obtained there. Meeting with other troops and hearing about their "stunts", answering questions about one's own unit and discussing which part of Blighty one knew, all such talk made for very happy evenings. It was in one of these houses that we heard a rumour that there had been serious trouble in two French battalions, which had been relieved by two of our battalions.

On our return to the camp after an evening in the town, a long pull uphill, we would have a chat on the duckboards before turning in for lights out at ten o'clock. We would look towards Ypres and see the sky lit up by gun flashes and Very Lights and try to guess if the worst display would be near the boys in the line. Our anxiety increased as the third week of the course started. We noticed about reveille that the gunfire was much heavier and that Jerry was being given a very heavy hammering – a din that reminded us of our barrages.

I liked the weekends very much because after dinner on Saturday and, except for meals, on Sunday we were free to go anywhere, only having to apply for a pass-out if we intended going a fair distance to some big town such as Meteren or Poperinghe. It was a Sunday afternoon when I strolled uphill and down dale to Mont des Cats; the countryside was very beautiful, wooded and green, and at the foot of the hill was the Estaminet des Trappistes, called after the Convent des Trappistes on the top of the hill. The windmill at the other side of the road was a very prominent landmark and I bought a picture postcard showing a corner at the top high with hedgerows with the windmill to the right and trees and just the top of the convent showing. "Quite all right here," I wrote, and had added, "but have a slight cold." It was not often I gave the bad news. It was said that a German prince who had been killed in the early days of the war was buried here in the grounds of the convent and, for that reason, that pleasant district was never bombed. Tommy always referred to the building as "the monastery".

Poperinghe – all of us had heard of Pop, as it was very affectionately known. It was a railhead from which hundreds and hundreds of troops set off on leave. At Pop they felt safe, having reached the first real step on their way home to Blighty and having turned their backs on the Salient, its conditions, its mud and the slaughter. A ten days' break from it all, to see friends, wives, sweethearts and relatives. How glad they were to be going and how quickly those happy days would pass.

The fourth Sunday on the course Mac and I decided to visit Pop and, having obtained passes and had our dinners, we set off for a very pleasant six mile walk. It was full of refugees and the cafes and estaminets were doing good trade. Many officers were making their way either to or away from Skindles, a very popular hotel for commissioned men. We walked round the square, the Grande Place, and turned down the Rue d'Hopital and on the right hand side saw a large house with many flags flying outside it. It was a typical large Belgian house with three floors in the middle and two at each side and all the narrow long windows were lattice shuttered. We stood at the entrance and realised this was Toc House, i.e. Talbot House, called after the Reverend S. Talbot, a chaplain of a division and closely linked with the Reverend P.R. Clayton (Tubby), also connected with Pop. We read the notice that anyone was welcome to go inside but we were afraid to, not knowing anything about this haven of peace at the time. Later, when it was too late, we regretted this.

We returned to our camp and that evening we noticed greater aerial activity by both sides and on succeeding evenings as well. The air was full of the drones of aero engines as their planes and our planes, bombers, were seeking out dumps, railheads, aeroplane hangars, roads and troop concentrations. We watched our own planes, tail lights showing to indicate to our searchlight crews that they were friendly, till they reached the front line, and then they switched them off. The German planes recognised them by the sound of their engines and coming our way without tail lights showing were the target of our searchlights and anti-aircraft guns, known as Archies. This name we gave to their light shells as well. We had often seen an open motor lorry carrying an Ack Ack gun pass the camp on its way nearer to the line. One night in particular we heard that strange, heavy drone of an enemy plane (a Fokker?). As we gazed towards Pop that bright, starry night our searchlights were very busy and one soon found the intruder and then almost immediately another light caught it in its beams. The enemy plane looked like a small silver toy as our Ack Ack guns and the machine guns attached to the lights got very busy on that easy-to-be-seen target. We followed with our eyes the paths of the tracer bullets and it seemed that the raider was doomed for he was having a very hot time, and we were quite excited as we expected and hoped to see it fall. Its heavy load prevented it from turning quickly and dodging out of the beams so, in order to escape, it let its load of six bombs drop one by one. We heard the six successive thuds and thought "What a packet to drop" and "What billet have they found?" The enemy plane rose a little and was then seen to come much lower, turn round and make for its own lines, sinking lower as it went. Then our lights lost it and, although it seemed as if it had been hit, I think it successfully returned to its own hangar. Shortly after that incident enemy aircraft became more daring and decided to put the wind up the searchlight crews. When a light caught the enemy plane in its beams the observer fired his machine gun down the beams to catch the men moving the beam. The new dodge worked admirably, for some sections had casualties and became very scared. To counteract the new threat of danger, sandbag walls were erected round the searchlights which were then worked by long poles. Though our tents were well camouflaged and well screened by trees, we became a little apprehensive because of the important targets near us – the Abeele corps headquarters and aerodrome, the Godewaersvelde dumps and rail sidings. Whilst we were on the course Jerry missed those targets and his bombs dropped in the open countryside between us and them.

The Thursday came when the boys went over the top: we thought about them and in the evening before retiring, we gazed towards Ypres. The sound of heavy bombardment reached us and we wondered what was happening beneath the huge arc of light, the flashes and the Very Lights. We did not know when the remnants came out of the line and that they had been put in billets near Caestre or we should have visited them.

The time flew only too quickly and the sixth week found us in the midst of our final tests. We were given our certificates on Saturday, October 13th, and all our party of six had qualified as Assistant Instructors. Each of us could now wear our cross flags on the upper right arm instead of the lower left arm, as would a first class signaller. As we were packing up to return to our units, I was called to the camp office. Great news indeed – I had come out top of the course and was to be kept at the school as an instructor, a cushy job at last. What did every Tommy in the line want but a cushy job behind the line? I would not be becoming a base wallah but the next best thing. I calmed down in my selfish thoughts when I returned to our tent and found the others ready to leave, waiting for me. I gave them my news and they were glad, they smiled and I looked glum. Probably they envied me my good fortune; their thoughts would quickly be of what they might be returning to and so with "Best of luck" and "All the best" we gave hurried handshakes, or rather grips, a final wave and they were gone. I felt lonely and lost until I was again called to the office. "Bring your kit into the R.E. instructors' hut and, as soon as you can, put up two stripes." Unpaid, of course.

The beginning of the next course was postponed and there was little to do. We yarned a lot in the hut and I was asked dozens of questions about the line. Talk turned to leave, and I said that very few of the battalion had been on leave so far. The R.E.s could not believe it, for they had already had two leaves and any time they would be going home for the third time since coming out. In fact one of the instructors was notified the next day that he was to go on leave. When he heard that I had not had a leave and that I had come out with the division, he told the Jock officer and he came to see me with the lucky N.C.O. and told me that the Corporal was quite willing for me to have his allotment for the 29th, and that they would find a few extra francs for me. I expressed my thanks to both the officer and the N.C.O.

I was shocked that the system allowed soldiers with the safest jobs to have leave every six months whilst most of the men who went over the top or suffered such terrible conditions in water-logged trenches got one leave in eighteen months if they were lucky. The P.B.I. again got the worst end of the stick and most probably when leave did come they got to Blighty and spoke little of the terrible times they had been through; others would do the boasting. How hard it was to understand the minds of the powers-that-be. If the young officers of the line got leave every three months, they deserved it – and their men ought to have had better leave too.

12

Blighty and Leave

I had a clear conscience in taking this leave for the good-hearted R.E. would soon be on his way home, he would not have long to wait for the next allotment to his section but some of us of the line had begun to think that we should never get leave, even that we were not too keen on breaking contact with the front because it would be there to come back to after the leave.

On the Monday I set off with full pack along the same route to Pop that Mac and I had taken one Sunday. Dear old Pop, for me, at last. I felt very light-hearted once I was well on the way and reported to the R.T.O. My green combined leave and railway ticket was with my extra francs and pay book in my top left pocket. I had no copy of *Instructions for Officers and Men Proceeding on Leave*, nor any heavy souvenirs. Neither had I a certificate to say that I was free from vermin or scabies because I was quite clean due to the long stay on the course. Just a little anxiety till the train came in and I was settled in a cattle truck with quite a number of artillery men. Off at last and a slow train. We reached St. Omer exactly at noon and drew up in its station. I sat with a gunner dangling our legs in the doorway and looking out into the street. It looked as if a factory was leaving as there were dozens of girls all dressed in brown. I said to the gunner, "Just look, wouldn't you think they were English girls going home for dinner?" He replied, "You poor b … .., they are. Haven't you seen any before?" I told him that I hadn't. Apparently they were W.A.A.C. – girls of the Women's Army Auxiliary Corps, over in France to help with the war. I did feel a fool, but I had not seen any before – they did not come near the front line.

With that touch of Blighty in mind we left St Omer and very, very slowly continued on our way in fits and starts. There were many stops and bumps as we huddled inside towards dusk and suddenly there was a slight crash – our train had run into something, but the collision was only a slight one. I sustained a few scratches and a cut arm which needed attention. How odd that my field dressing had to be used under such circumstances

We detrained at Dieppe and were soon on a boat for Newhaven. No waiting there and we were soon on a train for London. Here I exchanged my francs for English money and found the way to King's Cross by tube. What a bustle! Crowds of people were going in all directions and there was khaki everywhere. The tube train hardly stopped and how passengers got on or off was hard to imagine. What a crush – no chance of a seat or even a strap. I stood on a platform and eased the weight of my pack by placing my rifle underneath it at the back. I had to keep on the alert and watch for the names of the stations, fearing I should miss King's Cross. I found it alright, out again, rush upstairs, found a porter to question about a train for the north – he told me the platform and the departure time, 5.25 p.m. I got a seat back to the engine and near a window. Off came my pack and I put it and my rifle on the rack; I sank back, tired and feeling as if my eyes were dropping out. I had been travelling for about thirty hours with very little rest and with no chance of a wash, which state of affairs I remedied as soon as the train left for the north.

I slept fitfully, unable to find much comfort in the moving carriage. Some short naps and then I found myself being bundled out with rifle and pack on to the Doncaster station platform; I must have told someone in the compartment that I had to change there. After a long wait on a cheerless platform a connection arrived and I reached my home town just on midnight.

At the barrier were scores of people – fathers, mothers, lovers and even children awaiting loved ones. I had not written to my mother to say that I was coming home because I waited to be sure, and a telegram was out of the question because of the heartbeats of fear it would surely cause. I had more than a mile to walk and when I arrived at the house I knocked only lightly and again lightly, but I could not arouse anyone. I went round to the back and threw a pebble up at my mother's bedroom window. At the third effort and after softly calling "Mother, Mother", she came to the window. She peeped out, realised she was not dreaming after all and came down to let me in. Then came down mother's uncle and aunt and her schoolgirl niece, who often wrote to me calling me her "big brother". A grand welcome home, and hundreds of questions about the front to which I gave evasive answers as I had no wish to pile on a description of the horrors of war. I told them of the good times and of the cushy job I had. We talked for hours. A fire had been lit, mainly to heat up the water. We looked at the map on the kitchen wall and its flags, especially the large one which showed where I was when out there, and they always knew. At long and happy last they retired and I went to the bathroom. No standing up under a shower of warm water for a few minutes followed by a cold douche this time, no race against time, but just reclining at ease. Months had passed since the last visit to an Army shower. I did not like leaving the warm water once I was in – what a glorious feeling I had – and then into a soft feather bed with clean sheets as a covering, warm all over with no need to put my legs into the arms of my cardigan in order to get extra wamth. Yet I was restless and tossed and turned over and over again. I had heard men say that when on leave they had to get out of their beds and sleep on the floor, and now I could understand this. I did not have a good lie in but got up and joined the others at breakfast, much to their surprise.

I did not know what to do on my first morning home – I felt lost and out of place. I stayed in to be near those at home. I would suddenly get up and go to the front door as if to go out but just as suddenly go back to the kitchen and sit down. I could not help noticing that there were trials and difficulties at home. The so-called white bread was poorer than the Army ration bread. Coupons were required for meat of all kinds and for sugar. Housewives queued up for this, that and the other. My coupons were added to the others of the household and the tin of bully that I had brought with me was welcomed.

At midday my great uncle, when he arrived from his work at the railway depot, told me that Mac, whose father worked at the same place, was also on leave. What cheerful news – the two of us were not to be parted in Blighty. Mac, like myself, was a home bird that day and did not come to see me till the next day – and what a surprise he had for me when we met. He had received a telegram recalling him to the battalion to which he had to report at once. I had not received such a startling recall and when he asked me if I would be returning I said I wouldn't not until I got a telegram. We talked things over and wondered what could be wrong. Within hours I guessed the answer: matters were going very badly for our allies, the Italians, and soon they were in full retreat being heavily defeated by a combined German and Austrian force (Caporetto). Some Italian divisions, fed up with the war, had lost the will to fight on and had given way. They had not the staying power like the Tommies who, I suppose, were just as fed up with the conditions and waste. We always felt that the Germans vented most of their hate on us. The Russians had failed us and things were looking rather black for the Western Front. Were they going to be worse still? Would the Italians pack in? What about the Yanks? We knew that a few thousands had arrived in France and that some had been sent to our infantry battalions to learn the business of war, but I had not seen any or heard much about them. I suppose that they would go to a cushy front and gradually learn, like we had.

I asked Mac about the battalion and he told me that after we bid one another goodbye at Boescheppe, he and the four others had gone by train to Dunkirk and then by barge along a canal to La Panne where the battalion was in reserve. The men were billeted in houses in the town and lived, as it were, by the seaside almost as if there was not war at all. In the line near Nieuport-les-Baines the battalion was on the extreme left of the Western Front next door to the North Sea. The trenches were not at all like those to which we had been accustomed. A wrecked railway engine proved to be very good cover whilst the holes formed by trying to prop up sand were a very weak protection. Middlesex Camp was the name given to the support billets. The troops billeted in houses lived in the cellars and it was possible to go a long distance under cover because holes had been knocked through the cellar walls that were common to any two houses. The sector was a quiet one and was just beginning to become warmer as one of our eighteen pounder batteries relieved a Belgian Spitfire battery and began to have regular daily shoots. We recalled that our second battalion had almost been wiped out there abouts and that Jerry had captured the commanding positions. Mac returned to the front the next day.

The news of Mac's recall altered my outlook somewhat. Till now I did not have to worry for I would be returning to a cushy job, but I now doubted whether my good luck would hold. The battalion had moved out of the X Corps area and I could see that I would have to re-join my battalion. I felt now that I could not keep smiling all the time, but I needed to put on a show before the family. My thoughts leapt ahead to the end of my leave and wondering what the outcome would be.

Of course I ran into old friends. They were all well-meaning when they came up, hands outstretched, and asked, "How long are you here for?" or, more usually, "When do you go back?", "Have you killed any Germans?" or "What's it like out there?" We weren't in the same world. I suppose that whatever answers we gave to the more serious questions were not believed, how could these people grasp the horrors on the Somme, the loss of so many lives, the water-logged trenches in the Salient the lice and all the rest of the horrors?

I visited my old secondary school to which I owed a lot – self-discipline, learning, sportsman-ship, courtesy, etc. It was the finest of all such schools, with its motto. Not for oneself, but for all. Peter Davies, the art teacher, known as "Drop a pencil, drop a mark" and "Scrape your chair and get one stroke", collared me and took me into his room:

"How long are you home for?"

"Ten days."

"Ten days, why I thought you were home on week-end leave. You haven't been out there, have you?"

"Yes, nearly a year and a half."

"What! But you haven't been in the line, have you?"

"Yes, mostly in the very Front Line."

"And you haven't been wounded?"

"No."

"I cannot believe it possible!"

His face was a picture; he found it impossible to believe that I could be alive. I ended the conversation with, "There are always a few survivors in every battalion." I wondered how many old scholars he had written off when he heard how long they had been out there. In the corridor I met Woodie, the manual instructor of the combined elementary and secondary departments. How I remembered him. One Thursday morning I had completed the first model of the woodwork course – a one inch diameter, twelve inch long wooden rule. I took it to him and he held it up in front of him, looking along it with one eye closed. He pointed out a slight bump. "Take a smoothing plane and just take off the thinnest of shavings there." I fixed the model in a vice protected by two strips of wood and applied the smoothing plane. What a disaster: a small piece of wood had been chipped out. I had slipped up because I had not examined the blade of the plane which jutted out a quarter of an inch. The boy who used it last let me down. Woodie, who ought to have been an instructor at a base camp, yelled out as he thumped a bench with a mallet. "Down tools, gather round!" I was told to lie on the bench face down and I received six strokes as hard as he could give them and then three strokes across each hand. "Dennis will never spoil another model, and neither will any of you. Get back to work!" I had to start on the plan for model number two but I could not hold the pencil steady for some time. However he failed to make me cry and if I had gone home and told my only parent he would have known about it – but I didn't I learned to take my punishment for I was in the wrong. There was Woodie in front of me, astonishment on his face at seeing me in khaki. I ignored his outstretched hand as he said, "Well Dennis, I never expected to see you in uniform." I replied, "Some of us have to have guts haven't we?"

I got used to being stopped on the main road and in the streets by mothers and sweethearts who, on seeing khaki, more or less worn, came to me: "What part are you from?" When I replied, "The Salient', they went on to ask such questions as, "Did you see my Jim – he's in such and such a regiment?" They did not realise how limited all Tommies were in meeting other regiments. Pathetic indeed, only those who cared worried.

The very first time that I had gone out of the house and turned away from the main road I was arrested by a voice, "Why, Gerald, don't you know me, and aren't you going to say anything?" Though I had never seen or spoken to her, I knew that Mrs. Spence was addressing me – she was the mother who sent me a telegram to the Front Line after our first attack on the Somme, the mother of our eighteen year old tallest boy. I was glad that I had guessed who she was, but I felt like a coward. What could I say? She had been notified that her son was "Missing, believed killed". Quite naturally she lived on in the hope that he would turn up. He had been killed and she was notified of that a few weeks later. I could not give her any hope because some of our own company had seen him fall as he rose from the trench at zero hour.

John Bell, the school friend who sent me books out there, had been two years at the secondary school when I arrived there and I was put in the same form. For two years he was top of the form and I was second and we became great friends. He left earlier than I did and went as an apprentice draughtsman to a firm doing work on submarines and became exempt from being called up. I knew that if I waited around near my house at one o'clock he would be passing and I should see him. I did so every day I was at home. He asked scores of questions about the front and I knew that he was the only person to whom I could describe what things were like. I told him that the Battle of the Somme resembled a huge game of draughts: our leader would advance a man and say to the enemy leader, "Take that" so that when he did he could take one of his opponent's men. The gigantic game would proceed, not with twelve men each, but with three thousand men each, and no-one would win, but honour would be satisfied and we would gain a little ground. Each evening we went for a walk into the country. I enjoyed the discussions we had and when I asked him about the home front I was shocked to hear that industrial disputes had resulted in strikes at the docks, in munition works and in some clothing factories. No wonder there had been a shortage of shells at times and a proportion of duds.

I spent many hours with my mother and one afternoon she took out of a drawer in her bedroom the letters, field cards and picture postcards I had sent. Where a censor had crossed off the name of a village or town on a card I printed the appropriate name on it. Then we looked at a map on the wall and I showed her whereabouts the places were. When I suggested that she could destroy the letters, she put them back into the drawer. I asked her to take charge of my soiled map of the Messines Ridge stunt and also look after the small souvenirs I had: a German Field Card, the five centimes note of Lille, and the aluminium pigeon message container which had to be fastened to the pigeon's leg with two clips attached to the container.

The end of the leave came, it had to come, it had been in sight for days. I was sorry for the sake of my mother and the others at home, but inwardly was looking forward to leaving behind the civvies for I had not been able to fit in. The gulf between them and the likes of me was too deep. They could not take in what I found hard to express in detail. I did not seem to mind as long as I was able to reassure my mother that the Italian front could not be so bad as anything I had met in France and Belgium. I packed up my kit and in full marching order I said my goodbyes at home. I would not have any of my family to see me off, but let John accompany me to the railway station. We walked all the way, disdaining to use a tram for part of the distance.

I never spoke to anyone all the way to King's Cross and then Victoria Station, where I got a great shock. When, just before 6 p.m. I showed my warrant to a Red Cap at the platform, he said, "What's this? You were due here at six this morning, not this evening." I could not believe it, yet I had made a very simple mistake; I had read "Report at 6 ... " and concluded that it was p.m. and never thought it might be a.m. "Come back in the morning early," he said, "I'll leave your battalion to deal with you." That sounded ominous, but it was better than his taking any action – it would not be worth his time. Ominous indeed, but the question was, what was I to do in the meantime?

The station was crowded and I recalled what Jack Ward told me when he arrived at Victoria Station on his way back to the front. A Salvation Army Officer had come up to him and said, "Going back off leave? Come with me," and when he had collected some ten such men he took them to an S.A, hostel to look after them for the night and to save them getting into wrong hands, such as those of women of doubtful character. However, I had no time to look around and stare and wonder what to do, for a chauffeur in liveried uniform came up to me, touched the brim of his cap and asked, "Going back off leave, young man? Then come with me. My master looks after one returning soldier each night. It is his way of doing his bit." Without hesitation or doubts I followed him to a spotless car and he held the door open for me to get in and then he drove into the darkness for twenty minutes. We pulled up at the front door of a mansion. On his ringing the bell a maid opened the door and I was taken upstairs to a beautiful bedroom and then shown where the bathroom was. I cleaned up a bit and then went downstairs and was taken into a drawing room where I was greeted by an elderly gentleman. He asked many questions about the war out there and we discussed many aspects of it. A dainty supper was provided for me and my host wished me "Goodnight and good luck out there" as he would not be about when I set off in the morning. I was called next morning at 4.45 a.m., given breakfast and taken by the chauffeur to Victoria Station in good time for my train. He too wished me all the best and, on my asking him the name of my host said that he preferred to remain anonymous. I was sorry about this for I should have liked to have written to him for such kindness to one so completely lost in our capital city.

My travelling warrant was stamped by a different Red Cap at the gate, a day later than it should have been, but no comment was made as he did not bother to look carefully at it. I was present and going back and that was sufficient. The train was crowded with soldiers going back to France. At first we were all, in my compartment, more or less very quiet busy with our own thoughts, looking backwards to leave and forwards to we knew not what. I took out of my pocket two recent photographs. Mother had insisted that I should be taken with her and also have one by myself. Hence my tunic and trousers had had a severe brushing and the trousers given a crease of sorts. I was surprised how smart and clean I looked. My attempt to grow a moustache, to Army orders, could not be seen.

Gradually our glum looks disappeared and we began to chat to one another – where we each had been where we were going back to, etc. We detrained at Folkestone and were marched by a Red Cap to a very large house on the front, no longer a boarding house for holiday makers but a barracks-like building for passers through. We sat down at some long tables and were given a drink of tea and something to eat. As we arose from our meal and were about to leave, the orderlies, whose job was certainly cushy, held out their cheese cutters and asked for, almost demanded in a jocular way, our English money, as we would not be needing it any more. This bit of fun was too much for some of the party, the air was blue and cheese cutters were flying all over the place. To add insult to injury, we did not like being escorted along the promenade by a Military Policeman – we did not think of escaping our duty.

As we reached the pier we saw many Belgian soldiers were enjoying a pleasant morning stroll. We boarded the boat that was to take us back. It was a daylight crossing this time and we looked backwards at the English shore and let our thoughts go further back still, to our homes. Above us were "the pigs", our splendid escort whose "eyes" were capable of detecting enemy submarines even below the surface of the water. They saw our transport vessel safely into the harbour at Boulogne. No welcome from the children and women folk this time; were they as disillusioned as some of us had been with "dear old Blighty"?

We marched up the hill to St. Martin's camp for another meal and a night's rest, breakfast and then down the hill to the railway station. The R.T.O. told me the time of the train I wanted for Pop and soon I was in a cattle truck and on my way to "our world". I got off the train at Abeele and thus saved myself an extra long trek to the camp at Boescheppe. It was late afternoon on Saturday, November 10th when I entered the office and handed my travel warrant to S.M. Green. He tore it up without looking at it and asked me if I had had a good time. I thanked his corporal who had given up his leave for me. "Hard luck," said the sergeant-major. "You have to return to your battalion. Didn't you get a telegram from us recalling you?" I truthfully replied that I hadn't. "You can stay with us till the morning and eat with us, then you will have to get a move on as your battalion is going to Italy."

So I had lost the cushy job on the Xth Corps staff, but I really did not worry about it. I knew what I ought to have done: as soon as I had been told that I was being kept on at the

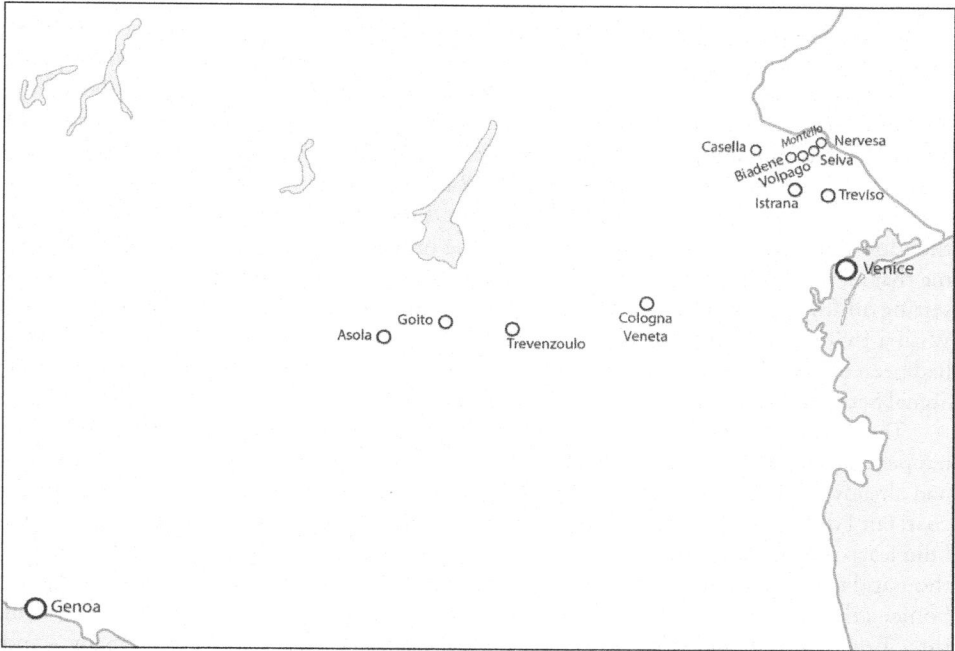

Map 6. Italy 1917-18

school I should have seen Lt. Kenneth MacDonald and asked him to put my name through for a transfer to the Royal Engineers Signals. It could have been done as easy as that, if I had keenly desired it, but I really did not want to leave the finest battalion of all. Somehow I always felt resigned to whatever turned up, or didn't.

I retired early and arose early and had my breakfast, eager to get on my way. I bade my new friends goodbye and set off for Pop and reported to the R.T.O. who told me that the Yeoman Rifles were in the Nieuport sector on the sea coast. A slow journey by district line found me at Dunkirk in the late afternoon. Here the R.T.O. told me that I could not go much further that day and that I had better report to our divisional office at Malo-les-Baines, a suburb as it were of Dunkirk. I went by tramway and made myself known at a very large house which had become the collecting centre for all Tommies of our division returning from leave. It was also a refuge for civilians who were scared during the night. Jerry planes bombed the place every night. A Belgian girl and I watched the sky that evening till we heard the sound of approaching enemy aircraft. Immediately a great barrage was put up around the town and the terrific din of the guns was like that of a bombardment of the lines. We went down into the cellar in which scores of civilians, whose homes had no cellars, and soldiers, sheltered. That night the guns kept the enemy planes at a distance and no bombs were dropped near us. Early in the morning the civilians departed and so did I. Again I travelled by tram way to Dunkirk. The tram was packed with soldiers and civilians and the inside seats were all occupied so I stood on the platform at the back and consequently travelled at a cheaper price, receiving a very flimsy piece of paper as a ticket. At the bridge over the water that separated the town from its suburb stood two Belgian sentries who casually sauntered through the tram and cast an enquiring glance at each rider. Then the tram continued on its way and passed the hospital and some very large emergency dugouts near the river bank. Much damage lay all around as obviously Jerry bombing planes had succeeded in dropping their loads near the railway station a few yards away. I got off the tram and strolled along the water side and looked into the dugouts, which had a British look about them. As I walked back to the station large crowds of excited Belgians stood about everywhere, but I never found out the cause of their alarm. The Railway Transport Officer told me where the battalion was and, after finding something to eat, I set off for Wormhoudt at 5.30 p.m. and then for Tedeghem where the boys were. At the orderly room Arnold Rushworth assured me that all was well and that I was very lucky in arriving just then because the battalion was setting off for Italy in the morning. "Did you get the two telegrams we sent you?" he asked. With a twinkle in his eye, he asked, "You live in Leeds, don't you?" The name and street had been correct, but the town wrong. It was almost nine o'clock when I finally reached the Signal Section and I was attached to H.Q. once again.

There was no time to chat or give news of Blighty, or to learn much about what had happened to my friends during my absence – all was hustle and bustle. Extra kit and things had already been given out and I was too late to be issued with a leather jerkin or sheepskin coat, but I did get a pair of fleecy lined mittens, fastened together with a long strip of leather. I did learn that as soon as the division had left the Salient and no stunts were in the offing, a thousand men had been sent on leave. I tried to reckon how many of the battalion had gone home; a thousand was a lot but when shared out (fairly or not) among the Divisional Staff, three Brigades' Staff and twelve battalions, our allocation could not have been many – and they were all recalled. How lucky I had been! Pip was another signaller who had gone on leave and his going was the result of a toss-up. One night when all the H.Q. Signals were asleep, a runner appeared from the orderly room with a message that another signaller had been chosen to go on leave. Corporal Fossie decided that the lucky one was to be Pip or Drake, who had returned to us after being wounded at Messines. Woodie, aroused from sleep, yelled out, "Toss for it." A coin was produced, tossed and Pip won. A few days later Drake had fallen from the high part in the farm building and had to go to hospital.

13

Italy – Cushy

T he early morning of Tuesday, November 13th, 1917 was dry as we rose long before dawn to pack up all our belongings, except a mug and a plate to use at breakfast. Excited, happy and carefree we paraded in full kit and finally left Tedeghem at 9 a.m. The band played at the head of the battalion and we stepped out like old times, even marching again to the bright tunes: *Tipperary* and *Take me back to dear old Blighty*, and we joined in singing lustily. On through Wormhoudt to a little place called Esquelbecq where in a railway siding our train awaited, a long line of cattle trucks – far too many of them as five would have been sufficient to carry all our men at "40 hommes" per truck. No over-crowding as about twenty men took to a truck and we signallers and runners of the H.Q. were all together. There was something about almost all the trucks that I had not noticed before on our travels. At the end of most of them was a short stairway of four or five steps leading to a small sentry – like box with two sides and a back, each with a small window. The other side, open, faced the truck. These little look-outs were for the guard of the train if any particular truck was the last. We left the sidings and slowly proceeded along the main lines. The doors were wide open and I dangled my legs outside the opening that faced the Front Line. Before reaching Hazebrouck and after passing through, our thoughts went to the Salient and comrades left there, and again as we skirted the Somme we had similar thoughts – "If you want the old battalion", well, we knew where they were and we'd always remember them.

Many were the jolts and stops as our slow train passed Paris on the next day. On Thursday we reached Lyons and the Rhone Valley. We admired the beautiful scenery and missed very little that was strange to us. We were all asleep as Marseilles was reached and passed and woke up within sight of the Mediterranean Sea and pulled up at breakfast time in a siding at Toulon, where we were to stop for a few hours. Eagerly we jumped down from the tracks and ran up and down the siding to stretch our legs after being cooped up for over three days. Then we returned to our truck for our dixies, which we took to the front of the train. Just under the step of the engine cabin was a pipe, through which the fireman let flow streams of hot water into our dixies. With this we made tea and were much indebted to the fireman for so often obliging us.

How blue the sky was, how mild the weather, and how peaceful. The quietness was suddenly shattered when scores of young boys descended upon us, all gesticulating and jabbering away. They all shouted out the same words and made the same proposals as they pointed back to the sheds of the sidings where quite young girls, some mere teenagers, waved to us. "Bully bif for my sister, you … … " said the boys. The two three letter words hyphened were new to me, but it was obvious what was meant in what I concluded was slang. There was nothing doing.

Here we saw for the first time some of the French navy, "matelots" in blue uniforms and wearing blue berets with red tassels. They looked much smarter than the French infantry. We waved to them and they exchanged our distant greetings. We were not allowed to leave the sidings. We would have liked to go into the town and do a little shopping especially for cigarettes as most of the men had none left as they had done more smoking than usual as there was so little to do on the journey down to the south. They improvised, bits of bootlaces were put between brown paper or any thin paper, even the make-your-own cigarettes had used up all their zig-zag papers, brown paper on its own was smoked, perhaps the most used makeshift was drying of the old tea leaves and putting them between some kind of paper. Though a non-smoker, I could understand the great want of these men – trench life had demanded that there should be something to ease men's nerves. It was very off that I of all people should have some cigarettes. On my return to the battalion the night before we left Belgium, a parcel awaited me. It contained a hundred County Life cigarettes, which were ten for three pence. I now opened it again and distributed to my special friends two cigs. per day. I could have sold them many times over, but I gained more satisfaction in seeing the looks of pleasure on my friends' faces.

On my leave I had bought a diary for 1918 and had written down in the few pages before the space for January 1st the names of all the places we passed through. My pal, Mac, on receiving the telegram recalling him had rushed into the town and bought an English-Italian/Italian-English dictionary. From the time we left Esquelbecq, we spent many hours learning the words for common things, eatables, etc. This was easy for we both had learned some Latin whilst at secondary school and, though Mac did not take that subject in the final exams, I had been in the special class of five students who had done so. It had been very hard work but I liked the subject very much and did well in it. I think I was looked upon as an oddity.

All aboard for the tour and we slowly passed through Cannes and shortly afterwards I dropped down from the truck, ran a few paces forward and ascended the short flight of steps to the guard's look-out. Then I stepped on to the roof and sat down facing the Mediterranean Sea. Others quickly followed and nearly all the roofs had Tommies sitting on them. What a tremendous welcome from its inhabitants: rousing cheers, much waving of flags of all kinds and hand clapping. How exciting and grand for our spirits.

So there was the Riviera before us; the weather was most beautiful and warm, the sea sparkled in the sunlight and the sky was cloudless. I had read about the climate of this land belt when studying the fruit lands of the world, and there it was. I feasted my eyes, looking first to one side of the railway and then to the other. The line hugged and zig-zagged along the coast, very close to it most of the time. Town after town, village after village, some of them bedecked with flags, beautiful with their palm trees and tropical plants. I lay flat on my back as the train passed through little tunnels bored through harder rocks; I gazed at Monte Carlo at night and was thrilled by the millions of lights and tried to picture the casinos with their gaming tables and the night life in general. At the last possible moment, I slipped down from my vantage point and entered the truck and the doors were closed for the night. I slept well, the abundant fresh air acted like a sleeping draught and the hard floor needed no feather bed. Not that I wanted to sleep too long for I wanted to be up and on the top of the truck again so that I didn't miss anything.

I don't remember anything much about meals which were always minimal, and the next morning, Saturday, I was back up on top. The coastal strip seemed to get narrower and we approached the foothills of the Alps. On the left lonely cottages, villas and farm houses dotted the cliff faces. I noticed a field containing many equally spaced out trees and, resting against them, ladders which were wider at the base and narrowing to the top. Women stood on the top and be at the trees with sticks and the fruit, damsons, fell on to large white sheets spread underneath the trees and round their trunks.

Shortly after passing through Mentone the train came to a sudden stop. We were near the French-Italian border and our steam engine had to be uncoupled and taken away. We waved goodbye to our hot water supplier. In place of the steam engine was put an electric engine and, as this was being done, along came N.C.O.s: "All riding on top of the trucks is now forbidden as there is a danger of electrocution." The twin cables carrying the electric current were little more than a foot above the truck tops. The electric link from the engine was like a cage with double poles and so there was less risk of the link slipping off the electric cable.

We crossed the border – San Remo and on to Genova (Genoa) after some fifty miles of glorious scenery and lovely weather. In the back areas through which we were passing the people lived in flats, very tall buildings five or six storeys high. In one crowded quarter washing day was in full swing and the women folk went so far as to wave their washing. As we drew away from them they waved goodbye but they held their hands differently from the way we do – their hands moved towards them as if to say, "Come back, come back."

On we went passing through Mantova (Mantua) during the night until we reached San Antonio where we detrained at six in the morning of Sunday. During our brief halt here it was rumoured that we were near Caesar's Camp and Alexandria, but we had no maps and could not verify this. Almost at once we set off for Goito, where the battalion was split into two parties. Two companies kept their packs and proceeded to a railway station to be taken to our next destination whilst the other two companies and H.Q. men discarded their packs and adopted battle order and set off on foot, led by the band. It was like some of the old times as we marched along, singing as we went. The roads became rather narrow and we began to ascend the hills, the road winding its way and so easing the ascent. We were hugging the rocky side on the left and looking to the right was the edge and almost precipitous drop down to a valley below. We were marching in and out of the mist and at times were, it seemed, above the clouds. As we started to descend and get lower down the other side, we came into brilliant sunshine and saw, stretched below us, a very, very wide valley with a very narrow river at the bottom of it. I had never seen anything like this before, and across the valley was a very long viaduct: it seemed to be too long for such a small river. I realised that the dry season was responsible for such an incongruous view.

We reached the plain (Lombardy?) and stepped out gaily. When we reached small habitations, the sound of the band brought out of doors many women and children. The strains of our martial music stirred them to following us for short distances. At one village we saw barracks of many hundreds of Italian soldiers; their greeting was far from welcoming – some would spit out at us and by signs they showed that they wished us to go back to where we came from. We suspected that they were disillusioned men and were now interned till they pulled themselves together. Perhaps they were fed up with the war and wanted peace. Who didn't? I thoroughly enjoyed that march of fourteen miles to Trevenzuolo, a small place where we stayed for one night. After I had joined in the water and blanket fatigues and had a meal, I had a look round; there was just a square (piazza) and a few houses off in short streets. The signallers were billeted in a Lady Chapel in the square. The post and telegraph office was an ordinary house with the necessary apparatus and was next door to our billet. Four of us entered the post office and embarked upon a conversation with the female operator. My knowledge of Latin-cum-Italian came in useful and we discussed her apparatus and the international morse code, which she used. Then she asked me, "How old do you think I am?." We looked at one another and discussed this feminine question with all seriousness. "Twentythree," I told her. What a surprise we got, for she declared that she was only seventeen. She was not in the least offended and laughed with us. Later we were to realise that girls and women who worked hard, especially in the country areas, looked much older than they were and that the climate affected their looks. Then she went to her stock of picture postcards and chose one of a girl and then wrote her name on it, Ida Ferrarini, with greetings. The writing was all flourishes. We left the post office and found outside groups of excited women and suddenly there stopped in front of us the village tomboy, who dropped off a boy's bicycle which she had ridden at great speed.

"Are you Germans?" she yelled. We shook our heads.

"Are you French?" Again we shook our heads.

"Who are you then?."

"Inglesi," I replied.

She was dumbfounded, as were most of the women who had gathered round. Their puzzled looks disappeared, but we could not tell what they thought of our being there. They dispersed to talk over this strange happening in their village.

The next morning reveille was at 6.45 a.m., blankets were handed in and we set off after breakfast and marched rather leisurely, band in attendance, until eleven o'clock when we halted, fell out by the roadside and stayed till two o'clock. By three o'clock we had reached a small village called Bragagnani, near Vallese, where we rested for the remainder of the day and the whole of the next day. Fred Johnson, Brookes, Dally and Cantlon of the signallers and Appleby of the runners joined the band as part-timers and helped it during the playing of selections three times the day for our entertainment.

The days were most beautiful, warm as soon as we got up, becoming warmer and warmer and around midday it was very hot indeed. Hence our marching from place to place was started early and followed by a long rest around midday, followed by further marching from late afternoon till we reached our destination for the day, no matter how far it was. It was really too hot to do anything but laze from eleven to after two.

Thursday, November 22nd arrived; two years since I volunteered for the duration of the war, and yet another Christmas almost upon us. Still no sign of the end of it. That morning we set off again quite early for a seventeen mile march to Cologna Veneta, without any breakfast as no rations had arrived for us. On arriving there we were given some Italian soldiers' rations, very meagre indeed. A pay-out in the afternoon cheered us up and we had ample time to go shopping. The signallers were billeted in the Law Courts, in the side rooms off the main court. Food was scarce in the town but there was plenty of birra for those who wanted it, and also vino, a very cheap, common wine which was purple in colour and which stained the drinkers' tongues and lips. The troops had been warned earlier to go steady with the wine as it went quickly to the head.

I received five lire (the equivalent of four shillings and two pence). I went into the mainstreet and soon found a ristoranti which, owing to the war, was little better than a cafe and I had to be satisfied with hot chocolate or coffee. I chose the former which was served up in a large basin, and I thoroughly enjoyed it. Coffee, served as a liqueur, was brought forward in very small glasses not much bigger than thimbles.

No mail from Blighty had as yet caught up with us and also I had not been able to write home since I came off leave. I found a shop from which I bought three picture postcards:

one of the Corso Nuovo, the municipal buildings and the Church of Cologna Venete; the second, a model by Nanni, a pretty girl wearing a white high-collared shirt with red reveres and black and white striped tie, her black hat was like a flattened trilby with a broad white band dotted with black circles and an oval blue badge in the front – a very attractive picture and very pleasing to the eye; the third was of two carnations, one pink and one red with a spray of light green leaves. The first two I put into my pocket and the last one I carried into the post office next door. I addressed it to my mother and on the other half of that side wrote the date, "all O.K." and signed it "Gerald". Then I bought a 5 centisimi stamp (green) and put it on the card. I slipped it into the Italian post box. It arrived safely, through the ordinary civilian channels and was franked Cologna Veneta – 22.11.17 – Verona. All so simple. Many of the men went hunting for cigarettes and found they could buy only a local brand called Populari, but they were not so popular as their name implied. They ought to have been called horrors for they were far worse than the cheap issue brands so readily gambled away in Plugstreet Wood.

Despite the hard floor of our bedroom, we slept well and were ready for another early start the next day. After marching twenty-three miles and in sight of San Germano, where we expected to stay, we were told that a mistake had been made and that the Queens were going to be billeted in that place and that we had to go another eight miles to Campolungo. We probably grumbled just a little over this slight upset, which set us thinking – why all this marching? Quickly a rumour gave us an answer, the Italians allowed the British forces which were coming to help them only two trains per day and so there was great difficulty with transport of materials, food, guns, etc. and there were not enough trains to carry the infantry as far as the front. We knew that there was a difficulty in bringing the rations forward because we had had another day without bully and bread, let alone Army biscuits. On this occasion our quarter master gave the following reason:

It had been agreed to swap rations with the Italians so we received, each man, a small tin of meat or fish paste, about one and a half inches high and of just over half an inch in diameter, and a two inch wide piece of Italian bread, brown and twelve inches long. The bread seemed to have more holes in it than actual bread. I think that we lost on the deal. A poor exchange.

Only sixteen miles the next day when we passed through Barbarano and went over the hills to Monte Galladella, a march through very lovely countryside and very much enjoyed. The signallers and other sections were billeted in a real chateau. Its owner had fled with his family, fearing that the Austrians, who had almost reached the plain, would come still further. The rooms contained most beautiful and expensive furniture. We were allowed to wander through the rooms and I was greatly shocked to notice in a splendid drawing room the remains of a grand piano – someone had wanted some firewood. Upstairs I was amazed at the primitive closet on the second floor. Half the floor of a small room was covered with a slab of stone, in the middle of which was a round hole six inches in diameter. A few inches forward of the hole were two foot shapes in stone raised two inches, and one on either side. A yard long plunger was at hand to push down one's excreta. From another room I saw outside a huge tank into which the excreta went.

On our arrival there we had been given a fresh order: all troops leaving their billets would in future wear side-arms. Some ill-feeling had arisen between the Italians and the British. In some cases the former were rather touchy and showed signs that they did not want us, and it was rumoured that they did not like the show of friendliness Tommies showed to the signorinas. Stilettos had been brought into action and it was deemed advisable that Tommy should have the means of defending himself. I did not leave the billet that night except for wandering round the beautiful gardens of the chateau. Sometimes when I realised that we should be on the march again the next day, I did not think it worthwhile to take my equipment apart just to use my belt and then have to put it together again.

Twenty miles to San Georgio delle Partiche and a welcome surprise that day, a Sunday, for the Reverend E. Sayer-Ellis appeared, probably from Brigade, and held an early evening service. His sermon was based on his reading from Job, Chapter 10, verses two and three. Two of our favourite hymns *Abide with Me* and *When I Survey* preceded the Holy Communion. We were delighted to see him, he was so much loved by all.

We must have felt very hungry in those days because when we heard the next day that bread could be bought at the town of Capos Ampiero only four kilometres away, many of us set off to see if the rumour was true. On the outskirts of the town we came to an Italian field bakery with a long queue of women, girls and a few old men. We joined that queue and no-one objected, not even a few Italian soldiers who also arrived after us. Each of us was allowed one round bread loaf; its quality was not of the best, but we liked it. We enjoyed the friendly spirit of the people as we tried to answer their questions. During our second day's rest an Italian battalion appeared and halted near us. We exchanged greetings and our band played martial music which we all enjoyed. Then they set off towards the line.

All the work in the fields was done by women and girls, backs bent double as they moved along the rows looking for whatever might have been left in the fields after harvest. It reminded me of the picture "The Gleaners". In other fields women and girls were tidying up after the Italian soldiers who had retreated that way and left behind much rubbish and evidence of their halting places.

Why we marched only four miles the next day to Lorio (or Loreggio), we did not know, but it gave us the opportunity to return to Campos Ampiero for more Italian bread. The following day there were whispers: the war was on and we were going into reserve. We set off at night by companies: no smoking was allowed and everything was quiet, the night full of stars. A weird feeling stayed with us as we marched for mile after mile until at last we saw in the far distance a light bobbing up and down. It was slowly approaching us and then we heard the "Eo, ito-eo, ito" as an old peasant urged on his cart, pulled by an ox. The bobbing light was from a hurricane-type lamp hanging down from one shaft of the cart. Eventually we reached Istrana and were billeted in houses. We slept till noon and in the afternoon I visited a church there and admired its gorgeous painted ceiling. Another move by night, again there was to be no smoking and in extended order. After twelve miles we reached Selva where there was some misunderstanding about billets. Twice the signallers were moved and then matched three miles to a deserted house near a village. I guessed a lot of the distances, but reckoned on three miles per hour (fifty minutes marching and ten minutes rest). Very seldom did we talk of kilometres but often joked about the number of "Irish miles" we did.

Early in our week's stay in reserve we had a pay day, but where were we to find anything to buy? One evening we strolled into Volpage where there were French and Italian troops and an ITI canteen though its stocks were very low and poor. Signal parades were resumed and on the third day the whole battalion, fewer than two hundred, paraded to be addressed by the Colonel. "Yeoman Rifles, you have had a very good time trekking through Italy. You are once again soldiers after a month's refreshing holiday and we must get down to serious work." He was quite right – we had had a very easy time and now we were back in the war.

Not far from our billet we saw two women looking around the fields and then returning to a small cottage two fields off. That evening three of us visited that cottage and asked the women if they had any bread to sell. They asked us in. I have never seen such a poor home – one room downstairs and one room up. The kitchen had a bare floor and hardly any furniture. I repeated that we wished to buy something to eat and they suggested that they should bake us some pollenta, of which we had never heard. At one end of the kitchen was a huge open fireplace and a large slab of stone on which a fire burned. Over it was a tripod and down from the chimney hung chains. One of the women took a huge metal pot-like cauldron and poured some water into it. Then she hung it on one of the chains above the fire. She gradually let ground maize flour fall into the water until enough had been dropped in to soak up the water. The other woman kept placing twigs and bits of wood onto the fire to keep up the flames. Very deftly the first woman with her left hand twirled the pan in a circular movement over the fire and with her other hand stirred the mass with a broom handle. Occasionally she added a little more maize flour or water until she had the mixture to her satisfaction. Soon the mixture was solid, heavy and ready. She lifted the pan and its contents off the fire and rolled the Christmas pudding-shaped mass onto a cloth – and there was our dish pollenta. I asked her how much she wanted and she said that five lire would suffice. We clubbed together, glad to get rid of our smaller centesimi notes, and they were delighted to receive some money. Those poor souls knew what shortages war brought. The pollenta was very heavy to carry and we took it in turns to bear it to our billet. We used a bayonet-sword to cut it and then we each took a mouthful and immediately looked at one another to see if we thought the same. It was awful and seemed to have no taste at all. Fortunately we had some pozzy and we each laid some thickly on a piece of pollenta. We got some of it down before leaving it for the others in the billet to try. We lay down with our tummies feeling blown out and heavy, and we felt quite unable to move about.

How beautiful the mountains looked, especially at sun rise. We often gazed towards the Alps and wondered how our new enemy fared there. Now and again we saw one of his observation balloons, the first sign of war for a month. We wondered why he needed an observation balloon because he had the high ground up in the mountains. When he did use a balloon we stayed indoors, otherwise we did some signal training out of doors.

On December 7th we moved forward to the Bavaria area in support, relieving the 23rd Middlesex, and we were billeted in a farmhouse on the right-hand side of the road up the hill away from the village. The Italian owner objected (quite rightly) to us chopping down a tree in a nearby field for the cookhouse fires. He became very excited, waving his arms frantically and declared that he would see the officer. We apologised and heard no more about the incident. Not far behind our billet our own artillery men were digging a gun pit, not a comforting sight, and I went to have a chat with them. Not far from each corner of the pit, a long pole was erected and a huge camouflage net stretched over with its many imitation green leaves and brown strips of linen.

An unexpected and rare fatigue came our way: an R.A.F. wagon had fallen into a deep ditch and the help of the infantry was sought. The signallers were detailed for the job and we went to man-handle the wagon out of the ditch. We had just started to set off back when we heard shouts and on looking round; we saw that the wagon had again gone into the ditch. Again we dragged it out and soon it was on its way, without further trouble. Another day we had to go to a railhead and help the Royal Engineers unload drums of cable for signal purposes and then moved them to their G.S. wagons and load them up.

Night working parties started. Two nights in succession we went to the Nervesa line and dug trenches and strong points. As in the past we soon performed our allotted tasks for there were fifty of us, but we had to wait till our sapper-in-charge came and gave the order for us to return. We did not mind so much as the nights were beautiful, the sky clear and starry and there was no particular haste to get away – this wasn't the Ypres salient. We would turn our backs on the River Piave and gaze to where we knew Venice was. How we should have liked to see it. We knew there was no chance as it was wider stood that the city was taboo to the troops, an understanding with the Austrians that as long as Venice was completely civilian it would not be bombed.

We did pay another visit to the Mervesa area. The engineers had erected some baths there and we enjoyed the luxury of a thorough cleansing – my first bath since I had been home on leave. Another day we dug a new rifle range and later fired two groups of five. Just in good time, the Royal Engineers' printing section had prepared a Christmas card, a think piece of card four inches by six. A square of about three and a half inches in the upper half illustrated the Battle of Messines. It depicted many riflemen with rifles at the port and an officer holding his revolver level and ready to shoot, advancing to the ridge, immediately above which rose huge red flames from exploded mines, large clouds of smoke and masses of debris blown in all directions. At the top of the square, Somme, Messines, Hollebeke, Battle Wood, Tower Hamlets – names not to be forgotten. Partly in a smaller square cutting the larger one at the bottom and also cutting a rectangle below, was an oblong with "Greetings from the 41st Division. Christmas, 1917". In the rectangle below sat two Tommies in fleecy jerkins, tin hats, etc. enjoying Christmas fare from a parcel. Nearby stood a red hot brazier and in the right hand corner were some duckboards and the sandbags of a dugout. The designer was G. Thompson. We were able to buy as many as we liked and get them off to loved ones for Christmas. I put my Christian name on mine and added "Somewhere in Italy".

"Up a Line" – how strange those words sounded after such a pleasant interlude. In the evening of December 16th, the battalion moved up. The night was dark and the roads new to us, heavy snow had fallen and we had to move carefully in Indian file, each man stepping into the footsteps of the man in front of him, so that we did not make a wide path which enemy aircraft would be able to see in the daytime. Our H.Qrs. were in dugouts. Into the foothills men had literally dug first a passage some fifteen to twenty feet long and six feet high, shored it up with timbers and then dug separate little passages and rooms off it. These too were shored up with timber. These dugouts were in the sides of the hills away from enemy observation. The signal office was at the end of one of such saps and our quarters in the holes off it. I slept on the floor on the right just near the entrance where one of the off-shoots caved in.

We were active during the night hours when we had all our meals and we slept during the day, except when on duty. This arrangement had to be followed because the whole part of the front, the Alps, were occupied by the Austrians, some Germans and, it was said, some Turks. They looked down on us occupying the plain and the Monte Belluno foothills. We were really at their mercy but so far we were not aware of the war at all. Our Companies were between us and the right bank of the Piave in similar little valleys and dugouts. In deeper valleys out of sight of the enemy they were in small bivvies. On the bank of the river were posts and small strong points, but not a continuous trench. During one of our spells in this part of the line, a shell from one of the Austrian light batteries struck a bivvy and we suffered five casualties, our only losses here. Our nightly patrols tried to cross the river or to reach an island nearer to our side, but the river current was so strong that we never succeeded. We suspected that during the day the enemy manned posts near the river bank and then retired to the rear and less vulnerable positions. No Very Lights shot up into the air, no machine guns sent their missiles of death over our way. Always a weird stillness, almost always bright and frosty nights. We never saw an Austrian until late one night our patrol found an enemy officer climbing up the river bank on our side. We could not say that we had captured a prisoner for he had come to give himself up. There were no identity marks on his clothing and nothing at all in his pockets. He was brought back by way of the headquarters and he looked very pleased with himself. He was out of it, and no doubt gave Brigade Headquarters the minimum of information – his name and rank.

One dull day I ventured out of the dugout and noticed several small craters on the hillside opposite to our position, so there had been enemy shells at one time. I went on to the left and came across the most solid trench I had ever seen. It was a work of art built by the Italians in imitation of a Roman ditch. It was exceptionally made from stone from the hillsides, the floor was perfectly level and the sides straight too, but diverging towards the top. The bottom was three feet wide and the top was four feet wide, and it was four feet deep. What a lot of work had been put into it, yet it was far less serviceable than the old St. Eloi trenches and such an easy target for the Austrian gunners. I walked along it in a straight line, for there were no bays, for many yards when suddenly a whizz-bump; I had been spotted. The enemy was awake, so I hurried back, bent low, and returned to the dugout.

All night through our dugout was stuffy, clammy and foul so that each morning without fail I just stood outside the entrance and inhaled the fresh air. Early, after dawn, I would watch for the sun to appear and cast its rays on the mountain tops. What a glorious sight and gradually the sun's warmth would make itself felt and drive away the chill. The little disturbed snow had begun to melt. Christmas Eve came and we were relieved and all but one signaller had to stand outside whilst he handed over I saw that the incomers had bright buttons but did not recognise the unit; some said the East Surreys had taken over. This was unusual for the Bankers worked "in" and "out" with us. The melted snow had made the paths damp and heavy and then the frost made them sticky. The mud clung to our boots and we had to keep stopping to scrape it off. Progress was slow till we left the valleys and came to the better roads of the plain and eventually we reached the town of Volpago where, early on Christmas morning, we were billeted on the upper floor of a silk factory no longer used in manufacture. No more than twelve of us were put into a large room big enough to hold eighty men. After eight days in the line, not the usual five as in France or Belgium, we were very tired and hardly had the energy to draw blankets, one per man. The floor was concrete and very cold so we got down to it in pairs. After taking off my boots I took off my cardigan and put my feet in the armholes and buttoned it around my feet. We soon fell asleep and would probably have slept until dinner time but for our band which was playing the old familiar carols of the season outside our billet. We remained in our "beds" and relaxed. There was no hurry for no rations had arrived and our dinner would be the usual bully beef stew in due course. Quite an ordinary day for us, except for more carols in the afternoon and a feeling of goodwill.

No orders were issued for Boxing Day so we had a leisurely breakfast then, suddenly, we were startled by a most terrific din. Whatever was the cause of it was very near and in the air. The rattle of machine guns, the heavy sound of aero engines and the shouts of the people outside made us dress quickly and get outside to see what all the commotion was about.

Arriving on the outskirts of the town we saw an incredible sight. Up in the air, but only just at about one or two hundred feet, were forty planes milling round and shooting at one another, or rather some with green, white and red stripes (Italian), some with red, white and blue stripes (French), and others with red, white and blue circles (British) totalling about twenty, were attacking and being attacked by twenty Austrian planes. What a dog fight! The Allied fighter planes were uppermost, streaking over, around and under the enemy bombers. The deafening din continued and soon planes were falling down to earth in flames or dropping, damaged in some vital spot. We stood on the roadway and the wrecks were there, just in the fields near us. It was a one-sided fight for our planes had the advantage of a higher position from which to attack, and our pilots were cooler-headed. Eleven enemy bombers bit the earth without damaging one Allied plane and the nine fortunate ones set off back across the line. Some enemy pilots and crews died, some were in flames, quickly put out by the helping hands of our troops. A fallen airman would come staggering towards us and one came holding out his hands to shake ours. If we had had out rifles with us I am quite sure that we could have hit an enemy plane.

The disastrous fun over, we hastened back to our billet for our postponed Christmas dinner – bully beef rissoles and Christmas pudding. As I tendered my enamel plate to the mess orderly he dipped a large spoon into a cylindrical tin about nine inches in diameter and twelve inches deep and gave me a fairly large helping of the black-brown mass. It was very tasty; the pity was we had no sauce or custard to go with it. We understood that the Christmas Pudding was the gift of the Royal family.

In the afternoon we spruced ourselves up a bit and then returned to the scene of the morning's dog fight. We covered a fair distance, roaming at will and seeing many wrecks of planes and no-one prevented those interested in taking some sort of souvenir. Rumour had it that the Allied planes had raided the Austrian aerodrome on Christmas Day, a most ungentlemanly thing to do. Such raids weren't done on that front disturbing the peace of a holiday and upsetting the enemy officers' mess. Retaliation was immediately planned and early on Boxing Day morning the gallant Austrian officers, much fortified by Christmas wines, came over the mountains and swooped very low down towards the Allied 'drome. The result was a one-sided battle, a cake-walk for the Allies and a disaster for the Austrians.

We returned to our billet, outside which stood an Italian woman with a huge basket of oranges. I asked her how much they were and to my great surprise she replied, "One kilo for one lira". I thought it an odd way to sell oranges, by weight instead of so much each. More surprising still was the means she used to weigh them – she used a steelyard, a long piece of steel unequally divided into two parts, one much smaller than the other. At the juncture was a hook. On the end of the smaller part was hung a pan onto which she placed the oranges. She moved a weight along the longer part away from the juncture till when she held up the apparatus by the book the steel was level and the oranges balanced the weight required. Surely a very ancient way of weighing.

Our evening was also sweetened by more carols from the band. Our night's sleep was disturbed by the sound of bombs being dropped by enemy aircraft and on other nights too, whilst we were in Volpago, but no damage was done to the town. In the morning my bête noire (N.C.O.) came to me and asked how I would like to volunteer for a special fatigue, the Town Major's. I fell for it as he knew I would because I always offered to do anything, a fatigue or a working party. Four of us reported to the Town Major who told us what we had to do. Each morning for the next four days we had to fill in, one per day, a civilian latrine, and dig a new one. We thought that this was the limit – not only did we provide the Italians with a means of sanitation but we had to fill it in, dig a new one and cover it from view with canvas sheetings. Poor P.B.I. – we had to fight a hygiene war too.

We learned that part of the Transport Section had had a most appetising Christmas. A corporal had found a "straying pig," and pork went on the menu. Later an irate Italian farmer had demanded payment and the offended owner was paid out of battalion funds. Mail arrived from Blighty just too late for Christmas Day but letters and parcels now dispelled some of the loneliness we had been feeling. Parcels were doubly welcome and I had a stroke of luck. Our Padre had received many parcels from a girls' college in Wales. He gave me one of these tuck boxes, parcelled with loving care and sent with great friendliness. Mine contained a Christmas greeting card, hand painted, and very welcome food. Of course, the eatables were tinned, but at least there was no bully beef. I shared mine with my special friends: firstly tinned spring chicken, which was so excellent that we all said that we had tasted nothing like it; the second delicacy, tinned sausages. Both were eaten at supper time and we had no difficulty in cooking them. Every evening we took turns to scrounge wood so that we could have a fire in the middle of our room's concrete floor. We were fortunate to find a bucket and half filled it with water, in to which when hot we dropped the tinned goods after slightly puncturing them with the point of our sword-bayonets.

Most of our evenings were spent in the billet and we sat round the huge fire in the middle of the room. Someone hit upon a novel way of spending some of our time. Each of us in turn sat as close to the wall as possible or knelt so that the outline of the face showed clearly on the wall. Another person used charcoal from the fire to blacken in the shadow cast by the head, and there was a very good silhouette of the sitter's face. The walls of the room became like a portrait gallery by the time we had finished.

Not till the Sunday after Christmas Day did we hear the real sound of war. From well away to the left we heard the sound of heavy firing guns of many sizes being used, but we did not know till later on that French troops had gone into action and captured Monte Tomba on that day. Otherwise, as far as we were concerned, except from the very light explosions of enemy bombs dropped in the vicinity during the night, "All was quiet on the Italian Front."

After a very welcome nine days' rest the battalion moved up to another and different reserve line. It resembled the earlier one in that the signal dugout was again a small sap in the hillside containing four beds and three pieces of planking across a wooden box for the office equipment: telephone, power buzzer, forms, etc. Outside within easy reach were some scattered houses, all derelict and empty and under enemy observation. As there was not enough room for all of us in the sap, Mac and I had to spend our daylight hours in an outhouse of a farm. We had to use the upstairs room which we reached by going up a home-made rickety ladder, the foot pieces of which were very much worn. The icy cold wind blew through this room, which was a very unpleasant billet. Yet it wasn't so wet as the sap, which could have caved in at any time. Much snow had fallen. In a nearby sap the headquarters' cook did his best to prepare something warm for us and kept appealing for firewood. We scrounged round at night time and did some tree felling – that bit of work kept us warm. Our upstairs windy billet was far from rainproof for it had many holes in these walls, through which most glorious sun rises could be seen spreading brilliant colours on the snow-capped mountains.

Seven days later the battalion moved up into the line and occupied the same sap as before. It had been slightly improved – the walls strengthened and a screen built between the N.C.O.s' quarters and the office. We lived like moles and the only exercise we got was carrying the accumulators along very muddy roads to Brigade for recharging and bringing charged ones back. A not too distant empty house provided us with planks for the cooks; with the help of a pick-axe we soon ripped up the floor and our unofficial working party off our returned fully laden with wood. Life must have been very boring right up at the front positions with nothing to do. The River Piave was about eight hundred yards wide there and patrols were a waste of time for both sides. There was no chance of an encounter.

After eight days "in" we were relieved by troops of another division, so Fred stayed behind to show them the routes our telephone wires followed whilst Atti, Wakeling and I carried all our own equipment. Weighted down and led by our guides, because none of us ever did learn the paths to be followed in or out, and at night, we trudged through little valleys knee deep in mud which was like a sticky dough. It pulled at our feet as we tugged them out of the mess and we smiled when we learned that the Italians had called this route "Road No. 10" for it was a horrible path, winding in and out as it sought the low land. At long last we reached Volpago where we rested one night, or rather for the rest of that night, before moving back to Brioni near a village called San Vito. Here we met some real French troops who were as delighted to see us as we were to see them. We often had a chat with them and we learned that some of them were veterans of Verdun, that they had taken part in the capture of Monte Tomba, that they did not like the Italians and thought little of them, and that they would like to go back to the Western Front I couldn't tell them that we were not so keen on returning to Belgium.

My billet in Brioni was in a large house with three floors. There was no proper stairway, just a frail ladder from ground floor to the first floor and a similar ladder from the second to the third floor, where I had to sleep – a good job I was always steady on my feet. Every night we received a rum ration. I paraded with the rest and drew mine in my enamelled mug to give to Pip, who saved it till the morning and had it at reveille. I knew it was heart-warming and body-warming and helped to keep out the cold, but I did not drink it.

The battalion that had relieved us was from the 7th Division and we took over the sector recently held by the 23rd Division. We did not know what lay behind these sudden changes after such a short spell in the Isola della Scale – Lonigo area. Brioni was a very small village without any shops and the section, being short of sugar and candles, asked me to go to another village to see what I could buy. Soon the Saturday I went to Altivoli, a short distance away round two bends in the road. I entered the square, paused to look at a commemorative column and beyond it the church. A few feet away was the bell tower (campanile) a tall rectangular shape, crowned with a steeple. In a street off the square I found a shop, a general dealers, and bought some candles, but no sugar, and a picture postcard of Altivole – Piazza della Chiese: the square and the church I had been viewing.

A football league was formed, each company providing four teams and headquarters two teams so that almost all the men played at some time or other and got some good exercise. Parades were held in the mornings and the matches played in the late afternoons. A field was found but we had no goal posts though the transport section supplied some sticks to serve as such and for the corners of the pitch. One Saturday afternoon I played for No. 18 H.Q. platoon against No. 4 platoon of 'A' Company and we lost 4-1. That same afternoon No. 17 platoon (H.Q.) beat a 'D' Company platoon 10-0. Many were the bruises inflicted on our legs – Army boots were not the best of footwear for the game.

Ode Sunday after dinner MacG. and I set off for Cassela d'Asolo and were greatly surprised that this small place had associations with Robert Browning, the English poet, who had lived there. We stood before a house above the doorway of which was a plaque bearing these words:

Here lived Robert Browning
Supreme English poet,
June1889

Further along the street was a Browning School and there came to our minds at least three of his poems which he had had to learn off by heart at an elementary school: *The Pied Piper of Hamelin, Incident of the French Camp* and *How They Brought the Good News from Ghent to Aix*. We were still able to quote from them and even completely repeat them. I asked Mac if he had seen any rats in Italy, and we realised that neither of us had. Probably there was no food for them, maybe the terrain was unsuitable for their underground burrowing, or perhaps a Pied Piper had coaxed them all away to the Western Front.

Early in February the gallant little hero of Messines inspected us, General Plumer, the P.B.I.'s best friend. After he had carefully looked at each of us and departed, our band entertained us, and we wondered why he had come. Three days later we left Brioni and proceeded to the Costalunga-Larocco Line and took over the deserted hill village of Possagno. At some time it had been heavily shelled, and again more recently, when the French captured Monte Tomba. The villagers had left it when the Italians retreated. The signallers had almost marched through all the length of the village before they reached their billet, a very fine house on the left hand side just past the cemetery. Hills and valleys everywhere and the Alps across the river. We carried on with daily parades where possible, whilst the company men kept out of sight in the front line posts. The orderly room was higher up on the road and we fixed up a visual station just outside it and were in touch with another visual station more than a mile away to the rear on much higher ground. For the first time in the history of our specialist section we used heliographs, which were very effective over long distances on the fine, brilliantly sunny days. Our lamps were used only on those days that were too dull for the heliographs.

I welcomed the alternate days when I was detailed to take a full day's ration and go to take a turn at the distant visual station. Just after we set off we saw an Italian heavy gun in a pit dug into the roadside and heavily camouflaged. At intervals along the village street, massive canvases of camouflaged netting kept our activities hidden from the enemy. After two stretches of road going uphill and then down I came to an Italian signaller's hut, surrounded by grass. I used their apparatus, which was aligned on our village station. I was greatly struck by the combined lamp-heliograph-telescope instrument which worked perfectly and was labour-saving. Three of us took it in turn to flash back messages and receive replies – oblivious to the fact that there was a war on. We kept under cover and were never disturbed. We faced the beautiful snow-capped mountains and neither side fired a gun.

Opposite to our billet was a splendid school without scholars and its huge hall was the venue for our Saturday night dance with music supplied by the band. All around the walls of the hall were Latin proverbs and mottoes, beautifully printed. The following Saturday we held a dance and whist drive there, the latter at the request of the non-dancers and of those who would rather have had signorinas to dance with.

I sent off home a black and white card of a typical view of those parts. It had no village name on it and showed hillocks, hills and high mountains, valleys, houses clinging to the hillsides, coniferous trees and paths. Office censor N. Baker did not have to do any crossing out. On the back I wrote in pencil "A fairly common sight in the distance – a treat of a view. No letter lately. In the pink." I was always brief and to the point, and always well.

There seemed to be no difference between our spells in the line, in support, in reserve or out at rest – our whole time there was restful. After ten days at Possagno we left the line and spent one night near Riese before going into divisional reserve at Biadene in the Monte Belluno area. The very next morning after our arrival there, Mac went on leave to make up for the one from which he had been recalled after two days. I did not know then that I should not see him again till after the war ended.

The signallers were billeted in the Central Café in the main street. The house part was rather large with many bedrooms, store rooms, a scullery and a very large kitchen with a wide fireplace, stone hearth, chains, etc. The house was one of four together in a row, the other three being occupied by Italian soldiers. The first morning there the whole battalion paraded and, whilst orders were being given, an Austrian plane flew over and we wondered whether we had been seen.

The Italians used the church tower as an observation post and we took over in the afternoon. We had climbed the ladder to the top and just settled down when we heard a sudden sound. An Italian civilian had arrived, removed the ladder and locked us in, whether by design or accident we did not know. We had been too slow and confident. Perhaps the caretaker had seen the Italians depart and concluded that the church was not being used? There was a splendid view from this post but we were more anxious about getting out. We shouted many times and two hours elapsed before our calls were heard and matters put right. On our way back to the billet we saw a large dump of Italian stores and the soldiers in charge of it were those who were billeted next to us.

Ted Coulson had been busy in the billet, he had wired it up to the mains and we had the electric lights working. The night was so cold we again got down to it in twos and also pulled our cap comforters-cum-scarves well down over our ears. Shortly after midnight we were aroused by the all-too-familiar sound of enemy bombers not too far off, but not near enough to hit the village as they unloaded their bombs.

The next afternoon I was free and set off on a country walk. I came to a stream and witnessed a woman's washing day. She knelt against a large stone quite close to the water's edge. From a basket she took an article of clothing, dipped it into the water and then partly folded it and beat it on the stone. After several dippings in the waters and as many beatings on the stone, she threw it into another basket. I saw no sign of soap and the article looked quite white. This incident reminded me that in my travels I had seen huge posters bearing the words "Sunlight Savon" in France, "Sunlight Saponi" in Italy and, of course, "Sunlight Soap" in England.

Another day's training and parading resulted in our having a lively night. Again about midnight we heard the drone of the enemy plane and then – plump! The first bomb dropped in the countryside. Crump! – the second much nearer, and the third on the outskirts of the village. By this time we knew that the next and the next would be very close. The sudden thud and crash as a bomb had landed on the school just across the way and the fifth brought a great crash, it had hit the next but one house, occupied by the Italian soldiers. We hurriedly dressed and went out and gave what help we could – only a little because the Italian stretcher-bearers had been quickly on the scene. So we had been spotted.

The next evening after tea we stood in groups in the streets looking towards the front but watching particularly the large area of the intervening hillsides in flames, which spread and spread as far as we could see. We did not think that the heather, gorse and coniferous trees could be dry enough to catch fire and burn fiercely, so what could it mean? In the midst of all the excitement we were ordered to "stand to". We entered our billets and came out dressed in skeleton equipment and with rifles. At ten o'clock when we were ordered to "stand down" and we were told that the 41st Division and one other were to go back to France. It was known that the Germans were going to launch a tremendous offensive in March, and that would not be a picnic. Though we had experienced only two tastes of the Somme, the Battle of Messines Ridge, and two tastes of the Third Battle for Ypres – so little compared with the actions of our gallant Regular Army – we reckoned that another year on that front would see a hell worse than ever. Probably we felt the shock of this news more because of the thorough rest we had had in Italy, where we had seen not even a shadow of the war and thus could not grumble at the sudden change in our luck.

14

In Dock (Hospital Blues) – Genoa and Marseilles

The battalion started its return to the Western Front on foot, at first marching in full pack from Biadene to Loria, a distance of about twenty-five miles, having been relieved by the 23rd Division. The next day a short march of twelve miles brought us to Loreggo. In the evening before settling down in bivouacs I took a stroll round about and came to a farm. It seemed deserted, although in good condition, The farmer, his wife and children were living in with the cows, their cow-shed being the warmest part of the farm. When I took off my boots that night I found some difficulty in drawing off my left boot; the foot had begun to swell again. However in the morning I paraded with the others for the sixteen mile march to Campodero. It took me all my time to do the march and the next morning the battalion had not gone far before I collapsed and was told to wait by the roadside for an ambulance that was following our troops. Our 139 Field Ambulance came along and took me to a hospital at Abbazia Pissano, then on to our 39 Casualty Clearing Station at Istrana, leaving there on March 2nd by Red Cross train through Castelfranco, Camposampiero, Padova (at night) and eventually arriving at the 51st Stationary Hospital in Genoa.

On that day the battalion entrained at Poiana and Bojand Stations at 1 p.m. and soon crossed the border into France. I did not expect to be away from the battalion for long and wondered when I should catch up with it; all my foot needed was rest. On arriving at the hospital I was told to get into hospital blues, and even allowed out later. The ward was a small one and very crowded and I was told to occupy the bed immediately behind the door. No sooner had I settled in than some of the others called out asking where I was from. We got talking and then one soldier said, "You're from Yorkshire, and I'll make a guess what part – Hull!" He was not far wrong and I asked him how he knew. He replied that he'd know that 'u' sound anywhere. He continued, "A soldier who has a broken arm and has gone out of the ward is from Hull." When the artillery man came in and I approached him, he told me that he had been kicked by a mule. I enquired what part of Hull he lived in – incredibly he lived in a street through which I had passed four times a day on my way to and from school for many years. One of my best school friends lived there too and John Bell lived off it. When I found out his name I got an even greater surprise, for I found that I knew his brother very well indeed – they lived at a shop near the far end of the street just before it led into the Boulevard where the secondary school was. We had much to talk about. What a small world!

I was given a pass which allowed me out of the hospital in the afternoon and was able to admire some of the fine buildings and walk along the dock side. I had no money so had to be satisfied with viewing. There were lots of high tenement-like buildings and streams of washing hanging across from building to building. How different from that woman's washing I had seen near Biadene where she had laid hers on the ground and on hedges to dry, no lines or props needed.

The next morning after breakfast I was told that I could no longer be kept in Italy as my battalion and almost the whole of the 41st Division had crossed the border into France. I had to change out of my blues, don my khaki uniform and draw my kit. Late in the evening I was taken to the railway station and just before midnight I was on the No. 10 Italian Red Cross train, and I was sleeping as it crossed the border. I awoke early and again jotted down in my diary the names of the places through which we passed. It was a very slow train and often we were held up in sidings and it was dusk as we neared Toulon. I slept till we reached Marseilles, where an orderly told the ordinary walking cases to be ready to move off. A lorry came and we boarded it. It took us through the main streets to the outskirts of the city, along a part called La Mer Madrague – a road along the side of a bay in which was supposed to be the Chateau d'If, mentioned in Alexandre Dumas' *Monte Christo*. After passing a racecourse we entered the land that led straight into the grounds of the 81st General Hospital. Beyond were sand dunes, hills and another main road that seemed to swoop around and shut the hospital in. The surroundings were very fresh and beautiful and in many respects were like the rocky parts of the Riviera. I think that the hospital was a new one and had come into being when Tommies were being brought back to the Western Front from Egypt.

The clean white single beds were a complete change from the barns, empty houses and holes to which I had become accustomed; so too were the English nurses, as male orderlies bid formed the staff of the other hospitals I had been in. The nurses were more tender in dealing with our ailments and kinder in their ways. Much of the next four days was spent in resting though I was encouraged to do a little walking out each day and at the Sunday inspection I was told to be ready to move on the following day. In khaki again I was taken by an orderly on a little tour past two smaller hospitals, one for skin diseases and the other for venereal cases (both fairly full and some of the sights that I saw in the latter really shocked me), and finally to the No. 16 Convalescent Camp. Here I soon realised that I was a soldier again for the senior N.C.O. looked at me and said, "Get your dirty tunic washed.

There's a C.O.'s inspection later in the week." I had worn that tunic for twenty-three months and no-one had ever condemned it so that I could have had a new one, despite all the wear and tear – now I had to clean it. I washed it and had to remain in my tent till it dried hours later. On this day the battalion detrained at Mondicourt, not far from Albert and the Somme, and marched to Sombrin.

The next morning at the 9 a.m. parade the same N.C.O. came to see if I had washed my tunic, and appeared so satisfied that he asked, "Can you do anything useful, soldier, in the building line?" I did not know whether to be flattered at his mode of address or offended, but I told him that I could use a hammer, saw and other tools and even prepare drawings. I was taken to a site where more huts were being erected and also a hut for tools, although there weren't any tools. I was asked to go shopping for some; I was given a four day pass and fifty francs and told to go and buy tools, nails, screws, etc. I walked a short distance and then took a tram to the city centre and off the Rue de la Cannebiere I found a tool shop and purchased a few of the things I wanted and asked for a bill. That done I had a look round, walked up and down the Rue de la Cannebiere and admired the buildings, looked in shop windows and noticed where a postcard shop was, gazed at a huge monument illustrating allegorically the River Rhône and returned to the Rue de Rome, where I caught a tram which took me back to the camp. In the afternoon I was asked to make up and keep a book of accounts and also prepare drawings for hut building. A pay parade followed and thus, when I went shopping the next day, I was able, after obtaining more tools, to buy for myself six picture postcards for my home collection: the first one "Souvenir de Marseilles" had the city's name in two inch capital letters a quarter of an inch wide enclosing small views of the district; the second one "Marseilles – un coin du Cap Pinede" showed the Cape Bar and Restaurant and the corner where the tram terminus was (on the back of it was the triangular stamp of the censor, No.393, under the crown, but I had never addressed it. Each of the other four cards was a photo of the Fountain Cantini depicting the Source of the Rhône; the Rhône itself; la Mer Amphitrite and the Torrent. The fourteen sculptured figures were truly magnificent.

On my return I was greeted by Vic, another Yeoman signaller and we had many an evening stroll along the coastal road. He told me that one of his company had just gone home on leave, his first leave since coming out here twenty-two months ago, and that there were still members of the battalion who had not yet had leave. Most evenings when I was not too tired and on Saturday and Sunday afternoons, provided the weather was fine, I left the camp with Vic and enjoyed a walk round the bay. We had to wear a blue band on the left arm to show that we had permission to be out. Only once, a Friday evening were we too late – all the blue bands had been given out, so we stayed in the recreation room and played table tennis. The next evening, after leaving the camp gates, we suddenly realised that certain French women, usually dressed in black, hung about the roads and were keen to make friends with the soldiers. One of them leaned on the gate of a nearby house and beckoned. They were prostitutes and I was surprised that the authorities had not deemed it wise to warn the men. What made me realise who they were was the poster on a hoarding at the end of the road. It was a French order – all prostitutes of Toulon and other towns excepting Marseilles had to leave the district and return to their own towns. No doubt the presence of many Allied troops there had drawn them to this second port of France and one result was the building of a V.D. hospital. Rumour had it that the French authorities had arrested thousands of them and segregated them on the islands in Marseilles Bay where they now had to work on munitions.

Each Sunday morning the Chief Medical Officer inspected the patients and on the first occasion I was marked 'B' and warned that I would have to go on the next route march, which was a kind of test for fitness. I had been on an earlier one which had been too much for my left foot which had not been rested enough because of the work I had been doing in connection with the extensions to the camp and also, of course, the four trips into the city for tools and such. After breakfast on Thursday, March 21st, we set off. We went a short way round the coast and then began to climb the hills. We passed the King of Spain's chateau and at noon stopped at an estaminet for drinks as we ate our sandwiches. Down below stretched the huge bay of Marseilles with its many islands, beautifully warm on this Spring Day and we were free of worries. On our return the news was given to us that the Germans had launched a tremendous attach in the Somme area and that mist had helped them to surprise the troops in the line and much ground had been lost.

That was not the only alarming news, though the other was more personal. The old battalion had been disbanded – the Yeoman Rifles was no more. Five days earlier the five officers and 165 other rank; still on the Strength (out of 122 officers and 2877 other ranks who had served with the battalion the 21st Bn. the K.R.R.C.) had been sent to other battalions of the regiment. Later we learned that many of the other ranks had immediately applied for commissions and had been sent back to Blighty to Officers' Training Corps.

Some of the remaining men had been packed off on leave, their first, and just in time.

Vic and I wondered what would be our fate when we were discharged from hospital. Later I was informed that I had been transferred to our 18th K.R.R. Battalion, in the same division but in the 122 Brigade. It had gone into action on March 21st against the German push and had almost been wiped out, only twenty-two men surviving. What luck for me to have been unfit. Most of the old signallers had been transferred to the Royal Engineers, Signals Branch and I never knew how it came about that I had not. Whilst the Germans were successfully advancing, I failed the fitness test, and so did Vic. We had to wait twelve days for the next test route march which followed the same stretch of coastline for three miles and then proceeded to Pointe Rouge and up the hills to a lonely estaminet in a lovely gorge where we spent over an hour to eat the one bread and cheese sandwich and rest. Then we all gathered round the officer, who tested us on our ability to judge distances. General knowledge questions then followed, and finally he asked for volunteers to give short talks on anything but the war. At three o'clock we began our return to camp. On the following Sunday, Captain Wore inspected my left foot and declared that I was now fit and that the Senior Medical Officer would give me a thorough medical test the next day.

Another great offensive had been launched by the Germans (Arras?) and I was still at Marseilles. I had written home regularly but had not put any hospital address on any communication, especially to those sent home, for I did not want to scare my mother. As a result, I was not receiving any mail whatsoever and, now that the battalion was disbanded, goodness knows where my mail was going – probably to the 18th K.R.R.s. Many months later my mother informed me that in mid-March she had received a buff coloured Army Form B 104/80 No.76890 stating "If replying, please quote this number":

King's Royal Rifle Corps Record Office
Winchester Station
14.3.1918

Dear Madam,

I regret to have to inform you that a report has this day been received from the War Office to the effect that (No.) C12747 (Rank) Rfn. (Name) G.V. Dennis, (Regiment) 21 King's Royal Rifle Corps is dangerously (erased) ill at 81 General Hospital, Marseilles, suffering from "Inflammation of skin and connective tissue, left heel – slight. 7.3.18."

I am at the same time to express the sympathy and regret of the Army Council. Any further information received at this office as to his condition or progress will be at once notified to you.

I am,
Sir,
Your obedient Servant,
H.W.P xxxfs, Lt. XXX (rubber stamp) Officer in Charge of Records."

On the address side was the rubber stamp of the Rifles Record Office, Winchester, 14 March, 1918 and the one penny postage stamp was franked Winchester 9.30 a.m., 14 Mar. 1918. Though the name of the street and of the road were spelled incorrectly, the communication had arrived safely. Mother was not too upset by it because of the flow of letters, cards, etc. by which I always inferred that all was well or that I was in the pink.

When I stood naked before the Senior M.O. on the Monday and before he had time to use his stethoscope, he noticed on my legs and thighs many large, boil-like spots, and said, "How long have you been in this condition?" I replied that it was about four weeks, but that they hadn't given me any trouble. "Why didn't you report sick?" he asked, and I answered that I did not want to leave the battalion. He then examined my left heel and prodded it here and there and bent the ankle, twisting my foot a little, but I felt no pain. The M.O. turned to an orderly and said, "See that this man is taken to the skin hospital." I returned to my tent and began to get my belongings together, but before I had done this I heard a voice yell out, "Dennis, come here!" I went outside and there stood the S.M., face like a beetroot as he bawled out, "Stand to attention when I address you. Call yourself a soldier! Don't you know the Germans are driving our troops back and here you are going into hospital when you are needed up there. You're a disgrace! ... " He rambled on till my gunner friend came out of the tent and said, "Do you know what it's like at the front? Have you ever been there? Leave him alone, you silly b ... ..! What's he done to you? Have you been in the front line?" The S.M ceased slating me and told me to get packed up and then strutted off. He daren't say boo to the gunners, whereas if I had answered him back I have no doubt but that he would have put me on a charge. By his attitude, I do not think he had been up at the front, and most likely he had been a base wallah all through the war, and of the type which threw its weight about when given some authority.

The next morning as Vic left for another hospital too and many others left the camp for base at 9.15 a.m., I was admitted to the Stationary Hospital, 'S' Lines and put into a small marquee with ten Tommies and three British West Indians, all with Biblical names, and whistling hymns as I entered. I again donned hospital blues and the attendants were all males. That day the Battle for Armentieres began. The next morning some form of liquid was applied to all my spots, from which I had some burning feeling, but the treatment caused them to sting. All treatment was given in the mornings and I found there was very little to do in the afternoons and evenings. The entrance to the marquee faced the other tents but behind it was a single wire fence separating it from a small holding or farm, with the owner's house at the end of a field, or lawn. As I looked that way one afternoon two little boys came from the house and began to ask questions, and we carried on a conversation on many easy topics. Marius was eight years old and Felice was eleven. By this time I had stepped over the wire fence and we sat on the grass. Felice went indoors and brought his sister, Rose, who was nineteen, very dark and pretty. Later we were joined by Elise, who was sixteen, very fair, and la plus belle. Although she "dwelt (not) among untrodden ways" she was like "A violet by a mossy stone, Half hidden from the eye. Fair as a star when only one is shining in the sky." (Shades of *Palgrave's Golden Treasury*, from secondary school days!).

Weather permitting, I spent the next ten afternoons talking to the children on the lawn and eventually met their father and mother. So friendly did we become that one evening I accepted Monsieur's invitation to see his fields, glasshouses and cold frames and he told me his plans for the coming season, what crops he was going to grow, etc. He already had some plants in the glasshouses and the cold frames. I began to help a little and used to put the straw matson the cold frames as soon as the warmth of the sun had gone and the cold of the evenings set in. I was invited into the house but at first refused the invitation and when Rose brought me an excellent drink of coffee I explained that I was shy of entering their house because of my complaint. However after many hours in the garden the next day I did go into the house and found there seven orderlies from the camps, one of whom was very keen on Rose. We all drank tea, made from camp tea. No-one had offered to stop my going to the farm and I did not realise that any of the camp staff knew of my visits, but that evening I was much chaffed about Elise, who was not seen outside often except when talking to me on the lawn. After early treatment one Sunday I was put on a fatigue and had to go to help camp staff put up a new marquee at the No. 57 Hospital. It was an exceedingly cold day and I spent most of it in the farmhouse. The farming blood in my veins began to show itself as I indulged in weeding burning weeds, muck plugging, following the plough, learning to make a straight furrow – such a lot of hours I put in working there that I was almost one of the family.

On Wednesday, April 24th, the date of another great offensive by the Germans, the M.O. decided to change my treatment as I had made very little progress. Two days later I was ordered to appear before a new M.O. and he asked me, "Are you allergic to anything?" I told him that, as far as I knew, I was not. The new treatment had made matters worse and he changed the treatment again. (I had an allergy, of which I did not know; had I known I should have been saved a great deal of suffering many years later).

To celebrate May Day the camp staff had the lawn and farm grounds put out of bounds to the patients, all of whom were forbidden to leave the camp at all. At 4.30 p.m. Vic left his camp for base and I felt very lonely. Two days later Madame G. came to the fence in the evening and asked me what was wrong. She wondered why I hadn't been to see them and whether it was because I was ill, I explained that the patients had been forbidden to leave the camp, that I was very sorry indeed as I missed my visits to them, and I asked her to tell all the family how disappointed I was at losing my freedom. After she had returned to her house I realised that I had been very fortunate in being able to cross the fence to their farm whenever I liked. I hadn't had permission to do so, yet I had not been stopped. I retired early and just after nine o'clock the peacefulness of the camp was broken by the camp orderlies who rushed about from marquee to marquee shouting out, "Stand by your beds!" The seven of us, four Tommies and three B.W.I.s (as six Tommies had been discharged) did as ordered and a corporal came in and checked the roll. I had been seen talking to Madame and it had been thought that I had gone with her to her house and left the camp against orders, hence the check.

At long last I received a letter from home mother had used the hospital address given on the communication she had received about my affected heel. She thought that things were going rather badly for our troops and she was glad that I was away from the Ypres front. She was referring to the fresh onslaught south of Armentieres, where the Germans had struck where the Pork and Beans (Portuguese) troops had adjoined the English divisions.

The following ten days were really boring for, after morning treatment there was nothing to do for the rest of the day. I helped the B.W.I. with their letters, played cards with them and listened to their stories of home. Their one great complaint was that they were not given enough sugar. One of them presented me with his cigarette case, which was about six inches long and three inches wide. It would hold twenty fags. On the front of it was the regimental badge with the letters B.W.I. in the middle. Within six months, after I had been transferred to another regiment someone "won" it out of my haversack.

My spots were disappearing and I was very pleased when I was put on a fatigue to help a part of R.E.s take down the old wash house and bath house. When we were tackling the roof and removing the rafters, the sapper working with me let go of his end of one and it struck my head, grazing all my face and sending my glasses flying. Fortunately they were not broken. When the two buildings had been removed, we had to take up the concrete bases – not an easy job because we had no suitable tools. Then we levelled the area and the R.E. officer remarked, "Is that the best you can do?"

I was on another fatigue when the M.O. sent for me, examined me and said to the orderly, "I think he may go out after morning inspection." That night just before ten o'clock I was taken to the Q.M. stores and handed in my kit. Only then did I realise that I had missed any chance of saying goodbye to my French friends. I was warned to rise at six the next morning, once again to don my uniform and hand in the hospital blues. Breakfast would be early, there was to be no transfer to a convalescent camp as would have been the usual procedure, but I would be leaving Marseilles for a northern base. The lorry that was to take a number of us to the railway station was late by about an hour and we finally left the 'S' Lines at 9.30 a.m. on Friday, May 17th. What a lot I had missed and what a cushy time I had had for ten weeks. We had to hang about at the station as our camp N.C.O., impatient to be off, had to make frequent calls at the office of the R.T.O. to see about our leaving Marseilles. On one occasion he came back with the news that there had been a collision between a French troop train and an ordinary express not far out of the station. About thirty soldiers had been injured and the line was almost cleared of the results of the disaster. Shortly after midday he took us on to a platform and told us to enter a train. Three of us – a gunner, a D.C.L.I. (Duke of Cornwall's Light Infantry), and I chose the end compartment of what proved to be the Northern Express. We were to travel second or third class and if we stood up we could look over the tops of the other compartments of that coach and, if we had wished, by standing on a seat we could have looked right into the next compartment, which was full of French soldiers. It was also a corridor train. An ITI (Italian soldier) joined us and he and I chose window seats. I sat with my back to the engine and on my right was the D.C.L.I. The gunner passed a cigarette to the ITI and I managed to carry on a conversation with him as he puffed his cig. and praised its quality. Great excitement started up amongst the French soldiers, whistling and shouting, and we wondered why. Then there paused at the door of our compartment a French girl who appeared to prefer to join us. She seated herself between me and the D.C.L.I. Some Frenchmen leaned over into our compartment and called upon her to leave us and join them, but she refused to do so. The train started off and I looked through the window and admired the beautiful scenery and saw again the beautiful sweep of Lion's Bay. We passed the wreckage of the troop train and as the train rounded a bend we got a fine view of Avignon Cathedral. Then on we went through Valence to Lyons and the Rhone, which we reached in about two hours.

I turned my attention to my companions who could only nod and smile at the French girl as she spoke to them. She told me that she was twenty-five years old, that she was a revue actress and was going to Paris to start at a theatre on the Monday. As darkness came she told me that she was tired and must have some sleep. She huddled closer to the D.C.L.I. and leaned on him. He put his arms around her and she rested her head on his shoulder, lifted up her feet and asked me to remove her shoes. I did so and then she lay almost full length, using my companion as a pillow and me as a footrest. She soon fell asleep and did not open her eyes until the night was far gone. I dozed fitfully and dared hardly move.

The next morning when we were all awake and sitting up, we Tommies went, one by one, along the corridor to the toilet and had a wash and brush up. I went last and, as I was washing my face, the train began to slow down quite suddenly and my rimless glasses slipped off the edge of the basin and fell onto the floor and broke. The train was pulling up in Paris as I returned to the compartment just in time to have a few last words with the actress. She thanked us for looking after her, put her arms round each one of us in turn and gave us a kiss on each cheek. She also said that if any one of us happened to be near Numero XX in the Rue de Petit Eglise, district ... . she would be pleased to welcome us. She left the train first and we took up our packs and made our way down the platform to near the entrance to the station, whose name I never got to know.

Here we saw that the time was a few minutes after nine and then we took off our packs whilst an N.C.O. went to report to the R.T.O. As a result we were taken outside and told to get into a covered motor lorry which took us to the Gare du Nord. I saw nothing of Paris as I had entered the lorry first and was unable to look outside. Here we were given breakfast and told to wait there till six o'clock when we would be put onto another train for the north. We sat on our kits just inside the arched entrance. The weather was beautiful and, after strolling round the station a few times, we began to feel bored. I suggested that, as we had about seven hours to spare, we ought to have a look around Paris. The D.C.L.I. agreed but the gunner said that he would rather stay there and so he would look after our kits. The former and I shared out our meagre francs and set off. We walked under the clock, crossed a kind of small square (the station taxi stand etc.), into a Boulevard (Magenta) and turned left, taking in all we could see. I could not help noting that a street on the left was called St. Denis and soon we came to a very large square called La Place de la Republique with a monument set in the centre. Across in the far corner we saw a huge Union Jack hanging from a building, so we decided to investigate. About halfway across the square a Canadian Military Policeman came up to us and said, "I suppose you have passes?" Instinctively our right hands moved quickly to our left breast tunic pockets, where most of us kept our pay books, letters, etc., we unfastened the buttons and with an "All right chums" he left us. Whether or not one of our own M.P.s would have been so polite and unsuspicious and let us go, I doubt.

The building displaying the Union Jack was the British Army and Navy Club which shared rooms with the Hotel Moderne. We entered and a very fine place it was. In the reading and writing room I sat at a desk and wrote home; both the writing paper and the envelope had a bordering of red, white and blue. In the next room I bought a small, thin, green book of English verse and a picture postcard of the Eiffel Tower with a big wheel on the skyline. I wrote the date, 26.6.18, and the Field Post Office stamp showed 26 June. My diary, however, revealed that I had sent it ten days after being in Paris.

We went to the buffet and had something to eat and drink. We had spent too much time here and realised that we ought to be making our way back, so we saw very little of Paris and had to set about it the wrong way. We did not hurry back along the Boulevard Magenta and turned in to a station on the right. Our kit was nowhere to be seen – we had arrived at the wrong place. When I asked a Frenchman where we were, he said "la Gare de l'Est", so I asked him where La Gare du Nord was, and he directed us. I saw that the entrance of that wrong station was far different from the one we wanted, it had no great archway. Not many yards on I saw La Rue St. Denis, which I ought to have looked for.

What a shock we got when we went inside the station – no sign of the gunner, only two kits. That slight delay in going to the wrong station had caused us to miss our train. We waited a time and then I went to find the R.T.O. who told me the time of the next train, which we caught just after eight o'clock – but it was not a through train and we had to make a change for Le Havre. It was quite dark and I did not notice the name of the station (probably Rouen) for one reason; the platforms were crowded with Portuguese troops from a sector south of Armentieres where the Germans had broken through, striking at a weak link between forces from different countries. The great surprise here was that these foreign troops crowded around any Tommy they saw, beseeching them to sell their Army issue jack-knives. What a crazy notion! Of course we could not sell them – they were part of our kit and had to be accounted for and shown on all kit inspections.

When we reached Le Havre in the dark hours, I bid goodbye to my friend the D.C.L.I. because he knew where he had to go to whilst I did not, and there was no-one about to whom I could report. I slept the rest of the night on the station platform and in the morning I was directed to a clearing camp of huts and tents and white washed stones marking the pathways. I was sent to the 19th Casual Lines and posted to the 18th K.R.R.s of my own Division. I put my kit in a tent and then strolled out, looking around and ran into some other Yeomen – Arnold Rushworth the Orderly Room Sergeant (later to initiate the Old Comrades' Association), Reg Payne of 'D' Company, Duggie Newmarsh (later the creator of many excellent cartoons about the old battalion, Morgan (drafted from Wales and a stranger to me), Bert Rayner of 'B' Company and four signallers very well known by me – Coomber, Bill Drake, Duckie Morley and dear old Vic. It was grand seeing them and hearing the news of t'owd lads. The disbanding of the battalion had been a great shock and deeply affected the men who had been through such a lot together. I never learned how the hundred or more men of the line (excluding the men of the Transport Section) were split up. It looked as if they were sent in small parties to one of the other twenty battalions of K.R.R.s. Months later I heard that one of my great friends of 'C' Company, Sgt. Mick Kenington, had been sent to the 1st Bn. He was welcomed with "What battalion are you from?" When he replied "The 21st, sir" he was told, "I've never heard of it and now you will have to forget all you learned with it. You are going to be a real soldier from now on." Poor Charlie Hutton, well over six feet tall and given an R.P.s job at the transport was quickly shown that he would be given no preferential treatment in the 2nd K.R.R.s – too tall for the trenches? Not there. Syd Bell was sent all the way to Salonika to the 14th Battalion. Brantie (a Sunderland lad who stayed in after the War and went to India) and Babs Walker (of 343 Anlaby Road, Hull) to the sixteenth, and soon. I learned from Rushworth that the Brigades had been reorganised and now consisted of only three battalions – the last formed in each had been disbanded and so the Yeomen, who were the babes of the Brigade, had to go. So the finest friendships ever made were suddenly broken and it would be hard to find "greater love among men and boys" than we had had.

The next morning, Monday, May 20th, I was a soldier again as reveille was at 5 a.m. and breakfast at 6.15. I was wrong in thinking that I was to be on the move again. I was allowed very little time for breakfast as I had to parade at the Q.M.'s stores and have my kit checked. That done, I had to parade for a haircut at 9 a.m. ready for the M.O.'s inspection at ten. This was the most severe test I had ever had and one result was that I was booked to see an eye specialist on the Wednesday. On the Tuesday I had to have my box respirator tested and so had to pass through a gas chamber to make sure that it was safe. Also there were some Yanks – the first I had seen. My word, they did look posh and smart too, but somewhat pasty. They liked a natter and I began to pity the Germans when the Yanks got at them, or did I? They had not been in any action as they were considered not to be trained sufficiently, yet they had been at war more than a year. I thought of the seventeen and eighteen year olds of ours who had been killed on the Somme.

Captain C.F. Harper, R.A.M.C. tested my eyes very thoroughly and he asked me if I had ever been in the front line; I told him of the trench life I had led. "You ought never to have been there, and I assure you that you won't ever be there again," he said. Very cheering words, indeed. The next day I was told, "You have been marked in a low category and you are fit only for garrison duties. "To celebrate Vic and I applied for, and got, passes for an afternoon and evening in Le Havre. We had tea at the Crystal Palace, toured the town, the dock side and the shops. Vic asked me what I would like to do, and I said, "I would like to be posted to a Prison-of-War Camp and take the chance to learn German." On our return I was not surprised when I was told that I was to move the next day to the E.B.D. Camp (Base Details) No.17, where I soon clicked a fatigue at the dentist's hut – removing manure to some flower beds. The next day I was a waiter in the officers' mess and, no sooner had I finished this fatigue than I was warned that I would be moving on.

Before retiring I put my kit together, which proved to be a wise move because I experienced the earliest reveille I had ever had – 1.45 a.m. Breakfast quickly followed and our little draft walked to Le Havre, which we left at 6 a.m., arriving at Rouen four hours later. Here we detrained and were told that we could go into the town and be back for another train at 2.45 p.m. Our first thoughts were on something to eat, and we managed to satisfy our hunger by having a snack at two separate estaminets. The Cathedral spire seemed very tall and I recollected from school days that Joan of Arc was executed here in the fifteenth century. Hitherto my journeys in the last six months had been in second class carriages but back at the station we boarded a train of cattle trucks for now more than a hundred men had to travel. The next morning at 6 a.m. the train halted at Étaples. Gloom descended on us for this Base Camp had a horrible reputation – the discipline was too strict, the instructors were devils, and all Tommies were glad to leave the place even to go to their deaths. At the camp we were given a hasty breakfast and then told to parade for kit inspection. Quickly followed another M.O.'s inspection and a short arm's one. The C.O. inspected us and I was posted to the 6th Garrison Battalion – and only then was I shown my tent, one of many in straight lines in a camp that already looked depressing. I spent that evening with others digging shallow trenches round each tent, and later erecting a foot high wall of sandbags round each tent.

After Thursday's dance in the Y.M.C.A. hut, just as we got in to our tents, we heard the drone of enemy bombers flying overhead. A large hospital, railway sidings and dumps, the solders' camp and the cemetery all lay round Étaples – two genuine targets and the hospital immune. That night the hospital was hit through bad aiming. I lay in my tent, flat, relying on the sandbags to keep any fragments of bombs from landing inside. The bombs were only small ones and only direct hits on a target did much damage. On orders I spent two hours the next evening excavating chalk and deepening the trenches. That very warm night I took to the trench when the nightly bombing began. That occasion, as I lay almost full length in the shallow trench, the German bombs were dropping on our camp and on our lines. One bomb hit our cook house not twenty yards away and demolished part of it and destroyed the bread store. The sergeant cook and one mess orderly were killed. Bits of wood, metal struts, stones and shrapnel flew over the trench. The faint crumps grew fainter and fainter, the slight earth tremors ceased and the raid on our part of the camp was over. We could still hear a more alarming sound as some bombs were falling in the railway cutting, more of an aerial torpedo sound as they hurtled through an enclosed space. Nothing seemed to be done to stop the raiders.

The next morning there were many rumours: the hospital had suffered far more than the camps, the railway sidings or the dumps; the death roll there was exceptionally heavy; some 325 of the wounded and sick cases were killed that night; besides nurses and R.A.M.C. orderlies, very few of the stretcher cases, let alone those in the beds, had been able to help themselves. All the orderlies, heroes, and all the nurses, heroines, had stuck to the tasks of helping the surviving patients. Who's the blame? The Germans for missing the pigeon and hitting the crow – or our siting of the hospital?

Sunday, June 2nd, 1918 – a very busy day as we were all on fatigue for hours clearing up. When we had finished our teas, the orderly corporal read out the following order. "All ranks will parade at the orderly room at 9 pip emma with groundsheet, greatcoat and one blanket." What a stir that order created! What was it all abut? When we were all lined up and had been counted, the orderly corporal reported to the officer in charge. "All present and correct sir." We were marched out of the camp to near a wood about three miles away, and told to settle down. What had happened to the British Army? Wind up, sky high!

It had been rumoured for many days that the Aussies had been leaving their camp each evening but they got the blame for anything untoward. Here we were, well behind the firing lines, and consideration was being taken for our lives. The times I had had to grin and bear a bombardment, often without retaliation to help. We returned to the camp at 3 a.m. and there was no enemy raid. The next evening there was a compulsory parade to hear a Belgian officer give a lecture on his country in the Y.M.C.A. hut. Again we were taken out of camp at nine o'clock, and the next evening too. The following evening we had to parade in full kit at 6.45 p.m. and we returned at about the same time, 3 a.m. Still no further raids. There was more digging and draining of trenches during the day and at the next evening parade at the orderly room at 9 p.m. I was summoned inside and handed my Will from my old pay book which had been taken off me in Italy and sent to Records. I placed it in my new pay book. We marched out again for the night, and then what a shock we got on our arrival back just after dawn. The camp was surrounded by the Military Police – Red Caps at every entrance. We were halted and stood at ease. The camp personnel, N.C.O.s and other ranks, were told to fall out. They were checked and then allowed to go through the camp entrances and return to their huts. But, we unfortunate Tommies of the P.B.I. were squared up and ordered to hand over our pay books, and only then were we allowed to return to our tents. A quick breakfast followed and then we were on parade at 8.45 a.m. I was told that any time I would be moving to the 6th Battalion and that I had to parade at the orderly room at 2 p.m. on a charge of breaking camp. I was severely lectured about leaving the camp. I was asked whether I had anything to say. I ought to have replied, "No sir," but I did not. I pointed out that I had marched out on a parade by the camp personnel. I ought to have known better, no matter how just I felt my action. As a reward for opening my mouth I had to forfeit seven days' pay – three or four days' pay more than the others. We all should have been treated alike and no favouritism shown to camp staff who were the ones who took us out. Anyhow the powers-that-be had realised that they should not have got the wind up and did right to stop the exodus from camp.

When the pay parade took place the next day I had not got a pay book. When I got it back at 1 p.m. I was told that there was no money left, but that if I tried an hour later there would be something for me. What a quandary I was in because I was ordered to parade with my new battalion in full kit at that same hour. Of course, I turned up for the latter parade and I was moved to another tent (No. 5) in some other lines. Too late for pay again, but after three more visits to the company office I was given five francs, so I went to the camp cinema in the evening.

More and more rumours about the Aussies; it was said that they had strongly objected to being stopped at the gates and the demand for their pay books. A real fight had taken place between them and the Red Caps, who had come off the worst, some having to be taken to the hospital. For my part I could find no real enmity towards the Military Police – they had followed their orders which, to us, were grossly unfair because we had been paraded and taken out of camp. The powers-that-be were more at fault because of the manner in which they had dealt with a situation that should never had occurred – they should not have got the wind up. The Red Caps always were and always would be unpopular with the boys of the line because they were an additional means of messing them about.

Sergeants' Mess fatigue the next day was quite a change from all the trench digging, sandbagging, etc. of the previous weeks and the only snag was that the day was Sunday and I got no time off. I had had my meals in the cookhouse and found them much better than my usual meals. When I returned to my tent I heard that we were to move on the following day. I had not experienced the Bull Ring nor come under the instruction by the Canaries: I had not been shown how to fight, how to treat the Germans by the notorious know-alls of Eat-apples and had missed the hatred they created in the passing through P.B.I.

Reveille was at 4 ack emma and breakfast quickly taken and then "on parade in full marching order" at 6 o'clock. A sergeant-major called for specialists in signalling, the machine gun, snipers, runners, etc. to step forward and four separate little groups of them were formed up. I found myself in a section of twelve and we were marched to the station and left Étaples to join fresh battalions from Blighty so that they could make use of our experience. We detrained at Wormhoudt and marched through the town to some empty huts, arriving drenched through. I had noticed in the town a huge poster advertising "The Crumps", the concert party of the 41st, my Division (actually my old Division, although I did not know it just then).

We had to wait three hours for the arrival of some sugar and tea before a drink could be made, for there were no cooks. The next morning we were not roused till seven o'clock and after a scanty breakfast we paraded in drill order at 9 a.m. and more detailed particulars of our specialist qualifications were taken. A kit inspection followed at 10.30. The afternoon was spent in cleaning out all the huts for the companies when they arrived, what companies and of which battalions we were not told. At five o'clock I was told that I was to be a guide and that I had to be at Wormhoudt station at 6.35 p.m. The train arrived almost an hour late and I reported to the C.O. He questioned me about the huts, distance and, oddly I thought, asked me if there were any rumours about the new battalion. For once there were no rumours, and I told him that we were only a very small advance party at the camp. The great shock to me was that I was addressing a Jock officer and that the new companies were all clean and smart in kilts, all their clothing was new. I led one of the companies safely to its billet and about midnight I retired and slept in the hut where my kit was. The next morning I was posted to 'A' Company which I joined after drawing some rations for the day. After a day of fatigues I was called to the Q.M. stores in the evening and from a crate the Quartermaster took several kilts and told me to pick one to suit my size. He helped me. I had to kneel down outside after removing my trousers and underpants and a kilt was drawn around my back and the two ends pulled forward to meet in front of my body, then with the right hand I pulled one half round to my left side and with my left hand pulled the other half round my right side, I waggled my body and fastened the kilt with a large black safety pin. I stood up and the Q.M. was quite satisfied with what he saw. He told me that I should have to learn to make the kilt "pan" to my body. Then he asked for my tunic and with a pair of scissors he cut off the right angled corners and my tunic was now curved. I had to remove my field dressing from its little pocket and from then on carried it in my haversack. Later I stitched round the edges of the curves. Next came a balmoral, size six and three-quarters, which I found rather comfortable. I was given a pair of hose – or rather hose tops – to pull over my socks and fasten under the knees, using the red flashes for the purpose and having to have a three inch turnover. Each flash did the work of a garter, it was about fifteen inches long and just over an inch wide. It was taken round the hose top where it joined the turn-over, pulled not too tightly and then the end was tucked in. From it to show just below the lower pan of the turn-over was a similar piece of light red cloth, the actual flash, showing two points. A khaki apron was also supplied to cover the kilt and keep it clean and to save it from getting sodden and covered in trench mud under rainy conditions. The kilt iself was rather heavy because the back of it was double box pleated. Later I bought two small buckles and straps and sewed them on to my kilt, feeling that they were more reliable than the long safety pin. I made sure that my kilt did not flop about or stand any chance of falling down. I handed in my old cheesecutter after removing my K.R.R cap badge, my old trousers and puttees, receiving in their place a much shorter pair to cover my boot tops, and my underpants. In return I received a chit saying that I had not been issued with the short special type underpants and a friendly warning from the Q.M. not to go upstairs on the buses when I went home. I wondered why I had to have such a chit. Later on morning parades the officer taking them would nick his cane just under one's kilt to see if the issue pants were being worn. On such occasions I had to produce my chit. I learned to like the kilt it was very warm and I felt more free without underpants. It was said that the summer time was the best time to adopt a kilt, never in the colder months.

I cut off my black buttons and the Q.M. gave me a set of brass ones which I sewed on my tunic and greatcoat. I cut off the 41st Divisional sign from beneath my epaulettes and substituted a sign showing a Gamecock. I was told that I was Private G.V. Dennis, No. 50517 and part of the division that had been badly battered south of Armentieres. I was no longer in the finest regiment of the British Army, no longer a rifleman. In due course I had to learn the rifle drill of an ordinary unit – how to slope arms and to present arms from the slope,etc.

After months of being messed about I had now an permanent address to put on my correspondence. For months I had had very very little mail and now I could hope to start receiving letters again. My new cap badge showed St. Andrew behind a multiplication cross. It had to be kept clean, as had my new brass buttons, so I had to buy some paste or powder and no longer use Cherry Boot Polish, which I had been using on my black buttons and black cap badge. For the button cleaning I still had an issue button stick.

15

Étaples – Base, Bombs and my new Battalion

Reveille was late the morning after my being fitted out with the kilt, etc. and, as there was nothing to do after a bath parade, I applied for a pass out to Wormhoudt. It was granted and, bearing in mind the Crumps Concert Party poster I had seen, I wanted to see if any of the old battalion was in the neighbourhood. Having no luck, I decided to return to camp by way of Equelbecq where we had entrained for Italy. There I met Bruce, Wakeling, Iley, Rhodes, Ramsden, Scruff and Atti. What a shock they got when they saw me and how amused they were. We concluded that I must be the only K.R.R. to become a Jock.

Breakfast was early next morning as I had been ordered to parade in full kit at nine. I had to go to Ledringhem to a camp there and join a signalling course. I helped to see the tents were ready and joined in the cooking of the dinner. In the late afternoon I was told to join a sergeant in a tent. A lance-corporal was Acting Quartermaster and came along too. It was only then that I was told that I had to share the instructing of the other men with this sergeant. The course started on the Saturday and the programme was as follows:

7 a.m. to 7:30 a.m. – Flag drill
9 a.m. to 9:30 a.m. – Inspection: Drill order, rifle and box respirator
9:30 a.m. to 12:45 p.m. – Lamp, flag, flappers, etc.
2 p.m. to 4:45 p.m. – Buzzer, lectures on procedure

The sergeant took those who had some knowledge of signalling and I took the beginners with the lance corporal, the acting Q.M., being present on my parade for disciplinary purposes. Sunday was not a rest day and after the morning with the learners I had the whole group after dinner because the sergeant was suffering from the effects of merry-making the night before. He was up late the next morning and we made up for some lost time by having a Lamp Parade at 10 p.m. till 10.30 p.m. I was told that if I wanted any pay I had to go to the battalion on Wednesday evening and join the 6.30 p.m. pay parade. I went – a walk of three to four miles each way, and I joined the H.Q. queue. When I reached the officer at a small table he went through his papers and told me that I was not on that roll. I went to 'A' Company and received the same bad news. I went back to H.Q. and had to wait till all the paying out officers returned and then my name was added to a list and at 9.30 p.m. I was given ten francs, much needed as I had received only twenty-five francs in the last ten weeks. I liked to have a little money in my pocket although there was not the least chance of spending some, there being no shop or canteens anywhere near us. On my return, rather late, the camp should have been in darkness, but it wasn't – our tent was lit up and the sergeant was again in a very merry mood, singing at the top of his voice, scaring off bogles and willing to fight any Bosches that came along. It was early morning before he settled down and snored through the night. He did very little work the next day and I took all the parades. I was feeling so fed up in the evening that, although rain was falling heavily, I set off and went to the battalion just to see if there were any letter for me and the others, as I had been made "course postman", but no luck. There followed another merry night and I could not understand how or whence he was getting all the good spirits that knocked him back each night. He altered the programme the next day and I took flag drill, squad drill, musketry exercises and gas drill. In the afternoon I led all the men on the course to the baths. I was very tired and got down to it rather early, to be awakened by him just before midnight to tell me that I had to return to the battalion in the morning – he had forgotten to tell me during the day.

The course was finished and all the men were required by the battalion to set up company and battalion H.Q. stations. Reveille was at 5.30 a.m. on a bright Sunday morning. I packed my things and forgot my mess tin, which I had left to dry outside the tent after using it at breakfast. The lance corporal kindly brought it along and handed it to me.

At the crossroads not far from the camp old London buses awaited us and I rode on the top. We went a long way round dropping men at various villages till finally I reached the battalion. I reported at the H.Q. but the staff knew nothing about me and did not want me. I tried 'A' Company – not known; I tried 'D' Company – again not known. I was getting fed up, not least because I had not eaten since 6.30 a.m. I strolled back to the orderly room and was finally taken on the H.Q. and put on duty for the whole night from 8.30 p.m. till 8 a.m. I had the morning and afternoon off and did an evening duty. The next day I did an afternoon spell and had the rest of the day off. On looking round I realised that we were in a different camp, we had moved to near Hazebrouck. A morning spell was followed by ten hours' night duty. This rota was followed for several weeks and I could not understand why so many hours at one stretch had to be done during darkness.

Only occasionally were we aware that there was a war on. On two separate occasions an observation balloon had broken loose; the first time one of our aeroplanes followed it and eventually brought it down in flames; probably a German balloon. The second one drifted very slowly away behind our lines and was descending all the time. We could not see what happened to it.

One Sunday I had to report to the orderly room where I was given a buff envelope addressed to me. It had been following me around and contained a note from the K.R.R. Record Office informing me that I was in credit to the tune of £7/11/2d at the time of my transfer to another regiment. Very thoughtful indeed, but there still rankled in my mind the failure to implement my allotment to my mother.

One Friday afternoon we were watching one of our planes flying fairly low and then suddenly a body hurtled from it to the ground; a sad end to a brave R.A.F. officer (no longer the R.F.C.) The battalion was rather spread about and I had to go to different camps to instruct the new signallers and I was pleased when I was moved to a camp near Sercus because it was more central for me and also it was quite close to the village. Here I was informed that no longer had the word "Garrison" to be included in my address. In the village I bought many picture postcards and some silk cards. One of the latter, a pansy worked in silk, I sent home; another one with a kind of silk envelope containing a small dainty silk handkerchief, I sent to my grandniece for her birthday. One particular card of L'Ecole des Garcons de Sercus I also sent home. In July I had received thirty-three letters in less than a month, some had been weeks in reaching me and I replied to some of them with picture postcards. I had made contact again with several of the old battalion: Signallers Vic, Ted

Coulson, Scruff, MacWilliam, MacG. and Johnnie Watson, Frank Markham, Don Wardell, Skinny (James W. Hannah) and Ted Nixon of the college party. More Old Boulevardians had written to me: Cabby Parkin, Bobbie Abram, Fred Taylor, 'Nigger' (so called because of his sallow complexion) Burns, Jack Digedan and John Bell. Bobbie, a junior sub., knew that I was in the Salient and he let me know that he too was in that part of the front and hoped to catch up with me some time – like Cabby had after Messines Ridge.

I celebrated Lammas Day (my birthday) after morning and afternoon signal parades by going to the Gamecock's Concert Party which was very good. The next Sunday a special gathering was held – we were to be told something about the Cameron Highlanders. The peacetime Glengarry was all blue with a red tassel; the hose tops were green and red; and the sporran had two black and white brushes. We learned that all kilty regiments had different distinguishing features in hose, kilts, sporrans, etc. Another Sunday a Cameron Pipe Band came to our camp and gave selections of reels, pibrochs and martial tunes. Some exhibitions of sword dancing were given. We became familiar with *The Flowers of the Forest, Highland Laddie,* etc. I got to like the bagpipes and would have liked to be able to play them. *The Cameron March* was always played.

So far I knew so little about this battalion – and its officers and other ranks knew so little about me. I gathered that most of the men were new from Blighty and had had very little training. Some younger ones had come from camps for under-age soldiers and now that they were eighteen they were sent as drafts to line battalions. All those had been together for some time but fewer than ten, like myself, were outsiders. I did not know the name of any officer, not even the C.O., and I had not as yet made any friends among the other ranks. My orders always came from Sgt. McSirrus who eventually reported sick and left us for good. From then on we did not have a signals sergeant.

All N.C.O.s were paid according to rank – how different from the old battalion. When the Brigade Signals Officer came down to see how our training programme was proceeding he found me, a private, the only qualified instructor, taking the squad. He wanted to know why and what were the signal N.C.O.s doing. It had to be explained to him that the battalion had its full complement of paid signal N.C.O.s, so the battalion had a problem – ought it to promote its own corporal to be sergeant of the signals, or give me the job. Matters stayed as they were, despite the awkward situations that sometimes arose. I did not mind; I was quite happy as I was and followed all orders given to me.

After one of our frequent moves, the signal office was in a pigsty that had been cleared out. It was rather comfortable though the smell of pigs seemed to taint our clothing and fill our nostrils. The companies seldom had an office; a phone was fixed up in the hut or tent occupied by other soldiers. At last I was attached to 'D' Company for pay and I learned the name of its officer, Captain Null.

Somewhere there was a war on, though we hardly saw or heard any signs of it, but in the last week of August we heard that the Germans had suffered a tremendous defeat in the south. Motor lorries collected the battalion from the various camps and villages around Wallon Cappel and took us through the western outskirts of Hazebrouck into a clearing in the Nieppe Forest, La Motte au Bois, where we got out of the lorries and were spread out in huts. We were told that we were now in reserve and had to be on the alert to follow our winning troops who were advancing towards Armentieres. Many roads passed through the wood, which had suffered very little damage, and the trees were normal height and very leafy. The Germans had held it until very recently and many light railway lines lay by the sides of the roads. A very small hut was the signal office and three of us both slept and did duty in it – Johnson, Fenton and myself. Fenton was from Low Fell, Gateshead and it was he who gave me the nickname 'Mush'.

Each night Jerry put over dozens of gas shells into the wood and H.E. Gas alarms were frequent. One of our special duties was to keep Brigade informed about the gas position. Candles were in short supply and when a night's supply was finished it was hard work keeping awake, but by testing the line to Brigade every ten minutes or less, the danger of falling asleep was averted. I explored many of the forest rides when off duty during the day. Not far from the clearing towards Hazebrouck was a very large building like a chateau, but I did not go to see it.

A battalion of K.O.Y.L.I. (King's Own Yorkshire Light Infantry) relieved us, and we went back to the camps near Wallon Cappel. Whilst here my younger cousin in Leicester wrote to tell me that her boyfriend was in the K.O.S.B.s (King's Own Scottish Borderers) and I was able to track him down near Ebblinghem. On our first meeting we became friends, giving me great pleasure to have succeeded in hunting up a friend of a relative. There was so little to do – the days were so quiet, we knew so little about what was going on, I missed never being in the orderly room and hearing the news and the rumours. Gunfire was never heard and it seemed as if our side at least was saving up for some great stunt.

We went back into Nieppe Forest for one night only and then we went forward a short distance and lived in the open – sometimes the signal office was a hole scooped out of the hedgerow and a telephone installed with a line being run back to Brigade. We did many such short moves forward and on only one occasion did we hear much German machine gun fire. Then it was rumoured that when our troops came close to the machine gun a solitary German came forward and gave himself up – he was wearing a brand new Red Cross armlet. From that rumour developed the old, old story that such a sham stretcher-bearer never arrived further back, only his escort did. Much nibbling away at the enemy's lightly held positions took place every night, especially by the Aussies on our right – one night a few farm buildings, another night two or three hedgerows and a roadway, etc. Such little gains were too insignificant to be mentioned in the night's communiques, but they kept the enemy on the move, backwards.

The next time out I was informed that I was the first man to go on leave as I had been out in France longer than anyone else since my other, my first, leave. Ten months had passed since I was home and so I had just to wait till leaves for the battalion started. In the meantime I was sent on a special signal course to Brigade to receive instructions in the latest type of Fullerphone. Then, in anticipation of coming stunts and moving forward against the enemy, we took part in brigade and battalion visual co-operation. Such practices took place daily and the only break came on the Saturday afternoon when sports were organised. All were invited to watch them, but anyone who did not go was ordered to clean his equipment, etc. and be inspected later in the afternoon. A good turn-out for the sports gathering resulted.

In the evening some of us gathered brambles, and what a size they were. Heavy rain drove us back to our billets and it never ceased for four days; the Sunday Church Parade could not be held for it was to have been in the open. In the second week in September the camp itself became a sea of mud so we were put into houses in Renescure. After four days drying out we moved to a farm at Sercus. The front was waking up and we moved to near Laventie to be in support. The natural surroundings were very little spoilt as H.Q. moved along to take over from the K.O.Y.L.I.s. We passed through a little village and on its outskirts we halted and were each given a dixie of hot soup in perfect quiet. We moved on down a road and, as the companies continued, we turned right down a farm track to some scattered farm buildings: a large farm house, adjacent barns and large sheds for carts completing a large square with a very large midden in the middle. Through a small paddock other out buildings, stables and sheds made up the rest of the farm. Some very hard fighting had taken place around and nearly all the buildings were roofless, yet with some rafters remaining. The midden had been completely emptied. Inside the main farmhouse and the adjacent barns, Nissen huts had been erected and bricks piled on them. The cellar was quite a good shelter and it was occupied by the C.O., the Second-in-Command, a Signal Officer and a Liaison Officer of the Artillery. In the stable beyond the paddock were boxes of small arms, ammo and Mills bombs. These boxes were piled to form three sides of a square and a door placed across the top. Sheets of corrugated iron lay along the sides and at the back. In the space below was the battalion telephone and enough room for the man on duty to sit upright. This stable was not damaged as much as the rest of the farm buildings.

As we took over I was very much surprised at the showing of lights. Officers of the relieving battalion and our own flashed their torches around, showing the site of the H.Q. and the billets of the men. The luscious brambles on the nearby hedges were being picked by torchlight I said to Green, "I don't think much of this flashing of lights – they give the position away." I was overheard by a young officer, who asked me. "Are you windy?" I assured him politely that I was not and added that I knew that Jerry would be observing such lights. He was not pleased with my view.

I was up and about early the next morning, about half past six, when Jerry sent over two shells; the first dropped not far behind us and the second just in front. The same young officer approached me and asked what I thought of them. "Jerry has bracketed our position and he'll let us know about it later," I replied. He glanced at my service chevrons and said, "You are a very windy old soldier." We parted and I did not mention this incident to Green and the new men and began to think that I had been wrong in my judgement. Dinner time passed and it wasn't until three o'clock that a five-point nine passed over us and dropped in the field behind us. Then at intervals of about two minutes further shells exploded all around us: many were near misses, some hit the road on the left, and by four o'clock the farm buildings were being hit and bricks and woodwork were being scattered about. One of the senior officers left the cellar with a runner to go and find alternative headquarters. Soon the runner returned and reported to the C.O. who shortly afterwards gave the order to evacuate the farm. I did not hear the order, not being in the main farm building or in the cellar. I saw him lead the way out and away but did not realise that all of us had to go. Green was in the paddock on duty and I was with him and found myself staying behind, but not by order. Who gave the other signallers the order to go I did not know, I just thought that we should keep in touch with Brigade. It was not till later that I found out who had remained behind: a junior officer of the battalion, Green and I, and in the cellar with our officer was a gunner officer and his batman. Instead of keeping to the field hedge and ditch against the roadway some of the twenty or more H.Q. men strayed off, some crossed the field making straight for a ruined farm and some of those who went directly across the field behind the farm or by way of the paddock were wounded. For carrying one of the wounded back the H.Q. cook was awarded the M.M. As I was about to go and help him, Green called to me: "A message has come through." I read it: "Re memo, No. xxx the Divisional Specialist Courses postponed will be started as soon as the battalion comes out of the line." I waited till two shells had burst nearby and then set off for the farm cellar. Other shells sent wood and bricks into the air and round about me and I was hit by very small pieces on the knees and face. I delivered the message to our junior officer, who said there was no reply, and I set off back to the lonely Green. More and more shells were coming over as if Jerry was wanting to use up a dump of five-nines before pulling out his guns. More of the main buildings were being destroyed and Green and I seemed to be in the safer part. A second message came through just after six. It read: "Leave will start on 1st October." I again ran the gauntlet of shells and flying bits and gave the message to our officer, who again said that there was no reply and that he would hand it over to the orderly room later. No sooner had I got back to the phone than another message came through – this one was for the artillery liaison officer. It read. "Can you locate battery firing on your front?" I took it to him and he read it. Before leaving the cellar with his batman he drew our officer's attention to my having brought three messages to the cellar. Our officer briefly replied: "It's his duty." The Colonel's runner suddenly appeared with the message that the position could now be abandoned and that we had to fall back to the new H.Q. The three of us left the cellar and had just reached the far corner of the midden when a shell struck the debris over it. I ran to Green and told him to inform the Brigade man on duty that a new H.Q. station was now operating and that we were closing down. We joined the other two in the ditch by the roadside when I suddenly remembered that the battalion's two pigeons were behind the bomb boxes so I rushed back for them. It was almost seven o'clock and the strafe became heavier and soon very little of the farmhouse and its buildings remained standing.

It was Jerry's last fling as we reached the cellar of a farmhouse on the outskirts of a small hamlet not far away. We reported to the Signals Officer who told us that the N.C.O. had tapped into the old line and thus reestablished communication with the Brigade H.Q. (For this L/Cpl. Laider was later awarded the M.M.) The new billet was exceptionally wet and uncomfortable. A few days later we came out of the line and I enjoyed looking at the old German positions, especially around those parts I had known when I first came out – villages of which I had sent home picture postcards were now no more. I feasted many times on the luscious brambles. On Monday, September 30th, I was told that I was not to go up the line with the battalion but that I had to go to the transport lines and details, and be ready to go on leave. I exchanged my francs for English money and was ready to set off at any time. A very young officer who had arrived on draft saw me idling away the hours and asked. "What are you supposed to be doing?" I told him, and he replied. "You needn't waste your time. You might as well be learning something, I'll show you how to use a machine gun. The knowledge might be useful some day." He spent part of the morning and afternoon instructing me and at the end complimented me on my taking it in so well. I did not tell him that I was proficient in the use of the Lewis Gun, and bombing, and sniping. As I sweated on leave that evening, a runner arrived from the battalion with the message "Leave cancelled. Report at once to Divisional H.Q. Appointed instructor.for Signals Course starting immediately." As for myself, I was not too disappointed but I was very sorry for my mother whom I had earlier warned that I should be home on leave in October. To me it did not matter so much for I was not going up the line, another cushy time lay ahead. Besides, even though I did not know many of the new battalion, the friendship with them was better than that to be found in Blighty where, on my first leave, I had found it difficult to bridge the gap between the war as seen by a Tommy of the line and that as imagined in England. The people there were incapable of understanding what it was like. I had to find out where the Divisional School was to be held and then I packed up and left the Transport Lines.

16

School again – Meteren – Jerry in Retreat

I found myself near Meteren attached to the Division and ready for the course in signalling to begin, but before the details arrived from the various battalions, a great change took place on that front. All the divisions were moving forward very quickly and the line was changing daily, as the Germans were almost in full retreat. Our troops were finding it hard to keep up with them, having to proceed carefully in case of ambushes, etc. The enemy made great use of the hours of darkness to help him withdraw whilst our troops had often to wait till daylight to carry on with the pursuit. We heard that when our division was held up at the River Lys, Jerry struck back by sending a patrol over to our side one night and took prisoner one of our officers and his batman as they went round giving out a rum ration to the scattered troops. The batman's body was found later, but of the officer there was no trace. The following day our troops crossed the river and pushed on.

The school did not get started: the course was cancelled and the staff, of which I was one, followed the advancing troops in easy stages by motor lorry. We passed through Meteren, where I spent many happy days in June 1917, and now not a building remained standing. The town was razed to the ground, bricks everywhere and the only traces of the main streets were roughly three layers of bricks to every wall. Gone were the farm buildings, the old billet and the Y.M.C.A. hut; the whole village was no more.

Pioneer men had cleared the roads and we passed through Bailleul, which had also received a tremendous battering but not quite all its buildings had been destroyed – although many important ones had. It was getting dark as we neared Nieppe and Pont de Nieppe, where I had had my first bath in France. I wondered if the large brewer's vats were still by the river side and where the French girls were who had prepared the bath tubs for us. We entered Armentieres, but mademoiselle had left so there was no chance of a parley-vous with her, and our lorry stopped well before the centre of town. Our billet for a very few hours was an exceptionally large building and we surmised that it had been a large school because of the large hall, broad stairway, corridors leading to many rooms that appeared to be classrooms, and similar rooms upstairs. Jerry had used the ground floor as a stables and it was in a filthy condition and showed every sign of having been vacated in a hurry. I slept on that stable floor and slept very well, much better than on my very first night in the Army, also on a stable floor. My hip bones were now well rounded and I could rest on any hard surface. We were astir very early and before we had our breakfast of Army biscuits, a slice of bully beef and a mug of tea, I slipped out to look round. Churches, schools and houses were all in ruins; mills, factories and iron works had all been destroyed; anything useful and light enough had been taken away. Some buildings had been deliberately mined and blown up.

We mounted our lorry and soon came to the crossroads in the middle of the town where, instead of continuing along a tram-lined road, we bore left and went along the Rue de Lille. Outside the town we entered a real battle zone, desolation and destruction on all sides. Everything seemed to have suffered in some way – the fields were barren, the roads very poor, and all villages in ruins. We had to follow which ever roads were in the best condition, zig-zagging our way through Premesques and towards Perenchies. Every crossroads had been mined and blown up and I noticed for the first time French civilians helping to fill in the craters. Perenchies itself was forsaken – deserted. All the houses were broken down and it looked as if all humans had fled as if from a dread plague. A further five miles on I saw a very tall tree, unscathed, and as we were passing it I noticed that a platform had been constructed near the top and between it and the ground stretched a very long pole across which were nailed short pieces of wood. That was the ladder to the German look-out post and it could not be seen from the other side. Then my eyes were drawn to what had been telegraph poles. Some German, no doubt by order, had measured one metre from the ground and then sawed the telegraph pole down. A few poles had not been taken away and it was seen that the copper wires, before being taken away, had been cut off just ten centimetres from the insulating pots. How methodical the Germans had been! How spiteful, greedy and childish too! Destroyed bridges had been temporarily repaired so that the follow-up could be continued without much delay. Everywhere at crossroads, side roads, at light railways (Feldbahn) and in all streets in all towns I noticed all directions and names were in large German letters. No German soldier could get lost through lack of sign posting – the large white letters stood out well on dark backgrounds. All signs pointed to the fact that Jerry was following a well-planned retreat. We had already spent one night in our lorry and just after passing through Wambrechies, in ruins too, we settled down for another night in it. A sapper of a specialist bomb squad paid us a visit and warned us to be very careful – time bombs had been left in unsuspected places and other cunning dodges had been used to delay the follow-up: a harmless-looking broomstick against a house door might, if disturbed, set off a bomb; a clock left on a house mantelpiece should not be touched; a picture askew on a wall should be left alone. Time bombs had been left in all manner of places: "Keep away from all buildings and objects lying about till you know the specialists have examined them," he warned.

The second night's stay in our lorry seemed very eerie – we were thinking more of what the Germans had left behind than of the Jerries themselves. They had not managed to use up all their shells and ammo, some had to be left behind and it was from these that any trouble came. Jerry had primed them to go off later and some were doing just that; bits and pieces of shells and nose caps were often flying about and around us though not all at the same time.

One Sunday in late October we crossed the main Menin-Lille Road and soon passed through the main street of Nouvaux. Shortly after passing over a canal bridge we entered Roubaix and the first building I noticed was a very large one with a golden dome. The lorry stopped a few yards further on and the Divisional Sergeant went to find out what we had to do. He was away quite a time and I got down from the back of the lorry very carefully, remembering that I wore no underpants, because as soon as we stopped a crowd of women and children started to gather round, showing signs of great pleasure and welcome. They chatted away and flung many questions at me. They felt my kilt and touched my bare knees and enquired: "Ecossais?" I did not tell them that I was an imitation.

I enjoyed the talk with them – how happy they were, so glad to be free from the Germans. The sergeant returned and he, with the help of a Tommy in the lorry, got me demurely back into the lorry. We had not far to go and found a house for our billet. We emptied the lorry and took all its contents into the house. The French women woke us at seven the next morning with coffee and asked if they could be of any help to us. During our two days' stay there they were exceedingly kind to us.

The Germans were thoroughly beaten and we were glad to set up the school and beginners would soon be sent to get started at long last. Our little party left Roubaix by the main road to Lille and, after passing through the little village of Croix, turned off to the right after going a mile to the village of Wasquehal, marked on the map as a Commune so perhaps it was classed as a town. Before we had quite passed through the lorry stopped in front of some old pensioners' cottages, one of six in a row, two of us, instructors from different units, were allocated to No. 62 – we were in Rue Christophe Colomb, Christopher Columbus Street. We stepped straight into the main room, the living room, in which was a typical large French stove in the middle of the wall on the left, there was no furniture and in the far right corner was a washing sink and a tap. Halfway along the far wall was a door which led into the small bedroom, on the floor of which were two bags of straw for beds. The other five cottages were occupied by old people.

We dumped our kits in the living room and went out to view the district. We turned left and walked past a high wall and massive iron gates, behind which was a very beautiful house in its own grounds. The small school just beyond it bid been allocated to us for the details that were to arrive. Our cook house was next door and at the top end of the street was a large open space which became our parade ground. A large empty factory stood opposite the cottages and stretched almost to the top of the street.

Within two days the school was in full swing forty men having turned up for the course. Reveille was at seven a.m. and there was a roll call at quarter past when the men were dismissed to get themselves dressed. Breakfast was at eight and the first parade was at nine. Flag drill, station work and lectures occupied the time in the mornings and short route marches, rifle drill and gas helmet drill kept the men in touch with the other side of a signaller's life. After 4 p.m. and tea we were free for the evening. By the time we had cleaned up, loitered and chatted, it was very dark and, having to see to fatigues and the rations, there was no time to go to Roubaix so we played cards, or wrote letters and prepared our bags of straw for the night's sleep.

One of us had to go along the street to the school at ten o'clock and call the roll. We called out forty names and got in reply, "Present, corp," forty times and that satisfied us, but we knew that not only did half the beds look empty, but they were! Most of the men had found private billets; a real bed was better than a wooden floor with a straw bag as a bed. The civilian women had sought lodgers because a few francs paid by them weekly would help to keep the wolf from the door. The women did not hide the fact that they had had Germans billeted on them for many years and they drew our attention to the difference – some women had had to have German lodgers by order, whilst some women had lived with the Germans, the latter being "no bon". Many times I was asked if I would like a comfortable bed but I preferred our little room.

In the large house nearby lived a grandfather, his daughter and her daughter. The old man used to stand at the gate and greet me as I passed and gradually we began to converse. He told me that his son had been called up in the early days of the war and he and his daughter had not seen him for four years and did not know if he was alive or not. His granddaughter was now sixteen and he was glad that the Germans had been driven away from the district as he had felt the need to keep her indoors and out of sight. Many of the French women in the town also had not seen their husbands and other loved ones for years.

The weather had turned bitterly cold but I found that in the daytime I did not feel it so much, thanks to the kilt, but the cottage itself was very cold. We begged a wooden box for fire wood from the cooks and also some petrol. We managed to scrounge some straw, a few "eggs" which were made of coal dust, tar and straw, and we put our finds in to our stove, poured on a little petrol and then stood as far away as possible from the stove whilst throwing on lighted matches to see which one of us could manage to set the contents alight. A sudden explosion would follow, shaking both the stove and its chimney pipe and we soon had a blazing fire in it. Our aged neighbours were alarmed at first and I had to explain to them what we were doing. How they managed to live I do not know. They fully appreciated our little gifts of bully beef, bread and sometimes fire wood. Near our parade ground Jerry had had his stables and on the long heaps of manure grew many large mushrooms which I collected and handed in to the cookhouse. The cooks never gave me any in return, so I wished I had given them to the old people.

One November afternoon I felt very ill. I was so weak on my legs and so hot at times, yet feeling cold and shaky, that I was very glad when four o'clock came and I could get back to my billet I had a drink of tea and went straight to bed. I could not go sick even in the morning for we had no M.O. Somehow the old lady next door got to know how ill I felt and came to my bedside at nine o'clock. She asked me what was the matter and then went back to her cottage. She returned with a handful of herbs which she scalded with boiling hot water. "Buvez – vite," she said, handing me the mug. I felt that I daren't refuse though the taste was very bitter. What a night I had: I dozed, I sweated, I slept fitfully, I shivered, I turned over time and time again. The old woman had told me that I should be well by the morning and I was, almost. Whatever had been the matter with me had been sweated out. Thought I felt a bit groggy in the morning I went on parade at nine o'clock. She came in to see me and I thanked her for what she had done. She presented me with a handful of herbs, which I kept in my haversack for quite a time before throwing them away many weeks later – when my war was over.

The end of the week came and we all noticed how quiet things were. We had not heard the sound of guns for a long time and we used to sit around the stove and discuss the latest rumours. One rumour in particular was that some Germans had crossed over to our lines to discuss peace; very pleasing but was it true? A second rumour was that all British and Allied troops were going over the top on Monday at eleven, and that sounded to have more truth in it. That was to be an all-out onslaught to end the war. Old hands took some such optimistic thoughts with a pinch of salt; I did not believe in anything till it happened.

The stillness and the doubt were a little disturbing and everybody seemed to be waiting for something to happen. The weekend passed and we all paraded at nine o'clock that Monday. I had just marched off my section to near the old factory when we became aware of one of our own planes flying very low overhead. We could see both the pilot and his observer quite clearly and the plane began to circle over us; at the same time the observer leaned over out of his cockpit and waved his hat to us. This happened four times. We waved back and then the plane made off towards our own line. Was there any doubt what the observer meant? Was it over? The younger recruits declared, "The war's over, corp." (I was not a "corp" but was addressed as such). They did not even ask if I thought it was over. I was more cautious and quickly started on flag drill, and we put on a good show when the officer came round to see how we were going on with our programme. He did not say anything about the end of the war, nor did I tell him about the plane and its cheerful crew. At noon the news filtered through to us that an Armistice had been declared at eleven that morning, the eleventh of November: a time of day that coincided with the planned onslaught.

So it looked as if the early rumours about the Germans seeking peace had been true. We heard too that our bombers were to have set off at that time to bomb many German cities. I wondered how those troops, standing with rifles and bayonets fixed waiting for zero hour, felt when they were ordered to "stand down". It was all over. Many sighed with relief, no doubt. Did any cheer? I don't know, I myself felt too overcome and found it impossible to let myself go. The news was too good to be true. I failed to grasp the significance of it and for a time could not adjust myself to it – I felt numbed. There didn't seem to be an appropriate way of celebrating; there was a little hand-shaking, but no shouting or cheering. It was left to those well away from the fighting parts and those in Blighty to go wild with joy – except for those for whom the end had come too late; their loved ones having perished on the Somme, in Flanders, at sea or in earlier battles. Around us thousands of civilians had lost everything – their homes, possessions and loved ones too. Many of them cried.

That night I strolled across the road to the factory. The Germans had taken away all leather belts, nuts and bolts and lighter parts of its machinery. Railway lines too had been carted off to the Fatherland. A nearby canal had no water in it as explosive charges had blown in the sides. What a lot to be put right.

Armistice or no Armistice, the course programme had to be carried on and we all did our best despite the lack of heart in learning how to manipulate the rifle or how to be proficient in donning the gas mask. I had enlisted for the duration, nay, volunteered for it, and now the war was over, but I did not take the same attitude as the conscripted men – many of them thought that now this blooming war was over they should be returned home toute de suite. Many of them had not wanted to come and they wanted to be back to their jobs. They were liable to grouse at the slightest upset, like no milk arriving in the rations one day, it being rumoured that the train bringing it had been robbed on its way. When no fresh meat arrived when it was expected, they grew more considerate when they were told, unofficially, that it had been given to the starving civilians. Then they realised that, in some ways, they were more fortunate than the men actually in the frontline. How did they feel, kicking their heels with desolation all around them? Things were being done around us – concert parties were being organised and we were told where a show was being put on and given permission to go. The Diamonds gave a very fine entertainment in the Casino in Roubaix. The following day I went to the Tabs very first show at Croix.

On the Sunday we four instructors – Bombardier Cox of the Artillery, qualified instructor, L/Cpl. Tuxford of the K.O.S.B.s, a first class signaller, L/Cpl. McKenna, a first class signaller drafted from a Welsh regiment, and myself, a qualified instructor – went to Roubaix in the afternoon and had a group photograph taken and then had ourselves taken singly. The photographer told me that King George had passed through the town in the morning.

The next day all the details were marched to Lannoy to hear a lecture in the St. Charles School by Captain Bartlett on "Demobilization". I was very interested in the talk for we were told that many months must pass before we could all be sent back to Blighty: miners were to be given first priority; then teachers (and students would get their turn); the men who had signed on "for duration" were entitled to go before those who had been called up under the Derby scheme. Active Service Schools would be set up and men could join courses to suit their requirements. Volunteers to take such courses were to be called for and everything would be done to help men pass their time whilst waiting to go home.

On my return to the billet in Wasquehal there awaited me an official note informing me that I could set off on leave almost at once – I had received leave only once in two and a half years' active service and my second one was to be in peacetime! I received my travel warrant on Saturday, November 23rd and left the school in the afternoon. In full pack I set off and had just gone a short distance along the main Lille-Roubaix Road when a lorry stopped and I was given a lift to the Divisional Rest Camp at St. Andre on the outskirts of Lille. I was robbed of taking a walk into Lille by being put on a fatigue, an unusual one – to guard and keep going a large fire in the middle of the very cold room to warm it up as it was to be used as a temporary sleeping place for other details expected. Early next morning we left St. Andre by train and soon reached Hazebrouck where had had to stay till seven in the evening. The train did not reach Calais until ten and then I had to walk up to No. 2 Rest Camp. I enjoyed the compulsory bath next morning and after dinner hundreds of us, very care free now, boarded the King Edward for Dover, where the sight of the white cliffs was not so thrilling. A train to London, then a train for the north leaving from St. Pancras Station. I had to stand all the way to Leeds, where I changed trains. Three days' travel saw me home early on the Tuesday morning.

This leave soon passed and there was not enough time in which to do all I wanted to do. There was no hanging about on this occasion, feeling lost in another world. I spent a lot of time visiting old friends and calling at many homes to see if school pals had been demobbed. No-one had but I got the latest news about them.

I spent many evenings at the pictures or at the theatre. Dear John Bell went with me to the pictures. When I went to the Royal to see *The Maid of the Mountains* I was told that all the seats were full but one box was not taken. As I stood pondering a young man came up and said that, if I wished, he would share the box with me. I decided to do this at only a few shillings cost. He proved to be the younger brother of one of the college men of my year, one who had not enlisted when we others did but waited to take his finals. Under the Derby scheme he was called up and was in ordnance near Wimereux, Calais. That play I shall never forget. The singing of the gipsy girl I thought wonderful (Jose Collins?). The play made such an impression on me that I could hum every song in it. It has remained a great favourite of mine.

I visited my old school, my old headmaster, the East Riding College, and then went for three days to Leicester to see my half-cousin and her husband. Pictures I saw there were *Ghosts, Eve's Daughter* and *The Lady of the Camellias*. I had not settled what I was going to do when I came out of the Army so on my return from Leicester I went to an Army Office in North Parade and asked for an extension of leave so that I could contact the Education Authorities. I was not received very cordially, but was given two days' extra leave. I had gone to the wrong office – it was the Recruiting Office.

17

Lannoy – Waiting for my ticket – Demobbed

Thus, just fourteen days after arriving home, I left it late on the Tuesday evening so that I travelled all night and so avoided being lost in London, which I reached at eight o'clock on the Wednesday. The crossing from Dover was very mild and I did not gaze lovingly at the receding English Coastline. On the Thursday afternoon I dropped off the cattle truck train after it had left St. Andre and was nearing Wasquenal. By so doing, I saved spending a night in the Divisional Rest Camp and saved a day. My pensioner's cottage was empty and so was the school as all the details had returned to their units, but the R.E. sergeant was still there clearing up with the help of Green, one of my battalion and a great friend. So I stopped with them and gave them a hand.

In the evening Green and I went to Croix and heard a ripping concert party called the Gamecocks. On our return we were told that we had to go back to our own unit the next day. I bade goodbye to the old pensioners next door and to the old man and his family in the large private house. Green and I found our battalion a very short distance away in Belgium at the town of Nechin to where they had gone from the line shortly after the Armistice. Headquarters took me on to its staff and I did one turn of duty in the next three days. Instructors and teachers were wanted to help in giving refresher courses in various subjects but I did not accept Captain Null's invitation of a post on the teaching staff. Instead I became a pupil on the matriculation course so that I would not be tied if and when my demobilization came through.

On Wednesday, December 18th, before any course got started, the battalion left Nechin and marched to Lannoy in France where the billets were barrack-like and our soldiering more like in peacetime. The signallers had to salvage wire and lay lines from the battalion H.Q. to the Officers' Mess and to Brigade and also to other battalions. After dinner on Saturday, Green and I got permission and went to Roubaix. We found a cafe where we had tea and later enjoyed the films at a French cinema. A supper of chips followed, as the people had no eggs and could not even let us have one small piece of bread.

The signallers moved into a large house near the railway sidings. We fixed up the offce in the front room upstairs and used the other rooms as bedrooms and a mess room. There were evidences of German occupation everywhere: directions in German and large arrows pointing the way to German departments. Green and I again visited Roubaix on Christmas Eve. As there were no parades the next day, we strolled together towards Leers in the morning. Christmas Day dinner was just as meagre and as unappetising as usual and we were told that some effort would be made to lay on a special dinner on New Year's Day – the Scots' day of celebration. Incidentally, I had got used to morning burgo (porridge) with salt instead of sugar and liked it very much. Green and I decided to try our luck in Leers and, after trying at about fifty houses, we found a woman kind enough to supply us with chips, cafe and a little bread. We were so hungry that we could have eaten a second lot, but she could not oblige us.

Everything was so quiet these days and on our return we settled down in our new billet and Green asked me if I knew shorthand. I told him that I did not, so he offered to teach me. I readily accepted his offer and he started me off with PB, TD etc. A few days earlier we had sent off home our Christmas cards. The Divisional Printing Section had produced a card in a light brown folder, five and a half inches by seven. On its front, a one inch sided diamond containing the words "40th Division, B.E.F." stood with one point in the middle of two stems of oak leaves knotted just above the motto "Excel", the latter word being exactly in the middle of the front. Near the bottom was "Xmas 1918". A large bow of red ribbon decorated the side; that ribbon was passed through two holes and held at the other side a separate piece of paper for any message one wished to send and the word "From". Page three had a darker brown border, five and a half inches by four, in which a gaily coloured card was fixed. A very pale blue-purple outline of the British Isles and the Western Front and a very pale green and white sky showed off a brilliantly coloured Gamecock with reddish brown wings and lighter yellowish wings flying over, piloted by a Tommy, rifle slung, left hand holding a rein and the right hand holding aloft two oak leaves and an acorn. The talons of the huge legs of the bird firmly held a mail-clad Uhlan with brass helmet and long jack boots and spurs. His gloved hands stretched down to the earth. (The designer's name is indistinct).

Some extra tables and boxes were brought into the signallers' office: the phone was put into the far corner and the office became the Demobilization Centre for the Battalion. It was to be run by the signallers with their own officers in charge, and we H.Q. sigs. were exempt from all parades. It was a very easy job, departures being few and only occasional, and there was an understanding that only one signaller would be allowed to go home should an allocation come through for his district. The corporal was very keen that he should be the lucky one. Six men only went home in the first week and we had many idle hours, many free afternoons and evenings.

In the afternoons Green and I kept on with our lessons in Pitman's shorthand, but in the evenings we could go out. The next visit to the cinema in Roubaix was disappointing for there was a break-down in the apparatus and we had to come out of the building. We paid another visit to the Gamecocks, who presented a potted pantomime – *Ali Baba and the Forty Thieves*. It was really great and the chorus of six young "girls" appealed to all of us. One of them, the smallest, was a young officer who played his part remarkably well. I was the most privileged of the signallers because I was allowed to go into Roubaix almost daily, when work was slack, to make purchases for the office – indexing cards, suitable boxes to hold them, etc.

A scrounging party found amidst some rubble on a building site a large tin bath and so we converted one of the small rooms of our billet into a bathroom. We heated water in buckets on the fire. On New Year's Eve there mysteriously appeared plenty of beer for every man, a band to supply music and no lights out. We made merry until early next morning. Some of our section had earlier gone into town and bought many bottles of vin rouge. Johnson had taken too much and during the few hours we slept I awoke to find him crawling around and shouting "Let me be". No-one was offering to touch him until it was noticed that he was so drunk and helpless that he was wanting to get his bayonet and do himself harm as his stomach was giving him great pain. We four of the staff, now thoroughly roused, rushed on him and held him down. Later he was very sick, all over the place, and didn't we bless him? There was no reveille – and a good job too – so we had time to recover from the effects of our merry making and to relax. A special dinner was laid on for us and we did full justice to it. The band played bagpipe music throughout the afternoon.

With pass-outs Green and I went to Roubaix later and to the cinema, called the Hippodrome (Theatre). The pictures were French ones, silent, and had sub-titles in French at the bottom. I used to translate these, quietly, for the benefit of Green. Anyone who could hear me would think because I could read French easily that I could speak it just as well. Behind us we could hear some French civilians and some giggling then suddenly I felt a slight push at my seat but I took no notice. It was repeated and I again took no notice. Then I received a tap on the shoulder so I turned half round and a girl's voice amid much giggling asked, "Portez-vous le calecon?." (men's drawers/underpants) and I replied, "Je n'en ai pas." Much laughter followed my answer to such a cheeky question, a question I was to be asked in English scores of times and always the questioners did not know whether or not to believe me. When the show was finished and we turned to go out a very much made up young girl spoke to us and we thought she would have been rather pretty without all the paint and powder. She asked me if I would like lodgings at her home, but I told her I was from Lannoy and not staying in Roubaix. When we got outside, she left us and went to a sergeant who accompanied her to wherever she was going. Gradually other entertainments were arranged in the district and in the same week we went to our own Brigade Cinema Show and to one of a civilian party from Blighty which was more English and more up to date with the latest tunes.

Though I was sweating on demoblization I knew that I should have to wait till, by chance, an allotment came through for the English side of the border, and so far only real Scots had gone home despite me having the longest service out there. At 10 a.m. on Thursday, January 9th, 1919, I was told that I was to go home. My hopes were short-lived for exactly at noon that day I was sent for and told that I was not to go, the allotment had been switched to the sergeant cobbler of the transport lines. There must have been some wangling for my papers had been started on. So that evening I went again into Roubaix with Green, and this time we enjoyed a real French variety show in the Casino Palace. The next night we went again to the Hippodrome Theatre because there was a change of programme. The building had a very fine front: on the ground floor were two large arched windows in between which was the arched entrance to match. Above were six half-sized arched windows and balconies. At the top of the building was a large stone bearing the words "Circus Theatre". On each side of the main building was a bureau (kiosk); the one on the left carried posters about forthcoming attractions, films, whilst the one on the right gave notice of revues, etc. The whole faced the large square and where the Grande Rue met the square on the left was a huge shop "Au Grand Bon Marché" owned by M. Fevrier et Cie. It sold "Draperies, Nouveautes and Convections pour Hommes". The latter amused me, it did not refer to ices but to manufactured goods for men – suits etc. This shop was empty. Across the street at the other corner was a fine ornate building called the Automatic Bar. Its doorway, two side windows and the huge canopy were oriental in design, Chinese. It too was empty. The estaminet "Jules" was in the corner. A single tram line from the Grande Rue split into two, one line went straight on, and the other turned left into the square. This was the street by which Green and I came from Lannoy. Another street that we explored was New Street.

The first thing that Lt. Kinloch did when I entered the sigs. office on the morning of Saturday, January 25th was to put before me Army Form Z21. It was my Certificate of Transfer to Reserve on Demobilization – I was not for discharge, disembodiment or demoblization. It was only then that I saw that my new Regimental Number was prefixed by the letter S/. Name, rank, battalion, date of enlistment and my original regiment all there.

Then followed a statement that I had no decorations and that I had served overseas. In case of emergency I had to report to Kinross. My category, specialist military qualifications and year of birth followed. Finally, "He is transferred to Army Reserve on 14th February, 1919 in consequence of Demobilization", signed by J. Rogerson, Lt. Officer, i/c Infantry Records, No.1 District, Perth. Down the left hand side was a request: "N.B. Any person finding this Certificate to forward it in an unstamped envelope to the Secretary, War Office, London, S.W.1." Down the right hand side was a warning: "If this Certificate is lost a duplicate cannot be issued. You should therefore on no account part with it or forward it by post when applying for a situation.

This document must have come from Records, already filled in. Other papers and forms had to be made out and I bid the greatest of pleasure in preparing them myself and then just placing them before the officer for his signature. I signed a form declaring that I had no claim on the Army. I really ought to have thought more before signing it as my eyesight was much worse owing to Army service, my left ankle was never normal and, like many other soldiers, I suffered some discomfort of the legs through the constant wearing of tight puttees, and too the soles of my feet were milky in appearance – the skin not at all flesh-like. I had been told that, if I did want to make any claim, my demobilization would be delayed for at least three months till a medical board considered my case. That delay influenced me and I decided to get out of the Army as soon as possible. I had my much-interrupted career and my mother to think about. I was given two hundred francs, and felt very rich, and part of my rations for the journey was a seven pound tin of bully. I was ready for "my ticket".

I had one disappointment because that very morning I received a letter from an Old Boulevardian school pal called Bobby Abram. He had managed to track my movements from my letters to him and he wondered if we could meet some Sunday in Lille. Too late, for I had not time to let him know I was being demobbed – I would willingly have waited a few more days just to have been able to meet him.

After bidding goodbye to the few friends I had and given Green my home address, I left the billet at 9.15 a.m. on the Sunday and walked into Lannoy Square where a motor lorry picked up we lucky ones. We left there at ten and were taken to the Concentration Camp at St. André, Lille. Hundreds of men were there waiting their turn for a train. It looked as if more were arriving than leaving and I was put in Group 100 B, the second group for leaving. All we could do was to hang about, talk with new friends, look around to see if there were any old friends there, stroll about the neighbourhood and be there for meals. The village of La Madeleine adjoined the camp, which I think had been an asylum. Time was dragging especially in the evening, so I resorted to an estaminet a short distance away in that village. I was quite surprised to find no other English soldier there and easily found a corner near the stove. Quickly I realised that this nook was far more comfortable than the camp. Marie brought me what passed for coffee, a concoction made from roots, and she hung around to talk to me as her few customers needed very little attention. She told me that her father had not yet come home, that she and her mother had had a trying time during the German occupation when all foods had been scarce and that the nightly curfews had resulted in their having very few customers, and there had been a scarcity of drinks. I told her I was about to go home and asked her if she could lend me an iron – un fer. She did not understand until I showed her the pleats of the kilt and imitated pressing them. She said she would see what she could manage if I came another time.

When I returned to the camp I noticed at once that my kit had been tampered with and that someone had been doing some "winning" or scrounging. My water bottle had disappeared. Such a loss would not have happened in the old Yeoman Rifles, but I ought to have known better than to leave my stuff unattended. The next morning I was told that our group would not be leaving that day so I looked round and found someone who agreed to look after my kit as he was not going to take his eyes off his own.

I strolled to Wambrechies and ran into Dagnall, Pickering and Cox, draft soldiers who had been on the signalling course. They took me to see their very comfy civvy billet at 201 Rue de Lille. They were free and, as they knew an estaminet where we could eat, I decided to have dinner there. We had the usual – chips, bread and coffee, after which I went to see my old pensioner friends in Rue Christophe Columb. After a similar meal I left the town at 4.30 and, instead of going back to camp, I went to the estaminet. Marie had found an iron and heated it for me and then let me go into a little back room and get busy on my kilt. It was not so much that any disorder in the pleats worried me, but the fact that in the tucks there may have been some chats or their eggs. Owing to the fact that I had not been in any trenches for some time, my kilt was almost free and I felt quite satisfied with it. I left Marie at the latest time possible. She asked me for a souvenir and I gave her a book I had bought in Roubaix. She asked me to write to her and I promised to do so, and made a note of her address before bidding her goodbye.

My friend at the camp had left our kits only at meal times, but mine had again been tampered with. Someone had made sure that he had plenty of rations for the journey home for my seven pound tin of bully had vanished. I could not blame my friend for I had had a good day out. At ten that night I was warned that I was to leave the next day and that I had not to leave the camp. At 9.30 the next morning all my group paraded in full pack and the roll was called. After half an hour's standing thus, we were told to take our packs off and rest. Just before noon we were told to get out our mess tins and go for dinner. We loitered over the meal as the mess orderlies seemed to be in no hurry to get us away. Back at our kits on the parade ground at 1.30 p.m. we were told that we should not be moving off till half past four. I never liked having nothing to do and here the dear old Army, right to the end, was messing us about: standing us around, keeping us waiting. I think that this aspect of Army life caused more grousing than anything else.

We moved off to the railway siding and waited for the train to arrive and finally at seven o'clock we were all in the cattle trucks and off, the long, long trail was nearing its end. It was dark and our train moved very slowly at first, till it had pulled away to the right and joined the main line from Lille. The huge doors were closed and the train increased its speed to medium – slow, for cattle truck trains never did travel fast. We knew when any large town was being passed by its crawl. After Armentieres I let myself dream. Away to the right, not too far, was Plugstreet, Messines Ridge and Flanders' mud and many villages I knew so well. "Goodbye-ee, goodbye-ee, Wipe a tear ... Though it's hard to part ... " I was not sorry to be leaving those parts. Whilst passing Hazebrouck and St. Omer I slept only fitfully, gripping my possessions and using my valise as a pillow. Rain greeted us as we detrained at Boulogne the next morning at 4 a.m. and we tramped up the hill to St. Martin's Camp where we were given breakfast and waited and waited for orders for the final stages of our Army life.

At the first parade we each handed in three blankets – good riddance. Our tunics, trousers, kilts, etc. had to be fumigated – our lice were to be demobbed too, along with their eggs. This action worried me for I had heard that a kilt lost its fine colouring; under the process, so I tipped the orderly a few francs and handed in only my tunic. Besides, it would have been very cold just standing with the lower half of my body almost nude. Dressed again, we paraded and were put into groups; I was in number one which meant I was to leave on the next boat. More waiting about followed and it rained all the rest of the day. Another wet day and anxiety at all mealtimes regarding my belongings, and then I was told to be ready at 4.30 a.m. the following morning. Our draft was ready before time, but it was not till seven that we moved off and marched to the docks, led by a band. We were moved about from quay to quay and our boat arrived at half past eleven. Instead of going across the Channel to Folkestone, our boat sailed through the Channel, through the Straits of Dover, round Kent and into the Tilbury Docks, London late that night. How we hurried off the boat and the first thing we saw was a huge notice saying "Welcome Home". We were at once provided with tea and a packet of food from a buffet. The women attendants were really pleased to wait on us, there was a true homely touch and signs of gratitude in all their actions, their faces radiating welcome. We hurried through this meal, wanting to be on our way home.

A special train arrived and took us to Clipstone Camp near Mansfield which we reached at 6 a.m. We were expected and orderlies quickly supplied us with breakfast. Then followed a medical inspection, chiefly a small arm one to see if we were free from V.D. and the like. Our papers were checked and then we were told to be prepared for the handing back of all our issue equipment. In large sheds were two lines of trestle tables, each with the name of some part of equipment clearly shown. We had to proceed snake-like round the tables, parting with the named article on the right table, round the top and back to near where we started. Here a checking officer sat at another trestle table. A member of the camp accompanied each one of us round the tables to see if we handed in our parts, or to make a note of anything we failed to hand over. Just before we set off on this task a real Scot, also in a kilt, singled me out. "Hello Jock, short of anything?" he enquired. I told him about my "losses" on the way from the front. "Wait here," he said. He disappeared and when he returned he handed me some items. I thanked him and he said that he would be going round the tables with me. When we reached the checking officer, who asked: "This man short of anything?" he answered, "Yes, sir – his water bottle." The officer opened a huge ledger about thirty inches square in which were listed in alphabetical order all the parts of equipment a Tommy should have. "Bottle, water, for the use of, ten pence," he read. Turning to me he said, "No charge for articles under a shilling." Thanks to the fellow kiltie I needn't have worried so much, watching and guarding my equipment, and how clever he had been in not seeing that I had everything – did any soldier returning from the front have all his equipment, I wondered.

Not having a valise any longer in which to keep my personal goods, I was given two sandbags into which I put several books, some signalling manuals, boot brushes, cleaning materials, two private shirts, a set of black buttons, numerals (K.R.R.), small souvenirs, diaries, picture postcards, my writing paper, etc. Most of the Tommies had only one sandbag and I noticed that several were eyeing my two. I was asked if I would like a ready-made suit and when I refused the offer I was given £2 as well as a ration book and an unemployment book. My "Free from Infection" Certificate and my Identification Certificate were stamped and I was ready for the last stage of my journey home.

A special train took a lot of us to Sheffield where I changed trains and finally reached home just after teatime. Though no special words of welcome were spoken, the hugs from my mother and her aunt spoke volumes. As I ate my tea my great-uncle and niece sat in silence, then came the hundreds of questions. My cousin, Jonathan, came in later and we all sat talking and listening till two in the morning. The following day was a Sunday and I stayed in all the time; we had just a small family gathering with nothing to mar our peace.

Any soldier not wanting to keep his greatcoat had to go to the nearest railway station and hand it in. I handed mine in. I had been given Army Form Z50 at the dispersal camp and had to fill it in: Returned Great Coat: Regimental Number, Rank and Regiment or Corps. Name in full (surname first) in block letters. Received from the London and North Eastern Railway Company at Paragon Station, Hull the sum of £1 (One pound) in exchange for Military Great Coat, the property of the Government, which is herewith returned. Signature of Soldier.

My mother told me that by the morning post the day before I had arrived she had received a cheque for quite a number of pounds from the Pay Office, but on presenting it at the Post Office later in the day she was told that it had been stopped by the Army authorities. All I could surmise was that some pay clerk aroused from slumber had found out that the government allowance promised me in addition to my allotment to her had just come to light. He had made the calculation as to how much was due and sent off a cheque for that amount. A second pay clerk discovered that I was being demobbed and cancelled it, thinking it was not necessary to pay it. I was home and we let the matter drop.

The next morning when I arose I got out of the cupboard my civvy suit the one I had sent home from Helmsley after enlisting and receiving a uniform. What a shock! I could get it on but the waistcoat and jacket would not meet and the trousers seemed to come half way up my legs. I had grown and put on weight no doubt down to fresh air, exercise and simple meals. I felt I perhaps ought to have accepted an Army ready-made suit after all, or I should now want one. In a top coat and with my trousers hanging well down I went to a tailor's and got measured for a new suit. I had to wear my kilt longer than I intended to and continue to be cautious. The return to wearing trousers presented a little difficulty in that I had to continually remember to fasten up the fly. When I received my new suit I packed away my kilt in a cardboard box, safely protected by moth balls.

A strange reaction began to set in: a spirit of restlessness took hold of me and I found that I could not sit down for long, unless fully occupied with something, or even stay in one room very long. I had to be moving about and felt even worse in the evening. I would go to the cinema or a theatre but not see the programme through. After thirty to forty minutes seated, I would get up and leave and go home, walking all the way.

I called on friends and longed for the return of Mac G. I met him at the station and arranged to meet up with him. We had a long talk about the old battalion. After I left him in Italy he collected all my letters and carried them about with him. Then he had been transferred to the 16th K.R.R.s where he met S.M. Gibson. Whilst his battalion was falling back in the northern sector he had lost all my letters and his pack in Plugstreet Wood. His new battalion had become a flying one, being hurried from one danger spot to another, always covering up.

I kept in touch with Green of the Camerons and he encouraged me to keep up with shorthand, writing part of a letter in it. Through his giving my name and address to a French girl by the name of Mireille, I began a long correspondence with her. She worked in the office of a notary in Lannoy and had a very good knowledge of English. We arranged that she should write to me in English and that I would reply in French and point out and discuss any mistakes either one of us made in the other's language. She sent me a photograph of herself and I was very surprised to learn that she was only seventeen as I had thought her to be much older. We corresponded for more than two years till the time came when she did not reply to one of my letters. I kept my promise to Marie, who soon grew tired of writing, but she did mention the French book I gave her and said that she had read it – it was *Le Vicomte de Bragelonne* by Alexandre Dumas (Père). For many years I corresponded with Monsieur and Mme. Wattebled, the old couple who "adopted" me after the Somme and in whose cottage I spent many hours.

Some of the Camerons went to Cologne and then on to India. When I heard this news I regretted that I had left the Army so quickly, I ought to have enjoyed some touring at the Army's expense. During my month's furlough, on pay, I received from Perth a Certificate of Transfer to Reserve and was informed again that I had to report to Kinross in case of emergency. The slip of paper accompanying this was addressed to Mr. Dennis. I received also a statement of my accounts with special reference to my old pay book. This showed that I had been paid 1205 francs and 115 lire. On pay parades, Quarter-Masters had never been too generous – they did not let Tommy get into debt, so paid him less than that to which he was entitled. I ended up getting a cheque for money owing to me. My gratuity based on months of active service duly arrived. I was also informed that stoppages of ten shillings and three pence three farthings had been deducted. I puzzled over this odd amount, then recollected that I had been stopped seven days' pay at Etaples – seven days at 1/6d per day came to 10/6d, so I had gained two pence farthing. I wondered if that was due to the rate of exchange, or to the generosity of the Army pay clerk.

At last I got down to seeing about my interrupted career. In September 1915 I had borrowed money from the L.E.A. in order to help me through college and when I decided to enlist I wrote to that authority to ask what the position would be. The reply was a very kind one – the matter could wait till I "came back", such optimism! I was offered either a six months' course or a year's course or the full year's course in order to gain my teacher's certificate and, until I took the course, I could go at once as an uncertificated teacher at £90 per year. I chose the full teaching course, simply because I thought that I ought to do so because of the almost four years' break and felt I would be stale, despite the fact that I ought to get earning as soon as possible because of my mother. I did accept the offer of being an uncertifcated teacher for six months. As for the loan, that could still wait till I had got a certificate, and a few months extra, and then they would consult me about it.

What about the other eight who left the college and served in the Yeoman Rifles? They all returned to continue where they left off. Some went to York, one to Caerleon and Mac G. to Sheffield University. Did they return unharmed? Not all of them: one, who received eighteen pieces of shell on the Somme, finished with one foot shorter than the other and had to wear specially built-up footwear. For his frequent visits to hospital he received free travel warrants, but he had to pay for repairs to his footwear. One had the marks of having been severely gassed; another found his love for games curtailed because of a bullet damaging one of his arms. Some showed signs of grey hair in their late twenties. Most had jumped from boyhood into manhood without being youths and none will ever forget the war to end wars.

When the "peace" came I was very puzzled. I could not understand why the Yanks seemed to have such a lot to say. It gave me great pleasure to think that our Tommies, the Poilus, and the glorious Empire troops could have licked the Germans without the Yank soldiers. Hadn't the Germans shot all their bolts before the Yanks went into action? The dollar aid, I suppose, we needed. How could the isolated United States, 3,000 miles away, have much knowledge of European politics? The Germans were not the only country jealous of our shipping lines and our Empire.

18

And now – Aprés la Guerre

The end of the war did not and could not terminate the friendships that it had created, and few were the men others wished to forget. Mac, whom I knew in my school days, and I became so attached to one another that nothing can describe the one's liking for the other we can only try to show it. He never fails to look me up when he comes to Hull, three or four times a year. He turns up where I work or at my home and I never really know the day when he will put in an appearance, yet he comes. All we do is to talk, mostly of our Army days together and of the war itself. We refresh one another's memories of the days we cannot forget, and live again in the past. Only by that means do we feel drawn together. Other topics are too commonplace and not allowed to intrude more than is necessary.

When Ted came to live near Hull I spent nearly every Friday evening at his house. If we were not discussing the ever-common subject, we were busy making my first wireless set – for in wireless we could see something to remind us of the old signal days. Ted already had a transmitting set and a constructor's licence. He moved to Monk Seaton near Newcastle and I went to stay with him and his wife. His departure brought about a closer tie with Pip, whom I started to visit every Friday evening. With other more distant pals I exchanged letters and always Christmas greetings. By such calls, visits and thoughts do we chums of the old section endeavour to keep alive the goodness that was created amidst horror.

What of the Yeoman Rifles – those who had returned? Thanks to Arnold Rushworth, that fine spirit of comradeship fostered on the battlefields was not allowed to fade away. He brought the survivors together and was responsible for the formation of the Yeoman Rifles' Association. Every year an Annual Reunion and Luncheon attracted survivors to York – 320 in the first year, later it went down to 200 till there are now only a few. They turn up just for the pleasure of meeting old pals and yarning of old times. Perhaps they fight bits of their war over and over again, and "Do you remember?" can be heard on all sides. It's not the luncheon that draws them there, but the chance of renewing the old friendships and meeting again. The luncheon is merely to get them together, and only the toasts are important. We do not forget our "absent friends" or "silent guests", those who did not return with us. Their memories live with us forever more and we are not likely to forge for their spirit of self-sacrifice and comradeship was of the best. The world has never known such – and seems to lack now. All the Yeoman Rifles helped to make England the soldiers' Blighty, a far better England than it is now. We cannot describe that noble spirit that was born out there. We have not the words to express it, though Q.M. Cowling holds us spellbound when he gives the Toast to the Yeoman Rifles. When we meet one another, little actions speak louder than words. One does not mind going out of one's way to receive an answering smile; a handshake conveys still more; the lingering cannot-drag-oneself-away attitude is strong within us all. After the luncheon is a general meeting and then a gradual fading away of members as they have to leave for their own towns. Many reunions have been held and more will be held until we have all joined our "absent friends".

That York Reunion and Luncheon gathering was not sufficient for the display of that affection we feel towards one another. 'C' Company held occasional reunions at the Farmers' Club in Newcastle and Pip and I, Jack Wade, Tim Lawday, George Bramley and Duggie Newmarsh (our cartoonist) would manage to join our company friends, thanks to a railway excursion on the Sundays chosen.

'A' Company started having reunions at Helmsley where the good folk of the town love to welcome the boys they adopted in 1915. They want us, and we all like, to use the same billets that housed us when we were "featherbed soldiers". They have never forgotten us, nor we them. Can it be wondered that we had a special gathering there because we had picked that town for our Battalion Memorial? The days there were our most pleasant Army days and its houses homes from home.

Rather late in the day, as it were, an idea of a visit to renew our acquaintance with "out there" was raised. Captain Brooksbank was exceptionally keen on such a tour and Arnold again saw to all the arrangements. So in 1928 two small parties left Hull at different times to visit the battlefields, or rather make a pilgrimage to the cemeteries out there and also to our old quarters. They felt honour – bound to visit the last resting places of their "absent friends" and felt happy paying their respects to those gallant dead. I joined the first, larger party, eighteen in all with Captain Brooksbank. We reached Zeebrugge one Sunday morning and quickly made our way to the railway station where I recognised one of my old company. He was obviously looking for someone, so I went up to him and asked him, "Don't you know me?" He said that he was looking for us because he had heard that we were coming out. He was staying at Ostend and had come over just to see us. He found that he could not leave us as quickly as he thought so he accompanied us on part of our journey. On the way to Bruges, the train crawled along – perhaps to remind us that we were in Belgium again – and we noticed many concrete pill boxes. Having a half hour to spare in Bruges, we walked round, saw the well-known belfry, boated on the canal and returned to the station to find the porter who had kept an eye on our luggage. He wanted, nay demanded, five francs from each of us. We paid up, rather unwillingly. We went on to Roulers where we learned that we had missed our connection for Ypres and that we should have to wait some hours for the next train. We decided not to wait and went outside the station and hired taxi cabs to take us to our destination. No sooner had we set off than we realised that we were in the old war zone. We passed a large cemetery and our drivers slowed down so that we could have a good view. Ypres, the square, the old Cloth Hall, and our Hotel Splendide.

After lunch our time was our own and Frank Miller asked me if I would guide him to find the Artillery Wood Cemetery, somewhere near Boesinghe. We set off, passed the other Essex Farm and its cemetery and many others too, which we inspected. There were so many little cemeteries that we were a long time in finding the one we wanted. A Belgian directed us to it, and Frank found the grave we had set out to find, the resting place of the son of two of his friends who greatly desired a photo of the grave. We took snaps of it. We called at Essex Farm for a lemonade and the lady living there told us that she remembered the approach of the Germans in 1914 and she fled to Poperinghe. By the time we reached the hotel, we had been truly in the past. After an excellent meal we sat at the little tables outside the hotel, silent for a good while until I suggested an itinerary for the week.

On Monday we took taxis, leaving Ypres by the Lille Gate, passing Shrapnel Corner and halting near the St Eloi Crater. It was full of dirty water and I knew not what else. Someone fished out a shell case. We had our photos taken on the crater lip. We gazed down towards the Brasserie Sector and imagined a lot. We could see how much the Germans had looked down on to our positions. On to Wytschaete along a very poor road, passing many ruined houses and other signs of our war. We approached Plugstreet Wood from the opposite way to the one we used to follow and halted at the corner where the piggeries used to be. We entered the wood here, but not by the Strand. It was like a new wood, there being very few older and higher trees, but many saplings, bushes and creepers. We were as tall as the growth in the rear part. We visited Rifle House Cemetery, where I found Machin's grave. In another small cemetery we found other graves of our lads. All were beautifully kept and well cared for. We pushed on and noticed a difference in the appearance of the wood. The front part showed much more the ravages of the war; its trees were split, shell marked, shattered and half dead and the remains of trenches could be seen – but there was no sign of the German house or of the faked tree observation post. In crossing an old trench I tore my trousers on some barbed wire. We walked down a road, turned right passed Le Gheer and a small German cemetery and entered the village of Plugsteet. A turn to the right and we were back at the spot from which we had started. We had lunch at the foot of the hill and then spent some time at the new cemetery (Bedford) into which all the bodies in those little cemeteries were to be, transferred. Some stone lions stood guard at the entrance.

Into the taxis again – Plugstreet, Romarin, Neuve Eglise, Kemmel to La Clytte where we halted. We walked a short way towards Reninghelst and stopped where the Murrumbidgee Camp used to be and a few yards away was the little cemetery in which Patch Watson was buried. At Hallebast Corner we were not allowed to follow the old road to the right but had to go by way of Dickebusch to reach the road to Vierstraat. We left the taxis and crossed the open to Ridge Wood. We roamed about in it and at the end of the old path I was the only one to remember the turn to the left before reaching the road down which we used to hurry to the Brasserie, a new one. There were no traces of the old headquarters or of the P. and O. communication trench. We did find Strong Point 7 and barbed wire, angle irons and sheets of corrugated iron now being used as part of a farmer's fences, sheds, etc. We returned to the Brasserie and had drinks there, for old times' sake.

Immediately after breakfast the next morning the taxis awaited us and we set off for the Somme. We went by way of the one-time side of the German line. In Armentieres the Belgian customs officials at their douane scarcely troubled us, but the French ones thoroughly searched our cars and deprived our smokers of packets of cigarettes, saying that they had too many (Entente Cordial). At Neuve Chapelle the memorial to those of the Indian dead, who have no known graves, was the finest we had seen.

La Bassée – Lens, with its hundreds of new houses – when we were on Vimy Ridge we could not understand how the Germans had let themselves be driven off it because it was more of a natural fortification than Messines Ridge was; to the right the beautiful Canadian War Memorial. Through Arras and Bapaume, then I declared that I felt we were passing the scene of the farce of the attack on October 8th, 1916 – the Somme. No one agreed with me at the time. A short distance on was Factory Corner where we halted for lunch near the New Zealand memorial wooden cross. It was then agreed that I was right.

We walked along the road to Flers and at the top of a hill turned left walked across a field of crops – with permission from a farm worker – and came to the Colonel's grave, all alone in its glory and just where he had fallen on September 15th, 1916. We solemnly placed our wreath against its cross, above which was a tiled roof on four wooden posts.

We returned to the roadway and, before teaching Flers, turned to the left crossed a field and entered Delville Wood – almost a new wood. Bright green bushes and frail saplings grew everywhere whilst here and there occasional scarred trees with no leaves or branches reminded us of the old wood. As we were walking along I found an old, rusty twenty pint dixie that had belonged to a company field kitchen. There was plenty of evidence of what had happened there all those years ago. We came to an open grassy space across the middle of which was the glorious South African memorial. It looked quite awe-inspiring; its purpose seemed to envelop us. We went to one end of it, entered the shelter and proceeded to its top, from where a fine view of the wood could be obtained. We descended, passed through the tall arch in the middle and admired it from the front. On the top of the arch were the figures of two South African soldiers holding a horse. As we set off to leave that memorial we could not help turning round to look at it.

Our way led us straight into the Delville Wood Cemetery, in which we were especially interested. Its figures alarmed us for, of the 5,500 graves, 3,587 were of unknown soldiers. Each stone of the latter group had been erected to "A Soldier of the Great War". Most of the soldiers buried there were Tommies – 3,458 of them. There began my special quest – to see if Willie Spence was among "known" ones. There were some 21st K.R.R.C. graves but not the one I sought. I was puzzled – too many of the fallen were "Known only to God", their stones lacking even their regimental badges.

We made our way to the village of Flers. How peaceful it was that afternoon. Sheep grazed round the raised green on which stood our Divisional Memorial. To us the figure of a Tommy in battle order was a rifleman and the simple inscription "To the glorious memory of those who fell" engraved on the base was not necessary to remind us of the purpose of that memorial. Its site there, in Flers, brought back in a rush the memories of our old chums – for did it not signify the beginning of the end of the Yeoman Rifles?

Still sad, yet happier for having paid homage to our fallen, we took our taxis and set off back. We did make one more break because we recognised the scene of the attack on September15th, 1916 – Tank Day. Lying just off the roadway were heaps of shells, ten or twelve in a heap. There was still a strong smell of gas, so easy to recognise, and we were told by a civilian nearby that a shell had exploded there quite recently. In the side of the hill, which resembled an embankment were broken-in dugouts. We entered some of them and found rifles, equipment, tin hats, cartridges and bayonets. I found a part of a Lewis gun and was about to throw it away when someone asked for it for a souvenir.

We climbed to the top of that hill and found the land was level again. In conversation with a farmer in the corn field we learned that the present crop was the first he had had from that field since before the war. The land had only that year been made arable and for many years he had been clearing away rubbish, the remnants of the war. Satisfied that we had spent a good day on the Somme, we dragged ourselves away. We stopped for a few minutes in Longueval and then reached Albert, which seemed to be undergoing repairs even then in all directions. On through Beaumont Hamel to Arras and then back by the same route as we had come, we returned to our hotel. What a day of memories! So many places of interest; names that conjured up horror and losses in 1916. The names of places that the boys and men who answered Lord Kitchener's call – the survivors – knew only too well; the graveyards of those who did not survive but are there somewhere in one or other of the cemeteries.

Some of our party had been wounded at Plugstreet, or on the Somme, or at the Brasserie, so that just a few of us had other sectors to see. We decided to make Wednesday a free day on which we were to go off independently to suit our own individual wishes. I intended going to Roubaix to see again the places I knew as a Cameron Highlander, after the Yeoman Rifles were broken up and disbanded. The morning dawned very wet so some of us settled on a bus tour of parts of the Salient (the bend in the British Line with Ypres at the front of the arc, and held at a high cost). We visited places we had heard of but never seen – St Jean, St Julien, Zonnebeke, Hell Fire Corner, Sanctuary Wood and Hill 62. At this hill, the natural features of the district have been utilised in the formation of a Canadian memorial that somehow resembles a very large and beautiful rock garden. The view from the terrace was magnificent, Flanders being laid out below and interesting to see. Amidst all that beauty we fancied that we could see Tommies struggling against almost impregnable positions.

Nearby a Belgian preserves a little bit of the Canadian trenches just as they were during the war – a shallow bench with bays, posts, supports and water, but no dugouts; rusty rifles, bombs, cans etc. He spends some of his time extending the trench and adding to his private museum of war articles and souvenirs. What a faithful bit of the past it is.

We moved on and visited the Tyne Cot Cemetery near Passchendaele – many, many rows of graves, absolutely awe-inspiring. I had seen nothing like it. I counted 216 graves in a row and in all nearly twelve thousand impressive grave stones. At the rear were two pill boxes. The impressive stone panels had on them the names of about 34,000 unknown soldiers. What a shock! Then to Hooge and the K.R.R.C. memorial. The well-known and much fought for by both sides, Hill 60, a misshapen mass of clay, the railway cutting below. There are still enough souvenirs in the form of cap badges of both sides, tin hats, bayonets, shell cases, etc. to supply the needs of all visitors – but we did not want any. Shrapnel Corner again, old dugouts that have stood the test of years, then back to Ypres.

On Thursday we split up into little parties. One party went up to Pop; another to Outtersteene – where the villagers wanted to know why we had not put up there. Six of us went to find Dammstrasse, of which the civilians knew nothing. We found it to be a partly sunken road and a private way to a white chateau. We walked a fair distance along it, entering many of the pill boxes that remain. Some were in a very good condition and had been rebuilt after the old ones of 1917 had been smashed in. The old dugout from which I had escaped was not there. We took snaps and I stood on top of the place where I had considered myself lucky to have escaped injury. In the afternoon we paid a visit to La Panne and walked along these a front to the sand dunes. The evening was spent on the old ramparts of Ypres, taking in the air for the last time. During our walk, Captain P. Brooksbank asked me to write a few reminiscences for him as he was collecting genuine "scraps" from the men of the old Battalion in order to form "a living and human account of the Yeoman Rifles in the Great War". I promised that I would see what I could do in the coming winter months. I failed him in this respect – I spent my leisure time that winter writing all that I could remember of my "bit".

After "grand diner" we followed our usual course. We went to the Menin Gate Memorial and stood to attention whilst the Last Post was sounded by the Belgian buglers. On our first visit to it we had placed our wreath there. We examined the panels of names of men who were known to have fallen in the Salient – some 54,000 of them – but had no recognised graves; the "missing".

Our pilgrimage came to an end and we had certainly lived in the memory of the past and all our lost friends. Our quests had been made easy and so had our efforts to trace the parts we had known because the civilians helped us all they could. The farmers did not mind where we walked, the hotel people packed us up when we were going out for the full day.

We were sorry to have to leave the old haunts for everyone had enjoyed the outing, the pilgrimage, even the four fathers who had accompanied us because they wished to see where their sons had fought. What a fine spirit! It was unfortunate that we could not include the Italian front in our itinerary, for we had left a few old comrades there.

Appendix I

"Thank You" printed by Second Army, presented to all ranks leaving the Army

HONI SOIT QUI MAL Y PENSE
DIEU ET MON DROIT

Now that the time has come for you to leave the Army and go back to civil life, I wish, both personally and officially, to thank you for the service which you have given.

You take away with you the priceless knowledge that you have played a man's part in this Great War for freedom and fair play. You will take away with you also your rememberances of your comrades, your pride in your Regiment, and your love for your country.

You have played the game, go on playing it, and all will be well with the Great Empire which you have helped to save. I wish you every prosperity and happiness.

Major General Commanding ... Division

Correspondence received from Brigadier-General W.F. Clemson, C.M.G., D.S.O., in reply to an invitation to attend the Yeoman Rifles First/Second Reunion and Luncheon.

H.Q., 1st Rhine Brigade, Cologne 7th February, 1920.

I sincerely hope that you will realise how grieved I am at not being able to be with you all on the 21st. Will you please express my regrets to all members of the Yeoman Rifles and thank them for the honour they did me in sending me such a kind invitation.

You say a very true thing in your letter, that is, "The Spirit of the old Yeoman Rifles is there. The Battalion may be disbanded, it can never be destroyed." You are right and it is a great asset to the country. I remember the first time I saw the Battalion at Helmsley under its Colonel, the late Lord Feversham, for whom I had the greatest admiration, how struck I was with its keen regard for duty.

This keen spirit remained with the Battalion all through its service, and when with the greatest regret I saw it finally disbanded, it left a record for hard fighting, hard-working and hard playing: which may have been equalled but was never surpassed by any unit in the Army.

Whether in France, Belgium or Italy, the Battalion was always ready and willing to carry out anything that had to be done with the same spirit of determination and good fellowship. I assure you that they helped to make my work as Brigadier very easy and I always feel I owe a great deal to the Yeoman Rifles.

Appendix II

People mentioned in the text

In conversations, up to October 1993, G.V.D. provided further information about various people mentioned in the text. My own research has taken me into contact with other Yeoman Rifles survivors and their families: there follows a résumé of my findings.

M.E.H.

AGAR, Alfred – his home was at Wetwang, near Driffield; died of wounds 14th June, 1917.

ALLEN, Wilf. (Q.M.S.) – in 1983, when aged 94, was living at Davenport Avenue, Hessle; was with 'A' Coy for three years from Nov. 1915; was not injured throughout service. First night in army slept on floor of loft over Lord Feversham's stables, later in lodgings with Sunley family, near park gates. Recalled everyone's embarrassment at primitive washing and toilet facilities. Described in detail death of Lord Feversham (GVD's account coincides exactly), adding that the body was recovered by McEwan, Lord F's former estate worker at Duncombe Park. Enlisted in response to appeal in Yorkshire Post for clerical workers and farmers' sons. Employee (Accounts dept.) of Reckitt and Colman, Hull.

ATTENBOROUGH (Atti) – had contacts with Manchester United Football Club; he was from Leicestershire, where his father was a headmaster. GVD thought "the family of Attenboroughs are the same family."

ARNOLD, Frank – Forest Farm, East Cottingwith, near Pocklington; was 88 in 1982, when he told me he was the first man to enlist in York at the end of harvest 1915.

BAIRNSFATHER, Capt. Bruce – had served with the Warwickshire Regiment; full details of his career as a cartoonist are to be found in "The Better 'Ole" by Toni and Valmai Holt.

BAMBER, Hills (L/Cpl) – an Oswaldkirk man, seen on the "Countess" photograph; he died of wounds 21st Sept. 1916 after the Flers offensive.

BARKER brothers, Nichol and Wilson, of Helmsley; both survived. Nichol is said to have enlisted because he was romantically involved with two girls at the same time – he subsequently remained single.

BEAL, Jack – of Malton, attended reunions; a friend of C. Whitfield.

BELL, Syd – died 1984; lived at 55 Manor Road, Beverley was in 'D' Coy. throughout service.

BENSON, Sammy – attended reunions for many years; kept a poultry farm at Beckwithshaw, near Harrogate.

BRODRICK, Frank – died of wounds at Flers, the same day as the Earl of Feversham; he was from Holme-upon-Spalding Moor.

BROOKSBANK, Capt. – completed the account of the Yeoman Rifles referred to in Chapter 18; GVD says, however, that much of it was taken from a newspaper article by Norman Carmichael (q.v.)

BROWN, ??? – attended reunions at York with C. Whitfield, farmed in the Helmsley area, C.W.'s widow thinks the Countess photograph at Aldershot 3rd May 1916 names G.D. Brown, P.H. Brown and W.G. Brown, all of Helmsley and district.

BUGLASS, Geo. A. (L/Cpl) – of Kirkwhelpington and Morpeth, Northumberland. He was returned to England badly wounded, died 6th Oct. 1916.

BURTON, There were two Captain Burtons in the Yeoman Rifles until October 1916, Gerald Lloyd and (Robert) Claud,. The only one G.V.D. mentions (see pp. 11 and 58) is Gerald Burton, a Lincolnshire man who was in 'D' Company, as was G.V.D. after Flers. Claud Burton ('B' Company) a Yorkshire cricketer was badly wounded at Gird Ridge (See Eden *Another World*) and did not return. The first edition had '(Yorkshire Cricket)' after the name '? Burton', without initials. This was an error, as G.V.D was obviously referring to the other Burton.

CARMICHAEL, Norman – of 'A' Coy; his home was at North Linton, Morpeth, Northumberland, and for many years he was a leading figure in the Newcastle-upon-Tyne reunions, and his son Peter was present at GVD's funeral.

CAVE, James – from York; gave his daughter, now Mrs. J.Q. Craven, Quentin as her second name as she was born about the time he was in the battle at St. Quentin.

CHAPMAN, Alf. – died Nov. 1984, aged 88; lived at Crowle, Lincs., and faithfully attended reunions at York and Helmsley.

CHILDS, Harry – of Bridlington; attended many reunions.

CLARKE, Herbert (Sgt) – a Goole man, he was killed in action 19th Sept. 1917.

CORDUKES, Robt. W. – a native of Kelfield, his home was at Riccall, near York. Killed in action on 20th Sept.1917.

COLLIER, John W. (C/12966) – of Helmsley; killed at Ploegsteert Wood, 1st June 1916, when stray shell hit 9 a.m. rifle inspection; his letter to his father, dated that morning, giving interesting detail of conditions of Y.R. men, has been deposited by his nephew, Johnny Collier, Pottergate, Helmsley, with the Liddle First War Archives, at The Brotherton Library, Leeds University.

COOK, Francis R. – enlisted at Acomb, York, though a native of Gilberdyke, near Howden; killed at Ploegsteert Wood, 1st June 1916.

COULSON, Ted (Coali) – Corporal, then Sergeant; home address was 10 Scarcroft Road, York later worked for Taylor Bros., Hull. GVD referred to his son, Peter.

COVERDALE, Arthur – see WHELDON, H.S.

DALE brothers, Jim and Tom – had been professional soldiers. Jim, an excellent marksman, became deerkeeper on Duncombe Park estate – sold venison in Helmsley market (see "These Well-Beloved Hills" by M. Kirby).Died in 1947. Tom served with the Earl of Feversham in Boer War; emigrated to South America, then to Australia, where he enlisted and saw service in Dardanelles. Responded to Feversham's appeal, and transferred to 21st Btn. as an N.C.O. From 1920s to retirement was keeper of Helmsley Castle; he died in 1951.

DENNIS, Percy – returned to his home village, South Cave, where he died in the mid-1980s; he sent the postcard, page 94A, to his sister Florence, who was then living at

Roos, near Hornsea – it is dated 17th October 1917; it seems likely he was returning to England to a convalescent hospital after being wounded. No relation to GVD.

DUGGLEBY ??? – farmed near Malton and attended reunions with C. Whitfield.

FARRER, Atheling – Boston Spa was the birthplace and home of this holder of the Military Medal, who died of wounds 10th Oct. 1916.

FORSTER, Ernie – was wounded at Ploegsteert Wood, GVD said. For many years lived at Bishopthorpe, York before moving to Clarendon Square, Leamington Spa, where he was living in 1982.

FOWLER, Harold (C/12203) – awarded the C.S.M.; killed in action 31st July 1917; Thirsk born and bred.

FOX, Tom – wounded at Flers 15 September 1916 when Col. Feversham was killed – lost a leg. Returned to native Scarborough – income tax officer; died in his sixties.

GRIEVESON, Oliver R. (C/12600) – enlisted at Selby; was in section; killed in action at Flers, 17th Sept. 1916.

HALL, Harry – wounded, as reported in the Yorks. Gazette of 30th Sept. 1916 – " ... a genial young soul, who is well known in Malton, where he was employed by Messrs. W. Snow & Sons ... " Was landlord of The White Swan, Thornton-le-Clay, near York for many years.

HEY, Claude – l 'D' Coy; was wounded, and convalesced at Cliveden, where the group was photographed with Lady Astor and Lloyd George. Became a teacher – was relief headmaster in Selby area. Was 87 in 1983 when he was living at Bishopthorpe.

HILDRICK Frank (Sgt.,C/12000) – died of wounds, 27th September 1916; his fiancée was Miss Gladys Cooper, whose family had a shoe shop in Helmsley for decades; she never married. Helmsley native, he worked in the drapery department of a large London store before enlisting.

HILL, Arthur – killed in action 17th Sept. 1916, Rfn Hill's home was at Lilling, near Sheriff Hutton, York.

HODGSON, C.H. (Cpl) – signed autograph book for Tom Dale's (see DALE brothers) daughter Nellie in January 1916 when leaving Helmsley for Aldershot.

HORE, Herbert ('Tom') – walked from his home at Loftus, Cleveland to join the Y.R. at Helmsley; became Cpl; wounded in 1917 and convalesced at Rugely, Staffs and Duncombe Park (The Countess's convalescence hospital). Attended reunions; great friend of Bert Rowsby, and Geo. Thompson of Staithes.

JACKSON, Joseph – wrote to his family in Sept. 1916 from a Manchester hospital, wounded in the foot. His parents were Mr and Mrs James Jackson, Market Place, Helmsley.

JENNINGS, 'Lux' – of Wakefield; (see TEMPLE).

JOHNSON, Fred – of Scackleton, near Hovingham; sustained an arm injury. Originally trained as a tailor, he became head gardener at Wiganthorpe Hall, then at Brandsby, near Easingwold.

KEN(N?)INGTON, Mick (Sgt) – his family lived at 93 de Grey Street, Hull, where they ran a laundry; his brother worked at the Spa Ballroom, Bridlington, GVD said.

KILHAM, Sgt – was a cook; his nickname, GVD said, was "or Cure'em".

LAPISH, Arthur – of Old Malton, attended reunions; a friend of C. Whitfield. At a Y.R. social at the Primitive Methodist Chapel, Helmsley, in November 1915, his recitations were very popular (Yorks. Gazette).

LONGBOTTOM, George – 'A' Coy; died at Peasholme, Scarborough in 1982.

LOWDAY, Tim – was "a Hull lad" who, after the war, worked in the City Treasurer's dept at The Guildhall; in retirement he lived at South Cave.

MACHIN, Jim – GVD's "first casualty", was killed on 7th June 1916 in Ploegsteert Wood. His memorial stone in Rifle House Cemetery records him as Rifleman R.B. Machin, whose home was at Bicker, near Boston, Lincs.

MEGGINSON, William (Sgt) – he and his brother Claud (who enlisted in Sledmere's Wagoners' Reserve) both survived the war, later to farm in the Wharram-le-Street area of the Wolds. Former pupils of Scarborough College.

MILLER, Frank (Cpl. 'Dusty') – his home area was Dinnington, Sheffield.

MORLEY, 'Ducky' – was so called because he walked with a waddle, GVD said. A Scarborian, he was a railway booking office clerk. He is photographed sitting next to GVD as one of the 18 surviving signallers after 13 months at the Front.

NEWMARCH, Duggie – home was North Cave, near Market Weighton. An artist, he attended reunions regularly, providing many very humorous cartoons to decorate the annual guest list / menu. His memoirs are deposited with the Liddle Collection, University of Leeds.

NICHOLSON, Ernie (Young Nick) – of Thurston Road, Beverley, became a bank manager. Attended 'A' Coy.reunions.

PORTER, Percy Roy ('Pip') – of Pendrill Street, Hull. Worked for BOCM (animal foods) at Hull.

PRATT, 'Tiger' – from County Durham; when Anthony Eden said he seemed able to see in the dark like a tiger, the nickname stuck.

RICKETTS, Fred – the organizer of 'A' Coy. reunions at Helmsley for many years; his widow lives at Driffield.

ROBSON, Bert – 'D' Coy, was a 92 year old, car driving widower in 1983, living at Langton Road, Norton, Malton.

ROWSBY, Herbert – of Norton, Malton. Wounded Sept. 1916 along with his friend Harry Hall (q.v.). Retired after working for Norton Woolgrowers; died 1972, aged 75.

RUSHWORTH, Arnold S. – lived at Blackpool in the 1950s; keen organizer of reunions. Played Back for the 'Stripes' Rugby trial team at Helmsley in December 1915.

SCAIFE, Jack ('Scruff') – of Scarborough; emigrated to Canada in the 1920s.

SHAW, Harry – died at Caistor, Lincs. in 1984, aged 88; a native of Nawton, he worked as gamekeeper on the Beckett estate; severely wounded at Ypres – was awarded the Military Medal. Attended reunions faithfully.

STEPHENSON, Arthur – 'A' Coy, wounded twice; returned to run family joinery/ undertaking business at Hornsea. While convalescing at St Luke's, Bradford, met a fellow Y.Rfm. who had gone AWOL several months earlier and was now working at a munitions factory opposite the hospital. Died aged 86.

STEPHENSON, Charlie – enlisted at Richmond, was born at Scampston, Malton; he was killed in action, 17th February 1917.

STURDY, David – see WHELDON, H.S

TEMPLE, 'Solly' – described by GVD as "an awkward one", was from Leeds; visited GVD at Fairfax Avenue occasionally and gave anonymously to the Y.R. Association. His great pal was 'Lux' Jennings, both nicknames being derived from 'Sunlight'.

TOASE, Thomas E. (C/12163) – an Easingwold man, he died of wounds at Flers, 15th September 1916.

TODD, Alan – died in 1984, having lived at Whitby since the 1920s. The name Elijah Todd is still used for the tobacconist/stationery shop in Bridge Street, Helmsley, though no longer owned by the family. John Collier (q.v.) refers to Alan Todd in his letter of 1st June, 1916.

TRAIN, Arthur – ran a plumbing business at Hornsea, his native town; attended reunions.

TRAIN, Rfn. – 'C' Coy, was a Hull man whose father had a small-holding near the Botanical Gardens, and his mother kept a florist's shop.

TRENHOLME, Gordon – his home was at Oswaldkirk, near Helmsley; he was one of the wounded at Ploegsteert Wood, 1st June 1916.

TRUE brothers, George and H..??? – 'A' Coy, were from Grimsby; GVD kept in touch with George's widow for many years.

WADE, Jack – lived at Willerby, near Hull; GVD sent newsletters to his widow.

WAKEFIELD, Lance – became a doctor, in practice at Dewsbury, and kept in touch with GVD.

WALKER, Noel – lived at Kingston Road, Bridlington. An accountant, he died on his 87th birthday; three of his seven brothers died in the war.

WATSON, Captain Arthur Toward 'Patch' ('B' Company) of Bishopthorpe

WATSON, Johnny (the Rifleman who strayed into the enemy trenches) – became a teacher, eventually at Buckingham Street, Hull; a Rugby Union enthusiast.

WELDON, Jack – died of wounds at Flers, 15th Sept. 1916; from Ellerby, near Hornsea.

WHELDON, Hammond S. – a native of Farndale, he became a tenant farmer at East Moors, on the Feversham estate; his widow died at Nawton, December 1993. On Fridays (market day) he regularly met with two fellow survivors (Dave Sturdy of Helmsley and Arthur Coverdale of Sinnington, who sold ice-cream from a motor-cycle sidecar) – locals said of these three that they seemed to have accomplished so much, it was a wonder any other men had been needed to defeat the Germans! HSW and A. Eden were two of the youngest Riflemen in the 21st Btn.

WHARRAM, John (R/26557) – enlisted in 21st, was transferred to 18th Battalion. Died of wounds 3rd October 1916. From Fridaythorpe, near Driffield.

WHITFIELD, Charles – of Fridaythorpe; replied in verse to thank his sister for sending a scarf when he was at Helmsley, Dec. 1915. He recalled that on the evening of 14th Sept. 1916, at a special service, the hymn "Lead Kindly Light" was sung so touchingly that Col. Feversham asked the men to sing the last verse again: the next day he was killed (as were so many others) as he led his men into battle. A Wolds farmer, C.W. died in 1960.

WHITTAKER, Bert – resided at Thirsk Road, Northallerton, in 1982; in 'A' Coy. originally, was later transferred to another battalion. Held p.o.w. for a time; died in 1985, aged 90.

YEAMAN, 2nd Lt. – was slightly wounded in an early offensive; returned to the line; killed – head buried, body was never identified – "from the north-east" (GVD).